KU-789-989

LONGCARE SURVIVORS

The Biography of a Care Scandal

John Pring

© John Pring, 2011

Published by Disability News Service

All rights reserved. Reproduction of this book by photocopying or electronic means for non-commercial purposes is permitted. Otherwise, no part of this book may be reproduced, adapted, stored in a retrieval system or transmitted by any means, electronic, mechanical, photocopying, or otherwise without the prior written permission of the author.

The rights of John Pring to be identified as the author of this work have been asserted in accordance with the Copyright, Designs and Patents Act 1988.

A CIP catalogue record for this book is available from the British Library.

ISBN 978-0-9568922-0-1

Prepared and printed by:

York Publishing Services Ltd
64 Hallfield Road
Layerthorpe
York YO31 7ZQ

Tel: 01904 431213

Website: www.yps-publishing.co.uk

Contents

Acknowledgements

Many people have helped with my research over the last 17 years. I could never thank them all individually, and many have asked me not to use their names, but I would like to express my gratitude to everyone who has generously contributed their time and expertise.

Some people I must mention by name. My friends Lisa Sherper and Mel Gow have provided invaluable advice over the years.

During the last year, I have relied repeatedly on the expertise, support and advice of my friend and former colleague Katharine Quarmby, whose important and troubling book on disability hate crime, Scapegoat, will be published this summer.

This book would never have been written without the professional courage of Janice Raycroft, who staked her career on publishing the first Longcare stories in the Slough Observer in 1994.

It was only in researching this new version of the Longcare story that I finally understood the contribution made by June Raybaud, the aunt of one of the former residents, and a formidable barrister and campaigner. It was June's probing, questioning and persistence that helped keep the scandal in the minds of politicians and the authorities, and encouraged the families of the Longcare survivors to keep fighting. Again, this book would not have been possible without her.

The same must be said of Fiona Mactaggart MP, who I thank for the forewords she has written to both my books. Her commitment to the human rights of her constituents in Slough and the vital part she played in exposing the Longcare scandal will become clear.

Others I must thank include Steven Rose, Margaret Kennedy, Jamie Trounce, Clare Johnson, Dame Philippa Russell, Graeme McQueen, the staff at North Finchley library, and Martin Rynja and Gibson Square, for publishing my first book.

I will always be grateful to the families of the Longcare (and The Old Rectory) survivors for sharing their painful stories with me, and particularly to Pauline Hennessey, Avril and Brian Scott, Susan and Davyd Power, Benedict Alcindor, Ron and Doreen Deacon (both sadly now deceased), Lidia Tunstell, Norma Adams, Rose Terry, Dr Christian Carritt, and the families of four survivors whose names I have changed: Andrew, Tracy, David Jackson and Michelle Callaway.

The most important words in this book come from people with learning difficulties themselves. Among those with no direct connection with Longcare were Ian Davies, Chris Shane, Janet Pheasant, Nigel Lott, Craig Hart and Karen Spencer from Central England People First, Mabel Cooper, Andrew Lee from People First (Self-Advocacy), Michael Ratcliffe, June (whose surname she has asked me not to use), Scott Watkin, and Lynne Evans and Phillip Morgan from Rhondda Cynon Taf People First.

It has taken me many years to learn that the people who lived under the brutal Longcare regime were not 'silent victims', as I described them in my first book. Yes, all of them suffered appallingly at the hands of Gordon Rowe. But in many and varied ways, they resisted his cruelty, they found ways to survive. Among them was Dorothy Thomson, who I have now known for more than 10 years. She resisted Rowe's regime, and her bravery helped bring it down – against the odds. Without her testimony, this book would have lost its core. Her courage and selflessness have been a source of constant admiration.

And finally, again, to the (still) anonymous person who sent that leaked document to the Slough Observer all those years ago: thank you.

John Pring, London

johnpring@btopenworld.com

Foreword

It was before I was elected MP for Slough that I started to learn of the horrors behind the respectable façade at Longcare, two homes for people with learning difficulties near Slough, the town I hoped to represent.

The series of articles written by John Pring in the Slough Observer newspaper alerted me to the scandal. Many local people, including some who were involved with Mencap and other campaign groups, dismissed the stories. They had been deceived by Gordon Rowe, the owner of the homes, who impressed many in authority while he tortured people in his care who were not able to communicate what was being done to them.

I had long been a campaigner for justice and equality, concentrating on race and gender. While I knew disabled people faced unfair treatment, I did not realise how vulnerable people with learning difficulties could be. I suppose that, like many people who did not dig beneath the surface of what Gordon Rowe was doing, I assumed that there were systems in place which would protect them.

And indeed there were. One of the horrible things about the events that are described in this book is that people inside the system knew, or should have known, that they were happening.

John's work opened my eyes and those of others. This book shows not only the depths of cruelty meted out to people to whom we all owe a duty of care, but also describes how laborious and difficult it was to get anyone held to account for those wrongs.

When I entered parliament, as a result of what I learned from John's articles, I pressed for better treatment for people with learning difficulties in the criminal justice system.

I was also glad to be able to secure an inquiry into the Longcare scandal. It had not been easy to persuade the minister, Paul Boateng, to agree to the inquiry. He felt that change could be secured without it. I was hugely relieved when, during a meeting with Buckinghamshire's director of social services, her arrogant responses to his concerns infuriated Paul so much that he changed his mind and insisted on an inquiry.

It was worth it. The inquiry's recommendations contributed directly to four major pieces of legislation: the Public Interest Disclosure Act 1998 (the whistle-blowing act), the Youth Justice and Criminal Evidence Act 1999 (which included measures on how to achieve best evidence), the Care Standards Act 2000, and the Sexual Offences Act 2003.

But we cannot relax. What John Pring's work has shown is that someone who has his investigative and communication skills can bring to public attention a horror which would otherwise have remained hidden. And I was a determined new MP facing a sympathetic new government which was willing to change things.

But not every disabled victim of abuse will have access to a clear voice like John's. I hope that this book will make a wider audience aware of the importance of these issues, of the ease with which abusers can exploit people with learning difficulties, and of the need to ensure that not only are perpetrators brought to justice, but also that mechanisms are put in place which give victims both protection and a voice.

Fiona Mactaggart, MP for Slough and shadow minister for equalities

Introduction

The editor of the Slough Observer, Janice Raycroft, took one look at the first page of the report, and reached for a cigarette. 'I knew immediately that the bomb had gone off,' she would say later.

The smoky air was tinged with the scent of chocolate expelled by the Mars factory, just 200 yards away from the Observer's offices in the middle of Slough's sprawling trading estate. Raycroft crossed her legs, took another drag of her cigarette and turned back to the note attached to the report. It was hand-written in capital letters, and dated 31 August 1994:

SIR/MADAM,

FOR OBVIOUS REASONS I AM UNABLE TO SIGN THIS NOTE. HOWEVER, I THINK IT IS AN ISSUE OF SOME IMPORTANCE. THERE APPEAR TO BE SERIOUS IMPLICATIONS, A POSSIBLE COVER-UP, AND NO SIGN THAT OTHER LOCAL GOVERNMENT OFFICES HAVE BEEN NOTIFIED ABOUT THIS MATTER. IT WOULD CERTAINLY WARRANT SOME FURTHER RESEARCH.

SINCERELY,

'CONCERNED'

The note accompanied a copy of a leaked Buckinghamshire County Council report written by Jennifer Waldron, head of the council's inspection unit, the department responsible for inspecting residential homes for disabled and older people and children.

A junior reporter with just nine months' experience, I was handed the story only because my 'patch' of south Bucks covered the two homes for adults with learning difficulties referred to in the document, which were run by a company called Longcare.

I had never met anyone with a learning difficulty, other than fleeting encounters with occupants of a residential home in Cheddar, the Somerset village where I grew up in the seventies and early eighties. I had felt uneasy when passing them in the street, but I never examined this discomfort. It soon became clear that most of the population shared my unease and ignorance, both of people with learning difficulties and of the multiple levels of discrimination they endured.

I was also unprepared for the suffering my investigations would reveal. Just as unexpected was the resilience, integrity and generosity possessed by many of the men and women I met. I would learn that it was not their impairments, but the barriers they encountered in society, that disabled them.

It became clear that people with learning difficulties had the lowest-paid jobs—if they could find work at all. Their clothes were often second-hand, their healthcare second-rate and their housing substandard. Many were hidden away from 'normal' society. If they were lucky enough to live 'in the community', their neighbours resented their presence and either ignored or bullied, ridiculed and abused them. Some of this has changed for the better in the 17 years since I started working on the Longcare story, but all too much of it has not.

The story of the report that landed on my desk at the Slough Observer in September 1994 was the story of Gordon Rowe, a mental health nurse and later social worker and residential home owner, of the people who came to live in the three residential homes he was to run, and of their families. It was also the story of how Rowe beat those residents, neglected them, stole their money, threatened and intimidated them into silence, and much, much worse. And it was the story of how these disabled people were abandoned, ignored and degraded by society at every turn.

As I investigated the events that took place at the Longcare homes, it soon became clear that what happened there was not an anomaly, a combination of freakish circumstances that were unlikely to be repeated. Other people just like them were being exposed to similar humiliation, deprivation and violence.

My first book on the Longcare scandal, Silent Victims, was published in 2003. It received a few positive reviews, and was serialised in The Times, but did not have the impact I had hoped for. By this time, I had begun to specialise in writing about disability, first as a freelance journalist and then on the national publication Disability Now. Although the horrors of Rowe's regime were never far from my mind, and we campaigned on DN for tougher sentences for abuse, I thought I had put Longcare behind me, and that the final chapter of the story had been written.

It was not until early 2010 that I again opened a copy of Silent Victims. Flicking through its pages reminded me how unsatisfied I had been with my book. I never felt I had done justice to the former residents, despite working so hard on their story for nearly 10 years.

I knew that a civil legal action had unearthed huge quantities of new evidence, just after my book had gone to press. Labour's 13 years in government were also drawing to a close. Labour had come to power just three years after the scandal was exposed and I wanted to discover how the social care and criminal justice systems had changed over those years, and whether attitudes to people with learning difficulties had improved. Most importantly, I wanted to find out what had happened to the former residents. Had they been the victims I described them as in my book, or had they survived the terrible abuses inflicted upon them?

As I took a deep breath and plunged back into my files, I also decided to look more closely into the origins of institutional care of people with learning difficulties, in a bid to position Rowe's regime in some kind of historical context. Longcare could not, I suspected, be dismissed as an aberration.

This book is divided into six sections. The first looks at early attitudes to people with learning difficulties, and the rise of the eugenicists and the huge long-stay hospitals that came to dominate the care environment for much of the twentieth century. The second investigates the background of Gordon Rowe, revealing his long and brutal history of abuse. Part three describes the horrific regime at Rowe's Longcare homes, through the testimony of those who lived and worked there. In the next section, I describe what happened to Rowe after his regime was exposed, and investigate what went wrong across the many agencies that should have prevented the abuse, or put a stop to it many years earlier than they did. Part five examines where we are now, what has changed and what still needs to change in the social care and criminal justice systems, and looks for signs of hope in the self-advocacy movement. Finally, in part six, I tell the individual stories of some of the Longcare residents, following their progress over the last 17 years.

As for my sources, the first section relies heavily on previously-published research, all of which I hope I have credited and all of which I am indebted to. This section, and much of the rest of the book, is also reliant on my interviews over the last 17 years with former residents and their families. I have also used extracts from police statements, witness statements compiled for the civil case mentioned above, and reports and other documents too numerous to mention. Much of the third section is based on interviews I carried out with former members of Longcare staff. But this book would not have been possible without the research, investigations and other communications of countless scores of people, and I hope I have appropriately credited those contributions.

I have not used everyone's full names. I have generally named those convicted by the courts, those who have died, and those who worked in senior positions for public bodies, as well as those who have given me permission to identify them. This means I have only used the full names of Longcare residents who gave me permission to do so, or whose families did so on their behalf. Those whose names I have changed I have marked with an asterisk when they first appear in the text.

More than 16 years after Rowe's horrific regime was exposed, the story of the Longcare survivors remains a shocking indictment of how our society treats disabled people, particularly those with learning difficulties. I hope the following pages do justice to that story.

Extract from
REPORT ON INVESTIGATION INTO ALLEGATIONS OF SERIOUS ABUSE AT LONGCARE LTD – Social Services Department, Buckinghamshire County Council, June 1994

'The extensive investigation which has been carried out has resulted in a considerable body of information which indicates that for many years the homes operated a totally unacceptable regime which meant that a substantial group of vulnerable people were at times denied some of their most basic human rights, as shown in the following paragraphs...

'The impression gained is that the prevailing culture was one in which the basic humanity of residents was denied. It is difficult to distil the information given and still convey the enormity and scale of humiliation, deprivation, torment and punishment to which residents were subjected.'

Author's Notes

1:   The terminology used to refer to the type of impairment I have written about has changed many times, including at least six times during the twentieth century. This is reflected in Longcare Survivors. I have avoided the use of outdated, offensive terms where possible. Where it has been necessary to include such terms for reasons of historical accuracy or because of their inclusion in direct quotes, I apologise for any offence this may cause to people with learning difficulties or other disabled people.

2:   The use of an asterisk next to a name indicates that it has been changed to protect his or her identity.

PART ONE

THE RESIDENTS

Chapter One

'Idiots'

'The feeble-minded are a parasitic, predatory class, never capable of self-support, or of managing their own affairs... they cause unutterable sorrow at home and are a menace and danger to the community. Feeble-minded women are almost invariably immoral and if at large usually become carriers of venereal disease or give birth to children who are as defective as themselves. Every feeble-minded person, especially the high-grade imbecile, is a potential criminal, needing only the proper environment and opportunity for the development and expression of his criminal tendencies.'

Walter Fernald, superintendent of the Massachusetts School for the Feeble-Minded; speech to Massachusetts Medical Society; 1912

'Campaigners have welcomed the broadcasting watchdog's decision to overturn its own ruling and condemn the use of offensive, disablist language on a Channel 4 show. Footballer-turned-actor Vinnie Jones caused outrage when he 'joked' on Celebrity Big Brother's Big Mouth (BBBM) – on Channel 4's sister channel E4 – that presenter Davina McCall walked 'like a retard', with McCall laughing and replying: 'I do not walk like a retard.'

Disability News Service, 26 May 2010

Before the story of Gordon Rowe and the residents of his Longcare homes can be told, it is important to describe what came before. How was it that society – in the supposedly civilised, enlightened years of the late twentieth century – could allow scores of adults with learning difficulties to endure years of almost unimaginable brutality and deprivation, in a place that the authorities would call their home?

What kind of road could we possibly have travelled that could lead to such a terrible destination?

*

The first experiments in community care took place not in the latter half of the twentieth century, but hundreds of years earlier. As early as the thirteenth century there were marked similarities in towns across England with the 'mixed economy of social care' that would be offered to people with learning difficulties in the late 1900s.

By the early fourteenth century, a system of tithes had developed through which members of a church parish would contribute a tenth of their income to parish funds. A third of this was distributed to parishioners in poverty. Some individuals – usually from society's upper echelons – made further charitable contributions. The evidence suggests that many of the recipients were widows and disabled people, and that the payments allowed many people who would have been unable to support themselves to live reasonably independently in the community.

But in addition to this early system of community care, monasteries and almshouses – also usually run by the church – offered care and protection, an early form of institutional care, to those in greater need.

By the middle of the thirteenth century, there were also about 400 hospitals, usually connected to the church or landed families, providing rest, clean beds, food and prayer. These hospitals often offered care and accommodation to people with learning difficulties, because the House of Commons would remind the King and the hospitals in 1414 that they had been founded to sustain 'impotent men and women, lazars [lepers], men and women out of their wits and minds [those with learning difficulties and mental health conditions], and poor women with child'.

But not every person with learning difficulties relied on charity. Through the Middle Ages, many earned a living, as most jobs were hard but uncomplicated agricultural work. Some of those unable to support themselves would undoubtedly have been rejected by their families, particularly in the frequent times of economic hardship, but it is clear that many of those who were too disabled to work were provided for by their parish.

There was also legal protection that supported those without the capacity to look after themselves. As early as the thirteenth century, the Crown was drawing a legal distinction between 'idiots' (people with learning difficulties) and 'lunatics' (those with mental health conditions) in cases involving the inheritance of property and titles. Court hearings decided whether a person was one or the other. If an 'idiot', the Crown would act as guardian, taking his property but ensuring his welfare with the proceeds. A 'lunatic', although treated in a similar way, could reacquire his property if he ever recovered. Parishes were frequently ordered by the courts to support those unable to provide for themselves. The courts developed a range of tests to decide these cases. The historian Peter Rushton says they often used competence in social skills and numeracy, particularly by the fifteenth and sixteenth centuries.

Although the Church in the Middle Ages was central to the system of social welfare, it had two contrasting attitudes to disability.

Many in the Christian Church saw a person's impairment as the work of the devil or a punishment by God. Key to the propagation of these beliefs was the publication of Malleus Maleficarium (The Hammer of Witches) in 1487. It was written by two German Inquisitors for the Catholic Church – members of the Dominican religious order – and is often described as a witch-hunter's manual. The Devil, they wrote, substitutes his own creatures – changelings – for children, and they can be recognised by their impairments. The manual states that women involved with witchcraft can also be recognised by their impairments, such as epileptic seizures or mental ill-health.

Tens of thousands of people, mainly women and many of them disabled, were put to death across Europe as witches. They were also used as scapegoats for plagues or periods of economic hardship. It appears, though, that there was only one major witch-hunt in Britain, during the civil war in the 1640s, in which the historian Malcolm Gaskill has estimated that around 100 people were executed by hanging.

It is believed that Martin Luther, the religious scholar credited with the Protestant Reformation, was influenced by Malleus Maleficarium, and when asked about a young boy with learning difficulties is reported to have advised a nobleman: 'Take the changeling child to the river and drown it.' Elsewhere he wrote: 'Idiots, the lame, the blind, the dumb, are men in whom the devils have established themselves...'

But at the same time that parts of the Church linked disability – and people with learning difficulties – to the Devil, other parts looked to the New Testament. Virtues such as faith, hope, charity and justice were central to medieval Christianity, with a consequent emphasis on feeding and helping those who were poor, ill or disabled.

At the end of the sixteenth century, the Elizabethan Poor Laws of 1598 and 1601 consolidated the system of social welfare and required that all parishes provided a minimum level of support for those in need, funded by the imposition of rates. Each parish had to administer relief through an overseer, who had a duty to look after those unable to support themselves by working. Old, sick and disabled people were to be housed in 'convenient houses or dwellings', and this undoubtedly included many people with learning difficulties. As the historian Eric Midwinter[1] said:

'Slowly, the poor law came to influence the lives of everybody. It was the only social service...'

In the fifteenth and sixteenth centuries, there was frequent migration of labour from countryside to towns and to London in search of work, but problems developed when the economy was not strong, and despite the poor law system many people with learning difficulties are believed to have been forced to wander the highways as thieves and vagabonds, or to turn to prostitution. By 1600, says Paul Fideler[2], 'poverty had become a ubiquitous calamity in the towns', with the social order becoming polarized between a small elite and 'swarms of destitute poor tramping the streets'.

Marjorie McIntosh[3] suggests that 'relatives, neighbours, and wealthier households continued to offer most of the informal or person-to-person aid as they had in previous centuries', while religious and parish organisations and town governments 'increasingly offered more structured or formal relief'. Her research into the support provided in the Elizabethan town of Hadleigh in Suffolk found evidence that, between 1579 and the early 1590s, 24 people with physical impairments or learning difficulties received financial relief or personal care, while several leading citizens took in girls with learning difficulties or physical impairments as long-term servants.

The historian Peter Rushton carried out a similarly fascinating study of the use of the Poor Laws in the 1600s and 1700s[4] in the north-east of England. He found that Poor Law court cases concerning people with learning difficulties were usually brought by relatives faced by financial difficulties. They often talked of their son or daughter's inability to perform everyday tasks such as going out on their own or dressing themselves. They often used the word 'innocent' to describe their child. One mother in 1702 asked for financial support to allow her to stay at home with her 'innocent' 12-year-old son, who was so 'past Government that without a continual eye had unto him she is in daily fear of some ill to be done by him either to her, himself or to some others'. A Northumberland widow told the court in 1711 that she cared for two grandchildren in their 30s 'and neither of them can tell to twenty' or were capable of gaining work in domestic service.

Rushton says most Poor Law cases relating to people with learning difficulties stemmed from family poverty and the failure to arrange an effective package of care. 'Idiocy was overwhelmingly a domestic problem: all those whose residence is given were with kin or in domestic care. There are no hints that custodial confinement for idiots was ever considered by parish officers or magistrates...'

The Poor Law authorities were determined to keep people 'hidden away at home', supporting the family if necessary, but not replacing it, which Rushton says seems to have matched the wishes of most relatives. He contrasts this apparent benevolence with the usual treatment doled out to those with mental health conditions, who were often kept in jails, 'domestic confinement', workhouses or asylums.

Throughout the seventeenth and eighteenth centuries, then, there were mechanisms in place which helped at least some people with learning difficulties when their family care systems broke down through poverty or death. The courts could order aid to be paid to fund nursing and lodging with parish nurses. It is unclear how often this safety net was taken advantage of, but it was there and there is documentary proof that it was used as another early form of community care.

By the early eighteenth century, there were more than 700 workhouses in England, with 200,000 places, and many of those forced to take shelter in them were people with learning difficulties. The introduction of the Workhouse Test Act of 1723 meant that anyone who wanted to claim poor relief had to enter a workhouse and carry out a set amount of work. This and the harsh regimes were supposed to act as a deterrent against irresponsible claims of support. In the years between the passing of the act and 1750, about 600 new parish workhouses were built. By 1776, there were about 2,000.

Before the Industrial Revolution, which took hold in the latter half of the eighteenth century, most jobs required only simple skills, so many people with learning difficulties were able to find work. But the process of industrialisation – with declining agriculture, increasing numbers employed in manufacturing and service industries, and fast-growing towns and cities – meant people with learning difficulties were relegated to the bottom of the labour market. Lindsay Brigham[5] says the emphasis in the new factory system on speed, timekeeping and production norms 'proved a hostile environment' for many people with impairments who had previously been able to contribute to agriculture or small-scale industry. More families were now supporting relatives who were unable to contribute financially to the household. Many people with learning difficulties subsequently became destitute, ending up in the workhouses, asylums or prisons, dumping grounds for the victims of industrialisation. Peter Rushton, though, suggests that most people with learning difficulties continued to be cared for in domestic settings, as few of the new generation of asylums admitted 'idiots'.

The true situation can only be guessed at. As Rushton says, he and other historians must rely on the written historical records and the responses of families and officials, while people with learning difficulties themselves remain 'obstinately silent'. As he says, 'the fate of the poor is all too often to be defined by those to whom they are a problem.' Peregrine Horden agrees: 'In any century earlier than our own, then, family care that was adequate to its task leaves few traces.'

It is only as the nineteenth century progresses that a fuller picture of how society treated people with learning difficulties begins to form.

A new institutional network was developing, of workhouses, lunatic asylums, and prisons. They were organised on a much larger scale than the parish workhouses, private madhouses and local jails they replaced. Their regimes were harsh and often brutal. The County Asylum Act of 1808 was designed to deal with this neglect and abuse. The act gave local powers to establish county asylums, but as most county authorities refused to build them, people still often ended up in the workhouses, and the few asylums that were built quickly became overcrowded, leading to more of the institutional abuse they had been set up to address.

The Times published more than 100 accounts of workhouse cruelty during the 1830s and 1840s. There was, says Bernard Harris[6], a drab, workhouse uniform, meals had to be eaten in silence, family members were separated and everyone slept in dormitories with little privacy. The work was hard and unpleasant, with stone-breaking or flour-grinding for men and scrubbing and laundry for women. The comparisons with the institutions that would be set up for people with learning difficulties in the twentieth century are striking.

In 1828, the County Lunatic Asylums Act had introduced a certification process, which meant that someone could be admitted to an asylum only on production of a certificate signed by two doctors, or just one doctor if they were a 'pauper'. Again, it was a precursor of a more widespread regime that was to be introduced at the beginning of the Edwardian era and would last through much of the twentieth century.

In 1845, the government introduced the mandatory building of county lunatic asylums, while licensed homes, hospitals and asylums receiving those who were 'a lunatic, idiot or person of unsound mind' had to have a certificate signed by two medical practitioners, with the Lunacy Commission acting as a national inspectorate.

Gradually, more and more of those who had no form of financial support and had either mental health conditions or learning difficulties began to be housed in huge public institutions, rather than in smaller private settings, although better-off families, says historian David Wright, would employ their own servants or nurses as care workers.

In practice, there was little or no distinction made between people with learning difficulties and mental health conditions, and for much of the century the term 'lunacy' was used to describe those with both impairments, as it was in the 1845 Lunacy Acts. From the 1860s, though, there began to be a much closer emphasis on classifying people with learning difficulties into different types, particularly by the medical profession. Those with the highest support needs were called 'idiots', those who were less disabled were termed 'imbeciles', and those with the lowest need for support were described as 'feeble-minded'.

By 1881, there were about 30,000 classified 'idiots' in institutions in England, but less than 1,000 in specialised asylums for people with learning difficulties. The rest were still in workhouses, asylums and prisons. Even so, the vast majority of people with learning difficulties were living outside institutions, being cared for in the community, usually by their families.

Undoubtedly, some families saw asylums as a way of relieving the economic burden of caring for their relatives, but there was also a growing tendency for the government to see institutions such as asylums, workhouses and prisons as a solution to social problems. A third factor in the growth of the institutions was the growing influence of the medical profession in the nineteenth century. Many doctors had much to gain, particularly from the rise of the asylums.

At the same time that many people with learning difficulties were facing neglect and abuse in workhouses and asylums, some educationalists had begun to ask whether it might be possible to cure what they called 'mental deficiency', or at least to lessen its impact on some people. There was also concern over overcrowding in the workhouses and lunatic asylums.

This led, in the 1850s and 1860s, to the founding of five voluntary, large-scale institutions for 'educable idiots' across England. They were built with charitable support and were mostly for children and adults from the emerging Victorian middle classes. Earlswood in Surrey, built in 1853, was followed by the Northern Counties Asylum in Lancaster, the Eastern Counties Idiot Asylum in Colchester, the Western Counties Asylum at Starcross in Devon, and the Midland Counties Asylum in Staffordshire. They focused on health, nutrition, exercise, practical training and 'moral education'. The aim was to lift the burdens of financial dependency and lifetime care from their families. These new asylums were also located in the countryside, where their occupants could benefit from the fresh air and fresh food, and be put to work in the fields and gardens. And they were many miles from the corrupting influences of the city. From the 1870s, these asylums were supplemented by institutions for 'pauper idiots', such as those at Leavesden, Caterham and Darenth.

The momentum was steadily growing towards the segregation of people with learning difficulties from both society and the other institutions of Victorian England.

David Wright[7] has researched the reasons given by families who wanted their children admitted to an asylum. It was usually the mothers and sisters who described problems with feeding, dressing and toileting on the reception certificates. There were stories of children with learning difficulties getting lost, running away, wandering into other people's houses and failing to recognise danger. One described how 'if a horse, carriage or cart was coming quickly along the road she would not draw to one side to get out of danger'.

Despite the rise of the new asylums, argues Wright, 'the nuclear family persisted as the primary locus of care for idiots throughout the nineteenth century', with the task usually falling on mothers and the eldest daughters.

One of those with more enlightened views about people with learning difficulties, and the need to teach them what would today be described as independent living skills, was Dr John Langdon-Down. He started work at Earlswood in 1858, as superintendent physician. But when Langdon-Down arrived he found it in poor condition, and noted how reports by the Lunacy Commissioners had described 'appalling conditions', with inadequate water supply and sewage 'discharged into open pits'.

Langdon-Down would go on to open an institution of his own, Normansfield, in 1868. His institution was aimed at children of the wealthy, and the residents lived in the same house as his family. His aim was to 'provide the highest possible culture, the best physical, moral, and intellectual training, and to open out fresh realms of happiness for a class who have the strongest claims on our sympathy, and for whom until lately so little has been done'.

Other 'idiot asylums' created less welcoming environments. St Lawrence's, also in Surrey, opened in 1870 and catered for more than 1,000 people in 13 four-storey T-shaped blocks. St Lawrence's was designed to control, and segregate, a sign of the gradual shift in public sentiment about people with learning difficulties that would soon accelerate.

Following the introduction of compulsory education in 1870, some campaigners began to focus on those they claimed could not benefit from the typical classroom environment, and were unable to find work after leaving school, leading to vagrancy, crime, prostitution and poverty. This scapegoating of people with learning difficulties led many campaigners to argue that such people would be far better off receiving 'treatment' in asylums.

Meanwhile, disciples of Charles Darwin were developing his theory of evolution, asking whether it was possible to improve the 'quality' of the population by 'supplanting inefficient human stock by better strains'. Sir Francis Galton, a cousin of Darwin, whose words these were, coined the term 'eugenics' in 1883 to describe this theory of improving the qualities of future generations.

Medical textbooks compared people with learning difficulties to 'primitive' people, and there were growing calls for efforts to prevent those who were 'unfit' – such as 'primitive' races, those with learning difficulties and elements of the working classes – from giving birth.

Dr Alfred Tredgold, whose textbook 'Mental Deficiency' was published in 1908 and reprinted many times over the next 50 years, wrote in a magazine article that those who were 'unfit' could impede the progress of a race by 'withdrawing for their support the energy and resources of the more capable members of the community', an argument later taken up by Hitler's Nazis in Germany.

People with learning difficulties were one of the groups that were seen as a threat to society, and somehow less than human. Women with learning difficulties were increasingly being described as immoral, while women who were said to be immoral were often labelled as 'feeble-minded'. At the same time, there were widespread fears that the working classes and criminals were reproducing more quickly than the respectable middle and upper classes.

Mark Jackson says there was a particular focus by the eugenicists on the risk posed by those considered to be 'feeble-minded'[8] – because of their alleged promiscuity and fertility and inheritable impairments – while 'idiots' and 'imbeciles' were less likely to reproduce. He says 'the feeble-minded' were seen as 'unable to benefit from education or to gain employment' and 'lacking in will-power and self-control' and likely to drift into crime and poverty.

The medical profession was central to the growing calls for specialised institutions and segregation. During the 1890s, the BMJ and The Lancet published many letters and editorials calling for specialist provision.

New dedicated organisations began to campaign for action on the 'menace' of the perceived tide of social misfits threatening society. They demanded legislation, and either segregation, sterilisation, or the banning of marriage to people with learning difficulties.

In 1896, the National Association for Promoting the Welfare of the Feeble-Minded (NAPWF) was founded. It played a critical role over the next two decades, although at first it campaigned for small, working homes for 'the feeble-minded'.

Campaigners such as Mary Dendy spoke of children with learning difficulties being exploited and neglected by their parents. Dendy's 'eloquent and insistent advocacy of permanent care', says Mark Jackson, was delivered with a 'pioneering zeal'. She 'portrayed the feeble-minded as the principal source of crime, poverty, disease and immorality', and described them as 'this terrible evil of our society'. She argued that permanent segregation would lower the crime rate and poverty and prevent the transmission of 'feeble-minded' genes to future generations, relieve over-crowding in institutions and protect them from themselves and society. Jackson says that her 'expansive knowledge and undiminished zeal effectively established permanent segregation as the dominant model of care and control in the first decade of the twentieth century'.

The influence of Dendy and others like her gradually grew, both outside and within Parliament. In April 1903, a petition signed by 140 prominent figures was sent to the home secretary, urging him to establish an official inquiry. The following year, the government agreed to act, setting up a Royal Commission on the Care and Control of the Feeble-Minded.

Organisations such as the National Association for the Care and Control of the Feeble-Minded had considerable influence over the commission, which sat for four years and heard 248 witnesses. When it reported in 1908, it made 96 recommendations, including calls to expand the definition of a 'mentally defective' person, and to give the state a role in identifying, classifying and regulating people thought to be 'mentally defective'. It suggested links between 'mental deficiency' and crime, poverty and increased fertility, and called for compulsory detention of people with learning difficulties 'for as long as it is necessary'.

The commission concluded that there were 'numbers of mentally defective persons whose training is neglected, over whom no sufficient control is exercised, and whose wayward and irresponsible lives are productive of crime and misery, of much injury to themselves and to others, and of much continuous expenditure wasteful to the community and to individual families.' Criticism of the report was sparse.

The commission, says Tim Stainton[9], 'laid the groundwork for the systematic repression by the state' of people with learning difficulties.

Following the report, calls for legislation intensified, led by the NAPWF and the newly-formed Eugenics Education Society. There were frequent public meetings, protesting at the government's failure to take action to control the 'menace' of people with learning difficulties.

The pressure intensified with the report of the Poor Law Commission in 1909, which also called for segregation, while Winston Churchill, then a Liberal home secretary, warned of a 'very terrible danger to the race'. He suggested segregation should be merely a staging post, while the public were persuaded of the need to sterilise women with learning difficulties.

Campaigners claimed segregation was more humane than sterilisation or regulating marriage, but Jackson says that in 'a society preoccupied and divided by class relations', segregation was a reminder of the 'moral superiority, professional expertise, and political authority of the middle classes', and offered them a way to 'consolidate class boundaries and to exercise greater political control over the dangerous classes'. For many Edwardian reformers, he says, 'benevolent concern and relentless control' were 'two sides of the same therapeutic coin'.

But there was often little that was benevolent in the public comments of many of the leading campaigners for segregation. Dr C T Ewart, in 1910, said that 'national progress' could only take place when 'means are taken to increase the fit and decrease the unfit. The establishment of suitable farm and industrial colonies is the only method whereby society can be protected from the feeble-minded.' Dr Alfred Tredgold told a meeting in Manchester the following year that 'the insane, the feeble-minded, the paupers, the criminals, and the whole parasitic class of the country are continuing to propagate with unabated and unrestricted vigour' while the 'industrious' classes were having fewer children. And in the same year, Dendy warned: 'We must free the country from these dangerous weaklings, and we must save these weaklings from their dangerous surroundings.'

Eventually, the production of a private members' bill forced the government's hand and the new home secretary Reginald McKenna introduced a government bill in 1912, which promised to give the home secretary potentially unlimited powers to authorise detention of anyone found to be 'mentally defective'. The bill would have made it illegal to marry a person with learning difficulties, and would have allowed others to be prevented from having children. Lack of parliamentary time meant the bill failed, but the following year McKenna introduced another bill from which he said any reference to 'what might be regarded as the eugenic idea' had been removed and was solely concerned with the 'protection of sufferers'[6].

Despite his protestations, the new mental deficiency bill suggested wide-ranging restrictions on the liberty of those identified as 'mentally defective'. It defined four types of 'mental defectives': 'idiots', 'imbeciles', 'the feeble-minded' and 'moral imbeciles'. All could be sent to segregated institutions or placed under the control of guardians in the community, under certain circumstances. These included the request of a parent if the person was under 21, if they were found neglected or abandoned or had no means of support, or if they were receiving 'poor relief' when pregnant or giving birth to an illegitimate child.

The state had found a way to imprison many of those seen as threats to the stability of society – the working-class poor, single women and people with learning difficulties. The act's 'clear intention' was to prioritise the admission of those who were young, 'morally defective' and 'high grade' [10]. In practice, this often meant single, working-class women who had become pregnant.

Despite the overwhelming support for the new laws, both in and outside Parliament, there were opponents. Two of the most prominent were the writers Hilaire Belloc and G K Chesterton. Chesterton said that the state – with the help of the medical profession – was giving itself new powers to control sex and imprison those who were powerless to defend themselves. He described the new laws as an attack on liberty, and became a close ally of the Liberal MP Josiah Wedgwood.

Wedgwood argued in parliament that authorising segregation of 'the feeble-minded' would be the 'thin edge of the wedge of the eugenic theory'. But it would be wise not to become too misty-eyed about Wedgwood's stand. His concern appeared to be only for those described as 'feeble-minded'. He described institutions for people with learning difficulties as 'full of people who are horrible to see, mentally defective persons, idiots, and imbeciles, people it would be the severest possible penalty to have to live in company with... these hells upon earth'[8].

Wedgwood staged a 'filibuster' through two all-night sittings of the Commons, making 120 amendments to the bill and delivering 150 speeches. He was not interested in the rights of people with learning difficulties themselves, but in fighting for civil liberties in general. He told fellow MPs that 'if this bill is passed into law, it will put into prison 100,000 people who are at present at liberty'. But he failed to halt the bill's progress, which was opposed by only two other MPs. It received royal assent on 15 August 1913.

The Mental Deficiency Act 1913 was to set the tone for much of the remainder of the twentieth century. It gave local authorities two duties: to certify all those considered 'mentally deficient', and to set up institutions for those considered not to be receiving adequate care at home. Recommendations for people to be certified might come from doctors, teachers, parents or prison authorities. Once they had been 'ascertained' as 'feeble-minded', an 'imbecile' or an 'idiot', they were 'subject to be dealt with' under the act and placed either in an institution or some form of community-based care, which usually involved supervision. Supervision was chosen if the person's home situation was thought adequate, although, says Mathew Thomson[11], this could sometimes be because there was no space in an institution.

People sent to these institutions, or 'colonies', were expected to work on their farms, or carry out other tasks such as cleaning, cooking or laundry. Although a person's detention had to be reviewed after one year and then every five years, those in charge of the institutions had the final decision on whether someone could be released. Many were unwilling to discharge members of such a cheap workforce.

Within a year, the Mental Deficiency Act caused the number of people with learning difficulties in institutions to rise by a third. From 1916 to 1926 the number rose from 6,500 to 20,000, then to 46,000 in 1939, and reached 57,500 by 1950. The number under statutory supervision in the community rose just as fast: from 16,000 in 1926 to 44,000 in 1939. A similar number were under voluntary supervision, with a few thousand under guardianship orders, in which guardians were paid a fee for providing a home and sometimes a job. Sheena Rolph[12] has described how disruptive young female orphans were often certified under the act, particularly if the authorities thought they would be difficult to place in service.

The influence of the eugenicists on the new state bureaucracy was clear: two leading figures from the National Association for the Care and Control of the Feeble-Minded – Mary Dendy and Ellen Pinsent – were appointed to the act's new Board of Control.

The board also helped establish the Central Association for Mental Welfare (CAMW), whose members were in favour of segregation and whose public statements, according to Jan Walmsley[13], often had a distinctly eugenic undertone. The CAMW was set up to provide cheap volunteers to implement the parts of the act that applied to care outside institutions, such as carrying out 'friendly' supervision of 'borderline' cases. Walmsley points out that no member of CAMW is known to have had a relative with learning difficulties.

As well as providing a willing source of labour to implement the control demanded by the Mental Deficiency Act, CAMW also campaigned on issues that were probably too politically sensitive for the government, such as calling for people with learning difficulties to be prevented from marrying, in the 1920s, and demanding voluntary sterilisation in the 1930s. It also nagged local authorities that were lagging behind in implementing the act. To CAMW members, says Walmsley, 'community care was always second best to institutional care'.

The Wood Report in 1929 led to growing alarm about the number of people with learning difficulties and the 'borderline' population who also needed care and control. The Board of Control would later admit, though, to 'a growing realization that the public care and protection of the majority of mentally defective persons must be organized outside institutions and colonies'. Mathew Thomson points to the first recorded use of the term 'community care' appearing in the Board of Control's annual report in 1930, which states that 'it is clear that society cannot afford to segregate defectives who are in other respects fit for community care merely to prevent them from marrying'. In a later report in the early 1930s, the board would say that 'it should be the aim of Local Authorities to reduce to a minimum the number of defectives who need to be retained permanently in institutions'. However, these admissions also led to growing calls for people with learning difficulties to be banned from marrying and to be sterilised.

Thomson argues that there was a slight shift away from institutional care in the 1920s and 1930s, because although the number of people in the colonies increased, the figure as a proportion of the population peaked in 1930 at 3.57 per thousand. Community care was cheaper than institutions, but only, says Thomson, because it was manned by a 'battalion of volunteers'.

CAMW members seemed to have acted partly as unpaid snoopers for the state. One of their duties was to locate people suspected of being 'defective' and then report them to the local authority, with councils often complaining that the problems they reported had been exaggerated. The CAMW volunteers – mostly middle-class ladies – also inspected people in their own homes, one of their duties being to ensure they had not formed relationships with members of the opposite sex. They also volunteered at occupation centres – another way for the authorities to keep track of people – became home tutors for children with learning difficulties, and provided 'aftercare' for those discharged from the colonies. Although the occupation centres were funded by local authorities, much of the work was carried out by these volunteers.

Even if someone with a learning difficulty was placed under a guardianship or supervision order and allowed to live in the community, they were still under the control of the authorities, with their placements regularly reviewed. Families always faced the threat that their child could be removed and placed in an institution if they did not cooperate and provide the necessary 'care and control' themselves.

Thomson says there was a reluctance to provide financial support to families to help them care for their child, with the authorities often happier to blame the mothers. Britain, of course, was in the middle of an economic depression.

The colonies themselves were brutal places. Certification as a 'mental defective' often meant being confined to an institution for life. Privacy was non-existent, the regimes harsh and the food poor. Patients frequently spent their entire day on the ward, if they weren't working in the grounds. Those who did work were not paid, apart from small extra rations. They were locked in, deprived of outside contact. They wore 'uniforms', as if in prison, and the sexes were strictly segregated. Staff training and salaries were poor. Patients were frequently ill-treated. Duncan Mitchell[14], a learning disability nurse himself, says: 'The system of control that existed clearly encouraged those who had a controlling nature.'

Many of the so-called 'high grade' patients were given some responsibility, as their job was to look after 'low grade' patients. Mitchell says some people classified as 'mental defectives' even went on to become probationer nurses themselves. But as he points out: 'Any power exercised by people with learning difficulties was always tempered by their restriction to the institution and by the possibility of withdrawal of privileges.'

It was the Second World War and particularly the gradual understanding of the horrors of the Holocaust and the Nazi eugenics programmes, which began to turn public opinion towards the realisation that segregating and institutionalising tens of thousands of people who had committed no crime was a terrible breach of their human rights.

The Aktion T4 programme led to the targeted killing of at least 200,000 disabled people in Germany, and probably many thousands more, and became the blueprint for the 'Final Solution', through which the Nazis hoped to wipe out Jews, gay people and other minorities.

Although scientists had begun to attack the scientific basis for eugenics, campaigns for legalized sterilization of people with learning difficulties were still successful in some European countries and US states.

Despite the tide turning against eugenics, says John Welshman, there was still 'no discernible intellectual challenge to the assumptions underpinning institutionalization as the optimum treatment'. That was until 1947, when the National Council for Civil Liberties (NCCL) launched a campaign against the MDA regime. Four years later, it published a pamphlet, '50,000 Outside the Law', which described the bureaucracy that had grown up alongside the acts – there had been a second MDA in 1927 – as a 'challenge to democracy' and 'one of the gravest social scandals of the twentieth century'.

The following year, the new National Health Service took over responsibility for long-stay hospitals and the colonies were transferred into the control of the new hospital authorities, while local authorities retained responsibility for providing services for those people with learning difficulties who lived at home. Parents were no longer expected to contribute financially to maintaining their children in institutions.

As Duncan Mitchell points out, handing responsibility to the new NHS only confirmed the 'medicalisation' of services for people with learning difficulties, the idea that they were 'sick' and needed to be 'treated'. And the NHS Act of 1946 had not dismantled the 'mental deficiency' apparatus. Local authorities still had their duties of ascertainment, supervision, licence and guardianship. The National Assistance Act of 1948 had encouraged councils to provide services such as occupation centres, hostels and social clubs, but there was no duty to do so and the quality and quantity of community-based services was highly variable.

The NCCL campaign helped persuade the government to set up the Royal Commission on Law Relating to Mental Illness and Mental Deficiency, in 1954. In its evidence to the commission, the NCCL said institutions were so dependent on the cheap labour of the patients that even if those in charge believed that a large number of them should be discharged, 'it would be impossible for release to be granted without bringing the institution to a standstill'.

The NCCL criticized the standards of care and protection and the extreme control over people's lives and liberty, and cited many examples of wrongful detention. It called for compulsory provision of good quality services in the community, and financial assistance on the basis of need. It concluded that people with learning difficulties were 'an integral part of the human race; their existence constitutes an unspoken demand on us. The extent to which we guard their right to the fullest and most useful life, the extent to which we guarantee to them the maximum freedom which they can enjoy and the extent to which we help their families to give them the love they need, is a measure of the extent to which we ourselves are civilized.'

When the commission reported in 1957, it recommended the replacement of institutions with 'community care'. The ideal, it said, was a family environment and the end of segregation. A hostel, or residential or foster home, was the next best thing. It called for improved procedures and safeguards around admission and discharge from the hospitals; better welfare services; more residential and training facilities in the community; and 'more social support' for people with learning difficulties and their families, all of which should be a compulsory duty for local authorities. It recommended that hospital care should be limited to those who needed specialist medical treatment or continuing nursing attention.

The provisions of the Mental Health Act 1959, though, were considerably weaker, and there was no closing-down of the long-stay hospitals, although the act did repeal the Mental Deficiency Acts. Local authorities were given a duty to provide a range of services and residential accommodation for people with learning difficulties living in the community. The act supported the idea of community care but provided little funding to put it into practice.

The act did abolish the certification process and replaced the term 'mental deficiency' with the marginally less demeaning 'mental sub-normality'. Most patients were now classed as 'voluntary' and technically free to leave the hospitals. Some of those with lower support needs did so, but were provided with little or no preparation for life in the community. For the hospitals they left, the loss of their unpaid, manual labour was a huge financial blow.

John Welshman argues that, before 1948 and the NHS, there was a 'mixed economy of care' for people with learning difficulties, with local authorities, voluntary organisations, hospitals and families all playing a role. It was only in the 1950s, he says, that the local authority became the major provider, with a virtual monopoly on provision.

The shift away from institutions and towards care in the community and the idea of enabling people to achieve independence also received support from right-wing politicians, who saw the opportunity for cost-cutting, and, says Jan Walmsley, 'an alternative to expensive involvement by the social services'. Some historians argue that the Conservative government failed to back its Mental Health Act with the necessary funding. The amount spent on mental health and learning difficulties services in 1959-60 was just £3.5 million, the same sum spent on compensating farmers for the ravages of fowl pest. By 1962, there were just 47 hostels and 11,259 training centre places for adults with learning difficulties, while John Welshman and Jan Walmsley say the work in adult training centres 'was dictated more by the needs of local industrial firms, through contracts, than by the needs of service users themselves'. Work, they say, 'continued to be seen as a form of atonement rather than as a stepping stone to a 'normal' life'.

The slow progress in moving away from large institutions and towards a more community-based model of support was given impetus by a series of important pieces of research through the 1950s and 1960s.

In 1954, Neil O'Connor and Jack Tizard published a survey of patients in long-stay hospitals in and around London. They tested their IQs and found many of the young 'feeble-minded' patients were not that disabled, while half needed no special nursing or supervision.

In 1960, M W G Brandon carried out similar tests on adult women who had been classified as 'feeble-minded', and found a quarter had been certified because they had had an illegitimate child, while the majority could be successfully re-integrated into the community.

The 'Brooklands Experiment' – which began in 1958 under Tizard's supervision and was funded by the National Society for Mentally Handicapped Children (NSMHC, later to become Mencap) – saw 32 children with learning difficulties and high support needs taken from a large, overcrowded long-stay hospital in London and placed in a small, family-type unit in Surrey, where they were given care that was as close to that provided by a typical nursery as possible. After a year, the children's average 'mental age' had increased by eight months, compared with a rise of three months for those left in the hospital. After two years, it was clear that their social, emotional and verbal skills had greatly improved, again in comparison with those left in the hospital.

Other influential research argued for a greater use of hostels as a way of avoiding admission to hospitals and to allow long-stay patients to return to the community. In 1963, the 'Slough Experiment', again funded by NSMHC, set up a hostel run by a husband and wife, with an occupation centre within walking distance.

Among the most influential research of the 1960s was Asylums, a collection of essays by the sociologist Erving Goffman that was published in the US in 1961 and is still widely quoted today. Goffman came up with the concept of the 'total institution', a residential setting characterised by degradation and segregation, and in which the resident/patient/victim was seen as morally inferior to the staff. Goffman said such institutions shared four characteristics: a rigid routine; patients or residents treated in blocks rather than individually; the 'depersonalisation' of those forced to live there; and patients/residents kept at a distance from mainstream society.

In the same year, Russell Barton, the physician superintendent of Severalls Hospital in Essex, listed the 'seven deadly sins' of long-stay hospitals: the loss of contact with the outside world; the enforced idleness of patients; the bossiness of the nursing and medical staff; the loss of personal friends, belongings and events; the excessive use of drugs; the poor atmosphere in the wards; and the loss of future prospects outside the institution.

Towards the end of the 1950s, there had emerged the first moves away from the institutional model and back towards a more 'normal' life for people with learning difficulties. Those who developed this new movement, which began in Scandinavia, called it 'normalisation'. They argued that people with learning difficulties should be supported to live lives that were as 'normal' as possible, in housing, education, leisure and work.

But resistance was so strong in local and national government, and among health and social care professionals and the public, that it would take many years before the legacy of the eugenicists would finally begin to crumble.

*

DOROTHY

As a little girl, Dorothy Abbott was abandoned by her parents and spent her childhood in a series of residential homes.

Dorothy believes she was deserted because she had cerebral palsy. Because of her condition, which sometimes made it difficult for her to be understood, she received practically no education, which only exaggerated her learning difficulties.

In 1963, when Dorothy was about 19, she became a resident of Botleys Park long-stay hospital in Chertsey, Surrey. She was to spend the next 20 years there.

Botleys Park had opened in 1939 and was planned and built solely for 'mentally defective' patients, with places for 1,200 people in the colony, and another 300 in an annexe, Murray House. Staff brutality was common and conditions were harsh. But even as a young woman, Dorothy resisted the injustice and brutality she encountered. She remembers sitting in the huge dining hall for Sunday lunch. 'The patients used to have all the gristle and the stalks of cabbages and the staff used to have the good. A nurse came to me and she said, 'You had better eat this or else.' I said, 'I don't want to eat it.' She came back within five minutes, pulled my hair back and tried to stuff it down me.'

Punishments were common if you disobeyed the nurses. 'They used to give them bath brush on the feet if they did wrong or give them an injection called 10ccs, or give you a cold bath,' she would tell me later.

On one occasion, Dorothy and a friend escaped, but were soon picked up by the police. When they were brought back to the hospital, Dorothy spoke up. 'I said, 'You're not going to give me cold bath or you're not going to lock me in a side room or do anything,' and they said no, because I had police witnesses there. They gave me a luke-warm bath, but they didn't give me no bath brush and they tucked me up in a nice warm bed, instead of stripping me in a cold side room [bare, locked rooms used to punish patients in many long-stay hospitals].'

DAVID

Another resident of Botleys Park was a young man called David Jackson*. He had also been living at the hospital since 1963, when he was admitted at the age of eight.

David was the youngest of nine children and had attended a mainstream nursery and primary school. But because he couldn't speak, he was badly bullied and beaten up by the other children. He would hide in a cupboard in the morning to try to avoid school. One of his sisters, Brenda, remembers seeing him standing alone in the playground at playtime. 'He couldn't say he was being bullied, but we knew he was,' she says. 'It was horrible, knowing he was there.'

His mother loved him, says Brenda, but could not stand to see him suffer. She was terrified of what would happen to David when she and her husband were no longer around. 'I can remember one day we went on an outing to the seaside and mum told me that she hoped David would go out to sea too far and drown. She never harmed him, never. She loved him, but she just didn't get any support.'

David's parents agreed, eventually, that their son should be admitted to Botleys Park. 'He wasn't taken away,' says Brenda. 'Mum knew he had to go so that when they weren't around anymore he would be looked after.'

Another of David's sisters, Janet, says: 'It was a difficult time. You don't want to send your child away but mum probably thought it was for the best. There were a lot of us in the family and we were living in a small cottage.' Botleys was clean but institutional, she says. 'A bit like an army camp.'

Brenda's husband, Andy, remembers visiting Botleys when David was 12 and being told his young brother-in-law was ill. 'The sister told me he wasn't very well so he was in bed. I went in and saw him in this long dormitory and I just burst into tears. It was like something you would see in eastern Europe. They were not the standards of care you would expect in a civilised country. They were out of sight, out of mind.' He suggested that David would make better progress with one-to-one care, but the nurses told him there was no point and it wouldn't make any difference.

Janet believes her brother was not neglected, and she remembers a couple of nurses who liked and looked after him. David was happy at Botleys Park, she says. Hospital records describe David as an 'amiable young man' who was 'highly motivated to communicate' and 'expresses his feelings in grunts'. But Janet does accept there was a 'lack of attention'. 'They would get them up in the morning and feed them and then they would just sit around all day,' she says.

*

Ten years after the Mental Health Act, the state of the long-stay hospitals was summed up by Dr Pauline Morris. Her 1969 survey[15] of 35 long-stay hospitals, again funded by the NSMHC (which changed its name that year to Mencap), found 61 per cent of patients were living in complexes of more than 1,000 beds; only one per cent were in single rooms; and 69 per cent were in dormitories with two feet or less space between beds. Only 21 per cent of patients had their own toothbrushes, shaving kit or hairbrushes. Many were living in 'barren conditions', with little occupation and few social relationships. Nearly half of the patients did not receive a single visit in a year.

Dr Morris criticised the 'isolation, cruelty and deprivation of the hospital organisation', but conceded that most of the public regarded the poor conditions with 'comparative equanimity'. 'Because almost everyone adopts an attitude of untutored pessimism about the possibilities of educating and occupying the handicapped, unjustifiably low standards of care are tolerated,' she wrote.

These low standards were to be further exposed by a string of scandals during the late 1960s and 1970s.

The Ely Hospital Committee of Inquiry reported in March 1969, and concluded that the hospital's regime had been characterised by cruel ill-treatment, inhumane and threatening behaviour towards patients, the pilfering of food and clothes by staff, and indifference by senior staff to complaints. It highlighted overcrowded wards, and a lack of privacy for patients, who were allowed few personal possessions. Buildings were old and poorly designed, few patients were discharged, and food and clothing were inadequate. Staff who tried to complain were intimidated into silence. There were poor links with the local community.

The Farleigh Hospital Committee of Inquiry reported two years later. It found that few patients received visits, and even fewer visited anyone outside the hospital. In one ward, nearly all the residents never left the ward. There was a lack of space, equipment and staff, and a 'harmful over-use of drugs'. Suspicious deaths were not reported to the coroner. Three nurses were eventually jailed for ill-treating patients.

These scandals forced the government to set up the Hospital Advisory Service, to inspect and improve the long-stay hospitals. And in June 1971, the Conservative government published a white paper, Better Services for the Mentally Handicapped. Its aim was to address the poor state of services and explain the need for a greater emphasis on care in the community and less on care in hospitals. The Department of Health and Social Security hoped its white paper might lead to greater public understanding of people with learning difficulties. It announced that the huge, long-stay hospitals should gradually be closed down and replaced by residential homes.

The hospitals were overcrowded and the demand for places in residential homes was already seven times higher than supply, so most parents of children with learning difficulties kept them at home, but were offered little or no support to do so. The white paper admitted that many families were 'under almost unbearable stress' but received little 'practical help and advice' to deal with it. It said little progress had been made in providing adult training centres, residential care and information and advice for families.

The white paper concluded that there was no need for new policies, just more money and more trained staff. Coming only a year after the Local Authority Social Services Act led to responsibility for people with learning difficulties being taken over by new social services departments from the old council health departments, it has been suggested that the white paper may have come too soon.

But most of the right words were there in the white paper, just as they had been in the report of the royal commission in 1957 and the Mental Health Act of 1959. What had been missing was the political will and funding to force those words into action. The white paper allocated £40 million a year to improve community services over the next four years, but the money was not ring-fenced and the government stressed that the main responsibility lay with the local authorities themselves.

In addition, social services departments placed people with learning difficulties way down their list of priorities. As one social worker put it later: 'Much of social work was taken up with the logistics of childcare, so the mentally handicapped person – who wasn't deemed able to grow and develop as a person – was not a high priority.'

Four years after the white paper, the government abolished the Hospital Advisory Service, when acceptable minimum standards were supposedly reached. But the scandals kept coming.

In May 1974, the Report of the Committee of Inquiry into South Ockendon Hospital again found worryingly poor standards of nursing care. The inspector blamed incompetent management and problems with the handling of complaints. The hospital, he said, was overcrowded and understaffed. Among other things, he blamed a lack of funding. Staff tended to rely on tranquillisers, rather than providing activities, to control the patients. Side-rooms on wards were used for patients who didn't 'behave' or co-operate. Often, there would be just a mattress and blanket on the floor of these punishment rooms.

The Committee of Inquiry into Normansfield Hospital in November 1978 was not about cruelty, but still found that 'the standard of nursing care was generally extremely low'. There was too much seclusion of 'difficult' patients. More than a century after John Langdon-Down founded Normansfield with the aim to 'open out fresh realms of happiness' for people with learning difficulties, the inquiry found its buildings neglected and dangerous, with patients sometimes soaked as they slept, because of leaky roofs. Faeces and urine were often left unattended for days. The inspector concluded that the hospital was 'generally speaking, filthy', and the wards bare and reminiscent of workhouses. Patients had no personal possessions and no privacy.

The 1971 white paper had drawn detailed attention to overcrowding, unsuitable buildings, poor living standards and chronic under-staffing in residential services. The government had pledged to make extra resources available, and said it expected hospital boards to reallocate money to long-stay hospitals. Either this money hadn't been enough, or the boards hadn't been committed to the idea of spending scarce resources on people with learning difficulties. Either way, many patients were still living in squalor.

But it wasn't just about money. Reginald Johnson, of the Richmond Society for Mentally Handicapped Children, told the Normansfield inquiry: 'A number of patients at Normansfield are patients there because their families simply could not cope... It is difficult for us to see that there is adequate co-operation between education, social services and health authorities... If there were more support services for parents of children at home, then I think it probable that a great many more parents would be able to keep their children at home.'

The white paper had emphasised the importance of different agencies working together. But their subsequent failure to do so, and the lack of support for parents, would enable appalling levels of abuse to thrive.

Despite the Better Services white paper, the long-stay hospital closure programme moved slowly: in 1971, there were 58,850 people in long-stay hospitals. Nine years later, there were still 51,500.

At the same time, the normalisation movement was growing. The Jay Report (the Report of the Committee of Enquiry on Mental Handicap Nursing and Care) in 1979 was influential, arguing that all people with learning difficulties should be enabled to live in the community, with support from non-medical care workers, and to be treated as individuals. The King's Fund report, An Ordinary Life, published the following year, also called for 'normal' lives for people with learning difficulties and 'ordinary' housing supported by local services.

*

DAVID AND DOROTHY

David Jackson's sister Janet had no idea what conditions were really like at Botleys Park, with neglect, overcrowding and ill-treatment ingrained into patients' daily lives.

Throughout the 1970s and early 1980s, the local newspaper, the Surrey Herald, carried reports of neglect and poor care at Botleys. In 1971, one young man, Alan Ball, died six days after being punched by a fellow patient. Their ward was so short-staffed that other patients had put Ball to bed after the attack, in which he suffered a fractured skull and 'lacerated brain'. An

31

inquiry by the hospital board severely criticised staff for the 'failure in communications' which delayed Ball's examination by a doctor and for 'inadequate supervision' on the ward. The hospital complained that it had less than 300 nurses to look after its 1,265 patients, 200 fewer than it needed.

There were occasional reports of sexual assaults on patients by hospital staff. In 1972, the hospital's part-time Roman Catholic chaplain, Father Stanley Tyson, was given a conditional discharge after his conviction for indecently assaulting two young female patients in the hospital chapel.

Later that year, a fire on the second-floor of the Murray House annexe, a former workhouse built in 1822, led to further public criticism, with the Daily Express describing how 'some children – admitted to Murray House at the tender age of seven or eight – are still waiting fifty years later for a first visit from parents, relatives or friends...' The hospital's chairman told the newspaper: '...the patients need more staff, more care, modern buildings: ours are ridiculously out of date and merely add to the strain already placed on a below-strength staff.'

By 1976, Botleys Park was so overcrowded and under-staffed that its nurses refused to admit any more patients until at least 100 extra staff were recruited and the number of beds reduced.

The following year, there were allegations of 'primitive conditions' at Murray House. The Surrey Herald reported: 'In South Ward, 38 high dependency patients sleep in beds head to foot, only inches from each other, with no lockers or cabinets of their own... [the] damp, overcrowded dormitory with its peeling paint and plaster opens straight into a large lavatory with rows of lavatory bowls ranged along the walls.' Conditions were further exposed in a TV documentary by the campaigning journalist John Pilger several months later, while the Herald reported on 'scandalous' conditions in the Botleys Park kitchens.

Documents from the hospital's archives reveal further evidence of poor care. In 1979, a divisional nursing officer told staff he had witnessed a 'disgraceful incident' in which 'a very reluctant male resident was being badly mishandled through the main thoroughfare of the hospital, being shaken and remonstrated with in an aggressive manner'. The following year, a female patient complained that a male member of the domestic staff had touched her inappropriately, and asked if he could take her to a pub 'to make love to her'. And in February 1980, a letter from a patient's sister accused the hospital of 'appalling mismanagement' and 'cruelty' on her brother's ward. Two months later, a nurse claimed to have seen a colleague in charge of a ward slap a patient in the face. A nursing assistant who witnessed the incident reluctantly corroborated the claim and told bosses he hadn't been surprised because there was 'a deal of teasing of patients' and he had 'seen residents cuffed about the head when they threw knives and forks about'. Strangely, the hospital decided there was insufficient evidence to discipline the nurse.

Two months later, the Herald reported how a barman at Botleys was given a suspended prison sentence after committing a serious sexual offence against a male patient.

In August 1982, the Herald described how a local Labour politician, who had toured Botleys Park, criticised the 'poor sanitary conditions and the shortage of staff in many wards'. The patients, he said, 'suffer from being at the end of a long queue for ever diminishing government funds'. The following month, three male patients in the Murray House annexe died from salmonella poisoning.

The reports of poor care kept coming. The following year, a leaked report on an inspection of Botleys by the government's National Development Team for the Mentally Handicapped described one ward as having the 'most disgraceful' toilet areas the team had ever seen, with three baths in a line without screens or curtains, and toilets not enclosed by doors or separated by screens.

Soon afterwards, there was national publicity for a report by a campaigning organisation, the Association for the Protection of Patients and Staff, into poor standards at 16 long-stay hospitals, including Botleys. Staff told how patients were overdosed with tranquilisers, and of physical and sexual assaults. Nurses and volunteers who found the courage to complain, according to The Times, found themselves 'isolated, banned or moved on by the defensive reaction of colleagues and authorities', while complaint mechanisms were 'ineffective'.

Bath-time for teenage girls on one Botleys ward was likened to 'bathing cattle', with the girls having to line up naked. The report said: 'Bathtime in this ward meant going through a porcelain bath tray and being hosed down. They were not allowed to sit in the bath and do what they needed to clean themselves... instead they were just hosed down like cattle.'

Other hospitals were just as bad, with descriptions of a 'punishment ward' at Manor Hospital in nearby Epsom where patients were forced to wear green boiler-suits and had to 'earn' their way out of the ward through a token system, by scrubbing floors and cleaning the kitchen, while patients in another ward had to 'earn tokens in order to get a meal', with many going hungry because they failed to earn enough tokens. At Bethlem Royal Hospital, in Kent, children with learning difficulties were tied to chairs and locked in padded cells, while the use of drugs and 'behaviour modification' was 'brutal and ill-considered'.

The health service union COHSE described the report as 'an outrageous piece of scare-mongering'.

*

One of the National Development Team's major criticisms had been of 'stagnation' in the process of discharging patients from Botleys back into the community. Only 10 people had been moved into more independent settings in the three years before their visit, according to The Times. The health authority apparently blamed a lack of cooperation by other agencies.

So it can surely have been no coincidence – in the light of the fierce public and parliamentary criticism – that six months later, a large group of Botleys patients were taken to see a newly-opened residential home called Stoke Place, in south

Buckinghamshire, near Slough. It was run by a former social worker called Gordon Rowe.

Dorothy Abbott remembers hearing about Stoke Place from some of the patients who had visited Stoke Place. 'I had a social worker and he took the other residents up to Stoke Place and they would come back and say how great it was,' she told me. 'I had to have a fight to get there because I was still with this boyfriend of mine, Jimmy. Because Gordon Rowe said, 'I only want one,' but then the social worker said, 'You will have to take them both, because they are both mates to each other.''

David Jackson was another of the patients found places at Stoke Place. And in December 1983, Dorothy and Jimmy, along with David and 14 other patients, arrived at Stoke Place. After sleeping for years in dormitory wards where their only possessions were kept in wooden lockers by their beds, they must have been overwhelmed to arrive at the grand country house, with its acres of gardens, woods, its lake, farm animals and their own bedrooms.

But David's sister Janet remembers meeting Gordon Rowe and disliking him intensely. 'He was a big, thick-set man,' she says, 'and he was just an absolute bully, you could feel it. I felt I had to be nice to him so that he would be nice to Dave. He wasn't the sort of man you wanted to cross in any way whatsoever.'

She also wasn't happy with the upkeep of Stoke Place. 'When we first went in there, Dave's bed was missing one leg and it was propped up with house bricks, and there was no light-bulb in the room.'

There must be a suspicion that the authorities at Botleys Park paid little attention to the care their former charges would receive at Stoke Place. They were under pressure to start shipping patients out and must have been reluctant to look too closely at the staffing numbers and standards of care, or indeed at Rowe's own background.

Sadly, for David, Dorothy, and the other former Botleys Park patients, this failure to see through Rowe's web of lies – as so many other professionals would do – was to expose them to years of neglect, abuse and brutality.

1   *The Development of Social Welfare in Britain, by Eric Midwinter; Open University Press; 1994*

2   *Social Welfare in Pre-Industrial England, by Paul A Fideler; Palgrave Macmillan; 2005*

3   *Networks of Care in Elizabethan English Towns: The example of Hadleigh, Suffolk, in The Locus of Care: families, communities, institutions and the provision of welfare since antiquity, edited by Peregrine Horden and Richard Smith; Routledge; 1998*

4   *Lunatics and Idiots: Mental disability, the community, and the poor law in North-East England, 1600-1800, by Peter Rushton; Medical History, 1988, volume 32, number 1, pages 34-50*

5   *Understanding Segregation from the Nineteenth to the Twentieth Century, in Crossing Boundaries: Change and continuity in the history of learning disability, edited by Lindsay Brigham, et al; BILD Publications; 2000*

6   *The Origins of the British Welfare State, by Bernard Harris; Palgrave Macmillan; 2004*

7   *Familial Care of 'Idiot' Children in Victorian England, by David Wright, in The Locus of Care: Families, communities, institutions and the provision of welfare since antiquity, edited by Peregrine Horden and Richard Smith; Routledge; 1998*

8   *The Borderland of Imbecility: Medicine, society and the fabrication of the feeble mind in late Victorian and Edwardian England, by Mark Jackson; Manchester University Press; 2000*

9   *Equal Citizens? The Discourse of Liberty and Rights in the History of Learning Disabilities, by Tim Stainton, in Crossing Boundaries: Change and continuity in the history of learning disability, edited by Lindsay Brigham, et al; BILD Publications; 2000*

10   *Assistance and Resistance: Making sense of inter-war caring strategies*, by Pamela Dale, in *Exploring Experiences of Advocacy by People with Learning Disabilities: Testimonies of resistance*, edited by Duncan Mitchell, et al; Jessica Kingsley Publishers; 2006

11   *Community Care and the Control of Mental Defectives in Inter-war Britain*, by Mathew Thomson, in *The Locus of Care: Families, communities, institutions and the provision of welfare since antiquity*, edited by Peregrine Horden and Richard Smith; Routledge; 1998

12   *Surprise Journeys and Border Crossings*, by Sheena Rolph, in *Crossing Boundaries: Change and continuity in the history of learning disability*, edited by Lindsay Brigham, et al; BILD Publications; 2000

13   *Straddling Boundaries: The changing roles of voluntary organisations, 1913-1959*, by Jan Walmsley, in *Crossing Boundaries: Change and continuity in the history of learning disability*, edited by Lindsay Brigham, et al; BILD Publications; 2000

14   *Ambiguous Boundaries: Retrieving the history of learning disability nursing*, by Duncan Mitchell, in *Crossing Boundaries: Change and continuity in the history of learning disability*, edited by Lindsay Brigham, et al; BILD Publications; 2000

15   *Put Away: A sociological study of institutions for the mentally retarded*, by Dr Pauline Morris; Routledge and Kegan Paul; 1969

Chapter Two

On Your Own

'Prejudice, discrimination and low expectations are the major barriers preventing improvements to the lives of severely disabled people with learning difficulties, according to a report commissioned by the government. But Professor Jim Mansell says in his report that adults with 'profound intellectual and multiple disabilities' usually get what they and their families want and need if they are supported to use personalised services. Research suggests there are about 16,000 people with profound intellectual and multiple disabilities in England, who all have great difficulty communicating, limited understanding, and high support needs. Professor Mansell said: 'A common experience appears to be that families are told that they cannot have the services they need because their needs are too great."

Disability News Service, 23 March 2010

It was not until after the Second World War, shortly before the National Council for Civil Liberties would start campaigning against the 'mental deficiency' regime, that the first pressure group began to represent the interests of the families of people with learning difficulties.

The National Association for the Parents of Backwards Children (NAPBC, which would in 1955 become the National Society for Mentally Handicapped Children (NSMHC) and then, in 1969, change its name again to Mencap) was set up in 1946 by Judy Fryd, the mother of a child with learning difficulties. The aim of these parents was to secure education for their children.

In 1955, the charity extended its aims to include campaigning for the state to provide care for people with learning difficulties, but also to 'prevent the birth of handicapped children'. Although they wanted better services and support to allow their children to live in the community, there was still a disquieting undercurrent: they thought that, in a perfect world, their sons and daughters would not have been born.

In its evidence to the royal commission in 1954, the charity drew attention to the 25,000 children and adults waiting for places at special schools and occupation centres. It called for local authorities to be forced to provide education, training and hostel accommodation for those people who needed it, and argued that better support for families would mean fewer people having to be admitted to institutions.

Families were left in no doubt right from birth, or diagnosis, that their child was a burden on society, their family and the NHS. Doctors and nurses would advise parents to put their child in an institution and forget about her, or take her home and do their best – on their own – to look after her; but not to expect any advice or support.

In the face of this culture of discrimination, NSMHC raised funds to fill in the gaps in services, such as respite care, nursery classes, clubs and outings, while lobbying the government for more support. This lobbying undoubtedly played a part in the expansion of day centres and local authority hostels in the 1960s. NSMHC also began providing services itself, sponsoring the so-called 'Slough experiment', which set up a 'family-style' hostel, a model which was soon widely copied.

Jan Walmsley[1] argues that NAPBC was 'part and parcel of the shift from seeing 'mental defect' as a hereditary taint associated with crime, immorality and disease, to seeing it as a tragedy which could befall any parents, its members as unfortunate people 'burdened' with a never-ending cycle of care, and properly deserving of publicly funded help'.

*

SIMON

Simon Scott had been born disabled in 1963, but his parents believed it was an impairment they could manage. Avril and Brian Scott tried to treat him as an equal to his brothers and sisters, and bring him up with children his own age.

Simon was a 'happy little soul' and would sit and play with his toy cars all day, stopping for nothing except food. 'He was very slow walking and talking and one of his hands hung down,' says his dad. 'He had his tantrums, and when nothing went right, he got frustrated and everything went, but he was good and he was happy.' But Simon still needed nearly 24 hours a day care, and an uninterrupted night's sleep for his parents was unheard of.

He later attended a special school close to home. 'He couldn't cope with a lot of children running around, because he couldn't keep up with them,' says Avril. 'He got frustrated.' Simon seemed to take in the lessons he was taught, but found it difficult to apply this knowledge. 'He would sit and listen to you and absorb what you were saying, but it was expressing his feelings he couldn't do,' she says.

When he was about six, Simon started having epileptic seizures. Many people with learning difficulties are susceptible to epilepsy, a condition in which the brain is struck by sparks of internal electricity, causing seizures, or convulsions, during which they can lose consciousness. Simon's seizures became so lengthy and frequent that, when he was 16, he spent more than a year at an epilepsy hospital. His parents withdrew him after a doctor failed to diagnose a poisoned ankle, and Simon nearly had to have the leg amputated.

Simon returned home, and spent two years at another epilepsy hospital in Buckinghamshire to try to stabilise his condition.

Despite his medical problems, Simon was always ready with a cheeky grin. Just over five feet tall, he was full of energy and a handful for whoever was caring for him. He was, Brian says, a typical 'bolshie' teenager.

GREG

By the time she gave birth to Greg, her sixth child, in February 1965, Norma Adams knew something about bringing up babies. So when she noticed that her son didn't seem interested in toys and wasn't 'babbling' the way her other children had, she knew something was wrong. Physically, Greg was fine – he was crawling around faster than any of the others at his age – but Norma's intuition told her he was different.

When she took Greg to her GP, he laughed at her. 'With your experience, you should know all babies progress at different speeds,' he said.

'No,' she said, 'with my experience that's exactly why I know something is wrong.' Despite her protests, he refused to refer Greg to a specialist.

When Greg was 11 months old, the family moved to a different part of London. Norma visited the family's new GP, who examined Greg and told Norma she could see nothing wrong, but arranged for him to see a specialist.

Six months later, Norma's suspicions were confirmed by a consultant. Greg was hyperkinetic – a condition which meant he rarely stopped moving – and 'mentally handicapped'. 'You'll have to put him away,' he told her.

When she told the rest of the family, she was the only one who was unable to accept it. 'From then on,' she would write later, 'it was as though I was split into two people. There was the one who was intent on doing and learning all I could to cope with our problem and the other one who refused to acknowledge that there was anything at all wrong with my son.' It took her another six months and an entire weekend of 'grieving' before she came to terms with Greg's impairment.

Norma remembers vividly what it was like trying to cope with a child who wouldn't sit still for a minute. 'By the time he had turned two, he was so active, he never stopped, never sat down, never stopped moving from the moment his eyes were open. And he didn't walk, he ran. He didn't sleep, except for short half-hour naps totalling maybe four or five hours in every 24, which meant I didn't sleep. I had other children at home, so it was a pretty stressful time.'

But she worked hard to cope with Greg's hyperactivity. To prevent the frustration that could lead to a tantrum, she reasoned that it was she who did not understand what her son was trying to communicate, and would plead with him to continue trying to make her understand what he wanted. So they established a rapport, Norma with her words and Greg with his gestures.

When Greg was a little over two, he began attending a special unit in a day nursery. This gave Norma a few hours of relief every day. She would write later: 'His super-abundance of energy made it impossible to do any shopping or indeed do any of the usual domestic duties without frequent interruptions. He had no sense of danger. He could climb like a mountain goat but he only had two methods of descent: he either just let go of whatever he was hanging from or leapt down regardless of the height. This meant that somebody's eyes had to be on him at all times and with the rest of my family either at school or at work it was my eyes which were needed.' Much of her time was spent teaching Greg to carry out his adventures with at least a degree of safety.

NICKY

Nicky Power had been born a healthy baby in January 1967. Eleven months later, on Boxing Day, her parents Susan and Davyd took her to spend the day with Susan's mother and step-father in Maidstone. When they woke Nicky up that evening, she appeared to be developing a cold. By the time they had driven back home in nearby Tonbridge, Nicky was unconscious and her right side paralysed. She was rushed to hospital and the Powers were told she might not make it through the night. At one stage, her temperature reached 109 degrees. But she survived.

'Thirty years ago, meningitis wasn't really heard of,' says Susan. 'We didn't know the symptoms or realise how rapidly it came on. It all happened within about two hours.' Davyd and Susan believed Nicky had made a full recovery.

But they soon became worried. Nicky would do nothing but sit screaming and rocking on the floor for hours at a time.

Susan and Davyd took her back to the hospital when she was 18 months old. Nicky was quite calm at first, but as the doctor started to examine her, she began screaming and bashing her head against the wall. The doctor said: 'Is this what you mean?' He told them to leave the room. A few minutes later, he called them back in and said: 'The best thing you could do is put her in a home, because she will only ever be a year old.'

The doctor's ignorance was only a taster of what was to come. 'I came home just in a heap,' says Susan. 'My worst fears had been confirmed.'

It was only when they paid to see a consultant in London a fortnight later that they were told about Nicky's impairment. After examining their daughter, he asked them: 'You realise that your daughter is severely brain damaged?' He said he would write to Kent County Council to arrange for Nicky to attend a special school.

The Powers would soon discover that having a 'mentally handicapped' child would change their lives.

'We found out who our friends were,' says Susan. 'They would ask: 'How's Nicola?' and I would say: 'Just the same' and they would say: 'I can't stand it when she screams.' We lost contact with a lot of people, including her god-mother.'

Susan didn't know anybody in a similar situation and knew nothing about her daughter's impairment. The authorities were not interested. All the Powers were given was a prescription for a strong sedative that left Nicky so drugged up she would do nothing all day but sit on the floor, rocking backwards and forwards.

STEFANO

Stefano Tunstell was born in October 1967. At first, he seemed like most other babies his age: he talked and smiled and seemed to like people. But from the age of about 30 months he started to become withdrawn. His parents Lidia and Leslie became more and more concerned as Stefano began to lose the speech he had learned.

Lidia was making frequent trips to see her parents in Italy and it was an Italian doctor who advised her to take Stefano to a psychologist. But when she returned to England, the family GP assured her Stefano was fine. It was only when she returned to Italy when Stefano was four that she was able to take him to a specialist. By this time she was becoming 'a little desperate'. The psychologist told her Stefano had 'an autistic tendency', but that it was not yet that advanced.

'He felt that with the right sort of help, Stefano would be able to come back to normality,' says Lidia. 'He had been such a sociable little baby – we never thought he was going to become so disabled.' The causes of autism are still unclear, although genetic and biological factors are both believed to play a part. No two people with autism are the same, but many share difficulties in using language, understanding social relationships, and using their imagination, and have a tendency to repeat familiar routines.

On their return to England, on the advice of a health visitor, Stefano was taken to a county council medical officer. Lidia says: 'She saw Stefano and she kept saying, 'It's very odd. It's very odd. He ought to go to a special school.' She was absolutely horrible. I was devastated.'

JANET

The family GP told Irene Ward she was just over-anxious. There's nothing to worry about, he said, your daughter is fine. But there was something in the way Janet moved, the noises she made. Irene had four other children; she could see the difference. She kept taking Janet back to the doctor, but he told her to be patient. 'She'll be fine,' he said. 'She's just a little slow.' He refused to refer Janet to a specialist. It was 1968.

As the months passed, Irene became more convinced that Janet was different. Eventually, she was referred to Great Ormond Street Hospital for Children. After Janet was examined, Irene was given a letter to hand to her GP.

Irene's daughter Pauline remembers sitting in her aunt's kitchen, watching her mother and her aunt discuss what to do. They finally decided to steam the letter open.

'The letter said Janet would not be able to walk or talk, that she would be a vegetable,' says Pauline. 'My mum was crying, she was absolutely hysterical.'

Tests had revealed that Janet was 'mentally retarded and epileptic'. While in the womb, the umbilical cord had become wrapped around her neck, interrupting the blood supply to her brain, leaving it permanently damaged.

Irene Ward was determined not to give up on her daughter, despite the 'experts'' gloomy conclusions. She could not bear the thought of Janet being sent away to a home. Her family was concerned about the extra burden, but Irene was ready to fight. By the age of four, Janet had learned to walk. By the age of five, she could say the words 'mum' and 'dad'.

Janet's father, Tony, had married Irene when he was young, and relied heavily on her. When Janet was diagnosed, the family worried about how he would cope. But he changed almost overnight. Unlike his other children, Janet was never punished with a smack, and Tony never raised his voice when she misbehaved. He celebrated the slightest progress in her development.

Janet's older brother and sisters spent hours playing with her, helping her learn the speech and dexterity the specialists had not believed possible. But they also paid a price for having Janet around.

Pauline, who was six years older than Janet, says: 'Janet was happy and active, but she was very, very demanding of my mother. My other sister was only two years older than Janet, but none of us could sit on mum's lap or hold her hand. She would just drag us off.'

The family could never relax. Janet only had to see an open door and she was through it. After an incident on holiday in which Janet had fallen from a first-floor balcony while Pauline was looking after her, Irene put locks on all the windows and doors at home.

Despite such restrictions, Pauline never resented Janet, although she and her siblings were protective of her. 'She used to have one of those disabled buggies with blue and white stripes. Everybody used to stare wherever we went – adults and children. One day, I was pushing her in the pushchair with my sister, and some children from my school saw us and started laughing and shouting 'spastic'. I let go of Janet to try and chase after them, but she leaned forward and fell out. She had a lump the size of an egg on her face. I got a real telling off from mum.

'We weren't ashamed of her, we were embarrassed. When you start courting and you bring your boyfriends home and your sister is always between you... Most long-term friends got on well with her, but we probably kept new boyfriends out of the way for a while.'

GARY

Ron Deacon was to discover that once you became a parent of a 'mentally handicapped' child, the National Health Service was a much less welcoming place.

He was 56 when his step-daughter, Angela, asked him for help. It was April 1968, and she had just given birth to a son, Gary. Angela told Ron she could not look after her baby – she did not know who the father was, and her fiancé was refusing to marry her if Gary was part of the package.

Ron and his wife agreed to look after Gary at their home near Maidenhead, in Berkshire. He appeared to be a healthy baby, although he had problems sleeping and cried a lot. When Angela asked Ron to adopt her son, when he was just a few months old, he agreed.

Ron said later: 'Angela's fella made it quite plain that he would not accept Gary, and I thought he would end up being adopted or going to a home. I didn't want that to happen.

'But I wasn't that young and I was worried the courts wouldn't accept me.' But they did, and Ron became Gary's legal father.

As Gary grew older, the Deacons realised that he wasn't learning how to chew solid foods. Ron would take him to his local pub, and sit in the garden, encouraging him to copy his actions as he chewed crisps. Gary was still not sleeping well, and Ron would often put him in the back of his car in the early hours and drive up the M4 motorway to Heathrow Airport to lull him to sleep.

Ron and his wife became increasingly concerned at Gary's slow development and took him to their GP, who finally told them the truth: Gary had autism and was 'mentally handicapped', due to brain damage at birth. The medical authorities had known about Gary's condition, but decided not to tell them. Ron had struggled to bring up his young son for nearly two years without the benefit of any specialist advice.

Ron Deacon soon learned that no-one would be there to help him look after Gary. His wife did not cope well with Gary's impairment, and when she died when he was five, the pressure intensified.

Even when Gary began attending a local special school, there was no time for Ron to relax. His day began by waking, washing and dressing his son, and making breakfast. Then he would see him into a taxi, before heading off to work as a taxi driver himself. Later, a friend would meet Gary from another taxi after school, and Ron would return home to make dinner and do the other chores, before preparing Gary for bed. A kind neighbour helped with some of the housework, but it wasn't enough. Ron couldn't relieve the stress by talking to his son in the evenings, because Gary would only ever learn to say 'yes' or 'no'. Instead, father and son would watch television, and Ron began to drink heavily. Eventually, he had a nervous breakdown.

Parents with children who do not have impairments like Gary's do not realise what it's like, he told me. 'There are times when you feel as though your head is going to explode with frustration, because you just don't know what to do next.'

All six families were quickly learning how wide the gulf was between the love that they felt for their son or daughter and the attitude of the outside world to that child.

1 *Straddling Boundaries: The changing roles of voluntary organisations, 1913-1959, by Jan Walmsley, in Crossing Boundaries: Change and continuity in the history of learning disability, edited by Lindsay Brigham, et al; BILD Publications; 2000*

Chapter Three

School

'Autism campaigners and politicians have reacted with anger and dismay after a Scottish local authority built a 'cage' to contain an 18-year-old with learning difficulties, attending high school in Stornoway. The teenager's family had asked for a safe space to be built as an outdoor play area for their son, who is kept apart from other children because of his severe autism. The family are believed to have raised £500 to help to pay for the facility, at the Nicolson Institute in Stornoway, on the Isle of Lewis. The boy's parents were however horrified by the result. Instead of the decking and play equipment they expected, they found a pen built from metal barriers, with a strong wooden door and a bolt.'

The Times, 2 November 2010

Between 1860 and 1880, there was growing concern over the presence of so many children with learning difficulties and physical impairments in classrooms[1]. After universal compulsory education was introduced in the 1870s, it became clear that teachers were ignoring children with learning difficulties. There were increasingly vehement calls for segregation of 'mentally defective' children, with campaigners like Mary Dendy claiming they were likely to be disruptive and turn to crime.

The first special schools opened in 1892, following a report by the Royal Commission on the Blind and Deaf which concluded that children with learning difficulties should not remain in workhouses or asylums, and that local authorities should educate them.

By 1896, there were 24 special schools in London, with others in Nottingham, Birmingham, Bristol, Bradford and Brighton. But the eugenics movement was becoming more influential, with its followers demanding greater segregation, and even sterilisation. Intelligence testing was used to argue that children who achieved poor results would never be able to improve, while education spending could only be justified to prepare for more permanent 'care' in segregated institutions.

In 1899, the Elementary Education (Defective and Epileptic Children) Act gave local councils the power to set up special classes for 'defective' children from seven to 16, but historian Mark Jackson says adoption of the act was 'piecemeal'[1], while Alice Paige-Smith[2] says parents often protested at the decision to send their child away to a distant, segregated setting. Education departments often had to take out court orders to force parents to agree.

Among the evidence heard by the Royal Commission on the Care and Control of the Feeble-Minded was testimony on the role of special schools. When it reported, it recommended that early schooling should develop into industrial training, while an institutional system was superior to a network of special schools.

The Mental Deficiency Act gave education authorities the duty of deciding which children aged between seven and 16 were 'deficient' and incapable of being educated in special schools. These children were to be handed to the 'mental deficiency committees' and were given brief and superficial intelligence tests to justify sending them to an institution.

The following year, another Elementary Education (Defective and Epileptic Children) Act compelled education authorities to provide special schools or classes and obliged parents to send their 'feeble-minded' children there.

But the eugenicists had not merely been waiting for this legislation. As Mark Jackson points out, they had been diligently establishing segregated schools. In 1904, there were 116 special day schools in England (catering for 4,307 'feeble-minded' children). By 1916, there were 179 such schools, with more than 14,400 pupils. In 1911 there were eight residential special schools, whereas by 1919 there were 21.

Children with learning difficulties were increasingly being forced to attend special boarding schools, usually in the country, and often a long distance from their family home.

The 'certification' process – often condemning children to a lifetime of care in long-stay hospitals – was not abolished until the Education Act of 1944, which obliged local education authorities to provide special education. The act set out 11 categories of disabled children, with the aim of avoiding the rigid separation of disabled and non-disabled, and replaced the term 'mentally defective' with 'educationally subnormal'. Civil servants suggested the term should apply to children 20 per cent or more below average ability. But the act still included many of the worst aspects of the mental deficiency regime, such as segregation and ascertainment, and was strongly focused on children's impairments – the 'medical model' of disability – rather than on the barriers they faced in society.

The 1944 act also stated that children with an IQ below 50 were 'ineducable' and only allowed to attend an occupation centre or receive 'instruction' at home, or even be sent to an institution. Those children with the highest support needs were therefore excluded from the new education system, with those who lived at home the responsibility of local authorities' health departments, and hospital authorities looking after children living in long-stay hospitals. There were wide variations in provision for those disabled children deemed capable of education, with hundreds on waiting lists for special schools.

By the 1950s, charities were beginning to open their own facilities, such as training centres, crèches and occupation centres, and campaign for improvements to council facilities. But it was not until 1970, when the Education (Handicapped Children) Act forced local authorities to provide schooling for all 'mentally handicapped' children, that more than 20,000 disabled children who had been deemed 'ineducable' were finally allowed to join the general education system.

The remarkable career of Maureen Oswin has helped to expose what conditions were like for the thousands of children sent to live in the long-stay hospitals.

Oswin began working with disabled children in 1959 at Queen Mary's Hospital in Carshalton, Surrey. She described how the children never left the hospital and lived their childhood in just four large rooms. Most of these children had physical impairments, although some also had learning difficulties. Everything was on a large scale, she wrote[3], with huge laundries and kitchens, and the children forced to share their clothing. 'They lived totally institutionalised lives,' she wrote, 'excluded from the rest of society.'

In the mid-1960s, many children with severe learning difficulties came to St Mary's. Oswin wrote: 'They came from the Fountain Hospital in Tooting, which was a fearful old Mental Handicap Hospital where hundreds of children had lived for years in sordid huts. Many had been kept in cots all the time, but others had gone to occupation huts every day, where they did tasks such as putting pegs into boards or threading beads.'

At the time, the more severely disabled children were categorised as 'ineducable' and only eligible for 'occupation' under the supervision of unqualified teachers.

Oswin's book, 'The Empty Hours', was published in August 1971 and received widespread publicity. In her book, Oswin described how 'there were children living deprived lives all over the country', with 12,000 living in long-stay hospitals. 'It is a sobering thought that there are actually children in this country in 1970 who have never been into a cafe, never bought themselves an ice-cream, have never seen uncooked vegetables, fish and meat, or a loaf of bread.'

When she returned to Queen Mary's after the summer holiday, she expected her colleagues to be full of enthusiasm and questions about her book. Instead, many were furious at what they considered her betrayal, and, she wrote later, 'were not a bit concerned about the children I had described'.

After leaving Queen Mary's, Oswin worked at the Thomas Coram Research Unit, where her first project was to visit long-stay hospitals to observe the care of children in the 'special care wards', where many children had severe physical impairments and learning difficulties. She witnessed children left all day to lie on mattresses in day-rooms or slumped in wheelchairs. Most of the children were dehydrated, but 'nobody seemed to realise that they were nearly always thirsty... I have seen teenage boys, who were able to drag themselves about on their knees, go into ward courtyards and suck at puddles.'

Most of the children she observed received about five minutes of personal attention in 12 hours. 'They were,' she wrote, 'totally excluded from all normal childhood experiences.'

In 1978, Oswin wrote a book about the special care wards, 'Children Living in Long-Stay Hospitals'. Again, it received widespread publicity, and again there was outrage from hospital nurses. She wrote later how 'hard-line bolshie nurses' from the nursing union COHSE would turn up at conferences where she was speaking and 'hassle in a most aggressive manner'. 'They were not interested in the deprived lives of the children,' she wrote. 'They just saw my criticism as a threat to their own careers, being afraid that campaigns to close hospitals might eventually succeed. It amazed me how nurses and doctors constantly denied that the children were neglected both physically and emotionally.'

But Oswin also wrote about the barriers faced by the nurses and teachers who worked on the wards that stopped them speaking out: the lack of training, the uncaring culture, the stigma they faced in their jobs, the built-in resistance to change, the lack of professional support and their low aspirations for the children.

According to Sheena Rolph and Dorothy Atkinson[4], Oswin was able to speak out because she was an outsider. Many of the nurses were used to a culture in which the children were mocked and made fun of, while some had been brought up in families of nurses, living in staff houses in the hospitals' grounds. They were professionally isolated and unaware of developments in the care of children with learning difficulties. It was these factors, she argued, that allowed such terrible neglect to flourish on the special care wards.

*

GREG

The local authority's attitude to Greg Adams changed abruptly the day the social services department learned he had autism, at the age of four. The condition had first been recognised by the medical profession only about 20 years before and research was still in its infancy, but the London Borough of Hammersmith and Fulham's social services department had its own day nursery with a specialist unit for autistic children, and was happy to accept Greg.

In the few hours he spent at the nursery, his mother had to try and pack in everything else in her life: shopping, cooking, cleaning. She also had five teenage children still living at home, including two step-children. They needed their mother, too.

Greg stayed at the nursery until he was five. He was still only sleeping an hour at a time and would then be awake for the next two hours. He was a loner, but – compared to some autistic children – didn't mind being with other people; he simply ignored them. As long as he had plenty of space to run in, he was happy. Greg didn't cry, or throw tantrums. He just wanted to be on the move.

But the stress and sleepless nights were taking their toll on his mother. 'I had had enough. I just couldn't take any more,' says Norma. 'I really felt I couldn't take any more. I asked if he could be taken into care for two or three weeks, so I could have a break. I had quite a battle, but eventually I got social services to agree. After that, he went away for a short period every year and I went away on holiday.'

When Greg was five, he was transferred to a special care unit, which meant he was away from home for slightly longer every day. He stayed there for two years, until a new school for children with autism opened in Hammersmith.

Greg spent four years there, but the family lived at the other end of the borough and the head teacher became increasingly concerned that so much of Greg's life was being wasted on the traffic-clogged streets of west London. She told Norma to consider boarding school.

'I was very definitely split over it,' says Norma. 'The practical side of me said 'yes, yes, yes,' and the mothering side of me said 'no, no, no,' but I knew it was the right thing to do. I knew I was too emotionally involved in him to teach him all he should be taught and could be taught. Even to this day, in a funny sort of way, there are two of me where Greg is concerned. A tiny bit of my heart will not accept there is something wrong with him. Who wants to accept there is something wrong with their lovely baby boy? But I always let my practical side rule in the end.'

A friend told her about a new unit for autistic children opening at Great Stony School in Ongar. Despite officers from

Greater London Council (GLC) trying to persuade her that the unit was both non-existent and already full, she eventually convinced them to accept Greg.

Greg was at Great Stony until he was 14, and seemed to do well. But then the GLC decided to change the school's format and, instead of admitting only children with learning difficulties, decided to mix in a few 'delinquents'. Norma decided there was no way she was going to let her son mix with young tearaways, and arranged for him to be moved to Bradstow School, in Broadstairs, Kent.

Norma knew Greg had learned more at boarding school than he ever had at home. As she wrote then: 'Most parents tend to think that no-one else is capable of caring for their child other than themselves. It is very ego shattering to find that not only can it be done equally as well but that more can be taught your child by a stranger.'

STEFANO

Stefano Tunstell's schooling began promisingly. The head of the local primary school in Epsom, Surrey, said he could attend her mainstream school. But when she left a few weeks later, the new head told the Tunstells there wouldn't be room for him anymore. After just six weeks, Stefano had to leave his new school.

He moved to a special school and progressed well at first, but soon began to react badly to the strict regime. 'He was always upset and he would come home crying. Often, he would be sick and vomiting,' Lidia remembers.

She decided to take Stefano back to Italy to see the psychologist who first diagnosed his autism. He told her the school was 'absolutely the wrong environment' for Stefano, but it was not too late to help him.

Lidia decided to remove Stefano from the school. After a visit to a Harley Street specialist, and a long fight with the local education authority, Lidia and her husband Leslie were allowed to move Stefano to an assessment unit at Queen Mary's, the children's hospital Maureen Oswin had written about several years earlier. However, Stefano seemed happier there and made progress.

The unit only took children until they were 12, and Stefano soon had to move again. 'It was a nightmare looking for somewhere for him,' says Lidia. 'There was no support from social workers. They were very unkind and insensitive. There wasn't any awareness of the situation and the hurt that having a child like Stefano was causing. It was almost as if Stefano had died and we had to cope with a different child.'

They also had to deal with other people's attitudes. 'People were not very sympathetic. He looks so normal and then all of a sudden he might do something like shout or pick up something he shouldn't do and get into a temper if he can't have it. You never know what he is going to do next. Other people would say: 'These parents do not have any control over their children.''

Stefano moved to a weekly boarding school for autistic children in Hampshire, and stayed there for four years. When he had to leave at 16, his parents battled with Surrey for him to attend St Margaret's School in Croydon, run by The Spastics Society (now renamed Scope).

He had 'one of the best years of his life' at St Margaret's, but when it closed down, Stefano had to move again.

By now the Tunstells were used to fighting to persuade the education authority to pay for schools they believed could cater for his needs. But it was always left to them to find him the most appropriate school. Lidia, a college languages tutor, told me: 'It was a nightmare, because every time we suggested somewhere, it was always too expensive, and there was nowhere suitable for him to go in Surrey. It took ages every time he had to move.'

She was not to know that the family's nightmare was only just beginning.

1   *The Borderland of Imbecility, by Mark Jackson; Manchester University Press; 2000*

2   *Choosing Inclusion – The Power of Parents in Special Education, by Alice Paige-Smith, paper presented at the International Special Education Congress 2000*

3   *Revisiting 'The Empty Hours', by Maureen Oswin, in Crossing Boundaries: Change and continuity in the history of learning disability, edited by Lindsay Brigham, et al; BILD Publications; 2000*

4   *Maureen Oswin and the 'Forgotten Children' of the Long-Stay Wards: Research as resistance, by Sheena Rolph and Dorothy Atkinson, in Exploring Experiences of Advocacy by People with Learning Disabilities: Testimonies of resistance, edited by Duncan Mitchell, et al; Jessica Kingsley Publishers; 2006*

Chapter Four

The Perfect Home

*'The aim should be to fix for each area as early a date
as possible after which the hospitals will not be asked to
admit any more people who need residential rather than
hospital care.'*

Better Services for the Mentally Handicapped
government white paper; June 1971

*'The last long-stay hospital in England has officially closed
its doors – although people with learning difficulties are
still living on the site. Orchard Hill, in Carshalton, Surrey,
'closed' on 1 May, fulfilling a pledge the government made
in its 2001 Valuing People white paper to shut all England's
remaining long-stay hospitals for people with learning
difficulties. The original deadline was April 2004.'*

Disability News Service, May 2009

In 1946, the National Assistance Act introduced a duty on local authorities to provide residential accommodation for disabled and older people 'in need of care and attention'. The act also gave councils the power to register and inspect private and voluntary sector homes. It was, according to David Walden and John Fraser[1], the first statutory regulation of residential care, although the modern regulatory system did not really begin, they say, until the Registered Homes Act in 1984, nearly 40 years later.

By 1971, nearly all services for people with learning difficulties were provided directly by the state and there was a huge shortage of residential places. The Better Services white paper said there were about 4,300 places in hostels and residential homes, compared with a need for nearly 30,000. It also argued that the word 'home' should be used instead of 'hostel', because for most residents they were supposed to be just that: a permanent home. These residential homes should be mixed-sex and small, taking a maximum of 25 adults in mostly single rooms, and should have the atmosphere of a 'family' home, said the white paper.

Most council hostels, though, did not have such a cosy atmosphere, with dormitories instead of single rooms, and the institutional air of a long-stay hospital.

The number of private residential homes slowly began to increase. In 1975, there were less than 20,000 places, including those for older people and people with mental health conditions and physical impairments, and maybe five times as many in local authority homes. But the real acceleration in the growth of private residential homes – and in the number of people leaving the long-stay hospitals – came after the election of Margaret Thatcher's Conservative government in 1979.

During the 1980s, the number of people with learning difficulties living in long-stays fell by nearly 20,000 to about 33,000. A major factor was a social security change which allowed benefits to be used to pay for board and lodging in private and voluntary sector residential homes. As a result, spending leapt from an estimated £6 million in 1978 to £460 million by 1988, and £1.3 billion by 1991[2]. One estimate suggests the number of places in private residential homes rose from 46,000 in 1982 to more than 160,000 in 1991[3].

Although the benefits change did create an impetus to move people from the long-stay hospitals, it was also a powerful incentive to place people in residential care, rather than in more independent community settings.

Many of the new private homes were set up by well-meaning people hoping to create caring environments; but there was serious money to be made, and many others – businessmen, social workers, nurses, anyone with a few thousand pounds to invest in a property – were simply scrabbling to get their hands on a slice of the pie. Gillian Wagner, who chaired an independent review of residential care for the government[4], said when her report was published in 1988: '...the number of homes for people with mental illness and mental handicap is growing steadily, often run by nurses or social workers from mental hospitals and mental handicap hospitals or community-based services.' Oldham social services had told the Wagner review: 'We are particularly concerned by the growth of private care for mentally handicapped people which seems to be modelled on that offered in the large hospitals.'

For many of the former long-stay patients, then, it was merely a move from a large institution to a smaller one, often run by people who had brought with them the culture of their former workplace. The homes they moved into were often more like long-stay hospitals than the family-type homes the 1971 white paper had envisioned.

In its response to a report by the Commons social services committee in 1985[5], the government made it clear that its policies were still based on the white paper, with the aim being to 'achieve a major shift from institutional health care for mentally handicapped people to a range of community care according to individual needs, with increasing responsibilities and resources for local authorities'. This commitment, it said, had been stressed in its Care in the Community green paper in 1981, which called for people with learning difficulties to be supported 'according to their individual needs' in a setting 'which provides the maximum opportunities for ordinary living among ordinary people'.

The Department of Health and Social Security told the committee that it 'fully recognised' the importance 'of ordinary housing in the wider community', and that the trend of government policy was towards 'this sort of provision rather than larger and more traditional settings... [the government] is firmly opposed to revamped institutions and to artificial ghettos, which have nothing to commend them except someone else's convenience and which have nothing to do with community care.'

By 1987, in its report on community care, the Audit Commission[6] was describing how services for people with learning difficulties were 'undergoing a revolution', with 'a major restructuring' underway 'in favour of care in the community' and places in private residential homes increasing by about a fifth every year.

The commission also pointed to the major challenge provided by the long-stay hospital closure programme, and the increasing burden on local authorities.

Those in private care homes, said the Audit Commission, were usually people with lower support needs. But only a quarter of metropolitan districts and London boroughs had such homes within their own boundaries, while most of the large long-stay hospitals were in the country, so an inner city authority's residents could be 'dispersed far and wide'. The London borough of Islington, for example, had clients in 12 hospitals across four different regions.

Meanwhile, parents were 'demanding better services such as respite care and the option of independent accommodation when their children grow up'. The commission pointed to the Jay Report from 1979, which had said that consumers – including people with learning difficulties – should be involved in planning services, with an individual plan for each person with a learning difficulty, short-term relief for carers, continuing support for families that was coordinated through a key worker, and small accommodation units. The Jay Report also called for 'a major change in attitude towards people with a mental handicap, who should be treated as individuals with dignity and respect, and who should appear and be treated in the most normal way possible with attractive age-appropriate dress, hairstyles, activities, etc'.

The Jay Report was, said the Audit Commission, 'relatively controversial' at the time, but many of its principles had since been adopted and even extended. Indeed, much of the report had been endorsed by the government in 1981. The commission said the vision espoused by the Jay Report and the King's Fund's 1981 report, An Ordinary Life, recognised people with learning difficulties as 'full and valued citizens who have as much right as anyone to an ordinary life in the community given their handicap'.

But the Audit Commission concluded that a consensus on what services should be like 'contrasts sharply' with the 'slow progress' on the ground, with 'a need to close the gap between policy and practice'.

The Audit Commission report also had interesting thoughts on the importance of inspecting residential homes and other services. It warned that 'the careful monitoring of standards' was 'more important and more difficult' when so many services were provided by the independent sector. Local authorities, it said, would need to ensure that 'adequate monitoring arrangements' were in place.

Sadly, many of those authorities weren't listening.

A report on community care by Sir Roy Griffiths[7] the following year placed a similar emphasis on the importance of normalisation, but concluded that community care was 'a poor relation; everybody's distant relative but nobody's baby', and suggested residential care was taking 'an undue proportion of available money to the exclusion of more satisfactory alternatives of keeping people in their own homes'.

The choice should not be between residential care and 'very little else', he said. Residential, nursing and hospital care should be reserved 'for those whose needs cannot be met in any other way'. But Griffiths did not call for the scaling back of the independent care home sector. Instead, he said, the aim should be 'to encourage further development of the private and voluntary sectors'.

Griffiths also stressed that nobody should be discharged from a long-stay hospital without a 'clear' and 'realistic' package of care and a named care worker who would be responsible for them. There was, he said, 'widespread concern that people have left long-stay hospitals with inadequate care and support being provided in the community'.

*

GREG

When Greg reached 16, his mother was told it was time for him to begin adult life. Norma had been a physical training instructor. She enjoyed walking and running, but, at nearly 60 years old, was finding it harder to keep up with her son.

'He was a climber, an escaper. I thought that if I had him home, which was what my heart was telling me to do, I would give myself another five years, top whack, and then I would be dead. Then who would look after him? If I let him go into permanent residential care, I was going to live a lot longer and would be able to keep tabs on him, make sure everything went all right. It was very difficult, though. I felt as though I was rejecting him.'

It was Greg's class teacher at Bradstow who told Norma about Gordon Rowe and The Old Rectory, a new residential home Rowe was running that was not yet full. She sent off for a brochure and was impressed with its rural setting and wide range of activities, therapists and trained staff. It talked about providing a 'constructive way of life for mentally handicapped adults' and helping residents develop their potential. 'Our staff,' Rowe wrote, 'will be expected to be aware that the resident needs to feel cared about as well as cared for.'

Norma visited the home – in a small village in Somerset's Quantock Hills – with Greg's social worker, and met both Gordon Rowe and his assistant Angela Adams. Norma liked Gordon but had reservations about Angela. She says it was just an instinct. The social worker liked Angela, but had her doubts about Gordon. They asked Gordon about the promised activities and therapists – of which there was no sign – and were told they would be up and running when the home was full.

'It was a heart-rending decision,' says Norma. 'It was quite a long way to The Old Rectory and I felt as though I was rejecting Greg. I still do to a degree. There is always the mother side of me that wants him with me and wants to look after him, and the practical side that wants to do what is best for him, which is not necessarily the best for me.'

Despite the initial concerns, shared by Greg's social worker, Norma never considered the possibility that her son would be ill-treated at The Old Rectory. 'It never crossed my mind that they would be anything other than kind to him. I just didn't see that this was a profession that anybody would take up unless they really cared. I was grateful that they were there.'

The decision was made, and Greg moved to The Old Rectory at the end of the school year. It was July 1981.

NICKY

It was becoming harder and harder for the Powers to cope with Nicky, especially for Susan, who took the full brunt of her 13-year-old daughter's tantrums. Nicky was punching her mother and pulling her hair, apparently frustrated at her inability to communicate and understand social skills like learning to dress herself and comb her hair.

Nicky had attended a special school since she was five, and lived at home, but Susan was on the verge of a nervous breakdown. She and Davyd talked to their social worker, who told them they had to think of their son, who was studying for his A-levels. She advised them to send Nicky to a boarding school. Susan wanted to 'plod on', but the social worker told her: 'You have had her for 12 years. You deserve a break. You can't continue the way things are.'

Susan and Davyd decided she was right and asked for help from Kent County Council. They had to explain to a tribunal why they wanted to send their daughter away. The council eventually agreed that Nicky could spend 12 months at a boarding-school, until their son finished his A-levels.

After Nicky had been at the school about six months, Susan received a call from one of her teachers. She told Susan they were having terrible problems coping with Nicky, and she would probably never be able to return home to live with her parents. The school agreed she could stay with them until she was old enough to move to an adult home.

'It caused me terrible heart-break,' says Susan. 'The whole thing is like living through a nightmare and it doesn't get any better, because you can't see an end to it.'

When the time came for Nicky to leave school and move to a residential home, her social worker told Susan and Davyd she wanted to find the 'right sort of place' for their daughter, somewhere with a 'homely atmosphere' and preferably with large grounds and horses, which Nicky loved.

'She came along one day and said the home she had in mind was in Somerset, but the people who ran it were now buying a home in Slough and she would like us to go and have a look,' says Susan.

Nicky was now a sweet-looking teenager, who in pictures taken at the time carries the slightly disapproving look of a school prefect, with a pair of clear-framed glasses and her brown hair brushed forward into a fringe. She visited Stoke Place with her parents and saw the horses kept in the grounds. The owner,

Gordon Rowe, and his partner, Angela Adams, told Susan and Davyd about the wonderful facilities. They had just opened, so there would be no problem finding her a place, said Rowe.

The Powers found Stoke Place 'shabby' and desperately in need of repairs, with dark and dingy bedrooms and peeling paint. But they were impressed by Rowe's plans for the future. He told them he had only just moved in and would soon be improving the look of the place. Susan thought Gordon was 'a nice man'. 'I thought he was caring. We both thought that,' she says. Susan later discovered that her step-father's first job as a head gardener had been at Stoke Place in the 1920s, when it was a grand family home.

A few days before Christmas 1983, a month before her 17th birthday, Nicky became one of the first residents of Stoke Place. She was given her own room at the back of the building, and her parents were told not to visit for six weeks, to give her time to 'settle in'.

ANDREW

Andrew* was another of the first residents to move to Stoke Place. His mother had been told by his school doctor when he was at primary school that he was 'educationally subnormal'. He had attended a mainstream school until he was seven and then moved to a special school for two years, before transferring to a residential special school until he was 17. His family were from Buckinghamshire, and lived a short drive from Stoke Place.

Andrew was a 'happy and contented' young man, who could 'hold a conversation', says his mother. He would occasionally lose his temper, but never for long. He was still 17 when he moved to Stoke Place at the end of November 1983.

His mother was quickly won over by Gordon Rowe, as many other parents would be over the next 10 years. She trusted him. 'I thought what a nice bloke he was,' she would say later. She says she took him at face value. 'He was always so nice to me,' she says.

ROSIE

Like Nicky Power, Rosie Valton had been born a healthy baby girl, in Whitechapel, east London. But a brain operation when she was just a few months old left her with a learning difficulty, epilepsy and a partially paralysed right arm. Her mother took her with her when she left England to return to her birthplace of St Lucia two years later. The Caribbean island was to be Rosie's home for the next 14 years.

When Rosie's mother and grandfather were killed in the great hurricane of 1981, it was left to her grandmother to look after the happy-go-lucky youngster. Caring for Rosie proved too demanding, though, and arrangements were made for the teenager to return to London to live with her aunt, Benedict Alcindor.

Benedict had a large family of her own, and within a year decided she would not be able to cope, and would need to find a care home for her niece. She was told of a new home that had opened near Slough. She met Rowe in January 1984, and he told Benedict there was a place for her niece at Stoke Place.

GARY

It was 1984 and Ron Deacon was now in his early 70s, a single parent, recovering from a nervous breakdown and caring for Gary on his own. Eventually, his social worker suggested that Ron should consider residential care for his son.

Gary was 16, the age at which he would have to leave his school, and Ron could find no other school willing to accept him. Ron decided to accept his social worker's advice.

'I was very upset about it, but I was getting on in years and I knew that, if something happened to me, being a one-parent family, Gary could have been stuck anywhere,' says Ron. 'I was relieved for myself, but it was very emotional. It's not nice having to part with your son.'

When Gary's social worker suggested Stoke Place, a nearby residential home, he agreed to have a look. 'I met Gordon and

Angela Rowe and they seemed all right,' says Ron. 'I agreed reluctantly for him to go there, but at least if he was at Stoke Place he would be nearby for his relatives to visit him.

'I didn't even consider the possibility that he could be abused. I never thought that anybody in their right mind could take advantage of a mentally handicapped person. With the money they were getting to look after him, I took it that he would be well cared for. I felt very guilty, but I wasn't worried about the place he was going to, just that he was all right. When he first went there, he used to wander around at night looking for me.'

Gary's first visit home was desperately difficult for Ron. 'After he had been there a few weeks, I had him home on a Sunday. Going back to Stoke Place with him at the end of the day was the hardest thing I have ever had to do. We got as far as the Horlicks bridge in Slough [about a mile from Stoke Place] and he started to play up. When we arrived, I had to ask Nigel Rowe [Gordon Rowe's son] to help me get Gary out of the car.' On Gordon's advice, Ron reluctantly agreed to visit less often, to make it 'easier for him to settle in'.

MICHELLE

Michelle Callaway's* parents were looking for a permanent home for their daughter, somewhere that would care for her when they were no longer able to.

As well as having learning difficulties, Michelle had been diagnosed with bipolar disorder when she was 18. Coping with the two impairments together had made life increasingly tough for her parents. 'We had weeks when there was no sleeping,' says her mother. 'It was very hard.'

Eventually, with Michelle approaching her 21st birthday, her parents decided something had to change. 'That's when the idea of Stoke Place came up. We felt we were in a position where we couldn't deal with it any longer. It seemed the right thing to do at the time, for her benefit as well as our own,' says her mother.

Their first impressions of Stoke Place were good. They thought it was well-run. They lived just a few minutes' drive from Stoke Place, and Michelle attended the local Mencap social club every Wednesday evening, as well as the county council's adult training centre in Slough. 'We wanted her to be local and not miles away,' says her mother.

'The place was a bit run-down looking, but we weren't interested in whether the carpets were fantastically good,' her father adds. 'It was the care we were interested in. We foolishly thought the care was there. We met Gordon Rowe and he was very friendly, all over you in fact.'

The Callaways found Rowe 'dominant', but helpful. They trusted him. They made the decision in the early summer of 1987. Michelle became the latest resident of Stoke Place.

STEFANO

Lidia and Leslie Tunstell knew they would soon have to hand their son over into someone else's full-time care.

Stefano had spent 18 months at a school in Telford, Shropshire, when his social worker finally gave his parents the news they had been dreading: their son was 20 and it was too expensive to keep him at a specialist school. Surrey's education authority was passing responsibility for him to its social services department. Stefano would have to be found a place at a residential home.

Although they were concerned, Lidia and her husband believed residential care would be in Stefano's best interests. 'We put our extremely vulnerable child in a home, not because we wanted to get rid of him, but because we thought maybe they could help him and he would mix with other people,' says Lidia. 'I was very worried, extremely uneasy, but he had reached the level where he couldn't go to school. We felt he needed more space and I felt selfish for wanting to keep him at home.'

Lidia and Leslie had visited one home, but its residents had fewer support needs than Stefano and they felt it was unsuitable.

The social worker suggested Stoke Place. After reading the brochure, they visited the home and met manager Desmond Tully, who they found 'charming'. He told them Stefano would have his own room and would work with a small group of residents.

'We said we would talk about it, but the social worker put a lot of pressure on us to send Stefano there,' says Lidia. 'She thought it was good and obviously the fees were much, much cheaper than the fees in Shropshire.

'The possibility of abuse never crossed my mind. I couldn't believe that such a thing could happen to a person with so many problems. I put my trust in them. I believed that these people who work with people with disabilities would respect them.'

After a trial run over Easter, Tully phoned Lidia and told her Stefano was 'very happy' at Stoke Place. Stefano's social worker told them it seemed the right choice. But Lidia didn't like Gordon Rowe and thought his attitude smacked of an 'old time nurse'. 'He wasn't unkind to me and he wasn't rude, but he didn't look like the kind of person to be in charge of young people.'

Stefano also seemed 'uneasy', and started to wet himself almost immediately. But Lidia had little choice. There was a huge shortage of residential places, after all. 'You have to follow the system,' says Lidia. There was always the fear that the local authority could withdraw funding.

The decision was made late in April 1988, and Stefano became a permanent resident at Stoke Place.

SIMON

Simon Scott had been moved from institution to institution, in search of somewhere able to cope with his particular support needs. Finally, his parents were told about Stoke Place.

They drove down to Buckinghamshire from their home in Hornchurch in north-east London one weekend in 1988, and spent the day looking around. They had lunch with Tully, who told them about the wonderful facilities. He said Simon's epilepsy would not be a problem. Just like so many other parents, they believed Stoke Place would be perfect. At the age of 25, they thought, Simon had at last found a permanent home where he would be happy.

JANET

When Janet Ward was five, she began attending a special school. Her mother joined her one day a week. Janet was extremely hyperactive, never slept more than four or five hours a night, and could never be left alone when awake. But Irene refused even to seek respite care, to allow herself a break. Janet was her daughter and she was determined that she was going to take care of her.

But by the age of eight, Janet had become even more difficult to care for. Her epileptic seizures had become more frequent, and her family believed she needed more care and stimulation than they could provide. Although the thought of putting her daughter in a home still terrified Irene, she believed residential care was the only sensible option, and Janet began a new life at a residential convent school in Hertfordshire for children with epilepsy and learning difficulties.

'Mum felt very, very guilty. She felt that she should have been able to cope, but she knew the opportunities for Janet were much greater than she could have provided,' Janet's sister, Pauline, would say later.

Although it was tough for the family to let her go, they immediately noticed the difference. 'It was like a whole new experience. It was the peacefulness of it most of all,' says Pauline. 'Janet was very demanding and wanted to be amused all the time. After a couple of weeks, we felt immensely relieved that we had reality. Mum seemed a lot healthier. She wasn't so tired. We did miss Janet, but there was also a relief every time she went back after a visit home.'

Janet was happy in her new home, surrounded by children her own age. She learned new skills like horse-riding, dancing and swimming, and attended full-time lessons. She made a lot of friends and often seemed annoyed when she had to return home. She learned to read simple words and perform basic sums. Her confidence grew. Soon, even Irene began to feel the move had been the right one.

There were frequent trips home: at weekends, holidays, birthdays. Janet was a bridesmaid at Pauline's wedding. And when Pauline had children, Janet enjoyed teaching them to say 'please' and 'thank you'. Then she turned 18, and her life changed again.

Janet had to leave the classes and her childhood behind and join the adult section of the home. There were no more riding lessons. Instead, she was given chores around the house. Most of her days were spent sitting in a chair, surrounded by people who had higher support needs than she did. Janet kept trying to visit her friends at the other end of the building. She was desperately unhappy.

But it was an even more challenging time for her mother. At the age of 46, Irene Ward discovered that she had cancer and had only months to live. She told her husband she had just one wish: to see Janet happily settled in a new home. Pauline told me: 'Mum wanted to ensure that she found a permanent home, because she knew my dad couldn't look after her and she didn't want to burden us.'

Janet hated the first home they looked at. Then her social worker suggested Stoke Place. It was, they were told, set in acres of grounds. Janet would have her own bedroom, instead of a dormitory, and there were classrooms where she could practice reading and writing.

When Irene, Tony, Pauline and Janet visited Stoke Place, Rowe told them about pub trips, the animals, the swimming pool, the discos and the holidays. It sounded too good to be true. Janet loved it.

'We were really impressed with the space and I liked the fact that there was a wide range of abilities and needs,' says Pauline. 'It was a real mixture and she would be able to meet a lot of people her own age.

'I thought Gordon was lovely and kind. He seemed very fatherly. He said that if a resident wanted to do something they could do it and if they didn't want to they didn't have to. He took me upstairs and showed me the classroom. There were four or five students doing artwork. It was a nice warm environment and there were a lot of colourful paintings on the wall. It just seemed so relaxed. There were all these choices. Mum was absolutely delighted to have found Stoke Place. She thought Janet was going to be very happy there.'

Pauline said her mother never considered the possibility that Janet would come to any harm at Stoke Place. 'You did think they might not look after them as well as you looked after them – there was a little bit of that – but never, never did she think of abuse. Apart from that, Janet would have told us. She was vocal. From the time she went to Stoke Place, she could speak properly. The possibility of abuse just didn't occur to us.'

As with most of the other families that arrived at Stoke Place to meet Gordon Rowe for the first time, the Wards found him charming, if slightly overbearing. He had an answer for every question, a brush-off for every criticism. He left them in no doubt that their children would be cared for, even loved, by him and his staff. Irene returned home reassured and Janet moved to Stoke Place.

TRACY

After a few months at her local primary school, Tracy had spent her education at a series of special schools in London and Surrey. After leaving school at 19, though, she was spending much of her time at home, with occasional visits to day centres.

Tracy was a 'quiet and sensitive' young woman. 'She always seemed to be fairly happy and content within herself,' her father remembers. But at the age of 22, she became increasingly withdrawn and tearful. Sometimes she would scream and throw herself to the ground. She was diagnosed with depression, which a psychiatrist said was caused by the death of her dog and her social isolation. Within a couple of years she had decided that she wanted her independence, and to leave home as her brother and sister had done.

Tracy's parents were offered just one choice of residential home for their daughter: Stoke Place. They were unimpressed when they first visited in 1989. 'It was very run down and the furniture in Tracy's room was appalling,' her father, Ken, would say later. But they were offered no alternative by Surrey social services. They were told that, because of 'financial restraints', Stoke Place was their only choice. Tracy became the latest resident that August.

LINDA

Linda Dagger was a quiet, withdrawn girl, says her sister Rose. She attended a mainstream school, could read and add up, but never understood money. 'She can spell the dictionary,' says Rose. But she never made friends at school. 'I used to talk to Linda at playtime and she used to be standing at the gate on her own. She never mixed and never had a friend.'

The doctors could never quite work her out, says Rose, although it seems that she was eventually diagnosed as having learning difficulties and mild schizophrenia. Her school never worked her out, either. Her reports were terrible, but Rose says her sister has always been bright. 'My dad used to say that when she is ready she will go and suddenly she will start flying.'

When Linda was 15, she had a nervous breakdown and was admitted to a mental hospital. She spent most of the next 26 years in hospitals and residential homes, including 16 years at a home in Norfolk. But when the journey became too much for her mother, her social worker suggested somewhere closer to her London home: Stoke Place.

Rose remembers meeting Gordon Rowe in 1991 and finding him 'very friendly' and telling her to look around the home by herself and ask any questions she wanted to. She liked what she saw – and was impressed by the grounds, the gardens and the teaching facilities – and agreed that Linda could move there for a two-week trial period.

Linda liked her new home, so the move was made permanent. She had a lovely en-suite bedroom, says Rose. 'I thought how lucky she was and she seemed to have settled down.'

LUKE

Luke Skiff had always been outgoing and sociable. He was born in 1971 in New Zealand, with Down's syndrome, and went to school in the US, before moving to the UK with his mother and attending a special school in London after his parents separated. His mother, Dr Christian Carritt, says her son is 'cheerful and loving and can be very endearing'. Although he doesn't have much speech, he communicates well with the language he has and the use of signs.

She began looking for a home for Luke in 1992. 'I was given all of these places to inspect, most of which were entirely unsuitable. They were frightful. I was really shocked by all these places and they were miles away. The good ones were all full,' she says. Eventually, Luke's social worker recommended Stoke Place, and said that the people who ran it were 'simply wonderful' and that the residents were 'allowed to do anything they wanted'.

But when she visited Stoke Place for the first time, and met Gordon Rowe, she was not impressed. She hoped it would just be an interim home for her son while she looked for somewhere better. She thought Stoke Place was 'Dickensian', with decrepit and run-down buildings, while the residents seemed 'under-nourished' and 'very badly dressed'. 'They all looked very sad and subdued,' she would say later. Although she took an instant dislike to Rowe, she gave him the 'benefit of the doubt' as 'everyone else seemed to think he was wonderful', particularly Luke's social worker. Despite her concerns, Luke became the latest resident of Stoke Place.

1   Reform and Regulation: Two journeys to one destination, by David Walden and John Fraser, in Residential Care: A positive future; The Residential Forum; 2008

2   A Walker, quoted in The Way to the Market: Who provides residential care?, by Terry Philpot, in Residential Care: A positive future; The Residential Forum; 2008

3   Laing and Buisson, quoted in The Way to the Market: Who provides residential care?, by Terry Philpot, in Residential Care: A positive future; The Residential Forum; 2008

4   Residential Care: A positive choice: Report of the independent review of residential care, by Gillian Wagner (chair); National Institute for Social Work/HMSO; 1988

5   Government response to the second report from the social services committee, 1984-85 session: Community care with special reference to adult mentally ill and mentally handicapped people; DHSS

6   Community Care: Developing services for people with a mental handicap; The Audit Commission; Occasional Papers, Number 4; November 1987

7   Community Care: Agenda for action: A report to the secretary of state for social services, by Sir Roy Griffiths; HMSO; 1988

PART TWO

GORDON ROWE

Chapter Five

Brighton and Broadmoor

'A teenager who repeatedly harassed a man with severe learning difficulties until the day he died has been locked up. David Askew, 64, collapsed and died in his garden in Hattersley, in March, after being hounded by local youths. Police were called to the house Mr Askew shared with his mother and brother after reports of youngsters causing a disturbance... They did not find any teenagers at the scene, but later arrested 19-year-old Kial Cottingham. Tameside magistrates heard how Cottingham was one of many teenagers who targeted the man they called Dopey Dave over a number of years. Cottingham... was detained for 16 weeks in a young offenders institution.'

Manchester Evening News, 21 September 2010

Alfred and Maud Rowe were a well-respected couple in Crowthorne. Alfred, who had fought in the French trenches during the First World War, was a railway porter in nearby Camberley. His wife had a reputation for being quiet, calm and hard-working. When she gave birth on 12 September 1934 to the seventh of what were to be ten children, she and Alfred named him Gordon Frank.

When Gordon was six, he began attending Crowthorne Church of England School, a short walk from his high street home. A former school-mate says he was a fun-loving boy who wasn't particularly bright and 'never showed a serious side to his character'. He had the same ginger hair as his four brothers.

The one thing that set Gordon and his siblings apart from their classmates was their love of performing. If the headmaster, Arthur Goodband, wanted a student to sing to the class or read out a poem, he would call for a Rowe. Their carol-singing earned their mother money every year to buy them Christmas presents.

The teenage Gordon was an extrovert. He and a friend bought a car, painted it garish colours and slapped on slogans such as 'Don't laugh, your daughter might be in here'. He played football for the local Crowthorne Saturday side, as a sturdy and reliable defender. One team-mate remembers: 'He showed a lot of team-spirit. I wouldn't say he was ruthless, but he was hard, fair and hard-working. He was a sociable and amicable kind of bloke and I got quite fond of him.'

In Crowthorne, there were two options for a school leaver of no exceptional aptitude or intelligence. Either you could work on the railways, as two of Gordon's brothers were to do, or you could find a job at Broadmoor.

The establishment of Broadmoor and the public school Wellington College in the latter half of the nineteenth century were the twin reasons Crowthorne had grown from a handful of houses into a small town. Broadmoor was Britain's first Criminal

Lunatic Asylum and had been built to take the pressure from the overcrowded Hospital of St Mary of Bethlehem in London. It opened in 1863, was renamed Broadmoor Institution in 1948 and renamed again in 1960, this time as Broadmoor Hospital. But its function remained the same: to hold and treat psychiatric patients of 'dangerous, violent or criminal propensities'.

During the latter half of the 20th century, Broadmoor held a morbid fascination for the media. The tabloids enjoyed running lurid stories of knife-wielding, escaped 'lunatics' bringing terror to nearby villages.

Despite its rural setting and the beautiful grounds designed for therapeutic effect, Broadmoor retained a reputation for staff brutality. It was a forbidding place, so much more a prison than a hospital. Its designer, Joshua Jebb, was also responsible for two of the country's most infamous jails – Pentonville and Dartmoor. His Broadmoor squatted on top of a hill, although most of its dark, red-brick buildings were hidden by high perimeter walls.

In the late 1950s, Broadmoor was also isolated from the rest of the psychiatric world. There were few reports of its work in specialist journals and it fiercely defended a belief that a strict disciplinarian regime could 'cure' those who passed through its forbidding gates. These patients soon learned that the only way to survive was to conform to this regime. If they didn't, they could expect to be beaten by the 'nurses'.

At the same time, Broadmoor inspired loyalty and affection in its employees. It was common for Crowthorne families to provide staff for generation after generation. Many lived in cosy Victorian cottages on the Broadmoor estate, and found both working and social lives could happily be spent within its boundaries. One Crowthorne resident told me: 'When people went to work up there, you generally never saw them again. Broadmoor was a very close-knit community.'

It was to this unique and claustrophobic community that Gordon Rowe applied for a job as a trainee mental health nurse when he returned from national service in the late 1950s.

One tutor remembers him as a good student: intelligent, alert, caring, and, of course, extrovert. He was said to have got on well with his patients and 'sailed through the course', qualifying as a registered mental nurse in 1962.

'As a student, you could not fault him,' the tutor told me. 'He was a bright lad with a sense of humour. I never heard anything about him which would cause me any disquiet. He was a good lad, and I liked him.'

During the next five years, it is harder to piece together how Rowe's life and career developed. He married in 1962 and left Broadmoor. He and his new wife, Pat, settled in Worcestershire, where he worked with adults with learning difficulties. The council has no record of him now.

In 1967, he moved to Brighton. And it is in Brighton where the story of Gordon Rowe takes its first disturbing turn.

It was 1974. Rowe was working as a mental health worker for Brighton social services, dealing with clients with learning difficulties and mental health conditions. He was certainly well regarded by his superiors, because when a regional ITV documentary team wanted to follow two members of staff, to examine the burdens placed on social workers, Rowe was one of those chosen.

In the film, Rowe portrays himself as a dedicated professional, struggling to help families on Brighton's deprived housing estates. His approach, he tells the camera, is one of 'complete informality'. 'I think when we arrive at a place, we are perhaps treated as a person of authority,' he says. 'I don't like that image. I like to dispense with that image of authority. I like to be considered a friend of the family. One that can be relied upon; one that can be trusted.'

During the documentary, Rowe is seen talking to a man with learning difficulties, whose dad has asked for respite care; a truant who won't stop smoking; and a family whose youngest son is running wild. In several scenes, Rowe is seen with a young boy or girl on his lap, a familiarity that would never be permitted today.

But the genial, popular social worker was not all he seemed. Behind the friendly, 'informal' facade lay a darker, disturbing truth: Gordon Rowe was a man driven by violent and perverted sexual urges that he was unwilling to control.

Evidence that he was raping and sexually assaulting his clients was not to be revealed until 1995, when a man contacted police investigating another case. He told them about the social worker who had subjected him to degrading sexual assaults in the back of his car, 26 years before, when he was nine years old. He described how the man, Gordon Rowe, would drive him to a deserted spot in the country, before raping him and forcing him to indulge in oral sex in the back seat. He described the car. It was the same vehicle Rowe could be seen driving in the documentary.

During the documentary, the narrator introduces another of Rowe's visits to his clients: 'The Adams family – Gordon became almost a second father to nine of the 16 children when Mr Adams went into mental hospital.'

One of the Adams daughters sits on the arm of the sofa, next to Rowe. Another, Megan, walks up and sits on his lap, putting her arm around his neck. He places his arm around her waist and continues talking. Angela, another of the 16 children, who is not shown in the film, was about 16 at the time and just nine when Rowe visited her family for the first time in 1967. More than 20 years later, she was to become his second wife.

As Megan sits on his lap, Rowe says in voice-over: 'I believe in some of the cases I deal with, I like to think that I am doing some preventative work, not for the immediate future, but perhaps for years to come, with some of the children I'm working with. Maybe I am preventing situations developing with themselves. Perhaps the families that they have will grow up considerably enwisened.' It was to take more than 20 years for the breathtaking hypocrisy of those words to be exposed.

The Adams family had been involved with Brighton social services since at least 1948, with contact throughout the 1950s and 1960s. The father, Dennis, a machinist by trade, had been in and out of hospital because of his schizophrenia. The first eight children, who were born between 1942 and 1952, were all placed in foster care. The next child, a girl, was adopted, but the next seven – including Angela, born in 1957 – all stayed with their mother. Neighbours remember the children as dirty and neglected, and said their house was filthy. They were known to the council as a huge, chaotic, 'problem family'. There were constant complaints from neighbours about the children's behaviour.

Angela's mother, Violet, certainly appears convinced of Rowe's contribution to her family. She stares into the camera as she says: 'If it wasn't for Mr Rowe, sometimes I don't know where we would be. Because, I mean, since 1967 when Mr Rowe entered my home, that was the best day's work anybody ever done for us in this family.'

But Rowe's interest in the family went far beyond the professional. He eased his way into the family's affections, doing little favours, asking the girls to babysit for him or helping one of the Adams boys out when he wanted to buy his first car. He also helped two of the boys set up a window-cleaning round. 'He had them all in the palm of his hand,' said one former resident of the estate. 'He became a father figure, but I knew he was an evil bit of work. Violet didn't seem to care what he did.'

Rowe began seeing Angela when she was about 13. She would babysit for him, but also spent increasing amounts of time with him during the day. Angela claimed Rowe was 'showing her the ropes' and telling her about his social work cases.

Rowe denied any kind of sexual relationship with Angela, but there were rumours that he had fathered several children with women from the families of other clients on the estate.

Many years later, Angela was to claim that she had not become close to Rowe until he rang her up 'out of the blue' in 1979, and asked her to work for him. But she had been in a relationship with Rowe for years and followed him into the care sector after leaving school at 16, working at a children's centre, an old people's home and a nursery, before taking a year-long residential social work course in 1976 at nearby Lewes Technical College.

By then, Rowe's job had been transferred to East Sussex County Council in the local government shake-up of 1974. Barbara*, a social worker who worked with Rowe in East Sussex, says he 'appeared to care very, very deeply and be very committed to the work he did' with people with learning difficulties.

'He was hard-working, diligent, he cared, he had a good rapport with the clients. We would have shopped him if we had known he was abusing anyone.

'We were a fairly tight-knit close group and we all used to meet up. You lived, slept and breathed social services. Gordon Rowe was a larger than life character and he could pull the birds. The only thing I can clearly remember is at a Christmas party. He was loud and over the top and was flirting with all the girls.'

Barbara found Rowe 'quirky' and 'very coarse', but many of his colleagues were, too. 'Social services in Brighton changed dramatically after Maria Colwell**, because they then started to recruit from Sussex University. But the old mental welfare officers were a crude lot. They went out to quite horrendous cases when there were not any drugs to use like there are now and they were quite difficult. You are talking about a profession in its infancy.' But, she adds, she would never have described Rowe as a brutal or violent person.

Stuart*, another former colleague, says Rowe was 'very well thought-of by the residents'. 'They loved him. He was very happy-go-lucky, just the type of chap they liked to be around. The first time I met him, such a cheer went up as his car pulled up: 'It's Mr Rowe!' He was a bit of an old-fashioned social worker. If he went into somebody's house and a light bulb had blown, he would get on a chair and fix it. He was very down-to-earth and helpful. He would talk to people at their level.'

*A seven-year-old Brighton girl who was starved, beaten and killed by her step-father in 1973. Maria Colwell's death led to a high-profile, influential public inquiry. The inquiry blamed her death, among other factors, on poor communication between different agencies – including Brighton social services – which had all been aware she was at risk. The Adams and Colwells had known each other, although they were not close.

In 1976, Rowe quit his job. Council records show no evidence of disciplinary problems. Their only existing information comes from his pension records. A spokesman said the absence of any personal files implied there were no 'known concerns' about his behaviour.

But police officers I have spoken to are convinced he was seeking out and sexually assaulting clients throughout his time in Sussex. He picked his victims well, choosing only those who had no-one to turn to or could not communicate well. And he used his position of authority to ensure that if anyone did complain, they would not be believed. It was a method he was to perfect in future years.

Rowe left the council in 1976 to try for the second time to study for a Certificate of Qualification in Social Work (CQSW). His first attempt had ended in mysterious failure. In 1970, he had enrolled on the two-year CQSW course at High Wycombe College of Technology and Art, but withdrew the following June. College records show that he cited 'personal reasons' for quitting. Brighton council wrote to the college, stating that it would be 'both in the interest of Mr Rowe and also of this Council that he should not return to complete the Social Work course... due to circumstances which are considered to be beyond his control'. Rowe's tutor wrote back to say that he and his colleagues 'fully support Mr Rowe's decision to withdraw as we believe that his personal problems are such that he is unable to reach the required standard either in his academic or in his fieldwork on the course'.

So what were these mysterious 'personal problems'? Brighton council says it has destroyed Rowe's personnel records, so cannot say why he left the college or why he was allowed to return to work. But one respected social care figure, who was on the High Wycombe course, says Rowe was expelled for cheating in exams and because of 'an issue on one of his practice placements'. Fellow students believed Rowe had had a sexual relationship with a client.

Brighton and East Sussex councils had become the first two in a string of public authorities that would fail to put an end to Rowe's abuse, and his career in social care. And Rowe was learning how easy it was to avoid detection, and how much easier it was to avoid punishment.

In 1976, on leaving East Sussex council, Rowe enrolled on the CQSW course at Lewes Technical College. One of his fellow students was Angela Adams, now 18, who was taking a social work course.

Lewes, since merged with another college, no longer has any records relating to Rowe and is unable to comment on whether it knew of his difficulties at High Wycombe.

After he completed phase I and II of the CQSW in 1977, Rowe enrolled at the University of Sussex to finish the qualification. The university says Rowe provided three satisfactory references, including one from East Sussex council, and there was 'no evidence to suggest that he had been previously excluded from another educational institution'. The following year, he completed his CQSW and returned to the place that seems to have become his spiritual home: Broadmoor.

Chapter Six

From Broadmoor to Somerset

'The government has defended a 10-year delay in setting up an inquiry into 'premature and avoidable' deaths of people with learning difficulties. The confidential inquiry... will look at the causes of such deaths and what should be done to prevent them, and will examine both social care and healthcare settings. The announcement comes 10 years after the government first noted concerns about evidence of avoidable illness and premature deaths of people with learning difficulties, in its Valuing People white paper, which pledged to examine the 'feasibility' of an inquiry.'

Disability News Service, 24 March 2010

Although he and Pat had now divorced, Rowe obtained married quarters on the Broadmoor estate by telling his superiors that his wife would soon be joining him there.

Ex-colleagues say his second spell at Broadmoor was 'uneasy'. There are tales of him running a pornographic video club at his house every weekend, charging colleagues 50p admission, and of an investigation into the theft of gold rings from a patient.

Broadmoor was essentially the same place Rowe had left in 1962. There was little therapy, because patients were supposed to be 'treated' through exposure to the rigorous regime. Everyone had to conform, and staff became just as 'institutionalised' as the patients. There were privileges for those who were good, with trips to the 'punishment house' for those who weren't. Patients had to obey the staff to survive.

Much of the daily routine would have been deeply disturbing to outsiders. Inmates were regularly given excessive doses of drugs to sedate them. Plumbing and toilet facilities were poor and there was little for patients to do apart from the daily routine of cleaning the wards. Beatings were common, but it was a 'golden rule' among nurses that there should be no marks left on the victims, and no witnesses. Relationships between inmates were often tolerated for a time, before staff 'broke them up'. The aim of most patients – many serving long spells for trivial offences – was to stick rigidly to the regime, survive and, hopefully, get out.

This was the Broadmoor Rowe returned to as a social worker. As with his previous spell, it made a great impression on him, and was to provide a blueprint for an institution he would set up for a very different group of clients.

One former colleague says he never suspected that Rowe was not the honest, committed employee he seemed to be. 'Working at Broadmoor could be quite depressing, but he seemed to approach his work in quite a good-natured and amenable way.' He says Rowe was 'at loggerheads' with the psychiatrist in charge of his 'villa' (wing). 'I think Gordon was trying to be more of a social worker, and they weren't regarded in very high esteem. Broadmoor was seen as more of a prison than a hospital and Gordon wanted to rehabilitate people. He came across as someone who was relaxed, rather than as a tough disciplinarian. But he probably conned me as well, because he knew I had different views from the establishment.'

Within a few months, Rowe began telling colleagues he planned to leave and open a residential home for 'mentally handicapped' people. Many other Broadmoor staff were doing the same thing, taking advantage of the huge shortage of residential and nursing homes.

In 1980, Rowe heard from a friend about an ideal property. The small hotel in west Somerset, formerly the village rectory, had been put up for sale by its businessman owner, David Fineberg. Rowe told Fineberg he had money to invest in a residential home. They met and Fineberg was impressed by Rowe's enthusiasm, and agreed to apply for planning permission to convert the hotel into a home for 20 'mentally handicapped' adults.

Residents of West Quantoxhead were horrified at the idea of 'mentally ill' patients living at The Old Rectory. They called a protest meeting and talked of the risk of 'dangerous' undesirables terrorising girls at the village school. But Rowe's apparent wish to create a caring environment won over the local council. Permission was granted and the home opened.

Within weeks, Rowe admitted to Fineberg that he had no money to invest. His financial backers probably never existed. Fineberg thought about pulling out, but Rowe convinced him the project would be enormously profitable, so Fineberg financed the home himself and made Rowe his care director.

Fineberg told me later: 'He was a very plausible person, in the same way that a con-man is a plausible person.'

Gordon Rowe hadn't come to Somerset alone. His assistant was Angela Adams and they shared a two-bedroom flat at The Old Rectory with Rowe's son, Nigel, and five large dogs.

The residents appeared to worship their care director. 'They all seemed to love him and called him 'dad',' says one of Rowe's friends. 'I thought the guy was magic.' He was not the only one. In 1982, a reporter from the West Somerset Free Press visited The Old Rectory and compiled a glowing feature about the work of the 'burly Londoner'.

Rowe told the journalist: 'What I set out to do, and what I think we are achieving, is giving these kids a place to grow up which they regard as home rather than an institution. Once here, they tend to grow up rapidly, as they realise they are no longer living in a children's world.'

He told the journalist how several of the mainly young men had developed 'almost miraculously' in their short time at the home. 'Aggressive behaviour is not tolerated. If they do try this sort of thing when they first come here, they soon learn it is better to behave properly. Anyone who looks likely to upset the rapport we have established or cause trouble is sent back on the next train.'

Rowe came across, as he would many times over the next decade, as a tough but caring professional, intent on providing a loving, nurturing environment. Unfortunately, the truth about his reign at The Old Rectory was far more disturbing.

Chapter Seven

The Old Rectory

'A leading activist has submitted evidence of 68 violent deaths of disabled people – and more than 500 other potential disability hate crimes – to a major national inquiry into disability-related harassment. Reports of the crimes were collected over just three years by Anne Novis, who leads on hate crime issues for the United Kingdom Disabled People's Council and is one of the coordinators of the Disability Hate Crime Network. Her evidence is based on reports collected from the media, blogs, internet message boards and personal experiences shared with her by other disabled people...'

Disability News Service, 7 September 2010

For the first 18 months, Norma Adams thought everything at The Old Rectory was fine. For the first six months, Rowe had asked her not to visit her son, to give him time to 'settle in'. Reluctantly, she agreed, but as Greg does not speak, she couldn't telephone him, either.

Greg seemed to settle in well, though, and the family visited regularly during 1982. But by the early months of 1983, Norma and Greg's social worker both began to question Rowe's failure to set up therapy sessions or expand the range of activities. Norma later discovered that most residents spent all day chopping wood or working in the gardens.

Norma arrived for one visit to find Greg 'like a zombie'. He had been heavily dosed with Largactil, an anti-psychotic drug often used inappropriately to sedate people with learning difficulties. Soon afterwards, she received a call from Barbara Smith*, who lived nearby and had taken a keen interest in the home. She had seen Greg wandering towards the main road and believed the residents were being neglected and that some of the men were being exploited.

In fact, Barbara and her husband David got on well with Rowe. David Smith found him 'an overtly friendly type of robust person' and was impressed by his 'great air of enthusiasm and optimism'. He believed Rowe when he said all he needed was enough money to carry out the changes he wanted to make. 'He really gave the impression that he wanted it to be nice for them, to make a new life for people who came from difficult backgrounds.' David twice took up invitations to inspect The Old Rectory, and was even asked to invest in a home Rowe was planning to open in Buckinghamshire. Astonishingly, Rowe gave the Smiths a list of local authorities with clients at The Old Rectory, so they could write to complain about the home.

'Rowe told me it was very difficult for him, because he didn't have enough money to run the place properly,' Mrs Smith told me. 'He said his own home would be nothing like this one.' On another occasion, he told the couple he was taking eight of the 'boys' on a free holiday, but hadn't been given any money to buy them treats.

The Smiths blamed other staff for the problems, and wrote to Somerset social services, complaining about the care. They said they had frequently seen residents running around outside in slippers and unsuitable clothes, while some had gone missing in the nearby Quantock Hills. The Smiths had been convinced by Rowe's air of vigorous affability and thought him blameless, even though he was running the home. They were merely the latest to join the long line of those who had been taken in.

Norma Adams also complained to Somerset social services, as well as Avon and Somerset police, the charity Mencap, and Greg's social worker. 'I had serious concerns about the standards of care and I thought Greg was having much too heavy doses of tranquillisers,' she says. She believes the resulting enquiries were 'superficial'. The London Borough of Hammersmith and Fulham told me it was unable to trace the relevant records.

Chris Davies, who was responsible for children's services in 1983 and later became director of Somerset social services, told me he had been through the files 'with a fine-toothed comb'. He said the only complaints received were 'general management issues and in particular around the impact on the neighbourhood of behaviour in the home'.

Meanwhile, Fineberg's relationship with Rowe was deteriorating. He suspected him of dishonesty, and noted his habit of drawing bundles of crisp bank-notes from his pockets. He describes him as 'behaving like Julius Caesar, some sort of emperor, but with sinister overtones'. Eventually, he discovered Rowe had written to social workers and relatives of residents at The Old Rectory, inviting them to an open day for the home he was setting up in Buckinghamshire, at which he laid on plentiful refreshments for his guests. Rowe, he realised, planned to take as many residents from The Old Rectory as he could to his new home.

Fineberg confronted him, took legal advice, and Rowe agreed to go. Fineberg then asked Michael Brown*, a former colleague of one of his employees, to take over. But Rowe was not yet ready to open his home and wanted to stay on for a few more weeks. It took a meeting with the chair of the local Mencap group for him to agree to leave.

Brown remembers the meeting. 'It was a very strange and bizarre situation to walk into and, although Gordon accepted he would abide by his decision to leave, he remained full of antipathy about his relationship with Fineberg. Rowe saw himself as all-important, a patriarchal figure. He told me: 'I am there when they get up in the morning, and I am there when they go to bed in the evening.' He was a very bombastic guy.' Rowe eventually left in late July.

Rowe's departure was not universally welcomed. Many of the social workers with clients at the home were unhappy at how he had been treated. Fineberg believed they liked his 'lack of polish'. And, after all, he was one of them.

When Rowe finally left, he took four residents, a lot of possessions belonging to those who stayed behind, and presents bought for them with the proceeds of a charity bed race. He was joined by various members of staff, including Angela Adams, Nigel Rowe and a bespectacled, teenaged care assistant called Desmond Tully. Tully had borrowed £8,000 from his bank and lent it to Rowe to help him start his business.

When they left, there was only one qualified employee. Rowe had taken on mostly untrained and unqualified boys and girls, filling their heads with techniques and theories he had picked up at Broadmoor. It was a method he was to repeat in Buckinghamshire.

Fineberg remembers driving to the home and watching Rowe load up a removal lorry. 'Anything that wasn't nailed down disappeared with him,' he told me.

Fineberg went about recruiting new staff, and for the first time the home was being run by experienced care workers. Brown says the home was in a 'disgusting' condition when he took over, a situation that had been allowed to continue because of the council's 'laissez-faire' attitude to its inspection duties and the general 'apathy' there was at the time about the standards of independent homes.

It took a few weeks after Rowe's departure for Albert*, a 34-year-old resident from the London borough of Brent, to confide in a staff member that Rowe had been sexually assaulting him. Albert had become upset after Rowe's departure. When staff calmed him down, he said he was missing Gordon because he gave him special privileges – such as giving him sweets and letting him work in the kitchen – in return for things he did for him. Albert gave a 'fairly explicit account' of masturbation acts which took place in Rowe's flat when the doors were locked. He said Rowe would make him masturbate him while he drew shapes on Albert's face, and he had to guess what they were. Albert spoke about these duties with some irritation because they would make him late for his tea. The allegation was passed to Brown and Fineberg. Brown contacted the police and Mike Furlong, Somerset's registration and inspection officer.

Furlong told Brown the allegations would have to be investigated by the police, not by the council. 'If it were now, we would almost certainly have done the investigation jointly with the police,' Chris Davies told me later. 'But at that time, we handed it to the police to do themselves. There was no suggestion that it was anybody other than Rowe, so there was no issue about the current protection of those people.'

At about this time, clinical psychologist Madeleine Thomas visited The Old Rectory to assess Albert. She had been there before, but had turned down Rowe's offer of work because she didn't trust him. 'Something about him made me feel he wasn't honest. I also didn't like the way he treated the residents. I thought he was rather autocratic,' she says.

The interview confirmed her fears. Albert appeared frightened and upset, and told her how Rowe had made him visit his flat four times a week for mutual masturbation. He had no idea that what Rowe was doing was wrong, and mentioned again the 'special privileges'. He said Rowe threatened to send him back to the long-stay hospital he had come from if he told anybody.

Appalled – especially when she discovered Rowe was setting up his own home – Thomas, who later became head of department for a Somerset hospital trust, informed Fineberg and rang Somerset social services. She has given evidence in court many times as an expert witness, and believes Albert provided details he could not have made up. She was convinced Rowe was guilty.

Two detectives interviewed Albert and the other residents. Brown says 12 other residents indicated to the officers that they too had been abused. Others who weren't as articulate as Albert pointed to their genitals.

On 3 October, the two detectives travelled to Buckinghamshire to interview Rowe about allegations of gross indecency. Angela Adams, introduced as Gordon's common-law wife, insisted on being present. Rowe was quizzed thoroughly, but told the officers nothing to corroborate the allegations. They passed a report to their detective chief inspector. He decided that no charges could be brought, so the inquiry was closed and Somerset social services were briefed. They notified Bucks County Council, as did one of the police officers.

The two officers were so upset at their failure to secure a prosecution that they returned to The Old Rectory with armfuls of presents for the residents. They told staff they believed Gordon Rowe was guilty, but just couldn't prove it.

When Fineberg realised there wasn't going to be a trial, he contacted Bucks County Council to warn them about Rowe, even though the Somerset authorities told him they would do this themselves. 'I was convinced Rowe's registration in Bucks would not be confirmed,' he told me.

Over the next few weeks, staff at The Old Rectory talked to all the residents about Rowe. 'There were other young men and women who were not able to give an intelligible account of what had happened to them,' says Brown. 'One of them demonstrated what Rowe had done to him with a mime and said, 'He do that, he do that'. We eventually decided there were about 15 residents who had been [sexually] abused. There was no corroborating evidence, but none of the staff were in any doubt. We all knew these things had happened. Unfortunately, short of getting them into the witness box, there was nothing that could be done. Even if they had gone into the witness box, Rowe had a tremendous amount of power over the residents and he would have employed that to intimidate them in court.'

Brown contacted Bucks County Council, whose registration department told him there was nothing they could do if the allegations were not proven. He says they inferred that he was motivated by malice, even though he had only met Rowe twice. Brown believes the department was told to expect his call.

Brown and Fineberg also wrote in late November to the social worker for a resident from a London borough, Kensington and Chelsea. Two weeks later, the council's director of social services wrote to his opposite number in Buckinghamshire, enclosing a copy of their letter and stating that they would be freezing any placements at Rowe's new home. In his reply, Buckinghamshire's director said his principal residential services officer, Stan Bristow, had taken up references 'from reliable sources, all of which spoke very highly of Mr Rowe', and that Rowe had himself told Bristow about the allegations, all of which he said were 'totally untrue' and 'were being made to discredit him in order to prevent him from taking residents from the Old Rectory, and admitting them to his new home'. Rowe, he said, had shown Bristow a police letter, informing him there was 'no case to answer'. Bristow had also called Furlong and the detective in charge of the investigation, he added, who told him the file had been closed after a 'thorough investigation'.

Brown says Rowe ran the home as a 'punitive regime', with residents given privileges which could be removed if they misbehaved. The home was 'a custodial place for people who had to be punished and it was Gordon Rowe's God-given right to punish them'. One male resident took a cake from the bread van and was sent to his bedroom for six weeks.

Brown, Fineberg, Thomas, Norma Adams and the Smiths were not the only ones raising concerns. Albert's social worker, Mike Danzig, had persuaded his superiors in Brent social services to write to Buckinghamshire. Brent also wrote to Somerset social services, and the Department of Health and Social Security. Nothing was done. Brent eventually decided to back off because of 'possible libel action', Danzig would say later. This could only have meant a legal threat from Gordon Rowe himself, a threat he was to use again to warn off potential whistleblowers.

Two months later, in November, Danzig visited Somerset. He saw Albert, and heard from Brown the wealth of evidence against Gordon Rowe. Brown told him he felt 'sick' that Rowe was going to get away with what he had done.

Eventually, Albert was moved to a hospital. Because of the abuse he suffered at the hands of Gordon Rowe, and the effect it had on his own behaviour, he was incapable of living in the community. I was told that he was likely to spend the rest of his life in an institution.

Chapter Eight

Buckinghamshire

'A mother who apparently killed herself and her disabled daughter by setting fire to their car had faced years of abuse from youths and children, but police 'did nothing' despite her repeated pleas for help, an inquest heard yesterday. The bodies of Fiona Pilkington, 38, and her 18-year-old daughter, Francecca Hardwick, known as Frankie, were found burnt beyond recognition in her Austin Maestro in a layby in Leicestershire in 2007. A gang of up to 16 girls and boys, including children as young as 10, had continually terrorised the family... They threw stones, flour and eggs at their house in Barwell, near Hinckley, urinated in the garden and taunted Frankie, who had severe learning disabilities, and her dyslexic brother, Anthony. Despite police logs of 21 calls in seven years, many referring to Anthony being bullied, no prosecutions were brought and the abuse continued.'

The Guardian, 18 September 2009

Stoke Place Mansion House, which came with 200 or so acres of land, had been bought as an investment by South Buckinghamshire District Council in the 1960s, and turned into a nursing home. After a fire, a funeral director took it on at a peppercorn rent, repaired the damage and converted it into a country club. In 1978, he sold the lease to businessman David George and his wife Chris, and two business partners.

The Georges turned Stoke Place into a two-star hotel. After initially thriving, the recession bit, and by the early 1980s they were desperate for a new business partner. For Gordon Rowe, its location – in Stoke Poges, on the edge of Slough – was ideal. It was near London and its plentiful supply of potential clients, and only a 25-minute drive from Crowthorne.

Rowe had been introduced to David George through a mutual friend. George was impressed. 'He could make one feel very emotional about the mentally handicapped and the lot they had,' he told me later.

Rowe even talked about his relationship with Fineberg and confessed to taping their conversations. 'There were lots of little things like that which should have warned me not to get involved. One should have twigged that he was a bit strange,' said George. They agreed to split Stoke Place into two, with the Georges running a country club in one half and Rowe setting up a residential home in the other.

'Gordon hadn't any money and we hadn't any money,' says Chris George. 'We got a joint short-term bank loan to do up the property. The council would not let us have the head lease and sub-let to Gordon, so we were co-lessees. It was sink or swim. Without them, we would have lost here and lost our house. At that stage, they saved us.'

Another businessman who helped Rowe was car-dealer Raymond Beck. Already past retirement age, Beck had been approached by his accountant, who also acted for Rowe. 'They apparently had to pay a sum up front for the tenancy and there was a shortfall,' he says. 'My accountant asked if I was interested and I said yes.' He paid £23,500 for a quarter share in the business. Rowe bought the shares back the following July and gave them to Nigel, but Beck says he made no profit. 'It was all done as a sort of charity,' he told me.

London solicitor Geoffrey Preston, who became the company secretary and advised Rowe on setting up Longcare Ltd – the company which would run the home – visited Stoke Place and was impressed by Rowe's plans. Preston, also briefly a Longcare company director, says: 'He seemed confident it would work and, what was more important, he convinced other people it would work. He didn't strike me as being anything out of the ordinary, apart from somebody who was really quite impressive in being able to put together something like that.' Preston says he parted company with Longcare in the late 1980s when Rowe found a cheaper legal adviser.

Before Rowe could apply to have his home registered by Bucks social services, he needed planning permission from South Bucks District Council to convert Stoke Place into a care home. The letter he wrote was perfectly pitched to appeal to local councillors – it talked about the jobs the new business would create, the educational benefits for the residents, and the 'family' atmosphere Rowe would bring with him from Somerset. It was persuasive, reassuring, down-to-earth and tugged gently at the heart-strings. No-one reading it would have had the slightest idea about the terrifying regime Rowe had presided over at The Old Rectory.

He told the council that none of the residents would have 'any previous history or record of aggression or anti-social behaviour' or 'sexual deviance'. Most of them, he said, had come from long-stay hospitals. He stressed the 'family life' The Old Rectory had offered, which would be replicated at Stoke Place, supplemented by educational and social training, such as trips to the cinema, Windsor Castle, and David George's country club.

Rowe talked about the 'very able working lads' at the Somerset home, who had worked in the kitchen gardens, cleared the woods and grounds of brambles, and cut logs for the fire. And he described their 'special projects', such as tidying old people's gardens, picking fruit, and maintaining the 20-mile length of the West Somerset Steam Railway track. At Stoke Place, the 'Working Lads' would clear the lake, the kitchen gardens and the woods.

All the residents, he said, 'have their own individual personalities, their likes and dislikes, their fears, hopes and aspirations'. Many would come from London, so Stoke Place would be ideally suited for visits from relatives. 'Contact of this nature is seen by us as essential to developing the individual and to help him reach his maximum potential,' he added.

'I could go on with the benefits for us, for the Stoke Place Country Club and for the surrounding community,' he wrote, 'but this may become boring and be misconstrued as an attempt at overselling ourselves, rather than an attempted straightforward and honest description of how I see the future and how we can complement each other.' It was a cleverly-crafted letter, but straightforward and honest it was not.

The meeting at which Rowe's application was discussed was the first after the local elections of 1983 and consequently many of the councillors were lacking any experience. Only two of them, the Conservative Rex Lingham-Wood, and an independent, Lionel Rigby, put up any opposition. They were sceptical that a country club and a residential home could exist as neighbours and knew that George had financial problems.

But Rowe knew exactly how to appeal to the other, less experienced, councillors. He quoted government reports and care experts and produced references and the cutting from the Somerset newspaper. The councillors were also impressed to read a letter from Rowe's banker, which stated that the home was potentially very profitable.

But a seemingly major obstacle was the copy of the report from Somerset police, which had landed on the desk of council solicitor Tony Levings. He questioned Rowe, but was fed the story of sour grapes and unfounded allegations. The district councillors – unaware of the police investigation and the allegations – voted to grant Rowe permission to convert part of Stoke Place into a care home.

The final and highest hurdle was to have the home registered with Bucks County Council. For that to happen, its registration department would have to view Rowe as a suitable person to be looking after people with learning difficulties.

Bucks County Council has never accepted it failed to make proper checks on Rowe's background. A spokesman told me they received good references, as well as a 'communication' from Fineberg. But they admitted that a reference from Somerset County Council, describing Rowe as 'a sensitive, able and caring man' with a 'good understanding of the needs of those mentally handicapped people placed within his care, together with a keen interest in their welfare', was written six months before the allegations investigated by Somerset CID came to light.

The council admitted that no-one from its staff visited Somerset to check on the allegations. Public relations chief Bob Bird said in 1996: 'At that time, the registration procedure focussed mainly on the qualifications of the people running homes and the suitability and safety of the buildings. Mr Rowe, himself, told us about the allegations made by the owner of another private residential home in Somerset, and about which Buckingham social services was, in fact, already aware. These allegations were discussed with Somerset social services and Somerset police, who told us they had been investigated and that the file had been closed after a thorough investigation.'

Chris Davies told me: 'Everybody felt pretty uneasy and people at the home felt he might have abused more widely. Mike Furlong was not in a position to have said that [Rowe was guilty] himself, but he would not have disagreed with that. Bucks were aware that while no criminal charges were brought, there was not exactly a clean bill of health. That in those days was a very common position to end up in, because of judicial views about the quality of evidence people with learning disabilities can give. It would have been a guarded message, as they often are, which would have said, 'That was the criminal finding, but that ain't the whole of the story."

Davies admitted that his council was conned by Gordon Rowe. 'Almost everyone who dealt with Gordon Rowe in Somerset thought he was absolutely wonderful. [If you had tried to take action against him] you would have had any number of statements from families, from agencies, saying this guy is absolutely tremendous. There is no doubt that he took us in.'

Bucks County Council received four references for Rowe, all of which had also been used with his planning application. Two were from professionals who had provided David George with glowing tributes a year earlier. Ieuan Williams, chief education officer at Broadmoor, had known Rowe for 20 years. He described his departure from Broadmoor as 'a great loss' and said he had been 'regarded with great esteem' by his colleagues and 'was popular and well liked' by patients. He said he was 'absolutely trustworthy, sincere and loyal'. Williams described The Old Rectory as 'a therapeutic environment' and said Rowe was 'idolized by the boys and girls who are resident there'.

A second reference was written by Richard Holley, who described Rowe's 'unique rapport' with people with learning difficulties and his 'natural flair' for social work. Holley was a senior officer in Kensington and Chelsea's mental health section. He had found places at The Old Rectory for two men who had been living in long-stay hospitals for 30 years. When he visited them, he remembers being impressed with the ease with which Rowe dealt with 'potentially explosive' situations. 'I remember one occasion after dinner in the evening, and two of the fellows got a bit excited, and one of them really clobbered the other one in the face. Gordon Rowe took one of them to the side and said to him: 'You must not do that. Say sorry to him.' Then he took him upstairs. I thought that was pretty good, that he had defused it straight away. It stuck in my mind, someone knowing what to do in awkward circumstances, because the one who had been slapped around the face was quite distressed.

'My lads were always happy when I saw them. They never had anything to say against Gordon Rowe, even when he wasn't there.'

The other two references were from Furlong and a Somerset fire officer. There was no reference from David Fineberg, and none requested by Bucks.

Despite the concerns of David Fineberg, Michael Brown, Somerset County Council, Mike Danzig, and the police investigation, Rowe was home and dry. Members of Bucks County Council went along with the advice of their officers. They believed Rowe was a fit person to be running a residential home for adults with learning difficulties.

On 28 November 1983, Gordon Rowe was registered by Bucks County Council to care for 38 adults with learning difficulties at Stoke Place Mansion House. It was to be nearly ten years before that decision was to come back to haunt them.

PART THREE

LONGCARE

Chapter Nine

Humiliation

'So many people call me horrible names such as spastic or retard or something like that, 'carry on taking the tablets'... swearing at me, calling me names... I have had neighbours in the past who have called me fat and ugly and spat on me.'

'Linda', speaking on the Grapevine Street Aware blog, a project set up for people with learning difficulties in Coventry to talk about hate crime, 6 January 2010

'The BBC has been criticised by the communications watchdog over a programme in which presenter Jeremy Clarkson made offensive, disablist comments about people with learning difficulties. Clarkson told viewers of the popular BBC2 motoring show Top Gear that the Ferrari F430 Especial should instead have been called the '430 Speciale Needs' because its 'smiling front end' made it 'look like a simpleton'.'

Disability News Service, 25 October 2010

At some stage in its past, the elegant front entrance of Stoke Place Mansion House had become the back door. It now looked out on an expanse of roughly cropped grass, and, beyond that, to a small wood and a girdle of trees that clung to the banks of a lake.

Visitors, who would once have admired the stately Mansion House as they approached in their carriages along a gently curving drive, now turned off a road growling with traffic, and drove through an entrance in a high brick wall and along a driveway that cut through a jumble of trees and undergrowth. Only then did they see the red brick façade of Stoke Place.

The building's three-storied torso had been constructed in the late 1600s on land known as Boone Jordens. Field Marshal Sir George Howard bought the house and 30 acres of land in 1764, and he and his descendants lived there for 200 years. They carried out several improvements and additions to the building, and commissioned the renowned landscape architect Capability Brown to redesign the gardens in 1771.

Among the additions was a pair of two-storey extensions, which sat like squat limbs on either side of the mansion's torso. They had been joined by bits of drainpipe, blocked up windows, and a main entrance which looked more like a fire escape.

A visitor driving for the first time along the pitted drive towards the front door of Stoke Place might just have sensed that something, somehow, wasn't quite right.

I had written these words a year or two before the publication of my first book on the Longcare scandal. I had always been slightly disappointed that they were cut from its final version. This image of Stoke Place as a building that had in some way stepped through the looking glass – where back was now front and perhaps the normal rules of society no longer applied – seemed fitting.

But the more I researched the history of how people with learning difficulties had been treated over the centuries – and listened to the advice of wise friends – the more this description of Stoke Place as somehow unique jarred with what I had learned: Stoke Place was no aberration.

This section of the book is perhaps its most important, and certainly the most disturbing. It describes what took place at Stoke Place. It portrays the daily violence, neglect and humiliation Gordon Rowe inflicted on its residents, based mostly on the testimony of former residents and staff.

I start by looking briefly at how Rowe used bullying and humiliation to undermine the residents, both in their own eyes and those of the staff. But, as in the rest of this section, it is crucial to remember the historical context: this treatment of people with learning difficulties as second or third-class citizens was nothing new; it was deeply ingrained into society, and had been for centuries.

*

Gordon loved to make fun of the residents of his Longcare homes. He thought there was nothing funnier than mocking Tim about his habit of buying ladies' jewellery.

'Gordon would stand behind Tony, who was blind, and make him jump,' one staff member recalls. 'He mocked Tim all the time and made him dress up in girls' clothes. He also took the mickey out of staff behind their backs, so the clients could have a laugh.'

Lottie, who was incontinent, was another who became the butt of Rowe's 'jokes'. If another resident was incontinent, he would shout: 'Smells like someone's got their Lottie perfume on.'

One frequent visitor remembers how Rowe used to tell residents to 'get your fat arse out of here', or 'get out the back, you big fat slob'. One of the women, whose real name was Natalia, was nicknamed 'Nasty' by Rowe. She hated it, but having seen Rowe call her by this cruel nickname, staff and residents started using it too.

Because of David Jackson's incontinence, Rowe would never call him by his first name. Instead, he was 'Jackson' or 'Animal'.

He nicknamed Dorothy 'Dysentery'; she knew exactly what it meant.

Dorothy says Gordon deliberately manipulated the residents' emotions. 'Gordon played with our feelings so much, me and Jimmy. He tried to actually send me mental. I was so strong that I wouldn't get it,' she says. It was only her dream of escaping Stoke Place that kept her sane. 'What kept me from going mental, once you went to those places you've got to be full of hate and you have to have a dream to cling onto. My dream seemed impossible to me. My dream was that, one day, I would be free, I would have my own flat, I would settle down, and I never let go of that dream.'

Steve*, a care worker, remembers Gordon appearing with a cardboard box of-out-of-date packets of crisps. 'Watch this,' Gordon told him, and winked.

Gordon walked around the room, handing a packet to each resident. He stopped next to Brian, looked at him briefly, and moved on to the next resident. By the time he had finished, everyone had crisps apart from Brian.

Brian looked at everyone eating their crisps, walked over to Gordon, tapped him on his shoulder and asked him where his packet was. It was only then that Gordon reached into the box and handed him one. 'There you go, Brian,' he said, and patted the man on the top of his head. 'Good boy.'

Another staff member recalls watching Peter walking down the stairs, his head bowed, one step at a time, one hand on the banister. Peter was blind, frail, and rarely spoke – although he was an excellent mimic. At the bottom of the stairs stood Gordon Rowe, wearing a dirty white vest and a pair of long, khaki shorts.

As Peter approached the bottom stair, he took his hand off the banister. Gordon let out a loud yell. As Peter jumped with fright and twisted round, Gordon flicked one of his legs away with his foot. Peter fell backwards onto the bottom stair, where he lay shaking.

'Sorry, Peter, didn't see you there,' said Gordon, and laughed, before sauntering back to his office.

As Katharine Quarmby points out in her masterly new work on disability hate crime[1], the mockery and humiliation of disabled people has often been closely linked to hate crime. It often proves merely the first stage in a process that leads to threats and intimidation, physical violence and even death.

How far, after all, was the kind of mockery and humiliation practised by Rowe from the organised publicity campaign of hate-filled denigration in Nazi Germany, in which Hitler described disabled people as 'useless eaters' who were 'unworthy' of life. And heading further back into our own country's past, how different was it to the medieval 'fools' who were beaten, mocked and laughed at, and the freak shows which became so overwhelmingly popular in Victorian times?

Name-calling, bullying and mockery – often, but not always, in public spaces such as buses and schools – is an accepted part of life for most people with learning difficulties. Quarmby suggests this became even more of a problem as growing numbers of people with mental health conditions and learning difficulties left the old long-stay hospitals and were assimilated into the community during the 1970s and 1980s.

When Rowe gave his residents offensive nicknames, or bullied them, or used them for his personal amusement, he was reflecting how many people with learning difficulties had been treated over hundreds of years.

But by exposing them to this kind of humiliation, he was teaching his staff not to respect the residents, and vice versa. This made it less likely that residents would trust the care workers, and less likely that those staff would object to the treatment they witnessed.

Rowe was steadily redrawing the boundaries on what was acceptable, setting an example as well as the standard for Longcare. The more he mocked and humiliated the residents, the less likely it was that a care worker would risk their job and object if Rowe stepped further over the boundary. It was only a short step from viewing someone as worthy of mockery and humiliation to turning a blind eye to a kick, a slap, or a punch.

1   *Scapegoat, by Katharine Quarmby; Portobello Books; 2011*

Chapter Ten

Control and Punishment

'Scores of people with learning difficulties are being forced into marriages against their will every year, government figures have revealed. Last year, 35 people with learning difficulties, as well as 14 disabled people with physical impairments, contacted a government helpline set up to deal with the problem of forced marriages. But the figures under-estimate the true scale of the problem, as the figures only represent those who used the helpline.'

Disability News Service, 25 October 2010

Life at Longcare was about control. Gordon Rowe was the boss. Many of the residents called him Daddy, Dadda, or Big Dadda, names he encouraged them to use.

Many were clearly scared when he walked into a room. 'Hello, Gordon. You want a cup of tea, Gordon?' they would say. They all had their survival strategies. For some it was about keeping out of Gordon's way; others tried any way they could to stay in his good books. For many of them, though, there was nothing they could do to avoid punishment. Just being who they were seemed reason enough for a slap, kick or punch.

Dorothy Thomson (formerly Abbott) remembers clearly what kind of man he was. 'I must say Gordon Rowe was a very, very dominating man,' she would tell me years after she left Longcare. 'He didn't like anybody not liking him. He liked every resident to like him. He also didn't like you if you was intelligent on making things and if you could read, or if you could do writing of any description. He hated that.'

He had to dominate his residents, to be in charge. Dorothy believes it went further than that: 'I think that he was a man that always wanted to be in the limelight.'

Jean was one of Longcare's better-qualified care workers. She worked in a senior position, across the road from Stoke Place at Stoke Green House, the second, smaller Longcare home, which was considered a more 'relaxed' place to work. Even so, it had taken her only a few months to become disturbed by things she was witnessing. At first, she thought Longcare was wonderful. 'You were shown around and shown the best of everything,' she told me. 'You read the prospectus and it sounded like a wonderful holiday camp... until you actually got to work there.'

She remembers sitting at her desk, trying to help John, one of the residents, learn about colours, pointing out pictures of a red double-decker bus and an apple in a book. John was a good-looking young man in his 20s, taller and stronger than most residents, and was one of the 'Working Lads' who would do gardening and other jobs in the grounds of Stoke Place. Some of them would do special tasks for Gordon and were given extra food and other treats in return. John helped with the security, which meant spying on other residents and staff and reporting back to Gordon. When he saw a care worker give a resident an extra cup of tea, he reported it. John was more than capable of living independently, but it suited Gordon to keep him at Longcare, and away from the classroom. Of course, it wasn't John's choice to be his helper. Such roles were chosen for the residents, and if they tried to refuse, they were punished.

Gordon walked in as Jean and John were looking at the book. 'You're wasting your bloody time,' he told her. 'He'll never learn colours.' Jean told him that John was a talented painter, a hard worker, and if he learned about colours, he could work as a decorator. Gordon slammed his hand down. 'No more colours,' he said. John nodded, quickly. 'Yes, Gordon.'

When Jean followed Gordon to the door, he turned round and stood so close to her they were nearly toe-to-toe. He was flushed and trembling. 'I don't want you helping him,' he said, and marched out, slamming the door behind him.

Later that week, John was moved across the road to Stoke Place, away from Jean and Stoke Green.

Rowe's need to control and dominate the residents extended beyond their education and what he called their 'social training'. He was only content if he was ruling every aspect of their lives.

In some ways, it was an exaggeration of the regimes of the old long-stay hospitals. Many of them, after all, had been little better than prison camps, rife with bullying, where staff had complete control over patients' lives. Many residential homes were little better. Despite the Jay Report's call for a 'major change in attitude' towards people with learning difficulties, many were not treated as individuals, with dignity and respect, and there was little evidence of people living a 'normal life'.

Rowe ensured that his residents' experiences were a long way from a normal life in a home-like setting, despite telling their families how much he loved their children.

Rowe seemed to gain a perverted pleasure from the control he exerted. He ordered staff to inform him of all instances of 'sexual activity', even if only a kiss on the cheek, and he kept track of which residents were going out together. If he didn't like a pairing, he would split it up and tell them who to go out with instead.

To his staff, many of whom were young and inexperienced, his orders made a kind of sense. After all, he was a trained social worker, he had worked at Broadmoor. As he told his employees, he had been working in social care for nearly 30 years. And, of course, he was the boss.

One of the residents, Rachel*, would describe later in a witness statement how James was 'kicked up the backside' by Gordon and other staff if he did not do as he was told. 'He would laugh and they used to grab him, sometimes by the arm. They would shout at him. They would kick him with the side of their foot,' she said. 'If he carried on playing him he would get sent to bed. Sometimes they would let him get up, other times he would have to stay there for two days or so. They would take his meals up to him.' Other residents would get told off and 'kicked up the backside for fun'.

Another punishment was being forced to miss meals. This would happen if a resident was late for breakfast. 'They weren't nice about breakfast if you were late,' said Rachel. 'Unless you were being washed and dressed by staff if you weren't down by half-past eight you missed breakfast. It was taken away and you would go hungry. Next meal at lunch. It would depend on time down. A little late you would get a piece of toast but if it was gone a quarter to nine you would just get a cup of tea.'

Dorothy also remembers being punished by having to miss meals. 'Gordon would attack me by saying you cannot have any tea because of doing that or he would say, 'Go upstairs, you're not to have nothing," she would tell me later.

Tracy, too, recalled in a witness statement how she was forced to miss meals. 'Sometimes the staff used to send me and other people to our rooms to punish us. They wouldn't allow us to have any tea and we would be very hungry. Sometimes I was sent to my room for the rest of the day and I would have to stay there. Sometimes I would have to stay there for days.'

Rachel often saw other residents being punished. Some of the men were kicked, she said. 'This wasn't done in private and if you were told off it was in front of everybody... Sometimes if you were naughty, you would be sent to bed for a week.' She remembers being given some gift vouchers by her family. Angela Rowe tore them up to punish her. 'This made me cry,' she said.

One care worker, Gary Moreton, described how Gordon would punish one resident, Michael, who would challenge him about why he was treated more poorly than other residents and wasn't receiving the 'privileges' they were receiving. This would enrage Gordon, who would hit him, pull him by the hair into his room, and tell the staff not to let him out. This imprisonment could last four or five days.

Tracy told how Angela 'used to shout at us all the time... On one day, Angela came running after me and shouted, 'You better get out or I'll get Gordon to hit you."

Lorraine Field, one of the care supervisors, also shouted at residents and punished them. 'She was very strict,' said Tracy. 'She used to send me to my room quite a lot. She used to shout at me a lot which used to frighten me.'

One of the residents frequently subjected to the punishment regime was Jackie, who had Down's syndrome. She was described by nearly everyone as a 'very funny, very happy' person who, like Michael, would question why she wasn't receiving privileges given to other residents, such as going out on trips. She had developed problems with her food – it would later emerge that

121

she had a medical condition that made it painful for her to eat. But her refusal to eat her food enraged Gordon.

Gordon would grab Jackie by her hair as she sat in front of an untouched plate of food at one of the long wooden tables in the dining-room. Sometimes, he would try to force-feed her. When that didn't work, he would pull her out of her chair and drag her across the floor and down the short flight of stairs that led up to the dining-room. Care workers said Jackie would often be screaming as she was dragged along.

Gordon would pull her down the corridor and through a fire escape into the garden. This often happened in the middle of winter, with Jackie wearing nothing but a thin cotton dress, a cardigan and a pair of slippers. Once it happened on Christmas Day. Jackie would be left there with her food and a wooden chair to sit on, sheltered only by a rickety, open-sided, wooden porch.

Dorothy remembers watching Jackie being dragged from the dining-room. 'She would literally scream at the meal table because she was petrified of Gordon Rowe and his common-law wife... so anyway, if she screamed they told her to keep quiet else they would put her down the bottom of the stairs and make her stand up to eat her food. So poor Jackie would scream and she was pushed outside and made to stand outside in the cold and the rain to eat her food.'

Angela Rowe was a willing participant in this punishment. One care worker remembered how Angela had come into the dining-room to speak to Gordon, minutes after he had dragged Jackie outside. After a brief conversation, Angela turned and clattered down the stairs. She kicked the back door open and shouted: 'You're a dirty cow for spitting your food out. You can stay outside.'

But Jackie was not just a helpless victim. She stood up to Gordon, despite his huge advantages of strength and power. She would tell him: 'Don't want to eat, don't care.' She would spit her food out. Eventually, as soon as she saw Gordon entering the dining-room, she would just pick up her plate and say: 'Going outside, Gordon.'

Michael was punished in a similar way. He was forced to go without his lunch and stand outside, and have to watch the others eating through the window. One care worker said he didn't do much to merit this punishment; he could have been just standing in the garden with his hands in his pockets instead of working.

Sometimes, Gordon would allow Michael to attend the pottery class. One of the teachers described how Gordon would ask him afterwards if he had enjoyed it. Michael would say, 'Oh yes I did, thank you Gordon.' 'Gordon would then say Michael could forget about going again and send him to work in the farmyard. Every now and again, Gordon would remind Michael that there were good things he wasn't having.'

Gary Moreton described how, after two years working at Longcare, he saw Michael's treatment worsen. 'Initially, it was Gordon making him stay outside in the garden and spend short periods of time in his room, but then he started to stand up to Gordon. Gordon would lose his temper and would kick Michael from one place to another.'

Michael was forced to spend more and more of his time in his room. There was no lock on his bedroom door, but the door at the end of the corridor had a bolt put on it and this was kept locked.

Another resident frequently punished by Gordon was Peter. Because he would wander about at night and sit on the sofa and masturbate – behaviour almost certainly caused by the abuse he was suffering – Gordon would make him sit on a chair in the corridor near the dining-room for days on end.

Gary Moreton described how Gordon would approach Peter, shouting at him. 'Gordon would go up behind him often and kick him in the small of his back towards a chair... Gordon would kick him from the top lounge to the bottom lounge... Gordon would kick him all the way, and Peter would be hollering in fright. He would have his arms stretched out in front of him, desperately trying to feel his way. If he was not kicked, he would be whacked around the head. Gordon would slap him so hard that he would fall over sometimes, lifting him right off his feet.'

Another blind resident, Christopher, was also punished by being made to sit on a chair. One care worker later described how she came across him sitting in the chair with his head in his hands. She put her hand on his shoulder and he pushed it away. When she knelt down next to him, Lorraine Field told her to 'get your bleeding hands off him', and told her he was being punished. Lorraine walked up to Christopher and slapped him on the back of his head.

Michael was also often forced to sit on a hard, wooden chair for hours on end. If he moved, Gordon would drag him back to the chair.

Often, the misdemeanours the residents had committed were simply unavoidable side-effects of their impairment.

Nicky Power had epilepsy and in the build-up to a seizure, she would often scream out because she didn't understand what was happening. On one occasion, when Gordon heard she was 'acting funny', he hit her across her head and dragged her across the floor by her hair.

Gordon had bought Stoke Green House in 1987 from the Conservative county councillor, Rex Lingham-Wood. It was on the other side of the main road from Stoke Place, about 50 yards from the entrance, and Gordon used it to house some of the residents with lower support needs. But any residents who misbehaved were transferred back to Stoke Place to be punished. They would return a couple of weeks later, drugged up to the eyeballs and hardly able to stand up straight.

Ben had a habit of opening the washing machine late at night to get his clothes out, so he could have them by his bed in the morning when he woke up. But sometimes he opened the machine when it was still full of water. On one occasion, he flooded the laundry, and Lillian, the duty care assistant, called over to Stoke Place for help. Desmond Tully rushed over and fought with Ben on the stairs. Lillian said later that Desmond hit Ben repeatedly with his clenched fist before dragging him over to Stoke Place – an allegation Desmond would later deny. Lillian claimed there was still a mark on Ben's jaw two weeks later.

When he returned to Stoke Green a few weeks later, Ben was hardly able to summon the energy to get out of a chair.

When a resident became too boisterous, cheeky, or showed signs of refusing to bow to Gordon's authority, he would drug them up with Largactil or another 'neuroleptic' drug used to control psychosis. Of course, they weren't psychotic, but there wasn't much they could do about it.

Anti-psychotic drugs such as Largactil can cause serious side-effects, such as difficulty talking or swallowing, muscle spasms of the head and neck, drooling, rashes, and uncontrollable body movements. But Gordon, with his Broadmoor experience, convinced staff, and other professionals, that they were essential to treat the 'symptoms' displayed by his residents.

Longcare was run like a correctional facility, with the residents there to be punished. Physical punishment was a constant threat. Psychological punishments appear to have been just as feared. One Rowe seemed to enjoy was locking a resident overnight in the Longcare aviary. One former resident was so terrified of this that in later years he would scream in panic at the mere sight of a bird on a piece of paper.

The punishment regime had been influenced strongly by Gordon's years at Broadmoor. Broadmoor, though, was a prison. The Longcare homes were supposed to be just that: homes.

But Rowe wasn't simply replicating what he had seen at Broadmoor. The language he used reflected the low esteem in which people with learning difficulties were held in society. Rowe used to tell staff how lucky the residents were to have him. 'Who else would look after them?' he would say. It was this kind of attitude that led to hundreds of thousands of people being imprisoned under the Mental Deficiency Acts: the belief that they were worth less, worthless even. Although Rowe's brutality and sadism set him apart from most of society, his core beliefs – and those of many of his staff – did not. Once he had established in his staff's minds the idea that people with learning difficulties did not deserve the same rights, the human rights, as other people, it became much easier to convince them that they deserved to be severely punished when they disobeyed his orders.

*

To stay in power, Gordon needed to know what his staff were doing, and saying. He could not risk them speaking out or making friends or alliances he could not control.

When Clare Johnson arrived for her job interview, Gordon asked her mother – an experienced care worker – to come in with her. He told them about the beautiful grounds, the holidays to the Isle of Wight, to Butlins, Cyprus, even Florida, and about the animals kept in the grounds and fed by the residents. They had rabbits – cute, long-haired rabbits – dogs of course, goats, horses, a donkey or two and a llama (Douglas) once owned by the Bee Gees. He was totally convincing.

But Clare soon learned that Stoke Place was not the glorious rural paradise Gordon had painted. She enjoyed working with the residents, but she started to wonder about the way her boss treated some of the residents: the slaps, the dirty jokes, the mickey-taking. But she was young and inexperienced. What did she know? After all, they called him Big Dadda. Maybe he was just playing the part of a strict, loving father.

She remembers using a video-camera to tape some of the residents in a classroom, as part of her college course in social care. Gordon had shown her the video-editing suite in his cottage in the grounds of Stoke Place. She had been delighted when he offered to edit her video.

As Clare held the camera, Gordon entered the classroom. He told her one of the residents needed some help. As she moved the camera away, she heard a loud smack. When she swivelled towards the sound, she saw one of the men cowering in his seat, with Gordon standing over him.

As the residents left the room at the end of the session, Gordon asked Clare whether her video was nearly finished. When she nodded, he held out his hand for the tape. 'Give me a week or so, and I'll have it ready,' he said. 'Save you all the bother with the cutting and the editing.' She hesitated for a moment before handing over the tape.

Gordon used as many young and inexperienced staff as he could. They were easier to intimidate, and were paid very low wages. If any of his employees dared question his behaviour, he warned them that he could make sure they never worked in the care industry again. Most had never been inside a residential home before, or met anyone with a learning difficulty, so they generally did as they were told. But Rowe also used more sinister techniques to control his staff.

Rowe spied on everyone. Not just with the video camera he often carried around, but also by listening to the conversations of residents and staff. He had an intercom installed so he could listen in to rooms all over Stoke Place. His staff found out and started communicating using Makaton – a sign language designed for people with learning difficulties – until Rowe banned it.

He often used spurious, but persuasive, explanations for such decisions. With his charisma and powers of persuasion, he was usually able to convince his staff that he was right. For instance, he told staff that using Makaton would 'embarrass parents seeing their daughter or son signing to them while they were walking down the high street'.

Those who weren't convinced were too scared to speak out. Colleagues would point to the speaker on the staff-room wall, if a colleague was mouthing off about the regime. 'Watch your mouth, Gordon's listening,' they would say. Rowe used to enjoy showing his staff the powers of his snooping devices. Often, he would confront them about complaints they had made behind closed doors, and enjoy their embarrassment at being found out.

But it wasn't just technology that Rowe used to spy on his staff and residents. He designed the whole regime to prevent careless talk. He selected a small group of favoured and able residents – including John and Andrew – to be his eyes and ears. They would tell him, for instance, if a care assistant had disobeyed his instructions and given a resident an extra cup of tea after lunch.

'The boys like John and Andrew, they were the spies to look out for places,' says Dorothy. 'Gordon Rowe wanted to get me like that. He said, 'I'll leave you in here. Keep an eye on the residents. Don't let them go to sleep, don't let them leave the room.' But I would let them go to sleep and Andrew would say, 'He's going to sleep, you better got to wake them up.' But I said, 'No, I'm not. He's allowed to go to sleep. I'm not going to wake him up.' But then I didn't know that it was Andrew would go back to Gordon Rowe and tell Gordon Rowe that I let the residents sleep through the day.'

One woman, who was in her 50s, was hauled up before Rowe because she had bought a packet of cigarettes during a shopping trip with one of 'Gordon's Girls', his small group of favoured female residents. Rachel remembers how she was rewarded with sweets for reporting back to Gordon what other residents had done.

Malcolm*, who worked briefly at Stoke Place and Stoke Green, said: 'Andrew wouldn't move unless Gordon had given him permission. He was Gordon's own little in-house surveillance camera. He had a walkie-talkie and everything. He would stand at the gate and take notes of the numbers of staff cars, when they came in and when they went out, and would tell Gordon Rowe what time they started and finished work.' He would even watch the staff during lunch, and tell Gordon how much they had eaten and how long they had taken.

'There was a lot of back-stabbing there, a hell of a lot,' Susannah*, one of the care workers, told me. 'He told the clients to spy on the staff and on each other. None of the clients told you anything for about a couple of years, until they thought you were really trustworthy. There was gossip going around, but we didn't really know if it was real or not. Gordon was so clever. There was one member of staff who was creating a bit of a stir and Gordon made out that he was mad. He was so convincing.'

Gary Moreton, who had discussed the cruelty of the regime with colleagues, agrees. 'Gordon was convincing and he convinced them that I was the trouble-maker. He could sit you down and talk to you for an hour and by the end of it you would think: 'He's got a point.''

It wasn't just the spying and the clever allocation of privileges and punishment that helped Rowe keep control. He also knew how to intimidate residents and staff by showing off his powerful friends. One trick was to invite pals from Slough police for social visits, or arrange trips to Slough police station. Staff at Longcare believed – with some justification, it turned out – that there was no point filing complaints about Rowe with Slough police.

Gordon also joined the Freemasons. The more people who knew how important his friends were and how many contacts he had, the easier it was for him to force them into silence.

When Rowe's police mates came to visit, they would stand in reception, the best-decorated room in the building, with oil paintings hung on the wall, and Gordon would tell them a dirty joke or two, explain how good he was to his residents, how he thought of them as his own family. Most importantly, he would make sure his staff knew exactly who his guests were.

Rowe knew his connections would raise other doubts in the minds of his staff. After all, if he had so many friends in the police, he couldn't be that bad a person, could he? Maybe he is right, they would think. Maybe this is the right way to treat residents. Who are we to challenge him?

Chapter Eleven

Neglect

'NHS and social care staff have been responsible for an appalling catalogue of neglect of people with learning disabilities, the health and local government ombudsmen say today after an investigation into six 'distressing' deaths. They included the case of a 43-year-old man with Down's syndrome and epilepsy who starved for 26 days in Kingston hospital, Surrey, because he was unable to speak... The investigation upheld complaints of maladministration against seven NHS trusts and two local authorities involved in the six unrelated deaths between 2003 and 2005. It also criticised the watchdog, the Healthcare Commission, for failing to deal properly with complaints.'

The Guardian, 24 March 2009

Every care worker I spoke to could recall how residents had been criminally neglected, whether through lack of food and personal care or how they were forced to spend their time.

Many relatives who visited Stoke Place before allowing their son or daughter to be placed at the home described the building as run-down and shabby. Gordon Rowe persuaded them of his plans for improvements, so they didn't worry about the dirty and faded carpets, the missing light-bulbs or the flaking paintwork.

But these signs of poor upkeep were evidence that Rowe was also prepared to subject his residents to sub-standard levels of care.

Dorothy Thomson remembers a fellow resident called Gary [not Gary Deacon]. 'He was a very nice boy, actually, and he couldn't speak,' she told me. 'And one day he was late for breakfast and he didn't have no breakfast so he had to go straight out in the garden and he was very, very hungry. So they used to keep horses and they gave the horse potatoes to the horses and Gary pick one up and start eating it. So the gardener reported him to Gordon Rowe and at dinner time when everybody was sitting down to a lovely dinner, all Gary had was this rotten potato on his plate. And Gordon Rowe said to him: 'Here, if you like eating potatoes so much, Gary, then eat that one.'

Dorothy took pity on Gary and secretly filled a bag under the table with food. After the meal, she gave it to Gary and said, 'Here, Gary, take this, don't say nothing to Gordon Rowe.'

Food portions were tiny, particularly for those who were not among Gordon's favourites. Sometimes, the food ran out, and staff would have to go round and scrape food off plates to make it go round. At some point, Angela Rowe made the decision to change the breakfast orange juice to water, again to save a few more pence.

Rachel says she lost three stone in just two years after moving to Stoke Place, and weighed just eight stone when she left. Many others lost huge amounts of weight, including Stephen, who was six feet five and weighed 12 stone when he arrived, and left Longcare 11 years later weighing nine stone seven pounds.

One care worker described catching George with a pocketful of potatoes and mud smeared around his mouth. 'When I eventually got him to open his mouth, he was eating raw potatoes. I heard from other members of staff that George was being punished and Gordon had stopped his food.'

One of Michael's relatives would describe in a statement how he lost three stone in weight in just a few months. They were shocked at the change to the 'lovely, happy-go-lucky' young man. His posture became stooped and 'almost doubled over'. She and other relatives visited him after returning from a holiday and were shocked to see that he 'looked like a skeleton'. 'Whenever we visited Michael we would take him food, Mars bars, sandwiches, etc. He would eat them almost secretly and make us take the wrappers home.'

Angela Rowe was becoming angry at how toiletries were being 'wasted', so she introduced a system where each member of staff was given a carrier bag containing a tube of toothpaste, a roll of toilet paper and a bar of soap. Each bag was used by several residents – sometimes a whole corridor – and had to last a month. There was one razor for five residents. If the toilet paper ran out, Angela would ration extra supplies to two sheets a day each. Inevitably, when this happened, some residents resorted to other measures to keep themselves clean, using their hands, flannels, towels or the curtains in their bedrooms.

Angela even ordered staff to collect all the bits of leftover soap and boil them up to make new bars, which fell apart almost immediately. Some staff would bring in toiletries themselves to make up for what Angela refused to provide.

Residents would frequently be dressed in each others' clothes, no matter how threadbare or ill-fitting. Many residents had new jackets, shoes and other clothes bought by their families, but they would be taken away almost immediately, and never seen again.

Gary Moreton remembers how George's father would phone up to say he was coming to visit. Angela would go to her store cupboard and take out some decent clothes and give them to George to wear. 'George would look tip top and be delighted, thinking he was getting some new clothes, but as soon as his father had gone, Angela would take the clothes back.'

As early as 1985, in a review carried out by Stoke Place, it was said that George had ripped his trousers 'but we have continued to make him wear them outside rather than be manipulated into providing a new pair (as we believe was his intention)'.

Years later, George had torn his clothes again. It was the weekly evening on which the residents were given fish and chips, although few of them received anything like a full portion. George sat down, clearly excited at the prospect of fish and chips. Instead, says Gary, Gordon put George's torn clothes on his plate and said: 'Eat those.' 'George just sat there with his head down, crying. He had tears dripping from his face onto his plate of torn clothes.'

Stephen, another resident, was sent home in shoes three sizes too small, causing permanent damage to his toes.

Gary also describes how Rowe dangled in front of Michael a new jacket that a relative bought him. 'Isn't this a nice jacket, Michael?' he said. As Michael rubbed his hands together with excitement, Gordon dropped it in the bin. Sometimes, he would give Michael's new clothes to other residents, and tell him that now they belonged to someone else.

Instead of the pottery and lapidary classes, the horse-riding, and the reading and writing lessons that Gordon told the families about, many residents were simply set to work.

The men, particularly, were expected to work outside in all weathers – those capable of doing so were called the 'Working Lads' – and were given inappropriate clothing. They chopped wood, raked leaves or cleared weeds in the gardens. They would only be allowed inside if there were visitors.

Rowe had talked about the Working Lads in his letter to South Bucks councillors in 1983. It was part of the supervised 'training' Longcare would offer. It sounded plausible enough, and so it seemed to many of the staff. Social and educational training, Rowe called it, disguising its true identity with a vaguely academic label. It was a tactic he frequently used to mislead his staff, professionals and other visitors, such as describing a punishment as a 'behaviour modification technique'.

One of the staff, Jean, would describe later how the Working Lads would be forced to work in the gardens whatever the weather. Even if it was cold they would wear their ordinary clothes and shoes, and had no protection or boots. In wet weather, they might wear their own anorak, if they had one. There were one or two jackets, she said, but not enough to go around, and she never saw anybody wearing them.

One of the Longcare gardeners would tell a similar story. 'They were out in the cold and the wet,' he said. 'There was no proper clothing in the winter.'

Gary said Michael could be out in the gardens in the middle of winter wearing just a button-up cotton shirt. He remembers him working outside when it was raining, in just a cardigan and no coat. Often the 'work' was little more than another 'punishment' Gordon had devised: Michael might be told to sweep up bird-droppings from the driveway with a dustpan and brush.

If it rained, and Gordon found the men sheltering beneath the trees, they would be punished.

Michael would often beg Gordon to let him go to the workshops. One day, according to Gary Moreton, Gordon was so infuriated by Michael's show of defiance that he picked up a stick and used it to draw a square on the ground. He told Michael to dig it over. Every time Michael finished digging the earth, he would start talking to other residents. Gordon would see him from his cottage and 'storm out in a rage', grab Michael by the hair and drag him back to the patch of earth and tell him to dig it all over again. 'He would make him do this time and time again and it would go on for days and days,' said Gary.

Former staff remember how Gordon, and lackeys like care supervisor Lorraine Field, would often ignore residents' epileptic seizures, dismissing them as play-acting.

One care worker describes watching from a window as Lorraine marched across the lawn towards a male resident who was having a seizure on the grass. Gordon joined her. Neither of them took any action to help the man. Instead, Gordon nestled his foot underneath his chest, and flipped him onto his side. He glanced at Lorraine and said something. Lorraine nodded, and she and Gordon walked back towards the house, leaving the man to finish his seizure on the grass.

Most members of staff could point later to many similar examples of neglect.

'The strange thing was that Gordon gave me the impression that he did care about the residents,' one of them would tell me. 'I happened to mention to him one day that it must be a very profitable business. He turned round and said to me: 'It's not a business to me. I like to look on it as a family home.''

Gordon could do this. Convince his staff that he cared about the residents, even while they watched him treat them like dirt. Staff may have heard rumours of more serious abuse, but had witnessed maybe a single kick up the backside, neglect and cruelty, which Rowe would explain away as the kind of strict, disciplinarian regime which worked well at Broadmoor.

Some care workers later justified their failure to report the regime to the authorities by telling themselves that they could either quit and abandon the residents they cared about, or stay on and make sure that at least one person was looking out for them. Money was another factor.

'At that time, with unemployment as it was, it was a difficult decision to just walk away,' one of them told me. 'And you had this feeling of protectiveness. When you walked in in the morning they would give you this feeling that they needed you. It was very difficult to just walk away from that. In the end, the reason I did walk away was that I was under so much pressure that I had to leave, and I went to sign on.'

One care worker later told how – before council inspectors were due to visit Longcare – staff would be told to hand out more toiletries, and place televisions in residents' rooms and hang pictures on their walls. The moment the inspection was over, everything would be taken down and put away again. Gordon would also order staff to remove pages from the report book – in which care workers were supposed to write up any 'incidents' that had taken place – fill in any suspicious gaps and add to entries they had already made, to cover up any incidents of abuse. He would also tell his staff what to write in the book.

Jean worked only briefly at Longcare and told me she tried, anonymously, to tip off the authorities. She contacted another council's social services department, but the warning was either not passed on to Buckinghamshire, or was dismissed as 'unsubstantiated'.

She describes being called over from Stoke Green to deal with an emergency. One of the female residents' parents had turned up unexpectedly. Their daughter had been locked in her room for a fortnight for 'messing around with the boys'.

When Jean opened the bedroom door, she was shocked by what she saw. The young woman was curled up in the far corner, her head hidden behind a blood-stained curtain. There were faeces everywhere: on the curtains, on the bed, smeared across the carpet. There was also menstrual blood congealed on her torn night-dress. Her feet were bare and covered in blood. She sat sobbing quietly, clutching the curtain over her face.

Jean looked at the room, at the young woman, and thought of her parents waiting downstairs. For a moment, she would tell me later, she thought of showing them how their daughter was really being looked after. Instead, she walked across the room. 'Let's get you cleaned up,' she said.

*

But the neglect at Longcare was by no means unique. After all, there had been a string of inquiries and exposes of just such neglect and poor care at long-stay hospitals all through the late 1960s and 1970s.

Dr Pauline Morris had written in 1969 about the deprivation of the long-stay hospitals, how patients were forced to share toothbrushes, and had described the 'barren conditions' and 'unjustifiably low standards of care'. These conditions were tolerated by society, she said. Many people knew, including, of course, the thousands of NHS staff who worked at these institutions. Morris said most members of the public regarded the poor conditions with 'comparative equanimity'.

At Botleys Park, where many of the Longcare residents had lived for years, there had been reports of neglect throughout the 1970s and early 1980s, with the Surrey Herald reporting in 1977 how people 'slept in beds head to foot, only inches from each other, with no lockers or cabinets of their own', and describing a 'damp, overcrowded dormitory with its peeling paint and plaster' which 'opens straight into a large lavatory'. In 1983, the year some Botleys patients left for Longcare, bath-time for teenage girls on one ward was likened to 'bathing cattle'.

In many ways, then, the neglect at Longcare was no worse than had been experienced – probably throughout the twentieth century – at many long-stay hospitals. The dehumanising levels of care, the failure to provide adequate food, clothing and toiletries, were a reflection of how society viewed the rights of people with learning difficulties. Rowe would have been more than aware of society's attitudes, and it gave him the confidence to run his homes in the way he saw fit.

Even so, when the appalling neglect and abuse that had been allowed to continue at Longcare became public knowledge, no-one could understand why the residents hadn't confided in their own families.

They seemed to see Gordon as a kind of second father. He punished them when they were 'naughty' and rewarded them when they were good. They accepted it, perhaps, because they had learned from birth that they had to rely on other people. Their survival depended upon submission to Gordon Rowe. All of them were threatened or punished in some way; either by Gordon telling them they would be sent back to Botleys or 'sent away' if they were 'bad', or by beatings, or by threats of violence to loved ones. There were also rewards for 'good' behaviour: holidays, trips to clubs and to the seaside, and extra food.

'They all respected him,' says one former care worker. 'They called him 'Daddy'.' Most of the residents seemed to believe they deserved their punishments. Michael had been locked in his room for days for some trifling 'offence'. When the care worker slipped upstairs to check on him, he pleaded: 'I'll be good, I'll be good. Honest, I'll be good.'

But the message that people with learning difficulties – people like them – were not deserving of the same rights as other members of society must surely have made an impression, particularly on those who had lived at the long-stays for many years.

Those who did try to alert their families to the abuse could not make themselves understood. Their reluctance to return to Stoke Place was seen as a wish to stay at home at the end of an enjoyable weekend. They were said to be 'playing up'. Others were too scared to do anything but nod and force a grin when asked whether everything was all right. All of them had learned that they had no right to expect anything better.

Chapter Twelve

Fraud

'Steven Hoskin had strong feelings about his killers. They had abused, exploited and humiliated him over a year, taking his money, treating him as their slave and making him wear his own dog's collar and lead. Eventually, having forced him to swallow 70 painkillers, they took him to the top of a railway viaduct and made him hang from the railings as one member of the gang, a girl aged 16, stamped on his hands until he fell 30 metres to his death.

'Yet these were the people the 38-year-old, who had severe learning disabilities, had boasted excitedly of counting as friends... Hoskin's case is extreme, but the phenomenon of learning disabled people being groomed by those who pretend to be their friends before being exploited by them financially, physically or sexually – 'mate crime'... is far from rare, experts say, and appears to be on the increase.'
The Guardian, 14 September 2010

Maybe it had always been the plan to squeeze every last penny out of Longcare. Maybe Gordon just noticed how lax the council's inspection regime was. Whatever the explanation, as the years passed, food and toiletries were cut or rationed, the upkeep of the building was neglected and staff numbers were kept dangerously low.

But it wasn't just saving money; it was making money, too. One night a week, the residents would be given fish and chips from a takeaway. They all paid for a full portion from their allowance, but only a favoured few received full servings. The rest received half a sausage and a few chips. A few always went without as a punishment. With nearly 70 residents at the two homes, that was a lot of chip money. And then there were the videos. Gordon sometimes showed some of the residents a film as a 'treat'. They were his tapes, from his own collection, but every Longcare resident was charged a couple of pounds for the 'rental'.

The more capable residents were used as part of Gordon's personal workforce. The women helped him and Angela with their cleaning, ironing and washing-up. Rachel remembers having to carry out unpaid work, helping with the drugs, 'working in the laundry, cleaning and washing up and assisting the less able residents'.

For some of the men, too, there was real work to be done. Rowe admitted to neighbours in a letter that he was bringing over 'a few of his more able lads' to help speed up the work on the extension to his large detached house in an exclusive Windsor cul-de-sac. The extension was being built by Angela's brother Keith. Rachel, one of the female residents, remembers visiting Gordon's house and seeing six of the Working Lads there helping to build the extension.

John was one of those who worked on the extension. He would say later that he wasn't paid at first, but eventually received £10 a week if he 'worked really hard'. He had a talent for painting, had worked as a decorator before he came to Longcare, and painted some of the bedrooms and hallways at Stoke Place. He even used his own brushes, and bought overalls with his own money. John also helped the builders and decorators who renovated Stoke Green House. Rowe didn't pay him a penny.

Another resident, Bob, spent a lot of his time at the Rowes' cottage in the grounds of Stoke Place. He cleaned, groomed the dogs, cooked Gordon and Angela's meals and looked after their son, Ben, who called him 'Butler'. Bob was often beaten by Angela and Gordon Rowe. Again, he wasn't paid for his work.

Andrew also worked on the Windsor extension. He was sexually assaulted by Gordon, who kicked him, threw chairs at him and pushed him down the stairs. Gordon warned him that he would have to leave Stoke Place if he told anyone what he was doing. Years later, Andrew cried as he told his mother: 'I couldn't tell you, mum, because I thought it would upset you.'

Rowe also made use of Bob, John and Andrew to help out his friends in the police force. Andrew told later how he had been taken to the home of a police officer to help with landscaping work in his garden. He and the others had also helped decorate the homes of the same officer and one of his colleagues. They were paid a pittance for their work.

As well as cutting corners and taking advantage of the residents' labour, Rowe also stole from them.

Dorothy told me how he would 'commit fraud with the residents' money'. 'Well, I found out that because somebody used to send me cheques: £300 cheques, £400. But he always used to say: 'I will look after it. Shall I look after it, Dot, and put it in the bank to save you from standing up?' So he would play me against my cerebral palsy, but he didn't realise he couldn't play me against my brain. So he put it in the bank for me, but then I found out later it was a bank that Angela Rowe used. And then he used to say, 'I will put it in the bank for you and you can come and look at the books now and then and see how much interest you are getting.' So a couple of times I used to go in the office and say, 'Gordon Rowe, can I have a look at the books?' So he used to say, 'No, you can't, they are locked away somewhere. They are over in my cottage somewhere. I'll get them later on.' But then he used to forget to get them. So that's how I triggered on that there was something wrong with that.'

Benefits payments also disappeared into Rowe's bank account. In late 2010, I was told by one of David Jackson's sisters that David was being forced to pay back £4 a week in overpaid benefits to the Department for Work and Pensions (DWP). Angela Rowe, or Angela Adams as she called herself then, had applied in 1992 for the care component of disability living allowance (DLA) on David's behalf. As a care home resident with local authority funding, David was not entitled to claim this benefit. But Angela claimed David was funding his own placement. As a result, nearly £6,000 disappeared into her bank account. David never saw a penny of the money. The DWP eventually refunded the payments David had been forced to make, after I drew their attention to what had happened.

But this cannot have been a one-off. It can only be guessed how many other such claims were submitted by Angela Rowe.

That wasn't all. Presents bought by relatives mysteriously vanished, including countless stereos, televisions and pieces of jewellery. When questioned, Rowe would say they were 'broken' or 'in storage'. Clothes, too, went missing. New pairs of trainers, coats and jackets, designer jeans. Anything valuable always seemed to be misplaced, and residents would return home for weekends dressed in borrowed, dirty and torn clothes.

Michael's relatives described how they bought him a television, a cassette recorder, a stereo, clothes, watches, radios, personal stereos. All were taken away because he was 'naughty'.

Gordon, of course, received hundreds of pounds a week in fees for each resident (£395 per week in 1989), and increased profit margins by cutting back on staff, food and toiletries.

He made huge sums of money, enough to finance a holiday home in Florida; boats; a Rolls-Royce; a sports car, jewellery and fur coats for his wife; a Ferrari for his son, Nigel; round-the-world cruises; homes for himself and Nigel in Windsor; as well as the mortgage-free purchase of Stoke Green House in 1987 and several small satellite homes in Slough.

Dot remembers how Angela would flaunt her wealth. 'Angela Rowe, she would dress up like a dog's dinner in mutton, like a flaming mutton really,' she told me. 'That's where the money was going. She had fur coats, she had pearls, she had diamonds, she was like a flipping walking Christmas tree, only you put lights on her.

'She was going out and she came in with her fur coat on and dripping with diamonds and perfume and that and she had all this make-up on, so I turned round to Jimmy and said, 'Put a couple of feathers up her arse and she would be a peacock.''

Dot and the other residents were given a pound or two in pocket money every week if they were lucky. 'I couldn't afford new clothes,' says Dot. 'I got them out of second-hand shops.'

In her new book on disability hate crime[1], Katharine Quarmby points out that people with learning difficulties, and other disabled people, are often targeted for their benefits money, as part of other connected hate crimes.

Many of the crimes she investigated involved socially-isolated people with learning difficulties who were 'groomed' by people who spotted the vulnerability of their situation. Although the Longcare residents were surrounded by scores of people every day, they were still isolated. Gordon Rowe had created an environment in which they had no-one to turn to.

Quarmby describes how many people with learning difficulties in isolated social situations, often living alone in the community, are approached by people offering them 'friendship'. As the relationship develops, money starts to go missing. Then the physical assaults begin and grow in intensity, often unchallenged by the authorities. In many cases, this progression – known as 'mate crime' – ends in violent death.

There are striking similarities with Longcare. Many of the residents referred to Rowe as 'my friend', something he encouraged. Others called him 'Big Dadda'. Then he would take advantage of the environment he had created, controlling their lives, beating and punishing them when they resisted, and stealing their money, their possessions and their labour.

Chris George says it took Rowe less than a year before he began to make serious money. 'We never thought we would get the [Mansion House] back, because Gordon was making so much money,' she told me.

Even discounting the illegal siphoning of residents' money and possessions, the Rowes were making a fortune. Longcare's official accounts show that, in 1984, the company made a profit of £37,845. The following year, this leapt to £103,864. At the time, the shares in the company were held by Gordon Rowe, Angela Adams and Raymond Beck, although Beck's 2,000 shares would soon be transferred to Nigel Rowe. On top of these profits, Gordon and Angela were drawing huge salaries from Longcare.

By 1990, Gordon, as chairman, was being paid £72,053 a year, with the highest paid director (one of the Rowes, although it is not clear which one), earning £88,547. In 1991, Gordon was paid £85,095 as chairman, with the highest paid director raking in £104,696. These sums of money were far too high to be made from a normal care home. They were achieved by taking the residents and squeezing them until they were dry. And the money the Rowes made on the side can only be guessed at.

There was nothing to stop Gordon Rowe defrauding the residents of Longcare. The county council's annual inspections never came close to revealing the fraud and theft, even though, in 1991, a council inspector told Longcare that too much of the residents' money was being kept in a company account. Gordon was also told that his wife should not be responsible for the personal savings accounts of residents who couldn't look after their own finances. She was the 'appointee' for nearly all such accounts. The following year's inspection discovered that he had not taken the slightest bit of notice and Angela was still the appointee for all but one of the residents.

There was never any danger that their scams would be uncovered. Any relatives' concerns were brushed aside, Slough police were nicely on-side, the county council was incompetent and toothless, and the staff naïve and intimidated. Gordon and Angela could sit back and watch the money flood in.

1   *Scapegoat, by Katharine Quarmby; Portobello Books; 2011*

Chapter Thirteen

Violence

'The health trust at the centre of an alleged abuse scandal at a day centre faced similar allegations at a nearby facility for disabled people just two years earlier. Disability News Service has been collecting mounting evidence of the serious nature of the allegations against former staff of Doncaster's Solar Centre, a day centre for people with learning difficulties and high support needs. Allegations include one disabled person being deliberately pricked with needles, pinned to a wall and hit around the head, punched and threatened. Another was allegedly thrown onto the floor from his wheelchair, and had his wheelchair kicked 'from one side of the room to the other' while he was sat in it.'

Disability News Service, 15 September 2010

Jean remembers sorting out the residents' medication in the office in Stoke Green one Sunday. Her desk was covered with bottles, packets and tubes. She heard the door being pushed open and saw Jackie walking towards her, a smile on her face. She had just finished the washing-up and held out her hands to show Jean. 'Washing,' she said. 'Finished.'

Jackie asked what she was doing and leaned her elbows on the table for a closer look. As Jean started to explain, she heard a yelp of pain.

Jackie lay on the floor in a pile of elbows and knees. Her smile was gone, replaced by a pained grimace. Behind her, grinning broadly, was Gordon Rowe.

He pulled Jackie up by an elbow and shoved her towards the doorway. 'You shouldn't be in here. Get out,' he shouted. Jackie stumbled out, but it wasn't quick enough. Gordon delivered another well-aimed kick at her backside as she disappeared through the door.

He looked back at Jean and smiled. 'I'll go and see if I can kick some more arses now,' he said.

The violence was part of the daily routine. It could be anything from a slap on the back of the head to a kick up the backside, a punch in the stomach to a severe beating in the wood. Gordon told staff the physical punishments were essential. Without them, he said, the home would descend into chaos. He told one care worker, who had watched him slap a resident across the back of his head for spilling his cereal: 'We have to show them who is boss. We have to show them who is in charge.'

For some of the residents, every day became a never-ending exercise in trying not to upset him. Cringing obedience, sucking-up, timid deference to Big Dadda, these were the tactics adopted to avoid beatings. Often, even this wasn't enough.

One care worker described how Nicky Power had been 'misbehaving' in the dining room. Gordon grabbed hold of her arm and then her hair and dragged her to a nearby room, shook her, and threw her onto the floor. Gordon was left with a clump of her hair in his hand. 'That's the way you have to treat her,' he said.

One evening, Nicky came downstairs in her nightgown and was pestering Gordon for attention. He told a care worker to take her upstairs. 'At this point she threw a tantrum,' one care worker said later. 'Gordon went up to her and started slapping her on her backside and she fell into the stairs and he was slapping her and slapping her... I returned two or three minutes later and Gordon was still hitting Nicky... Nicky was very distressed – she had bitten both of her hands during the tantrum, she was crying uncontrollably. I saw Gordon still hit her whilst she was lying down on the stairs.'

Another care worker described how Gordon had approached Michael, who was sitting at a table. There were raised voices and then a noise. When she looked round, a chair had been pushed over onto the floor and Michael had run outside. Gordon followed him into the garden. The care worker saw Gordon raise his right arm and Michael fall over. Gordon kicked him as he lay on the grass. Michael was confined to his bedroom for several days as a punishment.

Paul Robertson, one of the care workers whose whistleblowing would eventually spark a council investigation, remembers seeing Gordon punch a male resident in the face. 'One of the young guys had wet his bed during the night,' said Paul. 'Gordon walked straight in and punched him in the head. It split his head. I never saw the boy after that for weeks and weeks because Gordon wouldn't let him out of his room or let anybody up to see him.'

David Jackson, who was only able to communicate through signs or grunts, was a satisfying target for a bully like Gordon Rowe. David was also incontinent – mainly due to an undiagnosed medical condition, but also undoubtedly because of anxiety caused by how he was treated.

When Gordon heard about one of his accidents, he would fly into a rage. David was often sent to sit outside to eat his meal on the back doorstep, even in the biting winter wind. On one occasion, he had messed himself in a classroom and Gordon dragged him outside and made him sit on the step. A care worker, Lillian, said it was 'very, very cold'. Gordon told him: 'Stay there, you animal. You act like one and I will treat you like one.' Later that day, he dragged David into the bushes for 10 minutes and then sent him to the workshop. He told one care worker: 'That sorted him out. I have just done some of my therapy on him.'

Lillian would tell the police later: 'After this, David had marks on his face and arms. They were like thump marks. I saw bruising.'

Several care workers described how Gordon would grab David after he had messed himself and drag him outside, before hosing him down with cold water.

Gary Moreton described how on one occasion David had used an outside toilet in a desperate attempt to clean himself, but couldn't find any paper, so tried to use his hands. Gary and the residents in the nearby workshop watched through the window as Gordon dragged David back into the toilet by his hair and turned on a hosepipe. David was crouched, fully dressed, shielding his face with his hands. Gordon had the hose on him for more than 10 minutes.

Gordon often hit David when he messed himself. Sometimes, he hit him so hard he knocked him down. He told the care workers that David only messed himself to get attention, and there wasn't really anything wrong with him. You have to be strict, he said, or they take advantage.

On another occasion, a care worker had cleaned him up, only to be told by Gordon that they should have just hosed him down with cold water. Gordon had grabbed a metal shovel and dragged David across the lawn behind him. Through the dining-room window, residents watched and screamed as they saw them head into the trees.

The wood was about 50 or so yards from the back of the mansion. Through the trees ran one of Gordon's little toys, a narrow gauge railway. He loved to show it off when he held fund-raising open days (the money, of course, vanishing into his bank account). On a rusty siding in a clearing in the middle of the wood, sat a row of dark green railway carriages. It was towards these carriages that Gordon was dragging David.

Gordon knew he couldn't hit residents where a bruise would look suspicious. He knew the difference between 'accidental' and 'non-accidental' bruising from his Broadmoor days. A bruise to the elbow or knee could be explained away as an accident, but those to the back or kidneys were a different matter and might arouse the suspicion of a social worker or relative. So he was careful.

Gordon swaggered back in alone. He passed a care worker in the corridor, and said: 'Well, that's that sorted out. David has to have his dinner on the doorstep again. I've given him some of my psychology.'

The more serious physical attacks were carried out in secret, in the woods, or in Rowe's cottage, but every staff member had witnessed criminal acts of assault or ill-treatment.

One care worker saw Rowe walk George to a tree and tie him to it with rope. He left him there for about half an hour. The punishment was apparently because George had had an attack of diarrhoea in a woodwork class. Another care worker who witnessed a similar incident, said: 'George didn't want to work in the garden so Gordon hit and kicked him... and then he tied him to a tree with a piece of rope. I don't know how long George was left there, but I remember he was crying and whimpering. It was wintertime.'

Another staff member would say later in a statement how she came downstairs for lunch and saw George tied to a tree outside. 'No one of the other staff mentioned it until I did. Staff appeared to think that this was a normal event – even though some seemed disgusted they seemed to think there was nothing they could do about it. I was told that he was there because he had messed himself.... When I left the cocktail lounge after my lunch break (my break lasted one hour) he was still there.'

Stefano was another regularly punished by Gordon, sometimes for incontinence, sometimes, Rowe claimed, for masturbating. His mother would point out later that Stefano never masturbated at home and that she believed Rowe used this as an excuse to justify high levels of medication and to cover up the abuse he was suffering. Gordon would often drag Stefano out of his chair and hit him around the head and legs. Occasionally, he would pour cold water over his head. When incontinent, he was dragged outside and forced to stand there, whatever the weather, until his clothes were dry. Sometimes, he would have to stand outside to eat his meals. Paul Robertson said later: 'I witnessed this on numerous occasions and I also saw Gordon Rowe drag Stefano outside by his ears, hair and clothing like a naughty schoolboy. Stefano was left outside in all types of weather, rain and cold.'

But it wasn't just Gordon. Some of his managers, like Lorraine Field and Desmond Tully, and his wife Angela, also assaulted residents.

Rachel remembers Lorraine telling her to do something; when she refused, Lorraine told her: 'If you don't do what you're fucking told, I'll put your fucking head through the window.' 'I started to cry,' Rachel said later in a statement, 'and Lorraine said that if I didn't stop she would give me something to cry about. Later on, when I walked past still sobbing, Lorraine hit me on the side of my head with her open hand.

'On another occasion, I was in the Queen Anne classroom when Lorraine hit me across the back of my head. I nearly fell off my chair. The chair went back on two legs and I was frightened. She hit me hard enough to make me cry. She hit me because I didn't want to do the writing I had. Lorraine told me off. 'You'd better do your writing or you will not get your dinner.' Something like that.'

A care worker also described how she heard shouting and screaming coming from Nicky Power's bedroom. Nicky was on the floor, with Lorraine screaming at her to get up and dragging her along the floor.

Another care worker, Penny, would later describe in court how Lorraine had held Janet Ward face down on the floor after she had become angry and upset. Lorraine was pouring jugs of cold water over her to 'calm her down'. Another care worker described how Lorraine had thrown water over a second female resident, and how she saw Lorraine drag the woman by her collar along the floor.

Another former member of staff, Linda, described seeing Lorraine hit a female resident in the face. 'She told me that I would have to do this. I told her there was no way I could ever do that and told her never to do that in front of me again. She hit her a second time. Lorraine told me not to bother telling Gordon or Angela as they would only agree with the practice.' As a result, Linda decided she had to leave Longcare. 'I worked out my two weeks and then never went back,' she said.

Other staff members recalled how Desmond Tully had hit residents, including Ben and Stefano, and how Angela would frequently scream abuse at residents. One care worker described how she grabbed a female resident by the hair as she was climbing the stairs at Stoke Green, and pulled her back down the stairs. One resident told later how Angela used to hit her around the head or in the face.

Rowe's staff knew he had threatened a care worker with legal action for making 'allegations' against him. They also knew he had many friends within Slough police. What was the point of risking their job by reporting him to the authorities when they had no concrete evidence and wouldn't be believed anyway?

Besides, Rowe was always able to justify his actions, by referring to his training and experience, or disguising the assaults in fancy words, convincing his staff that what he was doing was therapy, not abuse.

153

He also seemed somehow to instinctively know how far he could go in public, and when he needed to retire to a private place to dish out a beating.

He had already neutralised the threat of Slough police and he knew from long experience how easy it was to evade the limp hand of Buckinghamshire social services. Behind the high walls of Longcare, Gordon Rowe thought he was untouchable. But it was the daily violence he inflicted upon the residents that would eventually help to bring down his regime.

Dorothy would describe years later what happened to her when she tried to stand up to Gordon Rowe's violence and speak out about his regime.

It was noon on a Sunday and her boyfriend Jimmy had gone home for the weekend. She was living in one of Longcare's small satellite homes, less than a mile from Stoke Place, and just over the county border in Slough. Dorothy had spoken to one of the staff and 'let it all out what Gordon Rowe was doing to the residents. I didn't know he was going to go back and tell Gordon Rowe. And that's what he did.'

She returned from lunch at Stoke Place and had put a video on and was about to sew name-tapes on some socks belonging to one of her housemates. Her house-mate Sylvia was in the kitchen, putting the kettle on for a cup of tea, when they heard 'three great knocks on the door'.

'I wouldn't answer the door because I had a vague idea who it was,' says Dorothy. 'So about a minute or so later the knocks came again: three great big ones. So Sylvia got frightened, she answered the door and in strode this Gordon Rowe, kicking the front door open and come into the living-room. So he says, 'Dorothy Abbot, I hear you've got something to say to me.' So I said, 'Yes, I hate you. I hate what you're doing to the residents.' I saw these scissors so I picked them up and Gordon Rowe turned round and he caught my wrist and he made me drop the scissors. I said to him, 'I nearly killed you, Gordon Rowe.' And if I didn't have cerebral palsy, I would have stabbed him. But he pushed me down on the ground and he didn't even allow me to get up to walk.'

She describes how Rowe dragged her down the doorstep and into the garden on her back. 'So the front door smashed and he did get me down the step eventually and my fingers were rubbed to the bone. I had very long hair and he got hold of the little bits at the back of my hair, he pulled my head right back right across the gravel. And then I had this pink blouse on and it was changing colour from pink to red virtually because of the blood I was losing. And he pushed me down on the grass, which was wet, and I was shivering with shock, and hypothermia was also working in.'

Even then, Gordon had not broken Dorothy's resistance. 'So I broken off a pair of glasses and I thrown them at him and I said, 'There, Gordon Rowe, I'm not frightened of you.' So he tried to pull me and I ripped all the buttons on his shirt and these fingers were getting more and more rubbed down. I had blood clots in my hair and it was like the ordinary bloodbath out there.'

Many of the families would tell me later they never even considered the possibility that their sons or daughters would be ill-treated or assaulted at Stoke Place. The thought of anyone doing something so cruel to someone in such a vulnerable position never occurred to them.

The journalist Katharine Quarmby would say something similar in her groundbreaking report on disability hate crime[1]. 'Many people find it difficult to believe that disabled people are attacked or harassed simply because they are disabled,' she wrote. 'Most people cannot imagine anyone hating a disabled person enough to want to frighten, hurt or murder them.' But the roots of the kind of violence perpetrated by Gordon Rowe at Longcare 'lie in contempt rather than fear', she wrote. Prejudice against disabled people 'is rooted in the view that disabled people are inferior; in some cases less than human. They are harassed, attacked, humiliated and even killed because their lives are considered less valuable than other people's lives.'

The hidden epidemic of disability hate crime that she and disabled activists like Anne Novis would uncover, described later in this book, would demonstrate that the violence inflicted by Gordon Rowe was no aberration. The particular circumstances that led to Longcare, and the depth, scale and depravity of Rowe's abuses, were unique. But the hatred or contempt that led to them were not.

1   *Getting Away With Murder: Disabled people's experiences of hate crime in the UK, by Katharine Quarmby; Disability Now, United Kingdom Disabled People's Council, Scope; 2008*

Chapter Fourteen

Rape

'Two men involved in the rape of a 16-year-old girl who was doused in caustic soda at the end of her 'nightmare ordeal' have had their sentences increased. Three Court of Appeal judges ruled that the terms being served... were 'unduly lenient' because the case was so 'horrifying'. The victim, who has learning difficulties, was disfigured for life in the gang rape in Tottenham, north London, last year.'

Sky News, 2 July 2009

Gordon had told Janet Ward that they were going to buy a house together, that he was going to divorce Angela and marry her, because he loved her.

Like many of the female residents, Janet was desperate for a life like those of her sisters, family friends, of women she saw on television. She wanted a boyfriend, a husband, a home, a baby.

Rowe was able to see inside the heads of Janet and his other favourites, the women the staff called 'Gordon's Girls'. As he had said about the residents of The Old Rectory in a letter to South Bucks council in 1983: 'They all have their own individual personalities, their likes and dislikes, their fears, hopes and aspirations.' Rowe knew the 'fears, hopes and aspirations' of Gordon's Girls and he used bribes, threats and violence to twist them out of shape and gratify his darkest urges.

Dorothy remembers a female resident she would see crying in the classroom. It took about a week to gain her trust. 'I was getting her confidence in me,' Dorothy told me, 'and she would tell me and the result was that Gordon Rowe was having sex with her. And the teacher there was saying to her, 'Stop crying, be quiet, don't be stupid, Gordon wouldn't do that.' But when it came out, Gordon was having sex with her. One day she was so hysterical, she said to me, 'Gordon Rowe has really hurt me,' and the next month she left. I don't know if he made her pregnant or what. She was gone to another place.'

Rachel was one of Gordon's Girls. She later described in a statement how the abuse started. When she first arrived at Stoke Place, she saw Gordon as a father figure. 'He always used to give me cuddles if I felt low or just wanted one just to be friendly,' she said. 'He was like a father.' But at some point he began to take advantage of her. 'I was sitting on his lap and when I stood up he gave me a cuddle, put his arms around me and undid my bra,' she said. 'I pushed him away, screamed and ran out. I didn't dare tell anybody.'

A couple of weeks later, Gordon started telling her how some of the other female residents were sexually frustrated. It was then that he started forcing her to have sex.

'He would tell me I was a very attractive girl. I thought he was just a friend. I always thought I was ugly because of things I got called at school.' He had sex with Rachel at the group home where she lived in Slough, in the offices and classrooms at Stoke Place, and once in the Rowe's cottage in the grounds of Stoke Place while Angela was out shopping. She described in her statement how Gordon would pretend to staff that they were going upstairs to 'work on the receipts', and they would go up to the classroom and Gordon would lock the door. She would often go over to the cottage to wake Gordon from his afternoon nap.

'At first I didn't know Gordon Rowe was having sexual intercourse with any other residents, but later on some of the other girls told me that it had happened to them as well,' she said.

At first, Gordon arranged for Rachel to visit the family planning clinic for a contraceptive injection. After a while, the Longcare GP began to give her the injections. 'I don't know why none of the staff questioned the need for me to have an injection or why Dr X didn't query this as this would have alerted them to what was going on.

'I should have tried to say 'no' to stop it all right from the beginning but I was frightened of him. He would shout at me and reduce me to tears. He would get cross and say, 'Oh, if you don't want it I'm not going to bother with you anymore.' I was scared. That's what I thought would happen.

'He said not to tell anybody. One day he told me that if the police came and asked me about it that I was to say, 'I don't know anything about it,' and make it sound like nothing happened. He used to say I would probably end up in prison.' As well as the threats, he also gave Rachel sweets and other 'treats', while she was better dressed than many of the other women.

She believes Angela was suspicious. 'Angela Rowe would pick on me,' Rachel said. 'Angela Rowe hit me around the head or across the face or from behind. Every time she did this she didn't warn me by saying anything to me first, she would just hit me. I didn't know what the rules were but I think she hit me because of what was happening with her husband. On one particular occasion she was cross about something and she threatened to put my head through a brick wall.'

Lillian, one of the former care workers, remembers carrying an urn of tea to the workshops one day and hearing giggling coming from one of the toilets. She heard two voices, a man and a woman. The man was telling the woman to keep her voice down. It was Gordon Rowe. As Lillian drew closer, she heard Janet Ward's voice saying: 'Do it some more, Gordon.' And she heard Gordon reply: 'Later, Janet, when they're all in bed.'

Lillian approached the door and put down the urn. She opened the door. Gordon was standing in front of Janet, his hands under her sweater, which had been pushed up over her chest.

Gordon quickly pulled Janet's top down and turned to face Lillian. 'These damn residents,' he said, and laughed. 'They always need your attention for something or other.' Lillian picked up the urn and hurried to the workshops. She told Gordon's son, Nigel, about the incident, but nothing was done.

Janet would tell police, after leaving Longcare, how Gordon would force her to have sex in her bedroom. 'One day Angela came into my bedroom and found Gordon in my bed. She hit Gordon around the head because Gordon kissed me. Gordon had sex with me as well and I didn't want him to. It happened lots of times in my bed, in the cottage and in the house down the road. It was horrible. I told Gordon not to do it, but he did. Angela hit me once in the cottage. She caught Gordon kissing me. I don't like sex on him, it was frightening... Gordon told me not to tell the police about it.'

One care worker said later that Janet had told her how Gordon would lie on top of her in her bedroom. She believed Janet had confided in other staff as well.

Many of the women – and men – were raped or sexually assaulted by Rowe. Mostly he picked on his favourites among Gordon's Girls and the Working Lads. He attacked them in their bedrooms, in the classrooms at Stoke Place during the evenings, or in his cottage during the afternoons, when Angela was shopping. They were given privileges in return, such as visits to a Windsor nightclub or trips in his boat. If they objected, he used violence. Andrew would often be called over to the cottage during the afternoons. If he resisted, Rowe would throw chairs, punch and threaten him.

Parvinder's face was often swollen with bruises. She always explained to staff that she had had a seizure and had fallen. 'Her face would be black and blue, but the rest of her body wasn't touched,' remembers Susannah. 'It looked as though she had been in a fight. I never saw her have a fit, but if I went off duty and came back, her face would be black and blue.'

Parvinder was described by care workers as 'beautiful', with long, black hair, and big, brown eyes, but she was frail and timid, too.

Late one afternoon, Susannah was looking for Gordon at Stoke Place. She had left the reception area and was walking towards the stairs, when she heard a sound. Parvinder fell into her arms, breathing hard. Susannah propped her up, held her at arm's length and looked into her eyes. Parvinder stared through her, just allowing the arms to hold her up.

'Parvinder, what's wrong?'

'OK,' she said, and shook her head. She leaned against the wall for support and pushed herself away and past, towards reception.

Susannah heard more steps, coming from the same direction, down the stairs. Gordon Rowe appeared; his face was flushed and he was out of breath, his white hair damp with sweat. He stopped when he saw Susannah.

'Gordon, there's a call for you.'

'Never mind that. Did you see Parvinder?'

'Yes.'

'Oh, good.' He hesitated. 'How did you find her?'

'She looked a bit dazed and upset,' said Susannah. 'What's wrong with her?'

'Nothing,' he said. He shoved his hands deep in his pockets. 'Nothing medical,' he added, and brushed past her.

Many of the staff had tales to tell of how they had met female residents returning to their rooms hot, flustered and sweaty, hours after they should have been in bed. When pressed, they might admit they had been at 'the cottage' with Gordon. Susannah had quizzed Michelle, one of Gordon's Girls, after she had disappeared during bath-time. When she returned, red-faced and out of breath, she eventually told Susannah that she had been with Gordon.

'She looked at me and said, 'He sup me,' and pointed between her legs. I put two and two together. After that, I never let her out of my sight, and she was always the last to be bathed. I tried to tell her to tell her mum. Then when her mum came, I said, 'Michelle's got something to tell you,' but she didn't tell her. Part of me thought to try and get help. The other part of me said if I do that I will lose my job and she will never get any help. I thought, how could anyone believe me that there's something wrong? All of us were caught. People were always leaving Longcare, saying, 'I'm going to report them, I'm not having this.' I said: 'Please, do it.' But nothing happened. A cook, a cleaning lady, a few carers, they all said they would do it. That's why we have got such terrible guilt. It will never leave us.'

Gordon believed he could do what he liked to his 'family' behind closed doors. If any of his victims complained to a relative or member of staff – despite the threats he had made – he would dismiss the claims as delusions, fantasies or grudges.

He knew very well that it was almost impossible to secure convictions in such cases – most of his victims would not be able to give evidence in court, and the others would be torn to shreds in the witness box by any half-decent barrister. Plus, he had his friends in Slough police. He still remembered how easy it had been to shake off the allegations in Somerset.

Lillian would describe in a statement how Gordon turned up at Stoke Green late one evening, saying he had come to see Jackie, who had 'been a little bitch today'. He disappeared into her bedroom and was in there for about half an hour. Lillian saw him come out of Jackie's room and remembers him being 'hot and flustered... and he was doing up his trouser zip,' although there was no toilet in Jackie's room. Gordon told Lillian: 'That's sorted her out. She'll be good now.' When Lillian asked Jackie what Gordon had wanted, she told her: 'He does things to me,' with the 'thing in his trousers'. Lillian said: 'She was sat in bed with her legs dangling over the side, laughing and giggling, which is unusual for Jackie.'

Tracy, another of 'Gordon's Girls', would later tell the police about the abuse he inflicted on her. 'When I was at Stoke Place, Gordon Rowe hit me and hurt me every day,' she said. 'There was no reason for it, it was just something he did. He was a cruel man. He used to slap me nearly every day. When Gordon slapped me, it was always in my bedroom and usually when I was in bed. He hit my whole body; he hit my thighs, my back, my bottom, my vagina, my legs, all of me.'

She described how he had come in and assaulted her when she was sleeping in a chalet during a holiday at Butlins in Bognor Regis. 'I remember him shaking me and shouting and then I woke up. Gordon then punched me very hard on my back. I had been sleeping on my tummy. It hurt very much and I was crying.'

Tracy remembers Gordon following her to her room 'nearly every day' that she was living at Stoke Place and Stoke Green. 'I was scared of him. He would make me get into bed under the covers even if it was still daytime.' She described in detail in a statement how Gordon had sexually assaulted her.

Lillian – whose words would later be backed up by Tracy in her own statement – described how she was on duty late one evening at Stoke Green, when Gordon Rowe knocked on the door. He told her he had come to see Tracy.

Lillian waited downstairs. 'He was up there for a while. When he came down he said something like, 'She's been naughty...or... playing up.' He was definitely in a hurry and said something like, 'That's her sorted out and I'm going home to put my feet up – I've had a hard day.' When Lillian went upstairs, Tracy was crying. 'I asked her what was wrong – at first she didn't say anything – then she said she had been naughty.' Tracy came downstairs for a cup of tea, and Lillian asked her what was wrong.

Eventually, Tracy looked up at Lillian and sobbed: 'I hate that Gordon.'

'Why?'

'Does things. Don't like it.'

'What kind of things?'

But Tracy shook her head. 'Scared.'

'What are you scared about?' said Lillian.

'Might have a baby.'

Lillian drew in a breath.

'Lillian?'

'Yes.'

'It's a good job I'm on the pill.'

But Rowe wasn't satisfied with mere rape and sexual assault. For him, the sexual humiliation had to be even deeper.

He would often make 'Gordon's Girls' watch pornographic videos. They would all have to take their clothes off, and

164

weren't allowed to leave the locked room until he gave them permission.

Then there were his own 'films', in which he forced female residents to have sex with male residents while he filmed them. Afterwards, he would force the women to watch themselves 'perform' on the videos.

One of the men once told a member of staff: 'That Gordon Rowe's in trouble. I would like to burn his house down in Windsor. He's doing things to me. I will tell you one day.'

'Paul used to cry and get all upset,' another care worker told me. 'He used to say that if he had done anything wrong, he would have to do things with *****, and Gordon would be stood there with his camera. John used to say the same thing: that he had to do certain things with *****, so that Gordon could use his camera. I believe they were genuine and scared, and just wanted somebody to talk to.'

It took so much courage for a resident to tell something like that to a member of staff, because they never knew who they could trust. And the staff turnover was so high that by the time a resident got to like and trust a care worker, they had usually left for another job.

It wasn't even as if Rowe pretended to be a saint. He was always talking about sex to the staff, and often told them how 'over-sexed' the residents were. He claimed this was a symptom of their impairments. Most of the care workers were so inexperienced that they didn't know any better.

But even this wasn't the end of the sexual perversions Rowe inflicted on the residents. Robert, another of the residents, who worked with the animals in the grounds of Stoke Place, confided in Lillian over a cup of tea that he hated 'that Gordon Rowe'. When asked why, he told her that Gordon made him do things 'like man and woman. But man and animals with me'. Gordon would film him doing this, he said. Lillian tried to persuade him to tell his social worker.

Another care worker told me how John had said that other residents were forced to have sex with animals and that Gordon made videos of them. One of the female residents also told a friend that Gordon forced residents to have sex with animals.

Rachel is angry that none of the staff questioned why Gordon was in the classroom with her late in the evenings, when she was just wearing her nightdress, or why they were locked in the office together. 'If they had queried this perhaps they could have prevented the abuse from continuing,' she would say later.

Nicky Power was another of those he would take into the classroom in the evening to 'help with the accounts'. One care worker would later say in a statement: 'The door to the room would always be shut and Gordon made it clear to staff that he was not to be interrupted.'

The staff were well aware of Gordon's suspicious behaviour. Gary Moreton would describe how Gordon would do the accounts in one of the classrooms. He would take one of the women, saying they liked spending time with him. He would tell staff not to disturb him. 'Occasionally he would buzz down on the intercom to ask for a cup of tea to be sent up,' Gary would say in a statement, 'and a member of staff would not be allowed to take it up, it had to be a resident.

'When he had finished he would come down complaining how hot it was in the classrooms... He would be red-faced, his hair would be all over the place and he would be wearing just his string vest and trousers. He would carry his shirt and jumper. This happened a number of times when he was doing his accounts. He kept on about the heating being hard to control in these rooms.'

Rachel said she couldn't tell anybody about the abuse because she was too scared. But she was surprised that none of the staff realised what was happening. She was often depressed, and would cry in public, she had trouble sleeping, and began having nightmares. She also complained of pains in her abdomen and irritation in her genital area – these symptoms were even noted down in the Stoke Place report book.

But she wasn't the only female resident showing signs of possible abuse. Council records from 1991 showed that Nicky Power was 'highly anxious' and would 'bathe and change her clothes two or three times a day in order to be sure of being properly clean'. And the Stoke Place report book recorded in 1990 how Julie, another of Gordon's favourites, was 'sore between the legs'.

Tracy told the police later how she had been too afraid to tell anybody what Gordon was doing. 'What Gordon Rowe did to me used to upset me but I was too afraid to tell anybody,' she said. 'I didn't like Gordon Rowe and used to be frightened of him... I was often very upset and crying but I was unable to tell anyone what was wrong but they would have noticed as I was very weepy... I was upset at Stoke Place and cried a lot but nobody really seemed to ask why or tried to find out what was wrong with me.'

She tried to run away several times, so the staff would lock her door and take her clothes away. On one occasion, she was picked up by the police. Several times, she made it as far as Wexham Park Hospital, a mile or so away from Stoke Place. 'I went there because I was worried that I might be pregnant after Gordon Rowe had touched me,' she would say later.

As far back as December 1989, Tracy's social services records note how she had thrown ornaments and clothes about in her bedroom, before Gordon had 'intervened'. She ran off to nearby Stoke Poges, where she was picked up by police. When she returned, she was shouting, 'Don't like me, don't hit me.'

Finally, she told her social worker that she wanted to leave Stoke Place and didn't want to attend her review later that day. 'However as I got closer to the home I felt scared about this and so I told my social worker that I had changed my mind.'

She remembers confiding in Lillian. 'I told her that I didn't like Gordon, that he had been touching me and that it was horrible and that it was a good job that I was on the pill because I did not want to have a baby.'

Many people with learning difficulties who have been raped or sexually assaulted find it impossible to come to terms with what has been done to them. Some attempt to cope by harming themselves, according to Burke and Bedard[1]. 'The self-mutilation... may be the only way a person can communicate what the abuse was, and to suggest the emotional distress it is causing.' They added: 'Often, abused individuals are told by the abuser that their actions are the way people show that they 'love' one another – when such sexual interaction ends, the client may resort to self-harm in an attempt to gain someone's love and attention.'

Curen and Sinason[2] discussed how 'all the usual range of signs and symptoms' that apply to children who have suffered sexual abuse apply also to adults with learning difficulties, such as bedwetting, stomach-ache, nightmares, inappropriate sexualised behaviour, excessive masturbating, promiscuity, running away and self-destructive behaviour. But instead of the alcohol or drug abuse that is often displayed by victims of child abuse, among people with learning difficulties this self-destructive behaviour will often take the form of self-mutilation, eye-poking or head-banging.

Many of these signs were displayed by the men and women who were being abused at Longcare.

Penny, one of the young care workers, had heard the steady, hollow ringing from reception. It appeared to be coming from the kitchen.

She found Janet Ward crouched beside one of the kitchen cabinets, her long, brown hair hanging down in damp strands. In a soulless, repetitive action, she was moving her shoulders backwards and forwards, striking her forehead against the metal door. When she saw Penny, she scrambled to her feet and made a grab for a couple of empty milk bottles. She knocked one of them off the table, smashing it on the floor.

'Keep away from me, Penny,' shouted Janet. 'Keep away.' And she turned and put both of her hands against the wall and banged her head hard against it.

Penny reached out a hand. 'Stop, please.' Janet slipped back down to the floor until she was crouched with her forehead resting against the door. Her shoulders shook as she wept into the arms she held across her face. All Penny could make out above the sobs were the words: 'Gordon said he love me.'

As for the residents themselves, it was probably in part the feeling of worthlessness that secured their silence, combined with Rowe's intimidation and threats. They deserved what he was doing to them, because they had learned that they were inferior to 'normal people'. And they believed they had brought the attacks upon themselves by something they had done to provoke him. Fear was combined with pain, confusion, guilt, anger, and an inability to express their feelings about what was happening – even if there had been someone listening.

Sobsey and Doe[3] found in one study that many survivors of sexual abuse felt it was 'useless' to report what was happening because they feared 'retribution' or being sent away from their home. The authors added: 'The experiences of those among this sample and elsewhere who reported the abuse to authorities and elsewhere suggest that such fears are often justified.'

What little research there has been suggests that sexual abuse of people with learning difficulties is widespread, and vastly under-reported, particularly among women.

In her book on disability hate crime[4], Katharine Quarmby describes how the 'casual sexual use and abuse of disabled women goes almost completely unchallenged'. Much of this abuse, she adds, remains 'largely invisible and untold'. Quarmby quotes Hilary McCollum, from the Equality and Human Rights Commission, who says that too little is still known about the perpetrators of violence against disabled women and children. 'Are people who sexually assault learning disabled girls the same as people who write graffiti and shove dog faeces through a wheelchair-user's letterbox?' says McCollum. 'Are their motivations the same or not, and what difference would that make to the intervention that would be put in place?'

A report in 2001 by the learning difficulty charities Voice UK, Respond and Mencap[5] said there was 'considerable evidence that people with a learning disability are at much greater risk of sexual abuse and assault than the general population', and that there was 'no doubt that the problem is severe'. The report suggested that abusers like Rowe 'may deliberately choose employment in the caring professions because of their vulnerable populations and the intimate nature of the work'.

Many of the Longcare staff couldn't bring themselves to believe that Gordon was actually raping residents. Susannah heard the rumours about bestiality. 'I hoped it wasn't true,' she told me, 'because it made me feel sick.'

Another care worker, Frances*, said: 'I saw an ad in the paper for carers. I had never done the job before. The first weekend I was there, I heard the most terrible rumours about him (Gordon Rowe), that he videos clients with animals having sex. The first thing I said was that these people must really hate him to say these things about him.'

None of the staff had ever seen him raping a resident, although Lillian had seen him engage in sexual contact with Janet Ward. How could they know for sure that the residents were not just making it up, or were confused about what had happened? So they gossiped, or tried to blank it out, or kept an eye on Gordon's Girls when they worked a night shift. They decided they couldn't risk their livelihood by making a complaint. They had bills to pay and children to feed. And maybe Gordon was just over-friendly.

And so Rowe was free to continue raping and assaulting his favoured few men and women. Until, finally, a few members of Rowe's staff decided enough was enough.

It hadn't been the first time Clare had seen bruising around the anus of a female resident. She knew what it meant, and this time she was determined not to let it go, as most of her colleagues had told her to do.

She told Gordon the bruises meant the woman had probably been anally raped. He blamed it on a cracked toilet seat and told her: 'The problem with you, my girl, is that you have done this new-fangled course and you want to find something wrong here. But if you did, you would be a very silly girl and you would never work in the care sector again.'

She had become ever more convinced that Gordon was responsible for the bruising, as he had been responsible for the incident in the classroom she caught on her camera, which he had wiped during the editing process.

Finally, a trickle of complaints started to reach Bucks County Council.

It started with two anonymous telephone calls from a former member of staff in December 1992. She had seen Gordon Rowe kick residents, punish them by making them eat outside, and order them to have cold showers. She had also heard that Rowe had sexually assaulted female residents.

A second former care worker made similar allegations two months later, followed by a third call a few days later. The following month, another former employee wrote to Berkshire County Council, a letter which was forwarded to Buckinghamshire and made further allegations of physical abuse and ill-treatment. This letter came from Paul Robertson, a friend of Clare's, who told the inspection unit that she also wanted to talk to them.

Clare helped Rose towel herself dry, then handed her the cheap dressing gown she had been given as a Christmas present by Gordon and Angela. Paid for, of course, from Rosie's money.

Clare followed Rosie as she walked into her bedroom and plonked herself on her bed. 'Time for the creams,' said Clare.

Rosie stuck out her feet, pointing her toes. She enjoyed having Clare rub the cocoa butter cream in. Afterwards, Clare would draw up her chair and put her own feet on the bed, as Rosie returned the favour.

Rosie always knew it was Clare's turn, because the young care worker would hold a finger up to her mouth and whisper: 'Ssshhh, don't tell anyone.' Rosie would nod and wink, and look towards the door.

Tonight, though, was different.

Clare put her feet up, as usual. But rather than reaching for the cream, Rosie sat there, kneading her hands.

'I got secret with Big Dadda,' she said eventually.

Clare's feet thudded onto the worn bedroom carpet. 'What secret? You know you can tell me, Rosie.'

She watched as Rosie picked up a pink tube of roll-on deodorant and looked at her, as if defying her to be angry. 'Big Dadda put up me,' she said.

Clare swallowed hard. 'Where did he put it?' She watched as the young woman pointed between her legs.

'Don't tell Big Dadda,' said Rosie, 'or I won't get my sweets.' And she giggled and threw the container onto the carpet.

'I won't tell him,' said Clare.

It was incidents like this that persuaded Clare to act. She had already started to keep a diary of incidents, on the advice of Gary Moreton, who had already left Longcare. 'I had wanted to complain,' she said later, 'but I was 17 and there was such a large staff there and no-one wanted to know. They would say: 'You can't say anything. We will lose our jobs. It's all right for you, Clare, but we have mortgages, we have got kids to feed.'

'It was a big step, and I was frightened of him (Gordon). In the end, I spoke to Paul and Gary. It was obvious that it was still going on. Then Alison had gone over to Gordon's cottage and came back with her top inside out and her bra done up wrong, and I thought, 'Oh, no.' And Rosie told me how he had stuck her deodorant inside her. I just thought it was wrong. My mum said, whatever I decided to do, she would stand by me.'

In July 1993, Buckinghamshire's inspection unit learned that Clare wanted to join those members of Longcare staff who had talked to them about Gordon Rowe's regime. They called her and she agreed to meet them at her home in Slough. 'It was very hush-hush,' she said. 'Then the police came and took me to Windsor police station under a different name. They had to take me there, because of the contacts Gordon Rowe had at Slough police station.

'Social services met me at home every week. I was seeing them in the morning and then going in to work at Longcare. It was making me quite ill.' But although she wanted to leave, the inspection unit knew it would be more useful to have her still working there, so she agreed to stay.

Clare gave a council inspector's card to a friend who also worked at Longcare. He called the inspection unit, and made a statement. Gordon Rowe's carefully constructed defences were finally starting to crack.

After Gordon was forced to quit Stoke Place because of the investigation, Rachel plucked up the courage to confide in Lorraine Field and some other staff about what he had done to her. Lorraine told Ray Cradock, Longcare's director of services, and the two of them talked to her about what had happened. The following day, Ray, Nigel Rowe and Lorraine discussed with her what she had told them. Ray told her that if she wanted to go to the police, she would have to leave Longcare. 'I didn't want to so I left it,' she said later.

Rachel began having nightmares. 'One dream was Gordon coming towards me and saying, 'I'm going to get you. I'm going to hurt you again.' In my sleep I would scream and wake up crying.'

There are at least two questions worth asking about Rowe's regime of sexual abuse. Why did he do it? And why was he not stopped earlier? Sadly, there are no answers to the first question, only guesses. It is probable that he was aroused by the power he held over the residents, possibly even by their emotional immaturity and naivety. But above all else, to do what he did, he must have felt that their lives, their wishes, were worthless.

As for the second question...

1   Self-injury Considered in Association with Sexual Victimization in Individuals with a Developmental Handicap, by Lillian Burke and Cheryl Bedard; The Canadian Journal of Human Sexuality; Vol 3(3), Autumn 1994

2   Adults and Children with Learning Disabilities, by Richard Curen and Valerie Sinason; in Domestic and Sexual Violence and Abuse: Tackling the health and mental health effects; Itzin,C; Taket, A; Barter-Godfrey, S (eds); London: Routledge; 2010

3   Patterns Of Sexual Abuse and Assault, by Dick Sobsey and Tanis Doe; Sexuality and Disability; Vol 9, No 3, 1991

4   Scapegoat, by Katharine Quarmby; Portobello Books; 2011

5   Behind Closed Doors: Preventing sexual abuse against adults with a learning disability; Voice UK, Respond and Mencap; 2001

PART FOUR

INVESTIGATIONS

Chapter Fifteen

A Leaked Report

'A documentary that highlights disabled people's firsthand experiences of hate crime will be broadcast this week on primetime television... One young disabled woman tells how she is too scared to go into her own garden or leave her house because of a campaign of harassment. Paul and Janet Williams, from Leeds, describe how they have to avoid walking past the local takeaway shops and pubs because of the abuse they have received. Ian Margerison, from Bradford, says he is too scared to leave his house because of thugs who bang on the door, throw eggs against his windows, spit at him and shout abuse. And Keith Shortman, from London, tells how he was kicked and punched by a gang of boys and girls.'

Disability News Service, 23 February 2010

Janice Raycroft, editor of the Slough Observer, was furious. She had just been handed a copy of the county council's confidential Longcare report, which had been left sitting for a day on a pile of council agendas waiting to be checked for potential stories.

A quick read of the report was enough for her to know that this was a story of huge importance, despite the serious legal obstacles.

Raycroft had joined the Observer nearly 20 years before as a young reporter. She was fiercely loyal to the paper, despite the increasing sense of doom surrounding its finances (it was sold a couple of years later to a Scottish newspaper group). As a young reporter recruited only nine months earlier, I was in awe of her journalistic reputation. But there was more to her desire to expose Rowe's regime than just 'the journalist's instinct for a great story – if we can call the Longcare scandal that', she would tell me 16 years later.

Her real determination, she said, 'was built on sheer anger'. 'Throughout the report I read of physical and sexual assaults, verbal humiliation, the full gamut of appalling behaviour being swept under the carpet by people in power. It was clear that people had been regularly raped, including women around the same age as I was at the time. There was I, a single parent, in charge of numerous people and with some standing in the community as a result of my position. I knew that if I had been raped or even 'just' bullied, the efforts of authority to effect justice and support me would have been 100 times greater than that accorded to the residents of Longcare.

'I could see that people whose human rights needed to be particularly reinforced and protected because of their vulnerability in fact were being treated worse than livestock. I realised that, only through chance, I was not the woman born with Down's syndrome and so had skipped through life, becoming an educated, respected, confident person unlikely to be unfairly challenged. Meanwhile, another woman could be raped and humiliated and then people with power could decide it would be best to simply tidy up the mess, file away a few reports and get on with their own, so much better, lives.'

I had only been handed the story by the news editor because my tiny 'patch' of south Buckinghamshire happened to include Stoke Poges, and the two Longcare homes. And I was much slower off the mark than journalists working on other local papers in Buckinghamshire. The first move was to confirm with the council that the report was genuine – as it clearly was. The second was just as important: get out to Longcare for a reaction.

The two Longcare homes nestled in Green Belt just a few hundred yards from the northern tip of Slough. In fact, Stoke Place Mansion House was just about the last building in Buckinghamshire before you reached Slough.

Because I was not the first reporter to arrive, I received a particularly frosty reception. There was no-one available to talk to me, according to the female member of staff who answered the door.

My first impression was of a cold, ill-maintained, forbidding building. I had gained a brief glimpse inside, but had not seen a single resident.

I had driven past the high brick walls surrounding Stoke Place on several occasions, but couldn't remember noticing the entrance, or Stoke Green House, a few yards further along the main road.

I returned to the office to track down Gordon Rowe's home address. All we knew was that he lived in Windsor. There were several G Rowes in the telephone book. The first lived in a small flat in Old Windsor, a village on the edge of Windsor Great Park. 'Rusty', though, couldn't talk to me about his brother, Gordon, as he had Alzheimer's. His wife invited me in, but told me they didn't see much of Gordon. 'We don't even know where he lives,' she said.

The next addresses were in a moneyed cul-de-sac on the western edge of Windsor: Harrington Close. There were two

Rowes who lived on the right-hand side of the road, one at number 10, the other at 12. I tried 10 first. A woman answered the door. She knew nothing about a Gordon Rowe. She had never heard of him. She later turned out to have been the wife of Nigel Rowe, Gordon's eldest son. I tried next door, number 12. This time, the door didn't even open. But when I returned to the office and telephoned the house, Gordon answered.

'I'm sorry, I've got nothing to say to you at all,' he said, and hung up.

After Raycroft had taken the report home to read thoroughly, she had decided that the Observer must 'publish everything we could'. She gave a copy to the Observer's owner, Peter Lawrance, both 'as a courtesy and because of the potential for legal action – attempts at injunctions and the possibility of libel actions'. The following day, Lawrance, who lived a mile or so from Stoke Place, called Raycroft with his decision. 'He told me to go ahead with his blessing,' she said. 'He was outraged and distressed by the contents. What I did not know at the time is that the newspaper was running without full libel insurance, so he took a huge risk in offering 100 per cent support.'

It soon became clear that neither Longcare nor Gordon Rowe were going to comment. And all three of our weekly rivals – who had also received copies of the report – backed away from publishing stories.

The legal questions Raycroft had to answer were serious: was it safe to print extracts from a confidential county council report we had no right to possess? And, even more importantly, could we be sued for libel by Gordon Rowe? The report was not a public document and we had already received two faxes from Rowe's legal advisers, threatening that he would sue if we ran a story.

'It was quite clear from the report that there were loads and loads of apparent witnesses, but all of them were terrified and anonymous to us,' Raycroft told me later. 'I realised that if we got this wrong I would lose my job and the Slough Observer

– then a campaigning and forthright newspaper trusted by the community – would lose a great deal of credibility.' She knew she needed serious legal advice. She called the paper's solicitors, Mishcon de Reya, and asked for libel expert Stephen Shotnes.

Time was running out. If Shotnes advised us to spike the story, we would have to follow his advice, no matter how desperately Raycroft wanted to publish. A series of calls and faxes were exchanged with Shotnes's London office. Eventually, as Thursday's deadline approached, he called the editor and gave her his verdict.

> *Slough and Langley Observer, Friday 16 September 1994*
>
> *REIGN OF TERROR IS UNCOVERED*
>
> *Secret report reveals a catalogue of torment and humiliation – handicapped people were kicked, punched and abused*
>
> *MENTALLY handicapped adults were subjected to a horrific reign of terror at two residential homes, a top secret inquiry has concluded.*
>
> *Today the Observer tells how a lengthy Bucks County Council investigation uncovered dozens of allegations that some residents of Stoke Place Mansion House and nearby Stoke Green House had been sexually assaulted, beaten and tormented between 1991 and last year.*
>
> *At the centre of the investigation was Gordon Rowe, of Harrington Close, Windsor, former director and managing director of Longcare Ltd, the company that runs the homes, on the Slough and Stoke Poges border...*

The advice given by Shotnes had been simple: you can run the story, but you must hope witnesses come forward to back up your allegations. 'If we published we had to go all out and then hope the witnesses came forward,' said Raycroft. 'It's the only time in my career that I have taken that dangerous gamble, but it was worth it 100 per cent in the end.'

On Friday morning, 16 September, just a couple of hours after the paper appeared in the shops of Slough and Windsor – The Independent had also run the story on its front page – a telephone rang in the newsroom. I was chasing leads in Aylesbury on my day off, so a colleague answered the phone. It was an ex-member of Longcare staff. He had read the story and he wanted to talk.

My initial reaction to the report had been one of revulsion and shock. But in those early days, this was aimed squarely in the direction of the 'perpetrators': Gordon Rowe, his wife Angela and manager Lorraine Field, who lived in Stoke Poges and whose initials featured prominently in the report. It was only in the following weeks that the true scale of the Longcare scandal – and the wider failures it revealed – began to fall into place.

For such a shocking story, though, the reaction from our readers in Slough, South Buckinghamshire and Windsor was muted. There was no outrage. We were not swamped with letters calling for 'something to be done'. In fact, in the three-and-a-half years that I covered the story for the paper, we received only a handful of letters about the case. Most were from people with a vested interest: politicians, voluntary organisations, relatives of Longcare residents. It was to take me nearly six years to understand why.

Chapter Sixteen

The Longcare Staff

'The heads of two care inspectorates voiced 'serious concerns' today about the treatment of people with learning disabilities across England. Anna Walker, chief executive of the Healthcare Commission, and David Behan, chief inspector of the Commission for Social Care Inspection, issued a joint statement voicing their fears for those suffering abuse and neglect. It follows an investigation into the Cornwall Partnership NHS Trust which revealed 'widespread institutional abuse' and significant failings.'

Daily Mail, 5 July 2006

Longcare's employees saw and heard much of what was going on at the homes, but only a very few made any effort to alert the authorities. By the time the inspection unit finally launched its investigation, late in 1993, Rowe had been beating, tormenting, raping and neglecting residents for nearly 10 years.

It was easy enough to blame these care workers for failing to act. But was that fair?

I have talked in depth to at least 15 former members of Longcare staff. Every one of them spoke about the atmosphere of threats and intimidation.

One ex-care worker said Gordon Rowe was 'the sort of man whose presence made you feel afraid. There was a certain aura about him. I was very surprised that the clients looked up to him as a father figure, because he was very, very strict in everything he did. They would be so afraid when he walked into a room. 'Hello, Gordon. You want a cup of tea, Gordon?' they would say. They were all out to score points, to get in his good books, because they had to survive in that place.'

That sense of fear and menace was used to control staff as well as residents. One former employee said: 'He used intimidation to keep them quiet. I know for a fact that one or two staff who tried to complain got threatening phone calls. He was a very powerful man and he had some very powerful friends.'

Rowe also told his employees how easy it would be to replace them. And he knew they would need a reference for another job. One young classroom assistant told me: 'We knew there were a lot of people out of work, so we had to toe the line. The way we dealt with it was to just close the classroom door and forget there was an existence outside the room.' Another young woman told me: 'It was like going into a factory. Input and output. Profit-making. We clocked in. We clocked out. As soon as five o'clock came, we were rushing to get out.'

Of course, not every employee disliked and feared Gordon Rowe. Many remained loyal. People like Lorraine Field, a former hospital cleaner with a fierce temper, who had been promoted far above her abilities to care manager. Rowe also employed several members of his own family, including Angela, Nigel, his brother Ted, and one of his sisters, Mavis, and her husband.

Rowe often made sure he could trust those in senior positions by taking unqualified staff and training them himself, as he had done with Desmond Tully and Lorraine Field. Field was 'seen as a 'yes woman'', said one former care worker. 'If Gordon had told her to jump in the lake, she would have done it. If you asked her why, she would have said: 'Because Gordon told me to.''

Tully was later to tell a court hearing that he was 'not proud of having worked there', and added: 'I carried out things I wasn't happy about. I was constantly employed to cover up situations. But we were limited in what we could do. It was Gordon's place, wasn't it?' Tully, who worked at Longcare for several months from 1983, and again for three years from 1987, added: 'You might say, 'Why did you work there?' You have to know how to get out of there. It was not the easiest place to get out of.'

Tully later claimed he had been concerned about standards at Longcare, and that he had talked to Anthony Barker, the council's registration officer, about the high staff turnover, the high levels of medication and the fact that Gordon was 'institutionalised'. But Tully was clearly not that worried: at around this time, he accepted a loan from Gordon that allowed him to buy his own residential home in Devon.

Taken together with his network of spies among residents and loyal care workers, and his use of the intercom system and surveillance equipment, Rowe's employees never knew who they could trust and when it was safe to talk.

If a member of staff did decide to confide in a colleague, their words often found their way back to the management. One male care worker, who worked for Longcare for seven months in the early 1990s, told police that Ray Cradock and Nigel Rowe had quizzed him about complaints he had made to other members of staff.

Gary Moreton worked at Stoke Place and Stoke Green for about two years, and finally left in March 1992. He paints a vivid picture of how Rowe operated. 'He was very clever – he manipulated people in such a way that they would be unable to stand up against him. He got a kick out of playing mind games with the staff. Another thing he did was to offer staff money if they were in financial trouble. He knew they would never be able to pay him back.

'He only ever employed people who desperately needed a job and had no experience of care work [some care workers had worked with older people and children before, but it was generally true]. He convinced them that his way was the way it was done – he openly told people that Longcare was run like a prison.' Like Broadmoor, in fact. Rowe often told inexperienced care workers that the violent 'techniques' they saw him use were accepted practice within the care industry.

The things Gary witnessed at Stoke Place slowly began to take over his personal life. Catriona, his wife, who also briefly worked at Longcare, remembers: 'He would come home and want to unwind, but we would end up talking about Gordon Rowe for hours, working out strategies to protect the residents. It was ridiculous.'

The staff knew about Gordon's 'friends in high places'. He talked openly about his 'contacts' and had made sure everyone knew he was a Freemason. His staff believed he had contacts at Bucks County Council and within the Conservative Party, of which he was briefly a member.

Rowe also let it be known that he had no qualms about flirting with the wrong side of the law. On one occasion, he paid an ex-Broadmoor patient with a violent history to patrol the grounds of Stoke Green at night to prevent an encampment of travellers from stealing his farm equipment.

After about a year working at Longcare, Moreton began a social work course and slowly learned the correct way to treat people with learning difficulties. It was at about this time, he says, that Rowe began to 'get sloppy'. Displays of violence became more common and began to occur in the presence of more than one member of staff.

Gary took advice from his college tutors. They told him to be careful, to stand up to Gordon and complain when he saw something he didn't like. He thought about leaving, but decided it would be better to stay and try to protect the residents.

Eventually, Rowe called Gary to his office, produced six pages of 'allegations' he had made about him to other members of staff, and threatened to sue for defamation.

When Gary refused to retract the allegations, Rowe's façade of control and power started to crumble. He turned bright red and began trembling and sweating, avoiding the other man's eyes while he shuffled his papers. Gary offered to resign. That was the last thing Rowe wanted. He preferred his opponents to stay with Longcare, where he could keep an eye on them. Instead, Gary was transferred to Stoke Green.

But it wasn't just Gordon Rowe the care workers had to contend with. Back-biting and bitchiness among the staff were rife. One told me: 'People hated each other. You could never rely on anyone, because what you said to one person would go straight back to Gordon. It got to a point where you didn't have any friends you could rely on.' Staff spied on staff, residents spied on staff and each other, and Gordon spied on everyone.

If one of the staff looked as though he might cause problems, Rowe spread a little gossip, hinted at a bit of wrong-doing, or perhaps told care workers their colleague was 'mad' or held a grudge. If that failed, he might try some subtle blackmail or explain that a resident's inappropriate behaviour was because he was 'over-sexed'.

Another trick Rowe used was to attack the credibility of the residents' parents, so his staff would not be tempted to confide in them. He spread vicious lies about some of the families to his staff, falsely accusing them of cruelty and abuse and inventing bizarre case histories for many of the residents to help cover his own tracks.

Monica*, who worked for Longcare for five years from the late 1980s, was another of the youngsters taken on by Rowe under the Youth Training Scheme. 'I am sure people say: 'Why did you stay for five years?' But my parents put a lot of pressure on me, saying I couldn't leave unless I had another job to go to,' she told me. 'Gordon had such power, and not just over the residents, over the whole staff. I think some of us were frightened we would never get another job in the caring profession.'

Jean lasted less than a year before quitting her job to go on the dole. 'It was making me ill. I had to leave, or I would have ended up doing myself in,' she told me. 'But I quit while Gordon and Angela were on holiday, because I didn't have the courage to do it while they were there. He would have talked me into staying.'

Scores of staff left Longcare over the years. It took months before a resident would feel able to confide in a care worker, and by that time they would probably have left for another job. Most of the trained care workers walked out almost immediately, and there was also a high turnover among less qualified staff. It was a standing joke that, at one time or another, everyone in Slough had worked there.

'The atmosphere was like walking into a factory,' said Monica. 'You couldn't wait to get out. I just feel sorry that I didn't do anything, that we weren't strong enough. But I think all of us were worried about what would happen to us.'

The mind games Gordon Rowe played on the staff were nothing to those he played on the residents. Gary Moreton says Rowe deliberately set out to humiliate them and break down their personalities until all signs of rebellion had vanished. Many felt so worthless they began to mutilate themselves with knives or razor blades. Then they were punished for that. If a member of staff complained, Rowe would take great pleasure in repeating the punishment time and time again, as if to say: 'That's what happens to the ones you try and stick up for.'

He told Gary how to whip their legs with wet towels. The advantage of this form of punishment – apart from the pain – was that it left no lasting marks. He told Gary on one such occasion: 'That will make them realise I mean business.'

Inexperienced care workers saw the way Rowe treated his clients and, even if only subconsciously, allowed it to reinforce their negative preconceptions about people with learning difficulties.

It was only the particularly strong-willed and enlightened members of staff – and often those who were also taking outside social care courses – who could see through this fog of abusive, controlling behaviour. It was from this small group – which included Clare Johnson and Paul Robertson – that the complaints that would eventually bring down Gordon Rowe were to come.

Paul only worked at Longcare for about three months in late 1992 and early 1993. But despite such a short period of time, he had already witnessed many examples of abuse. He saw Gordon punch a resident who had soiled his bed, and saw him force Jackie to eat her meals outside in the middle of winter. On one occasion, he brought Jackie inside so the residents could sing happy birthday to her on her birthday – 17 January – and so she could have a piece of her birthday cake. 'I brought Jackie inside and gave her some birthday cake, and she went back outside before Gordon came back. But one of the other residents told him what I had done and he was absolutely furious.'

Paul had wanted to wait until he had clear evidence in his head before he alerted the authorities, because he knew Gordon was 'so, so close to all the policemen and he knew people in power and he had been able to threaten people'.

'The final straw was Jackie on her birthday. Gordon told me that if I wanted to be a good manager I would have to manage the way he wanted me to manage... His idea was for all the residents to sing happy birthday and Jackie to be outside in the cold weather. I walked out that day. [He said that] I had to be tough and bully the residents and I just walked out and went straight home and phoned the police.' They told him to contact the council.

Paul says the only other member of staff he trusted was Clare Johnson. 'Clare was the person who warned me about Gordon's ways and the residents he had as spies and the residents he had as slaves.' He told the inspection unit that Clare also wanted to talk to them.

Other staff knew what Gordon was doing, but were not brave enough to act. 'He was so intimidating and manipulating,' he told me, many years later. 'They knew he knew some of the top policemen [and politicians]. He just threatened people. [Other staff would say], 'They won't believe you. People have tried it before and they have lost their jobs.'

There had been a widespread certainty among Longcare staff that no-one would be able to convince the police or council to investigate Gordon Rowe, that they assumed justice would never be done.

So when, one Sunday evening in November 1993, one of the care workers blurted out in a staff meeting that Buckinghamshire County Council had launched an investigation into the Rowes, the news was met with a stunned silence. It was broken by Longcare manager Ray Cradock. 'Investigating them? For what?' he asked.

Even before the inspection unit's probe had started, Gordon and Angela Rowe suspended themselves from Longcare. But Rowe wasn't going to let his empire go without a fight. He employed a solicitor to interview every member of staff and warn them of their obligation to maintain the company's confidentiality.

Three days before Christmas, the inspection unit was told that Gordon would retire at the end of the year. The following month, Nigel Rowe told staff in a memo how his father's retirement had been 'carefully planned' over the previous 18 months. It didn't fool anyone. Angela would eventually resign as a Longcare director and employee on 4 July 1994.

As the investigation dragged on well into the new year, morale continued to plunge. Nigel Rowe threatened to sack any staff who gave confidential information to outsiders. They took that to mean the inspection unit. Nigel was rattled. So was Cradock, who told care workers in another memo that their standards were slipping.

The report was finally completed in June 1994. Despite severe shortcomings in the investigation, the inspectors had gathered mountains of evidence. The tone of the report was horrific. Jennifer Waldron, head of the inspection unit, concluded that Gordon Rowe had been responsible for behaviour of almost unimaginable cruelty.

Nigel Rowe and Ray Cradock were predictably scathing about the report. They called it 'blatantly inaccurate' and said nearly every allegation had been made by staff with grudges against Longcare. They accused witnesses of collusion and cast doubt on their credibility. They claimed the county council was conducting a 'witch-hunt' against Longcare and denied nearly every single example of abuse detailed by Waldron's team.

Nigel Rowe had been working with his father for years, ever since – except for a short break in the mid-1980s – he had joined him as a care assistant in Somerset. Ray Cradock had been at the homes since 1990, when he began working for Longcare as a consultant. It was inconceivable that they did not know what was going on around them. Many of the staff I spoke to were convinced that Ray and Nigel knew what was happening. They knew because, even if they had not witnessed abuse first-hand – and that was unlikely enough – they had been told about it time and time again by members of staff.

Some of the care assistants admitted at least a grudging respect for Cradock. He boasted an impressive CV, with a social work career spanning 28 years, including spells in residential homes in the Honduras and Guatemala and experience of conducting inquiries into abuse at other residential homes in Britain. He was also married to Gordon Rowe's first wife, Pat. He was originally employed as a consultant to Longcare in 1990, before his appointment as director of services in September 1992, and, later, registered manager of the two homes.

But every former employee I spoke to remained adamant that Ray and Nigel both knew of a number of instances of abuse by Gordon Rowe.

Jean said: 'I reported it to Ray Cradock more than once when he was working as a consultant. It was no good taking it to Nigel. He didn't want to know. I think he just shut his eyes. Two weeks after I started, I told Ray about the day Gordon kicked Jackie. He knew about the physical abuse, because I told him. I also told him that David had been hit because he was supposed to have been 'misbehaving' in the garden, and how Gordon had taken David behind the bushes to be punished. I couldn't have been the only one. But somehow, whenever I told him something, it always seemed to get back to Gordon. That was why in the end I stopped telling him these things.'

Another former Longcare employee remembered Cradock interviewing every member of staff to try to find out why morale was so low. 'Every time somebody came up to him with a complaint, he would say, 'Can you put up with it a bit longer, because it won't be long before Gordon retires?' And Nigel used to say, 'You know what my dad's like, but he won't be here for much longer.''

The failure of Ray Cradock and Nigel Rowe to act over the allegations only served to suggest to their staff how difficult it would be to force the authorities to take notice of the abuse. But it must have had a more subtle effect. They realised that Nigel and Ray – their managers – were not concerned about such appalling abuse, and some of them surely began to ask themselves whether they might be right: maybe people with learning difficulties did not have the right to respect and decent treatment.

Inevitably, the investigation hit Longcare hard, with the withdrawal of many of its clients over the next 18 months. Eventually, two years after the inspection unit's report was leaked, Stoke Green was closed, and the management of Stoke Place was passed to REACH, a new company unconnected with Longcare.

In a letter to relatives in April 1996, Cradock spoke of the 'unsubstantiated allegations of abuse by former employees' and the 'life threatening letters and phone calls, intimidating police, social services and media activity, negative newspaper articles and television programmes' he and the company had been subjected to. He said Longcare had lost 70 per cent of its business. 'There is no doubt in our minds,' he said, 'that the authorities have closed ranks and made it impossible for us to progress.' He said his and Nigel's names had been 'unfortunately and unjustifiably' tarnished by the affair, and he insisted that Longcare had provided a good standard of care.

Both he and Nigel, he said, had decided to leave the care profession for good. There were few who mourned those decisions.

Some care workers had reported what they had seen to the authorities. Gary Moreton told me that a couple of staff went to Slough police station and were 'laughed out of the door'. They were told: 'Unless you have got any evidence, there is nothing we can do about it.'

This underlined the pointlessness of complaining. The staff knew about Gordon Rowe's connections, and they were scared of their boss and what he might do to their careers.

Lillian, a care assistant, was one of those who did not manage to force through a complaint. When I asked her whether she regretted this, she told me: 'Yes, I do, but the staff had the impression that, because Gordon Rowe knew so many people in high places, they would not believe the likes of us and he would get away with it.'

Fortunately, a small number of those who worked at Longcare – including Clare Johnson and Paul Robertson – did find the courage to whistleblow.

Clare remembers the immediate effect of the inspection unit investigation. 'All of a sudden, everyone had pictures on their walls, everyone had a choice of food.' Despite this, Rowe's sidekicks were still in positions of power. Clare remembers Lorraine Field saying to her: 'Do you really think it's going to change?' and warning her: 'Don't you think your life is going to be a bit difficult here now?' 'I don't care," Clare replied. 'I have achieved what I wanted to achieve.'

Clare left Longcare in February 1994, in the middle of the inspection unit probe. She and others who had talked to the inspectors before the investigation was launched paid for their bravery by receiving anonymous, threatening telephone calls from Gordon Rowe's henchmen. It was proof, perhaps, that those care workers who had been too scared to complain had had some justification for their concerns.

But whether through ignorance, self-interest or fear, those employees who had not acted to halt the Longcare regime had been guilty – of failing to treat the people they were caring for as their equals, as human beings.

Research by the Ann Craft Trust – which works to protect people with learning difficulties from abuse – and the University of Nottingham's centre for social work, has highlighted the importance of whistleblowing in halting abuse[1].

The author, Rebecca Calcraft, examined the Longcare case as part of her research. She concluded that 'whistleblowing can be a risky and extremely stressful experience, but that it is essential in protecting vulnerable adults from abuse'. Former care workers she spoke to who had left their jobs after whistleblowing 'talked about feeling torn, wanting to stay on in their jobs to 'protect' service users and keep an eye on what is happening in the service', just as several former Longcare care workers had told me.

Calcraft says care workers may fail to speak out because 'they lack knowledge of what constitutes abuse, perhaps because they are new to a job or lack training in the protection of vulnerable adults. The distinction between poor practice and abuse may not be clear, even to established workers within an organisation, but with little background knowledge or experience it can be difficult to establish what is poor practice and what is abuse.'

'Safe services can only be developed,' says Calcraft, 'where the organisational climate is such that workers can speak out without fear of reprisal and where they have the confidence that their concerns will be listened to.'

In 2003, I called Clare Johnson again. Now a successful social services care officer, she had an eight-month-old daughter, and was soon to open a nursery with her mother and sisters. She told me she occasionally came across former Longcare colleagues who were still working in the care sector. They now told her the case was blown out of proportion, that it was all 'over-publicised and misrepresented'. These were the people who did nothing about the abuse, the ones who stayed silent.

1   *Blowing the Whistle on Abuse of Adults with Learning Disabilities, by Rebecca Calcraft; Ann Craft Trust and Centre for Social Work, University of Nottingham; 2005*

Chapter Seventeen

Buckinghamshire County Council

'*A couple with learning difficulties have been awarded £97,000 in damages from a local authority that failed to protect them from 'horrendous' abuse. The landmark high court ruling held that Hounslow Council had been negligent in not shielding the couple... from foreseeable abuse by a gang of local youths. In 2000, the couple, who had been in regular contact with social services, were held in their flat and assaulted in the presence of their two young children. According to a court report, the couple were made to perform sexual acts, had pepper spray put into their eyes, were forced to drink urine and eat faeces and were slashed with knives... The case marks the first time that a local authority has been held to owe a duty of care to adults with learning difficulties and has set a legal precedent with respect to negligence across all local authorities.*'

Disability Now, July 2008

The signature that a senior Buckinghamshire County Council officer placed upon the document that allowed Gordon Rowe to open a residential home at Stoke Place Mansion House in 1983 was to have devastating consequences.

Eleven years later, the council would admit it knew at the time that Rowe had been investigated by the police in Somerset. The council also admitted that neither Stan Bristow, its principal residential services officer – who approved the registration – nor any of his colleagues, had investigated the claims, or visited Somerset to test the evidence.

But this was only the first in a series of tragic blunders by the council.

Rowe had applied to be the owner and manager of Stoke Place in February 1983. He told Bucks County Council that he was currently the manager of a home in Somerset and wanted to bring some of its residents and staff with him to Stoke Place.

The law demanded that a home manager should be a 'fit and proper person'. If it wished to turn him down, the onus was on the council to prove he was unfit, and not on him to prove he was suitable. But, crucially, if the council believed he was 'unfit', it would only have to prove so 'on the balance of probabilities'. Evidence of abuse from just one of Rowe's victims, backed up by follow-up interviews with key witnesses, would surely have been enough.

Rowe provided his four glowing references and, by late September, had been told by Bristow what he would need to do to bring Stoke Place up to the required standard. But he had also been told – in advance of the council granting registration – that he could begin telling local authorities that in a month's time the home could start taking clients. Tom Burgner, who in 1997 was to lead an inquiry into the council's handling of the case, told me this was definitely 'bad practice' and compromised Bristow's position. 'It should not have happened,' he said.

The following month, the police investigation ended. Both Fineberg and Brown contacted Bucks. So, too, did Somerset

County Council and one of the police officers. Rowe told Bristow he had been set up in a bid to stop him taking residents from The Old Rectory to his new home. Bristow apparently called Somerset County Council and the detective in charge of the investigation, who told him the file had been closed after a 'thorough investigation'.

A simple visit to Somerset would have provided plenty of evidence to prove 'on the balance of probabilities' that Gordon Rowe was unfit to be running a home. But that visit was not made, whether through arrogance, through incompetence, through over-work, or because Bristow had already told Rowe he would be able to open his home and was fearful of the legal consequences if he changed his mind. Whatever the explanation, the failure to conduct a proper investigation into Rowe's fitness was appalling negligence.

But Bristow had left himself no room for manoeuvre and the certificate of registration was issued to Rowe on 28 November 1983. Eighteen days later, a letter arrived at Bucks social services from the social services director at Kensington and Chelsea council. It expressed concern about Rowe and enclosed a copy of a letter from Michael Brown and David Fineberg, in which Brown said he was '100 per cent convinced of the truth' of the allegations that Rowe had sexually assaulted more than one resident at The Old Rectory. The Kensington and Chelsea director said they would be freezing any placements at Stoke Place. In his reply, Buckinghamshire's director said Bristow had taken up references 'from reliable sources, all of which spoke very highly of Mr Rowe', and that Rowe had himself told Bristow about the allegations, all of which he said were 'totally untrue' and 'were being made to discredit him in order to prevent him from taking residents from the Old Rectory, and admitting them to his new home'. Bristow, he said, had been shown a police letter by Rowe, informing him that there was 'no case to answer'.

Again, no attempt was made to investigate the claims.

Mike Danzig, the social worker for Albert, the resident who had first disclosed the abuse, was also concerned. Danzig persuaded his superiors in Brent social services to contact Buckinghamshire. Again, Bucks did nothing.

Brent eventually decided to back off because of 'possible libel action'. This could only have meant a legal threat from Rowe himself, a threat he would use later to warn off potential whistleblowers at Longcare.

Years later, Buckinghamshire would defend its decision to register Stoke Place by claiming the police had told them there was no evidence against Rowe. But a Somerset police source insisted that the council had actually been told that the investigation had produced evidence against Rowe, but there just hadn't been enough to prove a criminal case beyond all reasonable doubt in court, a vital distinction.

It didn't take long for concerns to be raised about the standards of care in Rowe's new home.

Peter Costello, a social worker from Hounslow for one of the residents, Derrick, visited Stoke Place in July 1984. Costello would write in his file: '...I tried to pin [them] down with a review date – they were reluctant. The staff sit about in the office drinking coffee and seem to resent any intrusion into that process. I am still not happy with this unit, and will have to resist colluding with the general ethos of apathy and lethargy which prevails...'

Four months later, Costello visited Stoke Place again. 'I noticed a serious deterioration in the condition of the office and the chaos which prevailed. Desk tops were covered with scattered papers, several days of dirty dishes (from the staff eating meals at their desks) and drugs in bottles sitting about.' Costello also noted how none of the recommendations from his client's review had been achieved, including a need to communicate with his family and send them a postcard. 'Mr Rowe did go to a cupboard to get a psychology report to show me and as he

199

opened the cupboard, all the papers fell on to the floor. There were several psychology reports on other residents. I tactfully pointed out that none of the tasks growing out of the review had happened. He mumbled and spoke of staff shortages.'

When Costello met Derrick alone, he told him he received no pocket money. Then he added: 'He hit me – my friend.' When Costello questioned Rowe, he 'was not at all embarrassed' and told him there had been a tussle when Derrick was two minutes late one morning, so was not allowed breakfast. 'This developed into a scene outside the dining room and Derrick tried to forcibly gain access to the dining room. It was at this point Derrick was assaulted. Gordon Rowe did not deny it – but I was not direct in stating that Derrick stated he was assaulted.'

'This man,' wrote Costello, 'doesn't talk or think like a trained social worker... He sees himself as part of the penal system and places greater emphasis on nursing than social work.'

Costello contacted Stan Bristow, who told him he had no particular concerns. Bristow said he had insisted on a 'higher staff ratio', and Rowe had failed to honour a promise to submit staff names and numbers. 'He proposes to chase this quite firmly,' wrote Costello. 'He agreed to visit within two weeks and to feed me back.'

By February 1985, Costello found Stoke Place 'more organised and efficient than on his last visit'. He was 'convinced that [Rowe] has been reprimanded'.

Despite this supposed reprimand, Buckinghamshire's leaked report, nearly 10 years later, would make no reference to Costello's concerns.

I spoke to Bristow early in 1996, two weeks before he was due to emigrate to France and several years before I would learn of the Costello claims. Now retired, Bristow was prepared to talk to me only briefly.

At the time Rowe applied to register Stoke Place, there were about 40 homes in Bristow's remit and he was directly responsible to the director of social services. He claimed the council was 'well ahead' of other councils in registration and inspection.

Bristow was not prepared to talk in depth about why he allowed Rowe to open the home, but told me: 'I take full responsibility. I care about people and that was it. If Mr Bristow was inspecting or opening that home at that time, things must have been in his eyes correct, because otherwise a) it would never have been opened, and b) it would never have been allowed to run.'

In fact, Bristow claimed, Stoke Place was one of a handful of homes he took a particular interest in, joining staff meetings and occasionally calling in 'on the off-chance'. He would visit once every six to eight weeks, spending a whole day there each time. He said he spent a lot of time with the residents and even attended social events in the evenings. His frequent visits, most of which Rowe would have been aware of in advance, may have been due to his concern over the Somerset allegations, but Bristow wouldn't comment on this.

'If there had been anything untoward going on during my reign, I would have sussed it and I would have done something about it,' he told me. He was adamant that he had not been short-staffed, and that another officer was appointed soon after Stoke Place was registered to work under him.

But Gus Gray, Bristow's equivalent officer with neighbouring Berkshire County Council, tells a different story.

In 1985, Rowe approached Gray for permission to open a large residential home for between 60 and 80 adults with learning difficulties on the site of a former approved school for young offenders in the village of Grazeley, west Berkshire.

Gray's department had recently written a document concluding that no home for more than 16 residents should be acceptable. Rowe told Gray and a colleague that he was sure they could 'find a way round the regulations'. He also implied that he had connections and would make things unpleasant for them if they did not register the home. But they told him registration would not be possible. Rowe was furious. Gray and his colleague warned their boss and submitted a report. Then Rowe contacted them again and was even more abusive. He said they would 'live to regret it'.

Gray believes registration and inspection in Bucks was seriously under-staffed. In Berkshire, there were four inspectors reporting to him, contrasting with just Bristow in Bucks.

Gray is convinced his department would never have allowed Rowe to open a home if it had been told about the Somerset police investigation. He told me: 'Their preparatory work was much less thorough in Bucks and I do not think that agreed registration conditions were stuck to anything like as rigidly as they were in Berkshire.'

Gray was one of the Berkshire officers who ran a training session on inspection and registration for neighbouring local authorities, as Berkshire was seen as having special expertise in the area. Bristow attended the session and Gray would later describe in a statement that he was surprised when he told him he was the only inspection officer for the whole of Buckinghamshire.

Bristow confessed that he was having difficulty keeping up-to-date with his formal inspections, and had no time to carry out the vital surprise inspections. His request for extra support had been turned down. 'From what I know, Bristow did not get a lot of support from his superiors,' Gray told me, 'so I think Bucks social services must take some responsibility for what happened.'

Bucks County Council told me in 1998 that it was 'difficult' to say how many inspectors they had in 1983. 'The actual business of inspection of homes in the county was part of the job of various managers,' a spokeswoman said. This contrasted with the view of Gus Gray, and indeed Stan Bristow, who seemed to have been under the impression that he had been the council's only inspection and registration officer.

In 1987, Bucks County Council made a further unfortunate decision.

Early the previous year, Rowe had submitted an application to register Stoke Green House. Members of the council's senior management group decided this would mean a large number of people with learning difficulties concentrated in a small area, and rejected the application.

Rowe didn't give up. In April, he wrote again to Bucks and persuaded a representative of Slough Mencap to write to South Bucks District Council in support of his planning application to convert Stoke Green House into a residential home. The charity said there was a shortage of residential placements for 'mentally handicapped' people, and until there were enough smaller units, such large homes were filling a need not being met by local authorities.

The same month, the director of Bucks social services wrote to the district council to say they had changed their mind. Although they still had reservations, they registered Gordon and Angela Rowe to run Stoke Green House.

The subsequent Independent Longcare Inquiry concluded: 'There was [now] a large number of vulnerable adults, in a relatively closed environment, under the control of one man against whom allegations questioning fitness had been made.' There was also no attempt to ensure that residents would be involved in the community or with outside agencies.

Again, Bucks had given Gordon Rowe the benefit of the doubt. Why the council behaved in such a cavalier fashion has never been explained. This, though, was far from the end of its failures.

In April 1991, the county council officially recorded the first abuse allegation against Gordon Rowe at Longcare, the incident in which Dorothy was attacked in her home by Gordon Rowe.

Dorothy later showed her social worker the healed wound on her hand and made other allegations of poor care – including Rowe pulling residents around and depriving them of meals as a punishment. Dorothy left Stoke Place, but her social worker sent a copy of his report to Buckinghamshire's registration officer, Anthony Barker, and asked whether any other residents, families or social workers had made similar complaints.

Barker agreed the homes were large and regimented, but said he hadn't heard any other such complaints. He visited Longcare to talk to Rowe and his staff. Employees lined up outside Rowe's office, to wait for Barker to interview them. Rowe was pacing up and down next to the queue, warning them to 'be careful' what they said. They all knew his office was bugged. The episode was a farce.

Even so, during his investigation, Barker received allegations from three members of staff about over-use of medication, physical assaults and punishments. Among the allegations were that Rowe had hit a man on the head with a slipper, that he listened to staff conversations on the intercom, that residents who were late were denied meals, that there were no staff meetings, and that Rowe had thrown a bucket of water over a resident for not eating. Barker also interviewed Dorothy. She repeated her allegations, and admitted grabbing a pair of scissors to protect herself from Gordon Rowe when he burst into the house. She also told him that four other residents were being ill-treated.

In a letter to Rowe, Barker said: 'I find it difficult to understand why there was so much physical violence when you were dealing with one so physically inferior in both weight and strength.' He drew his attention to various inappropriate methods of 'restraint, discipline or sanctions'. Barker also spoke to Ray Cradock, who told him Longcare was committed to raising standards and that Rowe was looking to buy a house, so he wouldn't need to live in the grounds.

In Stoke Place's regular inspection report the following month, the council said visits would take place every three months, with inspectors monitoring specific areas of care. It also said Longcare should arrange external advice for residents who needed help with their finances, as Dorothy claimed Rowe had been stealing their money. But there was no full investigation, even though the council knew Rowe had previously been questioned over allegations of sexual abuse at The Old Rectory.

The following year, the council received another complaint. On 4 December 1992, an ex-member of staff called the council anonymously and spoke to the head of the inspection unit, Jennifer Waldron. She said Gordon Rowe was punishing residents by sending them into the garden to eat their breakfast, had kicked a resident on the bottom and 'ordered cold showers'. Two care assistants had told her Rowe was sexually abusing residents.

Three days later, she called the unit and repeated the allegations, this time giving enough information to be identified. But the inspection unit concluded that the risk to the residents was 'not one of immediacy', although it did inform the police's family protection unit.

On 11 December, the unit received a third telephone call, probably from the same caller. New allegations were added, including further examples of abuse, neglect and ill-treatment. The unit was told that Jackie had been kicked on the bottom, thrown across the dining-room and put out in the garden to eat breakfast. There was also an alleged sexual assault on a resident.

On 14 December, a police officer told Waldron there was not enough witness information to proceed with a criminal inquiry. Amazingly, the inspection unit decided not to make a surprise inspection visit, in case they 'tipped off' Gordon Rowe. Instead, they decided to review the situation the following month.

On 8 January, the unit decided that if they visited the homes unannounced during the day they would be unlikely to meet many residents. But a visit 'out of hours' would 'alert the directors'. So they decided to continue with an inspection already arranged for 23 February, and announce that out-of-hours visits would be starting across the county, especially in homes for people with learning difficulties.

The following month, a second caller contacted the inspection unit and gave her name. She stated that Michael had been sent to bed for three to seven days for 'confrontational behaviour'. Staff were encouraged to write in the report book that he was 'unwell, again'. Further allegations were made about Jackie being made to eat outside.

A week later, on 23 February, a third caller provided information about physical assaults, financial irregularities, and insufficient staff. Although he declined to leave his name, he provided enough information to be identified. Yet again, the unit did not act.

On 29 March, Paul Robertson wrote to Berkshire County Council. His letter was passed to Bucks. It made allegations of physical and emotional abuse by Gordon and Angela Rowe, including claims that Gordon forced Jackie to eat her meals outside on her birthday. When her brother called to wish her happy birthday, Gordon instructed a member of staff not to pass the message on. Rowe had punched a male resident in the face for incontinence and put another man – probably Stefano – outside to dry his clothes when he wet himself. Other allegations included concern about the length of time Gordon had spent in a resident's bedroom after she asked him to kiss her goodnight. He said he was willing for his name to be used, and later told Bucks that Clare Johnson would also talk to them.

On 11 May, the council issued new registration certificates for Stoke Place and Stoke Green, in the name of Longcare Ltd, and under the management of Ray Cradock. The applications had been made the previous September.

The decision to allow the names of Gordon and Angela Rowe to be removed from the certificates was another serious error. It meant that, because Gordon Rowe was no longer officially in charge, it would be much harder to take action to close the homes. The certificates were also issued without asking Cradock whether he had been aware of any of the abuse allegations.

Again and again, the county council had found excuses for not investigating, even though its inspection unit had the power to enter Stoke Place and Stoke Green. Yet again, it had failed the residents of the Longcare homes.

On 15 July, Clare Johnson contacted the council and made serious allegations about the abuse of three residents and said Cradock had told her that if she reported concerns to anybody and Longcare collapsed, she would be financially liable for the losses. She said nine other staff had left over the previous few months and might come forward.

The following day, Slough police agreed to take part in a joint investigation with the inspection unit. It lasted just three months, during which time detectives merely took statements from Clare, Paul and the other caller who had left their name. The three other telephone callers were not tracked down. The statements contained a string of serious allegations of physical, financial and sexual abuse, neglect and ill-treatment.

In mid-October, the police told the council there was no-one further they could interview without alerting Gordon Rowe. They also stressed how difficult it was to secure prosecutions in cases involving people with learning difficulties, and told the inspection unit there was nothing they could do without further evidence.

On 1 November, the inspection unit met with Jean Jeffrey, Buckinghamshire's director of social services, to discuss the case. It was only now that Bucks decided to launch a full investigation. On 16 November, Waldron wrote to every local authority with a client at Longcare, saying they were investigating 'several complaints' about the care of residents.

The investigation finally began on 17 November 1993, almost 12 months after the anonymous call to Waldron, and more than two-and-a-half years after Dorothy Abbott had been attacked.

The inspection unit interviewed every current and former member of staff they could track down. They interviewed the

Rowes, Ray Cradock and Lorraine Field. But they failed to talk to the doctors, the dentists, the relatives, the social workers, and – most importantly – the residents themselves.

Now, when it seemed as though someone was finally listening, the residents of Longcare had, once again, been denied a voice.

The investigation team took 17 written statements, which included more than 140 allegations, involving 51 residents, stretching from 1988 to late 1993.

There was evidence of physical assaults by Gordon Rowe against more than a dozen residents, including punches, slaps, hosing down with cold water, holding a snooker cue around the neck of a resident and tying another to a tree. There were allegations of punishments, such as sending people to their rooms for days on end, being made to eat meals outside and being forced to sit apart from other residents. There was also evidence that Gordon Rowe had raped his female 'favourites'. Staffing levels, fraud, the exploitation of the Working Lads, inadequate clothing and toiletries, and problems with over-medication were mentioned, including a series of allegations against Angela Rowe and Lorraine Field. Witnesses had described how Field hit one resident around the head, failed to act when residents were sick, sent one man to bed as a punishment and chased another male resident into the garden. According to the report, one man confided to a member of staff that he was 'scared about upsetting Lorraine and making her angry; he wept, recalling one incident where she had hit him'.

'It is difficult,' wrote Waldron, 'to distil the information given and still convey the enormity and scale of humiliation, deprivation, torment and punishment to which residents were subjected.'

But now Gordon Rowe's name was no longer on the registration documents, if it wanted to close the homes, the inspection unit would have to prove that Ray Cradock and Nigel Rowe had known the abuse was going on and did nothing to stop it.

A draft report concluded: 'It is impossible but to conclude that all three directors (Angela and Nigel Rowe and Ray Cradock) must have been aware of the repressive nature of the regime which prevailed and by inaction, share the responsibility for its continued existence… the inspection unit's continuing concern is lack of confidence in the owners and manager's ability to protect the residents from the degradation which, on the balance of probabilities, they have suffered in the past.'

On reading the draft report, though, the council's barrister became concerned. He had originally been told that Nigel and Ray had probably done all they could to protect residents. Now, following detailed examination of the report books, inspectors were telling him the two men were almost certainly unfit to be in charge. The barrister asked for more proof.

But Jean Jeffrey, director of social services, was becoming increasingly impatient. She told Waldron to wrap up the investigation and prepare a final report.

In the absence of proof that Nigel and Ray had known what was going on, the barrister amended the draft report. There was, he was forced to conclude, insufficient evidence to force closure. The report now stated: 'Nigel Rowe and Ray Cradock are and were honourable men and decent men who found themselves in a position not of their choosing and in which they were for all practical purposes powerless to act against Gordon Rowe… they are seen as forces for good.'

The report's recommendations included requirements that Gordon and Angela Rowe and Lorraine Field should be banned from any involvement with the company or contact with the residents; that the residents should undertake assertiveness training; that there should be more inspection visits; and that staff training should be improved.

When members of the casework sub-committee met to discuss the report on 8 July 1994, they were handed a file containing a mountain of information, including the inspection unit's report and Longcare's lengthy response. The councillors were not allowed to read the report in advance. Only the two

Labour members argued that the homes should be closed; the others accepted Jeffrey's recommendations. At the end of the meeting, the councillors had to hand all the papers back to the officers.

Audrey Bainbridge, the Conservative councillor who chaired the sub-committee, refused to be interviewed for this book, after taking advice from council lawyers. But Pam Crawford, a Liberal Democrat member of the sub-committee, agreed to discuss what went on.

Crawford said she and her colleagues had discussed the report in detail and 'asked a lot of questions', but were told it was 'not our duty to bring retribution'. She said a major factor in the decision not to close the homes was the shortage of suitable places in other residential homes. A secondary concern was the fear of being sued by Longcare. 'There was no certainty that we would have been able to prove the case. It was our social services that had the concerns – no-one else's. If we had lost the lawsuit, that money would have had to have been paid for by our social services budget,' she told me.

'The other consideration was that once the inspection had got underway, the Rowes had distanced themselves. It was the Rowes who were the real culprits and therefore without them being there the danger was more or less gone. We asked a lot of questions about the son. We had no complaints about his behaviour and there was some evidence that on one or two occasions he had intervened.'

Crawford was clearly not in possession of all the facts.

Labour councillor Trevor Fowler also spoke to me. He was to discover later that Jean Jeffrey and her officers had not been 'totally straight' with him and his colleagues. 'There was revulsion and sickness on my part on reading the detail that was put in there, and I suspect other members felt the same as well. The real difference was in what do we do about it.' He and Labour colleague Dick O'Brien argued for closure, but were easily out-voted by the Conservative and Liberal Democrat majority. The report was sent to the local authorities with residents at the homes on 20 July, along with a copy of Longcare's comments. It was forwarded to Thames Valley Police on 11 August. Just over a week later, Bucks met representatives of the sponsoring authorities and passed on specific information about particular residents.

The county councillors who made the decision to allow the Longcare homes to stay open were not told two vital facts. Firstly, that the inspectors themselves believed that both Cradock and Nigel Rowe had known for several years about nearly every aspect of Gordon Rowe's regime. Secondly, that although the council's barrister had recommended that the inspection unit should seek extra evidence about the fitness of Cradock and Nigel Rowe, Jean Jeffrey had told the inspection unit not to do this.

Clearly, the Conservative and Liberal Democrat members of the sub-committee had been led by their noses towards their decision.

Four weeks after we published our first Longcare story, the Slough Observer reported that Bucks investigators had been given evidence that Nigel Rowe and Ray Cradock knew of allegations that Gordon Rowe had abused residents.

Jean Jeffrey had told a meeting of the social services committee only the previous week that her department had carried out a 'massive search' of the homes' records and failed to unearth any evidence that the two men were unfit to be running the homes.

It was only four years later, with the publication of the Independent Longcare Inquiry report, that the Slough Observer and the two Labour councillors were proved right. Fowler told me: 'One of the things the inquiry report showed was that there was a strong feeling within the inspection department that de-registration should take place, but we were never told that the inspection unit took that view. I have never felt so strongly that a view that I have held has been vindicated.'

It was all merely a confirmation of what the relatives of the Longcare survivors were later to discover: Bucks County

Council's decisions had been powered by a mixture of arrogance, cowardice and incompetence.

This conclusion was confirmed the following year, when the government's Social Services Inspectorate uncovered a catalogue of errors and complacency during its routine inspection of the council's inspection unit.

The report criticised the unit's failure to talk to residents and relatives during its inspection work. It also said the unit failed to talk to GPs, community nurses and social workers, which, it said, 'served to reinforce the limited contact between residents and the outside community'. The inspectorate concluded that the council had given a low priority to the inspection unit's work and had granted it insufficient resources when it was set up in 1991.

The unit had been set up as an independent, arms-length body – although under the direction of social services – following the NHS and Community Care Act 1990. The government had hoped such units would improve the standard of registration and inspection.

Bucks had originally intended to launch the unit with six inspectors and a unit head. Councillors decided instead to cut the number of inspectors to four. According to the inspectorate, the county spent less money on social services than any other comparable authority in the country.

It would be reassuring to know that those members of the social services committee who read the inspection unit's disturbing report on Longcare had learned something from that experience. Unfortunately, in February 1996 it emerged that members of that committee had completed reports on just 29 of the 153 visits they were supposed to have made in 1995 to check on conditions at council-run homes for older people, children and people with learning difficulties.

Buckinghamshire County Council – and Jean Jeffrey – refused to admit they had done anything wrong. When the Slough

Observer called in 1997 for an independent inquiry, the council was dismissive. 'The whole thing has already been the subject of exhaustive examination,' said a spokesman. 'Is a public inquiry really necessary?'

The inquiry that eventually followed would never have happened without the efforts of Fiona Mactaggart, the newly elected Labour MP for Slough, whose attention I had drawn to the scandal shortly before the general election of 1997. Within days of her election, she wrote to junior health minister Paul Boateng, asking him to set up an inquiry. She followed up with a parliamentary question. Boateng was initially cool on the idea. He thought Bucks could and would learn from its mistakes.

But Boateng did agree to question council representatives. 'He had a pre-meeting with me and Dominic Grieve (the Conservative MP for Beaconsfield, whose constituency included Stoke Place),' said Mactaggart. 'He said, 'this is a lengthy process, we don't necessarily need an inquiry'. I had a row with Paul, saying, 'you cannot be so feeble. This is serious, we have to find out what's going on.' He was intending to rap their knuckles, accept an apology and send them on their way.'

But Jean Jeffrey was not about to be criticised by a mere government minister. 'Not only do we have nothing to learn, but our behaviour was exemplary and everyone should learn from us,' she told Boateng.

The minister exploded, said Mactaggart. 'He said, 'I'm not being talked to like this,' and he just lost it, because of her arrogance. It was her complete refusal to admit that there had been something which was a deep offence to a civilised community for which she was responsible in any way that provoked him into insisting that they have an inquiry, and Paul Boateng angry is quite an interesting sight.

'I think Paul quite rightly realised as a result of seeing her face to face – which I don't think he had realised before – that there was a serious cultural problem in Bucks social services. He realised that Jean Jeffrey was not going to learn from it unless her nose was rubbed in it. And even when her nose was rubbed in it, she didn't.'

Mactaggart didn't let the matter rest there. She had planned to introduce a private members' bill aimed at improving regulation and inspection, but was unsuccessful in the ballot and was unable to put her bill before fellow MPs. But she became chair of the Voice all party parliamentary subject group, which was linked to the charity Voice UK and provided a forum for MPs to discuss the rights of people with learning difficulties who have been the victims of crime, particularly sexual abuse.

The inquiry ordered by Boateng – which looked solely at the last years of the Longcare regime and not the decision to register Stoke Place in 1983 – was led by Tom Burgner, a retired Treasury official. The previous year, he had written a well-received report which called for a more independent system of regulation and inspection of social care services.

In fact, there had been similar calls almost a decade earlier. Gillian Wagner's review of residential care, which reported in 1988, said there had been a 'great deal of criticism' of the system of registration and inspection. Many of those who gave evidence called for a national independent body to inspect homes.

Sadly, it was to be many years before the government would pay attention.

Burgner and his two colleagues concluded, after nine months' investigation, that Buckinghamshire County Council had made 'serious mistakes', although lessons had since been learned. He made 95 separate recommendations, most directed at Bucks. But there were also key messages for the government.

The Independent Longcare Inquiry delivered a trenchant criticism of the council's investigation. It concluded that its work had been unfocussed and tentative and had waited far too long to obtain evidence from the report books, and then failed to develop that line of enquiry. Crucially, it failed to interview residents and so was not able to determine whether they were at risk. The inspectors also failed to talk to social workers and relatives, or to experts who could have decided whether the residents would be seriously at risk if the homes stayed open.

The final report, the inquiry concluded, did not reflect the inspectors' view that the homes should have been closed. Their investigation stopped 'just as it began to focus on the supporting information it needed' to show that the homes should be shut and that Nigel Rowe and Ray Cradock were unfit to be running residential homes.

The inquiry also found that information about the allegations should have been passed on much sooner to the local authorities that had placed clients in the homes. They had only been given details of the allegations in late July 1994. This delay meant the families also had no idea what had been alleged, and allowed their relatives to continue living at Longcare for much longer than necessary.

Neither Jean Jeffrey, Jennifer Waldron, nor Audrey Bainbridge were present at the press conference held by the county council on the day the inquiry report was published in June 1998. Waldron was no longer in her post, although it was unclear whether she had left permanently or was on sick leave. Bainbridge had been promoted to deputy leader of the ruling Tory group. And the council announced that Jeffrey was leaving after more than seven years' service. There was not a word of criticism.

Jeffrey's own press release was startlingly self-congratulatory. Indeed, some journalists wondered if she had been handed the wrong report. 'The Burgner report shows that we took reasonable action in 1994, and recognises the determination and success of the inspection unit and of Thames Valley Police in pursuing the protection of people, within the constraints of the legislation in place at the time,' she announced. That was quite definitely not the conclusion reached by Burgner and his colleagues, who had heavily criticised her decision to stop the investigation just as it was about to seek the evidence it needed to close the homes.

Trevor Fowler said there had been 'great secrecy' about the terms of Jeffrey's retirement package, although it was believed to be 'really generous'. 'The senior officers and senior management of the council were privy to what the report contained (before it was published) and they chose not to lose one minute,' he told me. 'They acted to make sure that when the report was actually published, Jean Jeffrey was not there. Everyone knew that she had gone because of Longcare.'

But Fowler also believed the ruling Conservative group had got off lightly. 'Nothing stuck to the politicians and yet they had made the final decisions about these things,' he said.

The council accepted the findings of the inquiry and that the inspection unit had made mistakes. 'We are deeply sorry for this and apologise to the residents and their families,' it stated in a press release.

Burgner, who sadly died in 2001, told me: 'Although we made a lot of recommendations for changes in the law, my over-riding feeling was that if everyone had done their job properly and fully, the duration of the abuse could have been prevented. You can't prevent individual acts of abuse, but this entrenched culture of abuse should never have been allowed. It should have been stopped at source or uncovered sooner. The law gave all the powers. What was lacking was the skill and determination and experience to tackle a difficult case. It was a difficult case for any inspection team to crack, but they made a lot of mistakes.

'The distinction between what you need to secure a criminal conviction and what you need to challenge a registration, that was not clear in the minds of the inspection unit in 1993 and 1994. Of course, there were also checks that should have been undertaken and information that should have been followed up in 1983, when Stoke Place was first considered for registration.'

But he did feel there had been mitigating circumstances. 'Gordon Rowe obviously cultivated people he thought would be useful in the police, and possibly elsewhere, too. I think I would accept that his success in making himself to some extent a pillar of the community made life particularly difficult for the inspection unit team. They were dealing with someone who was influential in the community.'

Dr Philippa Russell, one of his inquiry colleagues, told me the council should have sought advice from experts, who could have 'asked far more probing questions'.

'Equally, I don't think Buckinghamshire felt competent to actually talk to the residents themselves, or rather question the residents – there's a difference between talking to and questioning.

'We felt very strongly that during every routine inspection, there should be a proper consultation with the residents, which should be in a private place and should not be with a member of staff sitting in. Now, of course, the residents may or may not tell you that something's going wrong. If they have come from very disadvantaged circumstances they may not know that what is happening is very wrong. But a lot of them will, and at least half of the Longcare residents – if they had been asked – were well able to say what was happening. They knew very, very well. And I think that is actually one of the greatest safeguards – to actually ask people themselves.'

Abuse is easier to detect – and deter – when systems are in place to allow the free flow of information between everyone concerned, whether they are residents, care workers, social workers, inspectors, police officers or relatives. Communication is vital.

Once such a system is in place, those responsible have only two further tasks: to listen and to act – immediately, and with determination. Buckinghamshire failed in all of these tasks, and in doing so failed the residents of Longcare, and needlessly exposed them to years of cruelty, neglect and misery.

Chapter Eighteen

The Police

'The Equality and Human Rights Commission has launched a three-point plan to address violence and hostility towards disabled people. The plan came in its new report, Promoting the Safety and Security of Disabled People, *which found that disabled people are at greater risk of being victims of targeted violence and hostility. People with learning difficulties and those with mental health conditions face the greatest risk, according to the report. But the report also revealed that many disabled people are reluctant to report violence and hostility because they believe authorities will not take any action. It found a severe under-reporting of incidents and said disabled people can often be deemed 'unreliable witnesses'.'*

Disability News Service, April 2010

The Longcare case was rapidly proving an embarrassment to Thames Valley Police, which had failed on at least two occasions to investigate properly the claims of sexual abuse, ill-treatment, neglect and assault against Gordon Rowe.

Meanwhile, the council's inspection unit had gathered a mountain of evidence, without interviewing a single alleged victim. It didn't take long for the force to acknowledge – at least internally – that something had gone badly wrong.

Within hours of the story appearing in the Slough Observer and The Independent, other newspapers and radio and television stations were following it up. We were already asking questions about Rowe's close relationship with certain police officers and his membership of a Masonic lodge. Chief constable Charles Pollard decided something had to be done and ordered a new investigation, under the name Operation Skip.

The officer Pollard chose to lead the investigation was Detective Superintendent Jon Bound. Bound's CV boasted a string of high-profile investigations. He intended to retire from the force in little more than a year and this was to be his last big case. He also had no links with Slough police and was not a Freemason.

Within hours of reviewing the case, Bound concluded that Slough had not dealt with the case properly. Because of the media pressure he knew his investigation would have to be exhaustive. In his opinion, Longcare was 'a sore that was not going to go away'.

Almost a week after the story broke, police officers raided Stoke Place Mansion House, Rowe's cottage in the grounds of Stoke Place, Stoke Green House, and Rowe's home in Windsor. They removed a mass of evidence from 12 Harrington Close, including several large crates of documents, boxes of videotapes… and a Thames Valley Police helmet belonging to one of Rowe's friends.

Thames Valley Police's first official, documented involvement with Longcare had occurred late in 1992, when Slough's family protection unit was told about the allegations made anonymously to the inspection unit. It had also been given details of Rowe's 1991 assault on Dorothy Abbott. A police officer made it clear to the council that they could not take the matter forward without a formal complaint, but agreed to read the files.

After the third anonymous telephone call, Waldron and the council inspector responsible for the Longcare homes met with a sergeant from the family protection unit to discuss the allegations. He told them there was not enough evidence to proceed with a criminal investigation.

Six months later, following allegations from four more former members of Longcare staff, Slough police finally launched an investigation, supposedly in collaboration with the inspection unit. It lasted about three months, but consisted only of interviewing members of staff who had made complaints, including Clare Johnson, who had come forward on 15 July, and Paul Robertson. The detectives' superior, a detective inspector, would later tell the Longcare inquiry: 'At this stage it was felt that the management of the homes should not be made aware of the enquiry and that the [two] investigators should concentrate on interviewing ex-members of staff, or any people who were unlikely to inform Gordon Rowe or the management of the homes of our enquiries. This was to ensure, as far as possible, that should a full investigation take place, no evidence would be lost. The enquiry was not to be made general knowledge to other police officers at Slough.' This was a clear acknowledgement of Rowe's close personal relationship with several Slough police officers.

But the inquiries hit problems almost immediately, when both officers were drafted into the investigation of the murder of a little boy, Aklaq Ahmed, whose body had been found in a Slough park. The Longcare file was reallocated to another detective constable, who again was chosen because he was neither a Freemason nor a friend of Gordon Rowe.

By early October, the new detective had taken statements from just two witnesses and Waldron was becoming increasingly frustrated. On 7 October, Waldron wrote to the detective inspector and said she believed residents were still being subjected to serious abuse and that her unit was having problems contacting the officer on the case.

A week later, the detective inspector met with a detective superintendent to discuss the evidence. The detective inspector contacted the Crown Prosecution Service (CPS) informally, and was told there was nothing it could do without the full papers and further evidence. The CPS was never asked for a formal opinion.

The detective inspector and two colleagues met with Waldron and four other council officers on 14 October. They said there was nobody else they could interview without alerting Gordon Rowe, that the evidence of people with learning difficulties was difficult to use in court, and that the investigation in 1983 in Somerset had also proved fruitless. They handed the case back to the inspection unit.

It was not until 12 August 1994, nearly 12 months later, when they received a copy of the inspection unit's report, that Thames Valley Police heard anything more about the Longcare case. Even then, no action was taken until the first stories appeared in the press, more than a month later, on 16 September.

The whole episode showed a frightening lack of regard for the human rights of the Longcare residents. It is certain that if Slough police had heard allegations that a non-disabled person had been subjected to such allegations of rape, sexual assault, physical assault and neglect, they would have acted immediately. But because the victims happened to have learning difficulties, the case was afforded a priority slightly below that of an overdue parking ticket.

*

Whatever had happened in the past, Supt Jon Bound was now taking the allegations seriously. His first step was to bring

221

together a team of four police officers, three of whom had backgrounds in family protection work and often dealt with sexually abused children. But none of the quartet, or Bound himself, had any experience or training in interviewing people with learning difficulties.

As with the two previous investigations, none of Bound's team had any links with Gordon Rowe or the Freemasons, and only the members of this small team were allowed access to the case computer files.

Bound set up his incident room at Langley police station, a couple of miles from the gates of Stoke Place. The core of his strategy was to try and interview every current and former member of staff who had worked at the two homes since 1987. It was to take them more than 12 months of hard graft.

They began tracing former members of staff. A confidential hotline advertised in the press produced many of the names. They also researched the issues surrounding people with learning difficulties: what is Down's syndrome? How are residential homes supposed to be run? How does the complaints system work?

A picture soon emerged of Rowe's regime, while the names of certain residents began to crop up in different interviews.

The team eventually compiled evidence of 40 residents they believed had been subjected to various forms of 'abuse', dating from 1983 to1994. Forensic psychologists assessed all of the alleged victims to judge their levels of 'competence' as witnesses. One of those psychologists was the renowned Professor Gisli Gudjonsson, from King's College London, whose expert testimony on false confessions had helped overturn the convictions of both the Birmingham Six and the Guildford Four. Gudjonsson would later tell the Commons select committee on home affairs that the investigation had been an example of good police practice. 'They asked us to go in, assess them psychologically before they interviewed them to identify what kind of problems and psychological vulnerabilities they might have and to give advice about, if they were interviewed, how should they be interviewed.' Those who were seen as capable were then interviewed on video by members of the police team, he said.

Even though only a small number were considered able to give evidence, it illustrated the ill-conceived reactions of the police officers in the first two investigations who had dismissed the chance of any residents appearing in court as witnesses.

The evidence was there. It had always been there, if only the police had come looking for it. Bound told me: 'It was quite clear that there was a considerable amount of physical and sexual abuse. It was also clear that Gordon Rowe had been having sexual intercourse with the prettier female residents. The majority of physical abuse was whacking around the back of the head and kicking up the backside, where there were no injuries.'

This created a problem. With no evidence of injuries, there was little chance of achieving convictions for physical assault. Bound realised the only option was to resort to offences introduced nearly 40 years earlier in the Mental Health Act, and prosecute the perpetrators for ill-treatment and neglect of 'mentally disordered patients'. The wording was another throwback to the days of the long-stay hospitals, but it was the best the inadequate British legal system could offer.

As for the sexual charges, Bound knew the victims would have to give evidence in court, because there were few if any other witnesses, and apart from their testimony there was only circumstantial evidence.

Towards the end of 1995, the police team were left with allegations against 15 current and former members of Longcare staff, including Gordon and Angela Rowe, Desmond Tully and Lorraine Field. Each was interviewed, but none of them admitted a single offence. In November, the 14-month investigation ended and thousands of pages of police evidence were sent to the Crown Prosecution Service. The team had interviewed 800 people, taken 519 statements and collated 1,178 documents.

But although Thames Valley Police had finally succeeded in investigating most of the allegations against Gordon Rowe and his sidekicks – relatives of the victims believe that the allegations of fraud were never satisfactorily probed – its problems were far from over.

*

Bound had been so concerned at the apparent links between Rowe and Slough police that, at the start of his investigation, he notified the Police Complaints Authority (PCA), which agreed to oversee an internal inquiry by the force's own complaints and discipline department.

For years, Rowe had used his links with the force, and Slough police station in particular, to intimidate both residents and staff. Officers were frequent social visitors to Stoke Place. Gordon Rowe even leant them one of the Longcare minibuses for fishing trips. One officer often arrived at Longcare to lecture residents whom Rowe told him had 'misbehaved'. On one occasion, an officer spoke to one of the men who had allegedly raped another of the male residents.

A former care worker said a detective had told her that nobody from Slough police had wanted to take on the case because it involved Gordon Rowe, while some of the Working Lads had carried out decorating and landscaping work at two police officers' homes, for little or no money.

None of this was proof of anything, but given the two abandoned police investigations, and Rowe's Masonic membership, the suspicions were clear.

When the 18-month internal investigation ended, in January 1998, it concluded that the allegations against Rowe had not been adequately dealt with in the first two investigations. A PCA spokesman told me: 'There was no evidence to suggest that officers neglected their duties, but, clearly, inappropriate decisions were taken. There were various accusations made which should have been investigated earlier.'

The PCA's report mentioned two police officers, Officer A and Officer B – neither of whose names were made public. Among the most serious accusations was that residents were taken by Rowe to both of their homes to carry out decorating and landscaping work. John, one of Gordon's Working Lads, had told one of Bound's team that he had been paid about £15 to paint the kitchen of one officer, and had also painted the same officer's office.

The inquiry also found that Officer A had used the force's national computer to carry out checks on the criminal records of members of Rowe's staff. And it discovered evidence that Rowe had invited this officer to Stoke Place on at least four occasions, to deliver 'warnings' to residents about their behaviour.

The PCA spokesman said: 'These were people who were very susceptible and very vulnerable and would obviously feel very threatened by police officers coming in and warning them. It was inappropriate and it is very doubtful that these warnings were given as part of the carrying out of their statutory duties.'

It later emerged that Officer A had been a member of the same Masonic lodge as Gordon Rowe. Rowe, in fact, had proposed him for membership in 1988.

The internal investigation was fraught with difficulties. Most of the witnesses were people with learning difficulties and so, the PCA said, the allegations could not be proved to a degree sufficient to bring any formal disciplinary charges. Instead, the two men were handed 'admonishments', temporary black marks entered on a police officer's disciplinary record, usually only for 12 months. They escaped with their careers almost intact.

No-one at Thames Valley Police was prepared to discuss the internal inquiry with me. I was told it was 'confidential'.

The force eventually sent me a copy of a 'protocol' developed with the county council, a direct result of Longcare, said a spokesman. 'There was a lot of discussion after the inquiries finished, asking what did we do wrong? What could we do? Were we as good as we could have been? (The answer was) no we were not.'

The Joint Protocol for Investigations of Abuse of Vulnerable Adults in Buckinghamshire would probably have led to concerted action being taken sooner if it had been in place in 1992. It provided guidelines on how to respond to an initial allegation of abuse, how to proceed with an investigation, how to set up and run a joint investigation with a social services department or health authority, and how to plan for court proceedings.

Although the third police investigation had been carried out with determination and the full backing of the force, the officers involved had still lacked detailed knowledge of how to investigate allegations of abuse of people with learning difficulties. They learned as they went along, but at least they tried.

The question remains: why were Slough police so reluctant to launch a full investigation into the allegations against Gordon Rowe?

There were several reasons: Rowe's close relationship with Slough police and his 'reputation' in the community; the reluctance of the officers involved in the first two investigations to make any effort to understand people with learning difficulties; and the failure of the English legal system to protect adults at risk of abuse.

But the main reason was quite simple. Slough police didn't care enough about the residents of Longcare, about people with learning difficulties. If they had, they would surely have acted sooner.

Chapter Nineteen

The Outsiders

'Almost half of doctors – and more than a third of nurses – believe people with learning difficulties receive poorer healthcare than the rest of the population, according to a new survey. Similar numbers have seen a patient with a learning difficulty being treated with neglect or lack of dignity or receive poor care, while nearly four out of ten doctors and a third of nurses believe people with learning difficulties face discrimination in the NHS.'

Disability News Service, 21 June 2010

'A 'damning' ombudsman's report has found a hospital guilty of widespread failings in the care provided to a woman with learning difficulties and high support needs who died after a routine operation. The findings of the parliamentary and health ombudsman came just weeks after the same hospital – Basildon University Hospital – was fined £50,000 over the 2006 death of a man with learning difficulties whose head became trapped in his bed rails. The ombudsman found that the care and treatment provided by the hospital to Lisa Sharpe before her death in 2004 fell 'significantly below a reasonable standard'. Her family claimed their concerns were ignored for nine days after she underwent a routine operation to insert a feeding tube – even though she had begun to vomit bile. When an x-ray was finally taken, it revealed she had pneumonia. Despite her condition, the hospital failed to provide any pain relief.'

Disability News Service, 15 July 2010

No matter how hard he tried to create a culture of isolation and secrecy, Gordon Rowe could not prevent everyone visiting Stoke Place. For more than 10 years, dentists, doctors, chiropodists, relatives of prospective residents and representatives of voluntary organisations all passed through the doors. So if Rowe was beating, raping and neglecting his clients, why did none of these visitors notice and raise the alarm?

One worker from the voluntary sector visited the homes regularly after Rowe set up his business in 1983.

By the time Rowe bought Stoke Green House, four years later, she remembers the London boroughs 'almost snatching his hand off' to take places because the shortage of beds was so acute. 'I could see the pound signs in Gordon's eyes. He knew he could get away with anything,' she would tell me later.

She saw many signs of poor care, but never imagined Rowe could be responsible for the scale of abuse eventually revealed. She once walked into reception to find him with a woman with Down's syndrome on his lap. He was totally unphased, and told her: 'Don't worry; she thinks of me as her daddy.'

'I told him it was totally inappropriate. What worried me was that he didn't think it was wrong,' she said.

She was also shocked at the way he spoke to some of the residents. He used to tell them to 'get your fat arse out of here', or 'get out the back, you big fat slob', but again, she blamed poor judgement and an unpleasant bullying streak. She sometimes saw residents in Slough who were dirty and poorly dressed, but added: 'If I had known there was real physical or sexual abuse I would have done something about it. I knew he had a flawed character, but I didn't believe it was anything worse than that.'

It is easy to conclude that she should have complained to the authorities, but she was hardly the first to be fooled.

Another outsider who often visited Longcare was Slough pharmacist John Ross, who supplied prescription drugs to the homes, and said he found Rowe 'a perfectly normal sort of chap, pleasant and polite'.

'The residents all seemed to treat Gordon on a friendly basis, and there was certainly no sign of fear or anything like that,' he told me, early in 1998. 'I didn't see a single incident that would make me raise my eyebrows, bearing in mind my job was to deliver medicine to a carer in the home and I was only ever there for five minutes. The first I heard of any problems was when I read about them in the papers. I was shocked when I read about the report.'

The residents would do anything to avoid annoying him in front of a guest – they knew what the consequences would be. It is possible to see how this fearful willingness to please might convince visitors that what they were seeing was a happy, well-run home.

Ross also said he saw nothing that alarmed him in the quantities of drugs he was asked to supply. 'Mental medicine is a science of its own; they are not normal doses. They were certainly well within tolerances, otherwise I would have queried it. It is difficult for me to comment correctly, because I wasn't familiar with the patients. My responsibility was purely to dispense the medication.'

Despite the huge weight of evidence, John Ross believes Rowe was innocent of all the allegations.

At a court hearing in 1997, three other healthcare professionals who regularly visited the homes also denied ever seeing anything of concern.

Henryk Cholewa, an optician at O C Wetherbys in Slough, said in a statement: 'The home always struck me as a friendly and well run place. If I had an elderly relative, this is the place I would choose for them to go.'

Jeswant Jessy, a community care nurse, told the court he had been paying quarterly visits to the Longcare homes since 1987 and had never seen anything that disturbed him. The residents, he added, were always clean and appropriately dressed.

And chiropodist Keith Stodgell and his wife said they treated residents every six weeks between 1983 and 1993. 'My wife and I never noticed anything at all to concern us,' he said. 'Everyone was clean and well presented. It was delightfully happy. I used to enjoy going there. There was a lot of laughter and a lot of fun.'

These statements appear to show how easy it was for Rowe to fool occasional visitors into believing he ran a thriving, well-managed home, particularly if he knew in advance when they would be visiting.

Scores of parents of prospective residents also visited, and were often shown around by Gordon Rowe himself.

Rowe was hardly likely to let them see anything incriminating, but he never bothered to disguise his core beliefs. One mother remembers him showing her a classroom where residents were occupied with nothing but a few beads. Some were tied to their chairs. She remembers Rowe saying: 'These are the very disabled. There is not much anyone can do for these.' She was astonished to hear such words from a care home owner.

However, she found Rowe courteous, he spent a lot of time with her, and his sales patter was as good as ever. But as usual, he lied about the facilities, his expansion plans, and Longcare's social life.

Few first-time visitors would be able to see through such lies. Although some of his attitudes may have been disquieting, he would never allow them to see the real Longcare.

Theoretically, no outsiders were better placed to see the real Longcare than the Georges. Their club was physically joined to the home, and David George picked up his post from the Stoke Place reception every morning. Country club staff would often look out of their windows and see residents on the lawn, while Rowe frequently visited the club.

David George died in 1998, and his widow Chris took over the running of the club. She told me that, although they were grateful to Gordon for saving their business, they knew they had to be on their guard as he had told club members he wanted to take over the whole of Stoke Place. He wanted his own club where he could entertain his friends.

All Chris George knew about the care home was that 'the place was a tip. We knew how dirty it was. It seems incredible that you can live next door and not know what was going on, but we knew nothing about it until one of my sons' friends phoned and said his dad had just seen Stoke Place on the news.'

David and Chris George frequently spoke to residents, particularly those with lower support needs, like John and Bob. But nothing they said led them or any of their staff to suspect abuse. Perhaps they didn't recognise signs of abuse for what they were. Perhaps even they were not close enough to see what Longcare was really like.

One of the regime's most striking aspects was the absence of contact between residents and their neighbours. This was particularly noticeable among those who lived in the small homes Gordon Rowe set up in Slough for some of his residents with less need for staff support.

It was clear from talking to neighbours of these small homes that they had never spoken to their disabled occupants. This was particularly true of those in Myrtle Crescent, in the middle of a Slough council estate. They saw their neighbours were different, and kept their distance. But in doing so, they deprived them of the chance to make friends among 'outsiders'. It was these friendships – and the trust they would have engendered – which might have provided an opportunity for a whispered confidence: 'Don't like that Gordon Rowe. Had sex on me.' The kind of conversations, indeed, that finally led to Rowe's downfall.

*

Of all the outsiders, the one who should have been in the best position to spot signs of abuse was the Longcare GP, Dr X*.

With his medical training, and regular access to the residents, he was in a unique position to spot suspicious physical symptoms or behaviour that indicated stress, sexual abuse or neglect, as well as the exceptional levels of medication and contraception Gordon Rowe was requesting.

But today, nearly 17 years after the Longcare regime was exposed, no thorough examination of the medical care received by the residents has ever been carried out by the authorities.

Dr X visited Longcare every week. Then in his thirties, he had joined a practice near the homes in August 1990. Gordon Rowe befriended him, and the GP was often seen by staff chatting over a coffee with Gordon and Angela in the reception of Stoke Place. He was said to be a golfing partner of Nigel Rowe, while Gordon would take him for meals at Blaze's, the Windsor nightclub where Rowe took favoured residents (paid for with their money).

There is not a single record of Dr X reporting any concerns to the authorities.

Former care workers were deeply critical of the GP. Gary Moreton said he would simply follow Rowe's instructions. 'Dr X would say to him: 'What do you think I should do?' and Gordon would tell him.'

Clare Johnson remembers watching him give contraceptive injections to at least five of Gordon's Girls, one after the other. He delivered the jabs in a toilet that led off the main reception area. 'He would have them pull their trousers down,' she says, while he continued talking about holiday homes in the US with Gordon, who was sitting in reception. 'The toilet door was still open,' says Clare, while the GP 'was not even talking to the girls, not even acknowledging that they existed'.

Clare says Dr X delivered the injections every few weeks. She worked at Longcare for nearly four years, and never saw another GP deliver healthcare to the residents.

Another Longcare whistleblower, Paul Robertson, said Dr X 'used to just come in and sign anything that Gordon asked him to. He would pop in for two minutes and would have a meeting with Gordon and walk back out again. He would believe what Gordon told him.'

Another care worker remembers Gordon, Lorraine and Nigel trying to force a female resident to have her hair cut. As they tried to push her legs through the arms of a chair, the woman became increasingly 'panicky'. Gordon called the GP. Somehow, during the ensuing struggle, the woman wriggled free and lost her clothes. Gordon, Lorraine and Nigel caught her, and held her down on the floor in the corner of the reception area.

By the time the GP arrived to deliver a sedative injection, the woman was still naked and lying pinned to the floor. He made no attempt to communicate with her or calm her down. 'There was no verbal,' she says. 'I was completely disgusted. She was on the floor in between the ladies' lounge and the stairs so everyone could see her.'

On another occasion, the same member of staff witnessed the GP giving flu jabs to the residents. 'They lined up and he gave them the jab. He didn't speak to them,' she says.

Another care worker noted in the Longcare report book how Peter had been ill in bed, 'coughing up black stuff'. The GP arrived and prescribed antibiotics. Peter's condition worsened and he was eventually taken to hospital and diagnosed with pneumonia. He was in hospital for several days and the hospital reportedly said he would have died if he had not been admitted.

Residents, too, spoke later of their dislike for Dr X. Dorothy distrusted him intensely, while Rachel said in 2003 in a statement that his predecessor had been 'very nice' and 'wouldn't let staff be present at the time of a medical examination as he took the view that we were all adults'. Then, she said, the new GP took over [in 1990] and 'he just did what the staff wanted and the staff didn't let me see [him] or if they did they wouldn't let me see him alone'.

After the inspection unit report was leaked to the press, many relatives raised their concerns about the GP's poor record-keeping and prescription of high levels of sedatives, contraceptive injections and other drugs.

They questioned why he failed to spot signs of abuse and neglect, and pointed to the bruises, the lack of cleanliness, ulcers, gum disorders, the rapid weight loss of new residents, the anal bleeding of the men and the vaginal infections of the women.

Rowe, of course, tried to hide as much as he could from outsiders. He was a well-respected figure in the community and it is possible that he blamed other residents for bruises or signs of sexual trauma.

One day in 1994, before they learned of the inspection unit's investigation, a care worker rang Pauline Hennessey and told her that her sister Janet had become 'disruptive' and 'aggressive' – almost unheard of behaviour for Janet – with outbursts nearly every week.

Pauline drove to Stoke Place with her father for a meeting with Janet's social worker, Nigel Rowe, Ray Cradock and Dr X. They told her Janet would enter a room and start throwing furniture around. On one occasion, she grabbed a knife from the kitchen and threatened to kill herself.

'I told them I didn't understand what was going on because we had never had these problems before,' Pauline told me. 'They all looked at each other and said: "We have no idea either."'

Someone suggested placing Janet in a secure unit. Pauline was horrified. Within a month, Ray and Nigel told Pauline that Janet would have to find a new home.

Only a few weeks later, Pauline was told by Janet's social worker about Buckinghamshire's investigation. She couldn't understand why the allegations had not been mentioned at the meeting. When she phoned Longcare, Cradock told her they couldn't say anything because it was 'sub-judice'. This was nonsense, as there were no court proceedings pending, or even a police investigation.

'Dr X's first allegiance is to Janet. I can remember him being so patronising and the pure lack of help,' Pauline told me. 'They all knew Gordon Rowe had been banned from the premises, that he was accused of sexual abuse and that Janet was one of the 'favourites', but they all sat there and said they didn't know what the problem was. I saw Janet falling apart and there was nothing I could do to help her.'

After Desmond Tully left Longcare in 1990, Gordon Rowe became more prominent in Stefano Tunstell's care. Stefano's parents became increasingly concerned at how many drugs he was being fed, his weight loss, behavioural problems and incontinence.

Lidia, Stefano's mother, says Rowe was 'quite rude' in the spring of 1992 when they questioned the quantity of drugs Stefano was being given. At first, the drugs made him sleepy. Then the drugs were changed and he would become incredibly agitated. For the first time, he was wetting his bed. His parents' concerns increased when he returned home for a weekend visit, as he did every four or five weeks.

When he first moved to Stoke Place, Stefano had come home clean and shaved, but this weekend they were horrified at the change in their son. The slight, curly-haired young man was dressed in dirty, torn clothes. He was unshaven and appeared drawn and tense. He weighed just six-and-a-half stone. He had always been slim, but his weight had never before dropped below seven stone. Stefano spent hours pacing backwards and forwards around the house or just sitting in a chair, avoiding the hugs of his parents, rocking backwards and forwards, playing with a piece of paper. Before Stoke Place, he had had good table manners. 'He started to eat in a way which was terrible,' said Lidia. 'It was like an animal, it was so fast, and he was getting so thin.'

Before he moved to Longcare, Stefano had been on 1.5mg of Haloperidol, an anti-psychotic medication sometimes used in low doses to lessen some of the anxiety associated with autism.

By 1992, after moving to Longcare, the dose had increased to 20mg, four times a day. 'That was when we started to see he was very heavily drugged,' Lidia said.

In the following weeks, they became even more concerned. They had already noticed Stefano's incontinence, which had developed only since moving to Stoke Place. They contacted Surrey social services early that summer, but were told not to worry. Now Stefano returned home for another weekend visit, and his horrified mother noticed he was bleeding from the anus.

She told Stefano's social worker and a meeting at Longcare was finally set up in late October. Ray Cradock was there, as was Dr X, who had prescribed the higher dose. The Tunstells were handed a 'dreadful' report, written by Gordon Rowe. It described Stefano's inappropriate sexual behaviour, his habit of excitedly running into toilets and then running straight out again, and smearing himself with his own faeces. These were all signs that should have suggested that he had been sexually abused. Instead, they blamed Stefano.

Rowe's report accused the Tunstells of undermining Stefano's care. He threatened to take them to court. They were 'horrified' that their sensitive son was suddenly being labelled a 'sex maniac', and received no satisfactory explanation for the bleeding. Stefano's social worker later told the police that she felt Dr X 'had Longcare's interests at heart rather than his patient's'.

Lidia says they questioned Dr X about the excessive medication. He said he could 'give Stefano as many drugs as he wanted and he said he wasn't even giving him as many as he thought he really needed. He was really horrible,' said Lidia.

Stefano was removed from Longcare in January 1993. After a short spell at home, he spent five months at an assessment unit, where staff began to decrease his medication. He was also inspected by a police surgeon and a community nurse, who told the family his anus was 'full of scars'. But by this time, it was too long since the alleged abuse had occurred to draw any firm conclusions.

The Tunstells have since been told that Stefano may have suffered permanent kidney damage. They fear it was a result of years of over-medication.

I learned later that another family had sparked a similar reaction from Dr X after questioning excessive medication. They too had been concerned about the high levels of Haloperidol their son was on – 80 mgs a day – and sought advice from a learning disability consultant, who immediately cut it in half. But when concerns surfaced about their son's health soon afterwards – probably related to the excessive levels of medication – the GP reportedly punished them by refusing to visit him for 12 days. When he did finally see him, he put the dosage back up to 80 mgs. After leaving Stoke Place several months later, the young man's medication was quickly reduced to just 5 mgs, twice a day.

Rose Terry is another relative who had concerns about medication. She remembers her sister Linda becoming 'very quiet' at Stoke Place, and believes this was because of the drugs she was being given. She told police in 1997 how Linda's weight dropped from nine-and-a-half stone when she entered Stoke Place in 1991, to just six-and-a-half stone when she left in 1995.

After Linda left Longcare, her care workers and new GP began to reduce the levels of sedatives. She is now on a much lower dose. 'She is a completely different person now,' Rose told me.

The terms of reference of the Independent Longcare Inquiry did not cover the medical care provided at the homes. But Tom Burgner, who led the inquiry, told me he had been concerned.

In the annexe of the inquiry report, he included the concerns of Stefano's parents (without naming the GP). The annexe also says that a female resident 'was given a contraceptive by injection without her guardians' consent', while her guardian suspected that her dosage of sedative was too high and during visits was reduced 'without adverse reaction'. The annexe also states that another family also had concerns about medication, but once it was monitored away from Stoke Place by a consultant, the medication was 'reduced substantially'.

Dr Philippa Russell, one of Burgner's inquiry colleagues, remembers evidence concerning the GP. 'His collusion with the privacy, or the isolation, of the houses was, I think, very significant,' she told me. She highlighted his habit of visiting the residents at Stoke Place, rather than asking them to attend his surgery. This increased their isolation and made it much less likely that another health professional – such as a practice nurse or dietician – would spot a problem.

'There were a lot of criticisms of him among the local doctors,' she said. 'They were worried about how he always went to Longcare. He saw the residents personally, individually, when he visited the home, in a way that other people wouldn't. I think it was inconceivable that he would not have had his suspicions. He may have had difficulty getting evidence, but he must have had some idea of what was going on.'

It was not until October 2003 that I discovered that, in 1996, Det Supt Jon Bound had approached the General Medical Council (GMC) – which regulates doctors – with concerns about the possibility of 'substandard record-keeping and irresponsible prescribing' by Dr X. The GMC had considered this information under its 'fitness to practise' procedures, but 'decided that the allegations didn't raise an issue of serious professional misconduct'. The case was closed with no further investigation.

Bound, who led the Longcare police investigation, told me that he and his colleagues were 'concerned about some of the prescribing aspects of what he was doing. We informed the GMC of our concerns. There was nothing that we could do criminally or as part of an investigation against him. All we could do was bring it to the GMC's minds and let them decide whether they wanted to investigate it further. We were very concerned about how he had dealt with the people there and his prescribing – authorising prescriptions without even seeing patients.'

Bound's concerns were not mentioned by the GMC when, in November 1996, Gary Deacon's parents filed a complaint about the GP. They were concerned at the 'negligent' way Dr X had handled Gary's medical records between 1990 and 1996. In the course of an investigation into the GP's failure to act on a letter from an epilepsy specialist – which he explained away as the result of administrative difficulties at his surgery – it emerged that he had made just two brief entries in Gary's medical records over those six years.

Longcare staff, though, had drugged Gary with anti-psychotics prescribed by the GP. Gary's parents were horrified to arrive one afternoon and find him hardly conscious and 'zombyish'. They switched to a new GP, who reduced the medication, and Gary's condition gradually improved.

Dr X apparently told the GMC that he had 'made appropriate entries for the infrequent occasions that Gary required medical attention'. The Deacons disagreed. A GMC representative told the Deacons: 'Clearly, although I noted your comments in our telephone conversation of 23 April that he would have certainly had 'treatment' more than twice in a five year period, the GMC is not in a position to comment on whether Gary's treatment over this period only necessitated two entries.' The GMC reiterated its 'guidance on the importance of keeping accurate patient records' to Dr X, 'with a view to his future practice'. But it took no further action.

Janet Ward's aunt, June Raybaud, a barrister, wanted the GMC to carry out a more thorough investigation. From the day the Longcare regime was exposed in 1994, she was suspicious of the role Dr X had played. As the years passed, she became ever more certain that he had failed his patients. In 2000, she contacted the GMC with her concerns.

By January 2001, the GMC was liaising with Nicola Harney, Janet Ward's lawyer. They told Harney in a letter that, because of their earlier 'investigation' – following the concerns raised by Jon Bound – they could not look at allegations of poor record-keeping and irresponsible prescribing again 'unless we receive significant new evidence'.

But it continued: 'If there was sexual or physical abuse and neglect and ill-treatment of the residents and... the principal medical carer [the GP] failed to act, then this would in principle seem like a new allegation as compared with those which concentrated on substandard record-keeping and irresponsible prescribing. There must be a duty for a doctor to report mistreatment of residents in a nursing home.'

By now, the Longcare families had obtained legal aid to sue the GP for negligence, and Harney had commissioned medical experts to write reports about the GP's treatment of Stefano and Michael. (Harney and her colleagues eventually focused the legal action on Buckinghamshire County Council, as their best opportunity for securing compensation.)

In December 2001, Harney sent a mass of documents to the GMC, including police statements, the inspection unit report, the medical expert's report into Dr X's treatment of Michael, and copies of Michael's medical records, as well as reports by learning disability consultants on the psychiatric trauma experienced by 10 of the Longcare residents. She also told the GMC it could see all her other clients' medical records (I believe the GMC never took up this offer).

In March 2003, the GMC wrote to Raybaud to confirm that the GMC's preliminary proceedings committee was considering her allegations. The committee had read the report written by Harney's medical expert into the care given by Dr X to Michael. The letter noted that 'the lack of medical records was his most stringent criticism of [the Longcare GP] but that he also had concerns with regard to prescribing and had concluded that [the GP's] practice was probably below what would be expected of a general practitioner'.

These conclusions, though, contrasted with those of a consultant psychiatrist in learning disability, Dr Peter Carpenter, commissioned by Harney to write a report on the trauma Michael had suffered at Longcare. Carpenter concluded that Michael had been subjected to 'the dangerous use of excessive medication', and noted the GP's 'very sparse' notes and 'little evidence that he was regularly reviewing their use'. Carpenter said the GP had noted that Michael should be put on a daily dose of 80mg of Haloperidol, for which a normal dose was 5mg. This later rose as high as 100mg a day. Carpenter noted that Michael was on 'some of the highest doses I have seen used' of Largactil and Haloperidol. Michael was also on Lithium, and Carpenter says there was 'no evidence that the Lithium was monitored, which if true is malpractice as Lithium can easily kill, particularly in combination with high dose neuroleptics [anti-psychotics, such as Haloperidol and Largactil].'

He concluded: 'All prescribing guidelines appear to have been broken, yet no psychiatrist was called in to oversee the medication.' He noted that, in 15 years, he had seen only one patient who was on a higher dose of medication and this patient 'was behaviourally disturbed due to being routinely assaulted on the ward by other residents at staff request'.

His concerns closely matched those of Michael's new psychiatrist, who told staff at his new home, the day after he left Longcare, to stop the Haloperidol, as 'it is bad practice to administer large doses of Haloperidol to someone who is on lithium as the two drugs in combination is known to lead to brain damage'.

The following week, the psychiatrist stated in another letter that he was 'very concerned about having virtually no medical information regarding this patient'. The following year, he wrote to police to state that he had been able to reduce the amount of medication 'without any difficulties. We are still reducing the medication at regular intervals... we have not seen any evidence of a mental illness.'

The GMC told Raybaud that it was 'concerned' at the evidence it had seen of high levels of prescribing and the 'issues around the medical records' but 'noted that these had not been included in the allegations'. It seemed to have overlooked that it had told Harney in January 2001 that it would be unable to consider allegations of record-keeping and irresponsible prescribing due to its earlier 'investigation'. It was not Raybaud who had failed to include the allegations in her complaint, but the GMC that had removed them from consideration.

The letter said the committee had adjourned the case to decide whether it could, after all, consider these issues.

Four months later, the GMC wrote to Raybaud again. The letter noted some of the criticisms made by Harney's medical expert, in his report on the care provided to Michael by Dr X, but claimed that the GP was not the only GP to visit Stoke Place, a statement strongly disputed later by former Longcare staff.

The letter also pointed out that the GP was 'probably given very little opportunity to see what was happening in the home and could not necessarily be criticised for having failed to pick up any signs of abuse' and that the GP's representatives had 'pointed out' that 'the Inquiry Report details how other organisations failed to discover any evidence of neglect or ill treatment even when they were specifically conducting investigations with these points in mind'.

The committee said it had decided, in the light of legal advice, not to allow the addition of the 'extra' allegations concerning record-keeping and irresponsible prescribing. The letter concluded: 'It further determined that in the light of the inquiry report and the police investigations, there was insufficient evidence and no real prospect of further, sufficient evidence emerging in support of the allegations for serious professional misconduct to be established in this case.'

But it also claimed that 'there had been no criticism of [the GP] by the Police or the Independent Inquiry', which was quite simply not true. The GMC had, after all, informed Nicola

Harney that Thames Valley Police had approached it in 1996 with concerns about 'possible substandard record-keeping and irresponsible prescribing' by Dr X.

Apart from contacting the GP, the GMC launched no investigations of its own. It did not even contact the members of the Longcare inquiry to ensure that it was not overlooking evidence. For the third time, it had failed to investigate the medical care offered at Longcare.

The GMC did pass its decision to Slough Primary Care Trust, which was at the time responsible for Slough's GPs. But the following year, the GP resigned from his practice, and the trust was forced to abandon any attempts to monitor his work through an action plan.

The trust's chief executive, Mike Attwood, told me in 2004: 'We now have a GP who is no longer around to be held to account. The regulatory framework just lets us all down. The formal position for us, which is really uncomfortable, is that the GMC have not investigated anything. The GMC ought to be held to account for why they decided not to pursue a hearing. And there is still an issue of what should be done at a national level when doctors of concern are not formally investigated and just move from PCT patch to PCT patch. Clearly, he was a GP we knew we needed to work with to ensure ourselves that he was working to improve certain aspects of his practice. Now he is in limbo.'

By 2010, Slough PCT had been subsumed into Berkshire East PCT. The trust told me the action plan had been 'led by the GMC' and 'related to personal as well as professional issues', although it had 'not been possible to find out what happened to this plan'.

The GP had started working in neighbouring Surrey in 2006. A Berkshire East spokesman told me that it worked within 'a tight statutory framework', and that although the secretary of state for health could investigate a GP or refer them to the GMC, a PCT 'does not have the right to strike off a doctor – this is the role of the GMC'. He declined to comment when asked whether the PCT was happy with this national regulatory system.

When I contacted Surrey Primary Care Trust in late 2010, a spokesman eventually confirmed that the former Longcare GP had moved there, was on its 'performers list' of GPs registered to practice in the area and was practicing as a GP somewhere in Surrey, although he would not say where. But he admitted that there was no action plan in place, although the trust had been aware that Dr X had had a 'conditional inclusion' on the Berkshire East performers list, that allegations had been made against him to the GMC, and that an action plan had been in place in Slough, although he suggested that the terms of that action plan had been 'fulfilled' before he left Berkshire.

Over the years, I have made repeated calls to the General Medical Council's (GMC) press office about Dr X. There was usually no comment, a typical response in such cases unless and until it decides to hold a public inquiry through its professional conduct committee.

The latest response came in November 2010 from Niall Dickson, the chief executive, after I informed the GMC that I had seen a huge amount of evidence that suggested the Longcare GP was not fit to practice, and questioned its lack of action. In reply, Dickson said the GMC had 'looked into concerns that were raised' in 1996 and so it would be 'inappropriate for us to now make further comment'. The GMC showed not the slightest interest in my evidence.

Dr X himself has declined to comment when I have approached him either directly or through his employers on at least five occasions, the latest early in 2011.

June Raybaud says she eventually 'lost heart with the GMC' and the obstacles it was putting up to a proper investigation, but is still 'outraged' at its failure to take action.

'This doctor apparently saw them all every week,' she told me. 'He could have noticed how they were losing weight… a lot of the women had [vaginal] discharges and the men had bleeding from the anus. A lot of people had similar things wrong with them. They were obviously suffering from malnutrition, boils and things wrong with their feet and teeth. He could see how poorly they were dressed, how their hygiene was bad and he never did anything about it. He really didn't care. It didn't matter what Gordon Rowe did tell him or didn't tell him. He was in a position to know.

'For a trained doctor, all that was going on there was so obvious. I always thought that was the biggest scandal of all.'

Fiona Mactaggart is also deeply concerned about the GMC's failure to conduct a proper investigation into the care provided by Dr X at Longcare. In January 2011, she wrote to the GMC, stating that the documents I had shown her 'raise very serious issues about his fitness to practice', and asking it to investigate. The GMC wrote back three weeks later to say that 'as a result of our previous consideration of this matter' it would 'not… be appropriate' to open another investigation into Dr X.

Because of its refusal to answer questions, serious and troubling questions remain about how the GMC dealt with the complaints about Dr X.

Why did it not interview the members of the Longcare inquiry? Why did it apparently fail to take up Harney's offer to forward copies of her clients' medical records? Why did it apparently only speak to representatives of the GP and not the GP himself? Why did the GMC state in its July 2003 letter to June Raybaud that the police had made no criticism of the GP, when Thames Valley Police had approached the GMC in 1996 with concerns about the doctor? Why did it not launch a full and proper investigation into Dr X's care of the Longcare residents when Thames Valley Police passed on its concerns in 1996? Or when the Deacons lodged their complaint later that year? Or when Raybaud lodged hers in 2000?

The final question the GMC needs to answer is whether it would have been so shockingly arrogant and complacent in dealing with a complaint made about a GP's treatment of patients who didn't happen to have learning difficulties.

Chapter Twenty

Gordon Rowe

'Brent Martin, a young man from Sunderland with learning difficulties, was about to start a new job as a landscape gardener and live independently for the first time in his life... Mr Martin had already bought new bedding for his flat and was looking forward to working and spending free time with his new girlfriend. Instead, on 23rd August 2007, he was viciously attacked and murdered for a five pound bet... Before his death he was partially stripped and chased through the streets. He was attacked by his killers in four different locations over a period of several hours, during which time he pleaded with his killers to stop hurting him.'

Getting Away with Murder: disabled people's experiences of hate crime in the UK; Katharine Quarmby/Disability Now, UK Disabled People's Council and Scope; August 2008

Gordon's sister, Maureen – deluded as only a sibling can be – once confided to a member of Longcare staff that she struggled to find an explanation for how her brother had changed over the years he ran Stoke Place. 'I can remember days when Gordon wasn't like this. On family holidays, when we were younger, Gordon would always have people with mental handicaps around him,' she said. 'He used to round them up like a sheepdog. When he opened his first home in Somerset, it was like a lifelong ambition for him – he was such a caring person. And when he opened Longcare, he brought all the family along and told them he wanted it to be a happy home and he wanted us all to work there.'

Maureen – who almost certainly didn't know then about the allegations from The Old Rectory, and, even earlier, from Sussex – believed money and power changed her brother. Gordon pushed his family away as the cash flooded in. His brother Ted was forced to take legal action to recover money he invested in Longcare. In the end, he is said to have received £14,000 and a new Toyota Landcruiser.

Many of the staff knew about the annual holiday at Butlin's, when Gordon had locked himself in the bathroom for three days. One care worker described later how Gordon broke down and cried when a female council inspector mentioned him retiring from Longcare.

But Rowe had been abusing children – and probably adults with learning difficulties as well – since at least 1969, and probably even earlier. Was there something in his past that could explain his apparent need for control, sexual domination and violence? Or was he able to commit such antisocial and violent acts without feeling any guilt whatsoever? Was he, in fact, a sociopath?

A letter Gordon Rowe wrote to a neighbour in Harrington Close nearly four months after the scandal was exposed provided the clearest evidence of the pressure he was under, but was also, of course, soaked in deceit.

He described how he and his family had returned home after three months away, 'following the horrific allegations so luridly and sensationally printed in the local and national Press'.

'There is a completely contradictory story to this situation but, right from the start, we were told to 'shut up' and 'make no comment whatsoever' and, thus, we have been unable to put our side of things,' he wrote. 'Certainly, our 'absence' and 'silence' implies guilt to most people but our legal advisers told us – and we firmly believe it – that the Press would <u>not</u> have published anything that was contrary to the story that they had told or of the image that they had portrayed of us.'

He claimed that none of the allegations had been witnessed by a second person and that if something had been going on, the care workers who left Longcare would have reported them to the authorities. He also denied intimidating his employees.

'Considerable 'contra-evidence' has been submitted to the Police but it is **still essential at this time** that these facts are not relayed to the Press who will again have a field-day by re-opening their coverage. Our opportunity to hit back will occur on completion of the present Police enquirey (sic),' he wrote.

Rowe had lost none of his cunning. He was trying to portray himself and Angela as innocent victims of a conspiracy. 'I am writing to you and placing my trust in your discretion and integrity <u>not</u> to inform the Press, but to give even just one Resident of Harrington Close the firm assurance that they do not have 'monsters in their midst'. We would dearly love for you to visit us to hear (and see) the other side of this appalling story after which, we feel sure, we may receive a little support that we so desperately need.

'We are living in a nightmare – curtains drawn, lights out, etc, and we are not certain what sort of any long-term effect it may have on Ben who we had to take out of school for the whole of last term. His Headmaster, fortunately, has been 100 per cent supportive and has seen, he says, the same thing happen to Teachers as is happening to us.'

21 February 1995. Harrington Close, Windsor

I pulled up alongside the kerb and looked across the road at the large, detached, red-brick house. The graffiti had been cleaned from the large French window. All the curtains were drawn.

For so long, Gordon Rowe had been merely a shadowy form, described second-hand by people who knew him. There were so many unanswered questions. Did he really believe he was innocent? Why had he done what he had done? And how would he behave when confronted?

I walked across the road, up the tarmac driveway and along the path to Rowe's front door. I knocked twice. After a couple of seconds, there were footsteps. The door opened. The squat, white-haired figure of Gordon Rowe was standing in the doorway, wearing an open-necked shirt and blue sweater. For a couple of seconds, my mind went blank.

'Mr Rowe, I'm from the Slough Observer. I wonder if....'

'Oh, no, no...'

The door slammed shut.

'Mr Rowe, have you got any comment about the serious allegations you're facing?'

Silence. That was to be my second and final interview with Gordon Rowe.

Six months later, Rowe tried to kill himself.

The previous day, 7 August, he had arrived at Maidenhead police station, confident he could talk his way out of the allegations, as he had done before. But he had a surprise waiting for him.

It was a long-arranged appointment. The police team had spent months investigating his background and interviewing witnesses, and they told Rowe about the thousands of pages of evidence they had compiled.

Madeleine Stewart was one of the officers who interviewed him. She told me: 'Our aim was to interview him in some depth and he indicated that that was what he wanted. We started the first day very slowly and went all through his background, and that took all day. He was polite and articulate, but quite old by this time and, like him or not, he had been through an extremely hard time. He had been hounded from his house, his whole life had been totally devastated, and obviously that had an effect on him.'

After eight hours questioning, he was released again on police bail, ready to continue the interview the next day. But, instead of returning home to 12 Harrington Close – or Harrington House, as the upwardly-mobile Angela called it – Rowe drove the two hours to Brighton, where he had friends and Angela had family. He stopped on the way to buy a jar of sleeping pills and some alcohol, and checked into a hotel.

Angela was distraught when he failed to return home. The two of them had pledged to carry out a suicide pact if either of them failed to clear their names. She phoned Maidenhead police station in hysterics and said her husband was missing and might have killed himself. A warrant was issued for his arrest.

Gordon Rowe was eventually found in a hotel room with a suicide note and a half-empty bottle of pills by his side. One Sussex police officer later described it as a 'half-hearted attempt to kill himself'. Rowe was arrested and taken to hospital.

He was admitted soon afterwards to the Cardinal Clinic in Windsor for a psychiatric evaluation and daily treatment. A few days later, neighbours in Harrington Close noticed a delivery of 12 tea-chests. Gordon and Angela had decided to flee to Crowthorne. Rowe was admitted to Fairmile Hospital in Cholsey, and later transferred to a hospital in Reading for outpatient treatment.

As Rowe continued to receive treatment for 'depression and anxiety', Det Supt Bound made repeated requests, through his solicitor, to continue the police interview. His psychiatrist repeatedly said he believed he was not fit to be questioned.

Five months later, Rowe tried to kill himself again, this time at home. The police only found out at the subsequent trial of his wife.

Eventually, Bound conceded defeat. Early in March, he rang Rowe's solicitors and told them that Gordon and Angela Rowe were to be charged. He also called the solicitors of Desmond Tully and Lorraine Field. Tully, who now ran a successful residential home in Devon, and Field, who worked as a receptionist in Slough, would be charged with ill-treatment and neglect. Angela Rowe would face similar charges, plus one of indecent assault against a male resident. But most of the charges were against Gordon Rowe, who was to be accused of three rapes and several indecent assaults and offences of ill-treatment and neglect. Bound said he could have been charged with 'hundreds' of offences. He told Rowe's solicitor that his client should attend Maidenhead police station on Monday 18 March.

On the evening of 17 March, Gordon and Angela visited Nigel and his family at their new home in Windsor. Nigel would later say that his dad had seemed happier than he had for some months. The two of them spent the evening using Nigel's telescope and discussing astronomy. At about 8.30pm, Gordon and Angela returned home to Crowthorne. They stayed up until early the next morning, discussing their life and talking about their grandchildren. Angela finally went to bed, leaving Gordon alone.

Angela woke the next morning and realised her husband was not next to her in bed. She ran downstairs and into the kitchen. On the table was a note, addressed to her, Nigel and Ben.

A little earlier that morning, at 5.45am, a man walking his dog had seen a Ford Granada parked at the side of Devil's Highway, a rough track that led off one of the main roads into Crowthorne. In the front seat, a stocky, white-haired man sat asleep, his head lolling to one side. The car had been parked back from the track, in a lay-by. As the dog-walker approached the car, he realised the man was slumped against the door, the engine was still running and a hose-pipe was dangling through the car window.

Rowe was already dead. The car is believed to have belonged to one of Angela's brothers.

The spot Rowe had chosen to kill himself was within sight of the walls of Broadmoor Hospital, and just a few hundred yards from the house in Crowthorne High Street where he and his brothers and sisters had grown up.

I walked up the gravel driveway past Nigel's red Ferrari. The house appeared empty, but I knocked anyway. No reply. I knocked again and peered through the glass panel, but saw nothing but an empty hallway. Stepping back, I looked up at the first-floor windows. Curtains were drawn across every one.

I turned and walked back down the driveway and across the road to my car. Just as I was settling into the front seat, a people-carrier appeared in my wing mirror. It slowed as it approached the bend, and turned into the driveway. Sitting in the front seat was Nigel Rowe.

I recrossed the road and walked back towards the house. Nigel was climbing out of his car as I approached. He stopped just a pace or two from his car, waiting, but not looking at me.

'Nigel, I wondered if there was anything you would like to say about your father's death,' I said, as I approached.

He looked at me for the first time, his face red. 'You've got a nerve coming here. Leave now. Get out of here.' He stepped a pace towards me.

'I wanted to give you a chance to say something about your father.'

He paused, and there was the crunch of gravel as he rocked slightly back on his heels. He took a breath. 'I'm sorry. It's been a difficult week. I was thinking of releasing some kind of statement to the press. OK. What I would like to say is that the intense press pressure had a direct bearing on my father's death. Led by yourself, unfortunately. He maintained his innocence in a suicide note. Never once in two years had he ever had one allegation put to him formally, either by Bucks County Council or by Thames Valley Police, and really I think the pressure over the last three years was just intolerable. It was too much to bear. Another thing he referred to was the Dunblane tragedy, and he thinks he is going onto a better world than the one he left behind.'

I forced myself to say nothing, to keep writing.

'He had not been charged with anything, but he did have a pre-arranged meeting planned yesterday with the police. His brother, Ted, died nearly a year ago to the day and he had just buried another brother two weeks ago, the third in 14 months.'

He paused. 'He had been tried and convicted by the press and you have to shoulder some of the responsibility.'

I wasn't paying attention to his accusations – that would come later – just concentrating on my shorthand. 'Have you had any reaction to his death?' I asked.

'Of course, he will be greatly missed. Tributes are pouring in from family and friends. The funeral will be a private affair.' The words kept tumbling out, all the months and years of frustration – and maybe guilt, too – released. 'He was very rational. The letter was very rational. He was not disturbed and the balance of his mind was not disturbed. A lot of the contributing causes were that for three years he had never once had an allegation put to him. I think it was the intense press speculation and media attention that had a direct bearing on his death.'

As I scrawled the final few words, he took three steps forward until he was a foot or so from my face. He leaned even closer and whispered: 'So, well done. I hope you feel proud of yourself,' and he reached out and patted me on the shoulder.

As it turned out, the funeral was not a private affair. There was a small knot of uninvited journalists waiting outside the church, although no-one from the Slough Observer, as we had decided our presence could inflame the atmosphere. Even so, one of Angela's brothers chased after a couple of photographers who were trying to take pictures of his sister.

Six of the Longcare residents were brought to the funeral in a minibus, including at least one of Gordon's Girls. The funeral was told they had come to 'mourn' Gordon because 'they all loved him'. The church was packed.

Angela had been threatening to kill herself and was – according to one acquaintance who attended the funeral – as 'thin as a rake'. As Gordon's coffin was lowered into the ground, she tried to jump into the grave after him. 'I think she was genuinely upset,' one of the mourners told me later. 'At that point, she thought she was going to inherit everything.'

After the funeral, at the wake held at a social club in Crowthorne, several of Gordon's friends from his national service in the RAF loudly 'sung his praises'. 'Everyone there loved him to death,' the mourner said. 'They praised him up to the hilt. There was nothing detrimental said about him at all.' There was no mention of the serious allegations that had been made against him.

Angela said she was seeing a counsellor because of depression and was concerned at the impact of the police investigation and Gordon's death on their son, Ben. But she made it clear that she still loved her husband and that the allegations made against them were 'all lies', invented by care workers who 'stabbed us in the back'.

A month after Gordon Rowe's death, a few reporters were almost the only witnesses to his inquest at Windsor Guildhall, just a few yards from the entrance to Windsor Castle. There was little evidence read out by coroner Robert Wilson. Frustratingly, Wilson only repeated extracts from the note Angela Rowe had found in her kitchen on the morning of her husband's death:

'Monday, 18 March, 1.40am.

My dearest Angela, Ben and Nigel,

the fact that I have disappeared and the discovery of this letter will immediately alert you as to what my intentions are and, by the time you read it...

It is a fact that I have been psychiatrically ill. I was first diagnosed last August. For many months and since then I have been receiving in-patient treatment for most of that time. I have been depressed and anxious...

You know well my belief in God and a new life after death and for that reason, and I am sure it has worried you, I do not fear death.

Your ever-loving husband and father,

Gordon.'

Wilson looked down at his notes and put the letter on top of a small pile of documents. He looked up at the three reporters, and said: 'I think he intended to take his own life.'

*

Incredibly, even more disturbing evidence would later emerge about Rowe's Longcare regime.

Dr Philippa Russell, one of the members of the Longcare inquiry, was told that Rowe had been running a prostitution ring from Stoke Place. 'I'm not saying I have evidence that there was an organised prostitution racket. You couldn't prove any of these things, but the allegations are such that clearly something happened. We had this from ex-members of staff, but we were also told it by a number of people from local voluntary organisations.'

Janet Ward, I remembered, had spoken to her sister Pauline about being taken out of the home at night and being put into a van by strange men. Other women had told similar stories.

'Of course, these rumours can roll like snowballs,' said Russell. 'All one can say is that there were worrying allegations and it seems extremely unlikely that there was not a strong element of truth about people coming into the house in the evening. A lot of the residents were clear that there were strangers, and some of the younger women say they were taken out of the house.

'I heard quite a lot about the people in the night, because of talking to people in their rooms. I was told how pleased everybody was to have locks put on their doors. There was a dog living there and one man said to me that he used to encourage the dog to sleep in his room at night, because then if anybody came in, the dog would immediately jump up.'

Russell believes the prostitution ring connected with Rowe's film-making hobby, and the suspicion that he was making and selling pornographic videos. Indeed, there were reports in The Independent that equipment capable of making multiple copies of videos was found by police when they raided Rowe's properties. 'It is unthinkable actually that these things weren't going on,' she said, 'knowing what one knows about paedophiles and Rowe's interests.'

Jon Bound, who led the Longcare police investigation, also told me that he believed Rowe had been producing pornographic films. 'I think there was something going on with the pornography,' he said. He believed Rowe had plenty of time to get rid of the evidence before his properties were raided by police.

Russell believes there are still associates of Rowe who worry that, one day, the role they played in this part of his regime will be exposed. 'I should think Gordon Rowe was engaged with a lot of other people,' she told me, 'and that there are a fair number of people down in Buckinghamshire who are still a bit shaky about what might come out.'

*

How was it possible to reconcile the two Gordon Rowes? There was the Gordon Rowe who was an influential and well-regarded member of the community, the centre of attention at every party, the sociable and amicable 'happy-go-lucky fellow', who wanted to create a 'happy home' for disabled people and could boast an impeccable CV and glowing references from senior social workers. And then there was the other Gordon Rowe: the rapist, the violent bully, the man driven by power and greed and lust to take advantage of people placed in vulnerable situations.

Maybe his violent thirst for sexual perversion, fuelled by a need to dominate and bully those weaker than himself, was fed by something that happened to him many years before. Maybe not. Either way, he was unwilling to control these urges. He was an arrogant man and claimed he didn't fear death. But if you scraped away the bullying veneer of arrogance and bombosity, he was weak. He knew he would not be able to maintain his persona of confidence, power, charisma and popularity through a lengthy and humiliating trial, and the resulting prison sentence. And that must be why Gordon Rowe took the easy way out.

Chapter Twenty-One

The Trial

'The Crown Prosecution Service (CPS) is often failing to allow people with mental health problems to give evidence in court, according to an inquiry by a committee of MPs. The Commons justice committee said in its report that it was 'concerned' to hear evidence that the CPS could be reluctant to recognise that people with mental health problems can be credible witnesses. The committee also heard evidence that the CPS was failing to identify thousands of witnesses – including many with mental health conditions, learning difficulties or other impairments – who could benefit from 'special measures', such as being allowed to give their evidence via a video link.'

Disability News Service, 6 August 2010

If Gordon Rowe's family and friends were devastated by his suicide, so were the police officers who had spent 18 months building a case against him. With Rowe's death, 90 per cent of their work was rendered useless.

They now had to pick up the pieces of the investigation and consider whether there was anyone else they could prosecute. Bound met the Crown's QC, Jonathan Caplan, and his assistant, Amanda Pinto. They decided to charge Angela Rowe, Desmond Tully and Lorraine Field, and also consider prosecuting Longcare.

Bound was disappointed when the director of public prosecutions ruled out charges against Rowe's company. 'We wanted to prove that out of the misery inflicted on 70 residents, Gordon Rowe had made a lot of money. We thought that if we were to prosecute the company and fail, we could push for a change in the law,' he said.

A Crown Prosecution Service spokeswoman told me several years ago that there was no law that could have been used to prosecute Longcare. This was not entirely true, as I was to discover later. 'Criminal law is all about individuals, not companies, apart from some very specific areas,' she said. So Rowe's company, which made huge profits out of his abusive regime, escaped any criminal sanction.

The trial of Angela Rowe, Lorraine Field and Desmond Tully at Kingston Crown Court – which began on 14 April 1997 – was always going to be something of an anti-climax. Because of Gordon Rowe's suicide, the jury would hear nothing of the sexual assaults and rapes and the most brutal aspects of the Longcare regime. His death also meant that none of the residents would be called to give evidence. Although it undoubtedly saved some of the survivors a distressing experience, it also deprived them of the right to have their day in court, to have their voices heard.

The trial lasted a month. The jury relied mostly on prosecution evidence from ex-members of staff and expert witnesses. There was little evidence submitted by the defence. Apart from the defendants' pleas of innocence, there were several character witnesses who praised Desmond Tully's residential home in Devon, and a couple of healthcare professionals who testified to Longcare's fine qualities. None of Gordon's former police friends, though, could find the time to make it to Kingston, although it had been rumoured that one police officer might give evidence on behalf of Angela Rowe.

In the end, after several days of jury deliberation, Angela Rowe was found guilty of two counts of ill-treatment and two of neglect. Although the police had also charged her with indecently assaulting a male resident, the prosecution had decided not to complicate the court case, and asked for the charge to remain on the court's files.

Rowe described herself in court as nothing more than 'a glorified housekeeper', but the jury didn't believe her story. They heard how she shouted abuse at residents and ordered Jackie to eat meals outside as a punishment; pulled another woman with Down's syndrome down a flight of stairs by her hair; and 'wilfully neglected' two residents by depriving them of toiletries to save money, while she and Gordon siphoned hundreds of thousands of pounds in profits every year to pay for holiday homes in Florida and the south of France and a luxury motor-cruiser.

Rowe cut a sad figure. She was taking Prozac for depression and other drugs to combat anorexia. Halfway through the trial, she escaped with a warning from the judge after allegedly confronting a witness outside the court. She had marched up to the woman, a former Longcare care worker, and told her: 'I'm going to fucking kill you, you fucking bitch. You're a fucking liar.'

Lorraine Field was found guilty of three counts of ill-treatment. The court was told how Field screamed at residents, hit those who annoyed her and took part in the punishments meted out to Jackie. A fourth charge, an allegation that she had sat on Janet Ward and poured jugs of cold water over her head to 'calm her down' was left on the files, after the jury failed to reach a verdict.

Tully was found guilty of a single count of ill-treatment. The jury had listened as a former member of staff described how he forcefully administered an enema to a middle-aged woman and slapped her on her bare buttock when she tried to struggle. He was cleared of punching two other residents, with a fourth charge left on the files after the jury again failed to reach a verdict.

Four further charges – two against Rowe and one each against Tully and Field – had been dismissed earlier in the case on the orders of the judge, because of a lack of evidence.

12 May 1997. Court Six, Kingston Crown Court

Angela Rowe's eyes appeared glazed as she walked between the young man – a friend of the Rowe family who had supported her throughout the trial – and her solicitor towards the court exit. To her right, several of the victims' relatives in the public gallery were on their feet, staring at her, but she didn't seem to notice them, either. She brushed past the small group of reporters and court officials and walked through the light wood double-doors. Her solicitor held one door open for her as he searched her eyes for a reaction to the guilty verdict.

'Angela, are you OK?' he said.

She sat in the chair, staring at the wall. Outside the door, police officers, lawyers, journalists and relatives of victims milled around in the corridor, discussing the guilty verdict.

Her legal team waited for her to respond, but still she sat there, not responding.

'Angela?' He repeated her name, louder. 'Angela?'

She didn't move. Then, in a high-pitched voice, the voice of a pleading child, she asked: 'Where's Gordon?' She looked around, seeming to search for a face that wasn't there. 'Where's Gordon?'

When Duncan Thomson, Angela Rowe's solicitor, visited her at home later that day, he found her apparently still in a condition of deep shock. Her barrister, Stephen Kramer QC, later told the court that she was 'alternately gibbering as if she was a little girl', asking for her dead husband, and telling those around her she 'didn't like the sound of doors slamming'. Some of those who know her well say this was clearly part of an attempt to wring sympathy from the judge. But one thing was certain. She knew she was about to lose her liberty.

The following day, the judge excused her from attending court because of the state of her mental health. Two days later, police officers had to break down her front door after claims that she had threatened to kill herself. They were soon able to confirm that she was safe and well.

Four weeks later, Lorraine Field was jailed for 15 months. Desmond Tully escaped with a fine. Angela Rowe was jailed for two-and-a-half years, despite Kramer telling the judge his client would rather die than suffer the shame of a prison sentence. He claimed she had been 'heavily influenced' by her husband. A family friend had told her barrister that his family had been looking after her and had been forced to keep razor blades and pills away from her in case she tried to kill herself. The court heard that Angela claimed there was now just £3,000 left of the fortune she and Gordon had built up through Longcare, despite the sale of Stoke Green House and two Florida properties. How she had managed to spend what must have been far more than a million pounds in just three years was not explained to the court.

Angela broke down in tears as she was led away by a security guard to begin her sentence in Holloway prison. Judge John Baker told her that her behaviour was 'disgraceful' and something that 'no civilised society can overlook'.

Despite the judge's words, Angela was transferred almost immediately from Holloway to a hospital, so she could be treated for her apparent mental health condition. But one acquaintance insists that she was not suicidal at all, and claims she was fabricating her condition to avoid prison. 'She was definitely not suicidal,' says the acquaintance, who has known her for many years. 'She was in the mental home and she was laughing and joking.' With Gordon having so many friends with expertise in the mental health field, it is not inconceivable that she had been coached in how to con the judge and the prison authorities.

'Angie was a bloody good actress,' the acquaintance says. 'She manipulated them. It was really cushy in there. She purposefully threatened to kill herself so she would get a lighter sentence.'

After sentencing the trio, Judge Baker demanded a change in the law. He said the Mental Health Act had provided him with inadequate sentencing powers and there was an urgent need for a parliamentary review of the relevant laws. The Slough Observer called for an inquiry into the role of Bucks County Council, a wish granted several weeks later thanks to the newly-elected Slough MP, Fiona Mactaggart. The following year, Rowe and Field would fail in their appeals against their sentences, while Tully would fail in his appeal against his conviction. Tully's failed appeal would mean that he would be banned from running his own care home in Devon, the home he had bought with a loan from Gordon Rowe in 1990.

Among the relatives of the survivors, there were some half-hearted expressions of satisfaction or relief, but no whoops of triumph. Several of them, including Janet Ward's sister, Pauline, had attended much of the trial and heard for themselves the evidence of former members of staff. It had been a deeply distressing experience for Pauline, particularly because the jury had been unable to reach a verdict on a charge that Lorraine

Field had ill-treated Janet by pouring jugs of water over her head.

Barbara McCarthy, whose son Shaun was abused at the homes, and who was at the court throughout the trial with her husband Terry, said after the sentencing: 'I'm glad they got sent down. They deserved it, regardless of how long it is. Now they might know what it is like to be locked away for hours and days on end, like some of the residents were.'

June Raybaud, Janet Ward's aunt, added: 'I think the judge took into account the seriousness of the offences and the fact that these people were so vulnerable.'

Jon Bound, who led the police investigation, also welcomed the sentences and paid tribute to the police officers whose painstaking work led to the convictions. He mentioned by name the trio who had been at court during the trial, acting as assistants for the barristers, and soothing the nerves of prosecution witnesses – Madeleine Stewart, Cathy Woodliffe and Denise Jenkins. It was, he said, 'one of the most complex investigations undertaken by Thames Valley Police, but was necessary to protect some of the most vulnerable members of our community'.

But he warned: 'If these matters are happening in Slough, then they are occurring elsewhere in the country, and we have already been contacted by other forces involved in similar investigations.' He called for new legislation, with tighter inspection and registration guidelines. 'Those involved,' he said, 'should not be allowed to make vast profits at the expense of other people's misery.'

Despite the transfer from prison, Angela was still in secure accommodation. When her mother died, soon after the trial, she was taken to the church in handcuffs by two escorts. She had the handcuffs taken off to allow her to sit at the front of the church with her family, but she was cuffed again afterwards as she was taken back to the hospital.

But there was perhaps some measure of justice. Angela would later tell friends that Gordon had betrayed her. She had expected him to leave his money to her in his will. Instead, he left most of it to his son, Nigel, while she didn't receive a penny.

She railed at her former husband and called him a 'coward'. 'We were going to do it together,' she told friends. 'We had a pact. But he went and did it on his own and left me to take all the blame.' She claimed she had been a 'scapegoat' and that Gordon was solely responsible for the abuse at the Longcare homes.

Chapter Twenty-Two

Justice for Longcare Survivors

'A project to set up the first hate crime reporting centres in Wales has seen an immediate sharp increase in reports of offences against people with learning difficulties. Torfaen People First – which is run by people with learning difficulties – set up the reporting centres through a partnership with Gwent police, with Home Office funding. Seven centres across Torfaen – a county borough in south-east Wales – now have staff trained to identify disability hate crime and support the victim to record and report offences. Just five weeks into the scheme, there have already been four reports of hate crime made by people with learning difficulties. This compares with six in the whole of the previous year. Two were reports of verbal abuse and two were complaints of harassment. All four are being investigated by police.'

Disability News Service, 13 May 2010

In the months following the first media reports on the Longcare scandal, relatives of the victims slowly began to make contact with each other. They linked up through the charities which made public statements, such as Voice UK and Mencap, through contacts they had made during visits to the homes in years gone by, and through stories that appeared in the press.

The relatives' anger eventually surfaced in a pledge to take legal action against Longcare, the Rowes, Thames Valley Police, Buckinghamshire County Council, Dr X and the local authorities that had placed residents at the homes. Their sons and daughters were going to need specialist care in the years ahead to cope with the after-effects of Longcare, so why shouldn't the organisations responsible for both causing and failing to halt the abuse help pay for this care? Such compensation would also be a recognition that what had been done was wrong. It might even act as a warning shot across the bows of other councils, police forces, and residential homes.

Although a tiny handful of relatives maintained a blinkered loyalty towards Longcare, most were horrified and heartbroken by what had happened, and relieved to find others in similar positions they could go to for support.

One of the first relatives to speak out publicly was David Jackson's brother-in-law, Andy, who set up an early support group for families of the Longcare residents.

Two others were Pauline Hennessey and June Raybaud. Pauline was a sister of Janet Ward, while June was their aunt. In the first days after the media storm caused by the leaking of Buckinghamshire's confidential report, Raybaud immediately started asking questions of the police, the Crown Prosecution Service, Jennifer Waldron at Bucks County Council, politicians, fellow barristers, academics and voluntary organisations. Her notes from the time also show that she immediately fixed on Dr X as one of the key guilty parties. She spoke to Slough police officers involved in the first, failed Longcare investigations. They told her that her 'best bet was a civil case' and that there was not enough evidence to prosecute Gordon Rowe. Newspaper reports are always exaggerated, one of them told her, and there was no need to reopen the case. But the same officer admitted that he and other police officers had been 'in and out of Longcare', and had helped with fundraisers at Stoke Place. Just three days later, the same officer rang Raybaud and told her that everything had changed. They had raided Rowe's properties, while he himself had now read the council inquiry report and was 'very positive' about investigating, and prosecuting, Gordon Rowe.

Raybaud, as a barrister – and someone with a sharp mind, almost inexhaustible reserves of energy and a deep commitment to human rights and justice – was well-placed to secure this kind of access to senior figures in the police, civil service, parliament and government, and over the following years her career would take second place to seeking justice for her niece and the other Longcare residents.

Pauline Hennessey also proved to be a determined campaigner, and joined Raybaud as a trustee of the charity Voice UK, which supports people with learning difficulties who have experienced crime or abuse. The two women launched and co-ordinated a support group for Rowe's victims.

The group of relatives decided on a name: Justice for Longcare Survivors (JLS). They wanted their family members to be survivors, not victims. By doing so, they gave solid form to the desperate hope that what Gordon Rowe had perpetrated at Longcare would not forever blight the lives of those he had pledged to care for, and that the former residents would, eventually, survive the terrible things that had been done to them.

Together, the members of JLS began the long journey towards an acknowledgement that what had been done to their loved ones was wrong, as well as a recognition by the government of the flaws in the system that helped Rowe commit his crimes and evade detection for so long.

At the first JLS meeting in 1996, a room – provided by the charity Mencap – full of 30 or so relatives discussed their memories of Longcare.

One man stood up to say that his son's television had gone missing at Stoke Place: Rowe told him it was being mended, and he never saw it again. Around him, heads began to nod. Soon, the common experiences were flooding out. Other relatives stood up and told their stories: the unexplained bruises, the missing pocket money, the over-medication. This was all vital information for the two solicitors – Nicola Harney, of Stewarts, in London, and Simon Richardson, of The Smith Partnership, in Derby – who would lead the work to prepare legal cases against Buckinghamshire County Council, and the other public bodies and individuals implicated in the scandal.

It was a frustratingly slow process, but at least those who attended JLS meetings knew that they were doing something, not only to make things better for their own sons, daughters, brothers and sisters, but to push for improvements that might prevent another Longcare.

By late 2000, the members of JLS had been meeting regularly for nearly four years.

Raybaud had continued to play a crucial role in the campaign for justice. In 1997, she had written to Paul Boateng, calling for the Longcare inquiry to be given 'judicial' status, so residents and relatives could give evidence. She also demanded that lessons be learned on the registration of care homes, and suggested a national register of care workers, clear policies on abuse, training for police officers and judges, guidance for prosecutors, and stricter sentences for ill-treatment, neglect and sexual offences against people with learning difficulties. She told Boateng that Buckinghamshire had behaved in an 'arrogant and secretive manner' and 'demonstrated a total lack of integrity throughout' and had 'certainly not demonstrated any willingness to learn any lessons'.

When Boateng replied, he told her he was determined to create 'a more comprehensive, more independent regulatory framework for homes and other social services which has the interests of users at heart'.

Raybaud told me many years later that her Longcare campaigning 'took my concentration away from a lot of things at the Bar', but that she never regretted the time she spent fighting for Janet and the other survivors. Typically, she was keen to praise other campaigners instead, and pointed particularly to Edwina Currie, at the time a high-profile Conservative MP, who had become involved in Voice UK after taking up the case of a constituent with learning difficulties. 'She was one of the unsung heroes,' said Raybaud. 'She understood exactly what we were trying to do. She trusted us, discussed these things with us, and always said 'use my name'. She opened a lot of doors for me. We used to go and see Barbara Mills [then the director of public prosecutions] all the time.'

Raybaud and other JLS members had been frustrated at the limited terms of reference for the Longcare inquiry. But they continued to put pressure on the authorities, and their most important victory had been to ensure the inquiry findings would be published. They had also shamed five senior officers from Bucks County Council into attending one of their meetings. The grudging apology for the inspection unit's mistakes that resulted from that meeting did not go far enough, but it was something. I was later told by a council insider that the only reason Bucks had not paid compensation to the victims at this early stage was because its insurers would not allow it to.

The regular JLS meetings helped Harney, Richardson and their colleagues compile the evidence necessary for the civil case (there were eventually to be 53 claimants in the 'group action', all of whom were former Longcare residents). If successful in a case against Bucks, it would be a landmark victory, the first time a registration and inspection authority had been found liable for failing to stop abuse in an institution.

During the summer of 2000, Harney and Richardson selected the 'lead cases', the handful of claims which would be heard in detail by the court. They also instructed Dr Leila Cooke and Dr Peter Carpenter, consultant psychiatrists specialising in learning disability, who would collate the medical evidence, and decide how much damage each former resident had suffered. The two experts would use the police's psychological assessments, crime analysis charts and summaries of allegations, medical records (sparse though they were), social services records (ditto, in most cases) and witness statements. They would also talk to relatives, and the residents themselves.

The solicitors – with help from JLS – decided that the lead cases against Buckinghamshire should be those taken on behalf of Jackie, Peter, George, David Jackson, Nicky Power, Michael, Stefano Tunstell, Tracy, Rachel, Christopher and Janet Ward. In the end, the trial judge would rule early in 2002 that he would hear only the details of Janet Ward's case. If that case was proved, all the other claimants against Bucks would also succeed.

A blow to JLS was their lawyers' advice that they would not be able to sue the Rowes, Lorraine Field or Desmond Tully, because they were not thought to have enough money to convince the Legal Services Commission to fund the cases. Many of the relatives believed that Angela Rowe had somehow squirreled away the Longcare riches. Tully, too, had previously owned his own residential home in Devon, now passed on to a relative because of his criminal conviction, and it was rumoured that he owned other properties.

But the members of JLS were determined not to let Longcare escape so easily with the profits it had harvested from the abusive regime. They asked their lawyers to find out what had happened to Gordon Rowe's millionaire's playthings – the holiday homes, the boats, the sports cars. They also decided to look into Tully's financial background. Richardson and Harney employed a private detective to conduct some preliminary investigations in Florida. It was another success for JLS, even though the search would ultimately prove fruitless.

The group had reluctantly decided not to sue the local authorities that placed clients at Longcare, or Thames Valley Police. Despite the dereliction of duty of those councils that dumped clients at the homes and abandoned them, it was felt they could provide useful information for the case against Bucks, and it was more sensible to have them on-side. Legal precedent suggested a claim against the police would not succeed. They, too, were considered a good source of evidence. It was another decision many relatives found hard to accept.

As the years passed, Buckinghamshire County Council seemed to take every opportunity to delay and prolong the legal battle, perhaps hoping the families would grow weary of the fight and give up, as had often happened with adults abused as children in care homes. By 2002, eight years after I had written my first Longcare story, the council was still refusing to admit that it was, at least partly, to blame, even though it had apologised to the families for its failures after the publication of the independent inquiry report. The council had twisted and turned and wriggled in an effort to avoid its moral responsibilities.

The numbers who attended the JLS meetings slowly dwindled. But there was always a solid core of parents, many of whom had retired, or were self-employed and found it easier to spare the time. Stefano Tunstell's parents, Lidia and Leslie, often attended; June and Pauline; Shaun McCarthy's parents, Terry and Barbara, who made it to nearly every meeting until they moved to Devon in 2000; Avril and Brian Scott; Rose Terry, whose sister Linda Dagger was a Longcare resident, and her husband Bill; Benedict Alcindor, Rosie's aunt; and Tracy's parents. Many others came a couple of times a year.

These get-togethers helped convince the families that they were making progress, kept them in contact with sympathetic friends, and, most importantly, proved they were doing something to make up for that one tragic mistake they had all made: trusting Gordon Rowe.

The lawyers for Longcare's survivors had gradually built up a strong case against Bucks County Council. They decided that the council had had a 'duty of care' to ensure Gordon Rowe was a fit person to be running Stoke Place; to inspect his homes with reasonable care; and to protect the residents from 'abuse, cruelty and personal injury'.

Janet Ward, according to their 'particulars of claim', was 'subjected to an abusive and harsh regime, inhuman and degrading treatment and punishment and suffered a deprivation of liberty and choice', as well as being 'physically and sexually abused' and 'inappropriately medicated and over-sedated'. They accused the council of failing to obtain references from David Fineberg, Rowe's previous employer, as well as his previous local authority employers in Sussex. And they claimed that Stan Bristow, Buckinghamshire's registration officer, had failed to record the nature of the allegations made against Rowe in Somerset, while there was 'no evidence' that he had attempted to talk to Fineberg about Gordon Rowe's explanation for the police investigation. Bristow, the court papers claimed, also failed to do anything later in 1983 when other organisations and individuals had contacted the council with their concerns about the case. They also pointed out that Bucks had failed to notify the police after the assault on Dorothy Abbott in 1991, and claimed that the council had failed to carry out its investigations between 1992 and 1994 with 'sufficient rigour'.

Buckinghamshire's defence was to argue that the law imposed no 'duty of care', and that it was only one of a number of authorities – including the police, the local authorities that placed residents in the homes, and the medical profession – that had obligations. It argued that there were 'significant financial implications' in inspecting residential homes and so it had a right to 'prioritise resources' as it saw fit, without the interference of the legal system. Being forced to justify 'finely balanced decisions' years later 'in a wholly different atmosphere and whilst ignoring hindsight imposes an unwarranted burden on registration authorities', the council argued. It also said it was right to rely on the police's decision not to charge Gordon Rowe in 1983, and that further investigations by Bristow in Somerset 'would not have resulted in a decision to decline to register Gordon Rowe'. And even if it had, the council claimed, a tribunal would probably have overturned the decision. The council was 'entitled to take the view that serious allegations had to be supported by cogent, direct evidence', while 'hearsay, suspicion and the observations of those not prepared to give evidence was not sufficient'.

The county council further claimed that, in the 1980s, it was accepted good practice to regard unproven allegations as 'irrelevant' to deciding how many inspections of a home there should be, while also arguing that unannounced inspections were seen at the time as 'generally counter-productive' to a good relationship between a home and a council.

Finally, in 2003, a trial date was set: 13 October, at the Royal Courts of Justice in London.

On the day the week-long trial was due to begin, Buckinghamshire County Council announced that it had agreed to pay compensation to the survivors of the abuse at the Longcare homes.

The legal settlement would eventually see the council pay 70 per cent of a series of agreed sums of compensation to those residents placed at the homes by other local authorities, while agreeing to pay 100 per cent of these amounts to the four residents Buckinghamshire had itself placed at Longcare.

The sums that were paid ranged from only about £5,000 for those who were thought to have suffered least, such as Simon Scott, to £55,000 for Rachel, who had been placed at the homes by Buckinghamshire. The total damages for the 53 people in the group action was just £782,000 (an average of less than £15,000 each), with the council also agreeing to pay all of the legal costs.

The damages were low because – as the claimants were people with learning difficulties – they were not inflated by any financial losses the former residents might have suffered in their careers as a result of the abuse. The lawyers had to follow precedents from other cases when agreeing compensation for psychological distress, pain and suffering. Stefano Tunstell, for instance, received just £15,000.

The council also refused to accept liability for what had happened at Longcare, merely agreeing that its 'shortcomings' had 'increased the risk' of abuse.

There were some brief words of regret delivered in court by Buckinghamshire's barrister, Simeon Maskrey QC, but the council's press release lacked an apology for its severe lapses and failings over a period of 20 years, and their long-term consequences for the Longcare residents.

David Shakespeare, the leader of the council, said he was 'relieved' that an agreement had been reached. 'It is regrettable that this matter has taken so long to come to its conclusion,' he added.

Harney says the council finally decided to accept defeat after its own expert handed over a report on how it should have dealt with the registration and inspection of the Longcare homes. The report was damning.

Some of the families had wanted the case to go to trial, to expose the council's failures in the full glare of the national media. But Harney says this was never an option. There was no guarantee that they were going to win the case, and the Legal Services Commission would never have accepted such a decision and would have withdrawn legal aid funding.

Harney says it was a 'groundbreaking' case, even though it didn't go to trial and so create a legal precedent. It was also part of a gradual shift towards holding public authorities accountable for the actions of their employees, she says.

Today, she is glad that 'justice was done'. 'It was absolutely right that we pushed it all the way. I am disappointed that it took so long but it did bring it more into the public domain that people with learning disabilities have the same rights as everybody else.'

Chapter Twenty-Three

The Other Local Authorities

'Later, I asked several colleagues who work as advocates and supporters of people with intellectual disability about what they knew. They confirmed immediately that harassment was a constant feature of the lives of every person they worked with. They told me about conferences and gatherings where people had shared horrific experiences, which to them were commonplace. People being Sellotaped to trees while people laughed, people being urinated on, people who had dog faeces put through their letter boxes, people who were beaten up. Faced with this constant exposure to the risk of abuse and violence, people with intellectual disability remained stoical and uncomplaining. Sometimes they were unable to make a complaint. Often, they were disbelieved, or were not taken seriously as witnesses. In most cases, the police were unwilling or unable to take effective action.'

Tom Shakespeare, The Guardian, 12 March 2010

As my initial research into the Longcare case slowly started to reach its end in 2000, proof began to emerge of yet another serious failure in the social care system.

The detectives investigating the allegations against Gordon Rowe in the autumn of 1994 had not taken long to discover that Buckinghamshire was not the only council to have deserted the residents of the two Longcare homes.

Madeleine Stewart, one of the officers who worked on the 18-month investigation, told me: 'It soon became clear to us that many of the 26 local authorities with clients at Longcare had had little or no contact with them for years. Some were not even aware they had residents at the homes.'

Gordon Rowe knew when he set up Longcare in 1983 that there was a severe shortage of residential homes for people with learning difficulties. Thousands of patients were being resettled into the community from the long-stay hospitals. This was exaggerating the tensions and the excess demand in the residential care system, and people like Rowe, with his social work contacts, were well placed to take advantage.

Gus Gray, who turned down an application by Rowe to open a large residential home in Berkshire in 1985, believes he knew that social workers from local authorities outside Bucks would 'fall over themselves' to place clients at Stoke Place. 'Stoke Place seldom had any vacancies, although Rowe was quite often prepared to squeeze people in, and that is always a dangerous sign,' he said. 'It means that somebody else is being squeezed.'

In fact, Berkshire was itself forced to place Gary Deacon at Stoke Place – against Gray's wishes – because it could find nowhere else for him to live.

'The reason inappropriate placements are made is that in terms of residential accommodation, there is no slack in the system,' he said. 'Residential care is more expensive than living at home and the social services budget is constrained. Because long-term planning is difficult, they are forced from time to time to have to find a long-term bed in a short space of time. That enables people like Rowe to say: 'Well, yes, I have got a room in the dogs' kennels or the stables."

Rowe also had a reputation for taking 'problem' clients rejected by other services. 'Many placing authorities which were forced to find places where problem clients could be accommodated didn't inquire too deeply into what was going on,' Gray told me.

Most residents were placed at Longcare by London boroughs, many of which were desperately short of residential homes within their own areas. Often, the only option was to find places outside London. Stoke Place, and later Stoke Green, both less than 20 miles from the western edge of the capital, were perfectly situated to mop up some of this demand.

Unfortunately, these London boroughs were also short of funds. They were also short of social workers.

One former social worker told me it was a time when there were 'an awful lot of problems and nobody was addressing them'. 'There were a lot of mentally handicapped people. London boroughs used to farm them out and there was no follow up. You couldn't possibly do anything more, because your caseload was too high. It was in the 'Planned Neglect' pile, because you knew you ought to do something about it, but it got shoved down to the bottom of the pile.'

Those who could not speak up for themselves were often assumed to be OK, so they found themselves at the bottom of this pile. And once they were at the bottom, it was almost impossible to find a way out.

Shaun McCarthy, who has autism, was moved to Stoke Place in September 1987 by the London Borough of Waltham Forest. Shaun's social worker visited Stoke Place in December 1987, and again, six months later. He visited him once more in March 1989. After that, Shaun wasn't seen by his social worker for more than 18 months.

Ron Wallace, Waltham Forest's executive director of community services, told me that all these case reviews 'concluded that Shaun was appropriately placed'. Shaun's parents, Barbara and Terry, remember being visited at their London home by his social worker every year. They were told that it was Buckinghamshire's job to inspect Stoke Place.

Following a review in November 1990, Shaun's social worker didn't visit him again until September 1994, after Bucks had sent Waltham Forest a copy of its Longcare report.

Shaun was fortunate that Barbara and Terry visited him every two or three weeks. They noticed the lack of staff, the occasional injuries to their son, how Shaun's new clothes would always be 'lost in the laundry', his weight loss and the high levels of medication. But they did not have the training or experience to conclude that Shaun was being abused. The person who might have been able to do that, had he visited Stoke Place regularly, was Shaun's social worker. But for four years, Shaun did not receive a single visit from Waltham Forest social services.

Wallace told me: 'Clearly, I would have preferred that reviews had continued at regular intervals. I wish I could say that had reviews and visits continued, the pattern of abuse at Stoke Place would have come to light. Unfortunately, even with the most intensive visiting, abuse has frequently gone undetected.'

He did at least acknowledge that the council had 'learned many lessons from this experience'. Waltham Forest now allocates social workers to all residents in long-term care – amazingly, this was not the case before – and seeks 'regular feedback' from relatives and inspectors. It is also trying to place as many people with learning difficulties as possible in homes within the borough.

Unfortunately, Shaun's was far from being the most worrying case.

The London Borough of Tower Hamlets was asked during the inspection unit investigation whether it had any clients at Longcare. No, said the council's social services department.

When this response was queried, the director of social services ordered a search of council records and discovered that there was a Tower Hamlets client living at Longcare. Rosie Valton had been living at Stoke Place since January 1984. She had been repeatedly raped and beaten by Gordon Rowe.

Tower Hamlets declined to discuss the case with me, or to detail the number of visits Rosie received from a social worker at Stoke Place.

One social services consultant told me – about 10 years ago – that Rosie's case was 'a significant example of the lack of safeguards' that existed. He said much of social work was spent in 'crisis intervention work'. 'There are many people that are placed somewhere and their cases are closed or they don't have an allocated care manager (social worker). That is happening in an increasing number of cases. It is one way of cutting down the workload.'

An experienced former social worker added: 'If you have a series of crises on your desk, people in residential care tend to have less attention. That's the kind of pressure that exists for most social workers. We have a duty to the well-being of everybody... but if there are people in acute need, they inevitably get the first bite of the cherry. It depends on whether you have enough social workers to keep the pressures at an acceptable level. I am bound to say there are not enough resources and there are not enough social workers.'

One care worker, who worked at Stoke Place for five years, told me: 'We never saw any social workers for the residents. If the social workers had bothered to come to us, I think we would have told them. I don't think half of them had social workers.'

But it was not just the London boroughs that were failing their clients.

Stefano Tunstell was placed at Stoke Place late in 1987. He was visited three times in 1988, as his social worker from Surrey

County Council oversaw efforts to settle him into his new home. But he wasn't visited again until February 1991. In the summer of 1992, his parents began to raise serious concerns about the standard of care he was receiving. He was finally visited once more in October 1992.

A spokeswoman for Surrey County Council told me: 'It's not usual for a person who is in a placement outside of the county to be visited more than once a year.' Unfortunately, it was often those placed a long distance away from their friends and family who were most at risk. But it was these clients who were visited least often, because it was too expensive for the placing authorities to travel to see them.

Surrey did not accept that it failed to act in Stefano's best interests, despite this period of nearly two-and-a-half years when he wasn't visited by a social worker. The spokeswoman told me Surrey was battling social services budget cuts throughout the 1980s and 1990s, as were other authorities. By 2000, each of its care managers had responsibility for close to 100 clients.

Nicky Power was another client failed by her local authority. She was one of the first Longcare residents, and lived there for nearly 10 years. She was visited by her social worker from Kent County Council in late 1983 and early 1984 (probably to make sure she was settled in) and then again later in 1984. There was a gap of more than two years until the next visit in 1987. She was visited twice in 1988, but at some stage during that year her social worker left the council for another job. She wasn't replaced.

Nicky was visited by somebody from social services in 1989 and 1991 for an annual review, but wasn't seen again until the Powers found out by accident three years later that she didn't have her own social worker. Throughout this period, Nicky was being raped by Gordon Rowe.

A spokeswoman for Kent social services said a 'team leader' would have been responsible for Nicky's case, but she would not have had a named social worker. Nicky's parents said they didn't receive any information about their daughter from the council for nearly six years. 'After the social worker left (in 1988), I think she was probably at the bottom of the pile,' said Susan, Nicky's mother. 'We didn't have any contact for a long time. We didn't think there was anything to worry about, so we didn't complain.'

Some local authorities do seem to have made regular visits to the Longcare homes to check up on their clients and monitor their progress.

The London Borough of Harrow, for instance, placed two residents with Longcare. One, who was there for seven years, was visited nine times, in addition to numerous letters and telephone calls. The other was there for five years and was visited 14 times. Again, there were many letters and telephone calls, and none of this seems to have produced any evidence of ill-treatment or assaults. This illustrates perhaps how difficult it can be for social workers to build up the kind of trusting relationship with a client that can lead to a disclosure of abuse, when they see them briefly only once or maybe twice a year.

Hertfordshire County Council visited its client three or four times a year while he was at Stoke Place, and 'spent some time alone with him on each visit' and again found no cause for concern.

The London Borough of Havering visited its clients – including Janet Ward and Simon Scott – two or three times a year, as well as attending annual reviews.

The disturbing message was that, even with regular visits, there was no guarantee that social workers would realise that abuse was taking place. Rowe was practised at covering up all signs of abuse when he knew outsiders were around. And every time a social worker visited for an annual review, it was arranged in advance with Longcare. Rowe had plenty of notice of when social workers were going to be poking their noses into his affairs. It was easy for him to ensure that he, his staff and his residents were on their best behaviour.

Tom Burgner was concerned about the lack of regular visits by social workers. 'Of course, we would have wanted the placing authorities to take a lot more interest in the people they had placed,' he said.

His fellow inquiry member, Dr Philippa Russell, told me that Jean Jeffrey, Buckinghamshire's director of social services, had written in December 1993 to every one of the local authorities with Longcare clients to warn them that they were investigating complaints about the home. 'There was absolutely not a flicker of interest,' said Russell.

She experienced a similar situation in the mid-1990s. 'It was a private children's home, which a lot of London authorities had put children in. A lot of concerns were being raised about what was going on at the home. The director of the host authority's social services department wrote to all the placement authorities and said he was very concerned about the home. He did not believe it was a safe place. They had not been able to get evidence which the local police thought would stand up in court, particularly because of the severity of the disability of the children. None of them could speak. He expressed the view really quite strongly and said if he had placed a child in such a home, he would have removed him. He didn't get a single reply and when he rang the various local authorities, they said, 'Well, we have nowhere else to put them.' I think that illustrates the dilemma.'

She told me – about 10 years ago – that the attitude of local authorities to the clients they placed in out-of-area services was 'one of the most shocking things about the management of residential care'.

James Churchill, chief executive of the Association for Residential Care, whose members were at the time – also about 10 years ago – responsible for about 14,000 residential places for people with learning difficulties, agreed. 'It's all a question of money and resources and time. Once the placement is made and the finances sorted out, our members' experience is that you are often left to get on with it.'

Fiona Mactaggart, Slough's MP, added: 'In effect what had happened was that a bunch of people had got lost, except to the finance department. They just featured as bills. I wonder sometimes how many people there are around Britain whose only contact with anyone who has any kind of responsibility for them is someone just paying a bill. Because I bet that wasn't unique and I bet it still happens.'

For every local authority that did manage to send a social worker at least once a year to check up on their client, there were two or three that didn't. I contacted nearly every one of the councils which placed residents at Stoke Place and Stoke Green. Many hid behind the excuse that it would breach 'client confidentiality' to discuss the case, even though I was not planning to identify anyone without their or their families' permission.

If you do not own up to your mistakes, you have no chance of ever learning from them. Buckinghamshire County Council proved that lesson. So I decided to list those councils which refused to answer the following simple question: how often was your client visited by a social worker while he or she was a Longcare resident?

The London Borough of Tower Hamlets, the Royal London Borough of Kensington and Chelsea, the London Borough of Hackney, the London Borough of Bromley, the London Borough of Ealing (which took 15 months to produce a 'no comment'), and the London Borough of Islington, all declined to answer the question. A spokesman for the London Borough of Hounslow said it had 'carried out all the required visits and reviews', but declined to say exactly how often it visited its clients, again for 'reasons of confidentiality'. The London Borough of Enfield refused to comment until legal action being taken against Bucks County Council was completed. In one case, that of the London Borough of Lambeth, the council said the family of the resident had asked it not to release any information, which of course is an acceptable response.

A study published by the Norah Fry Research Centre[1] found that disabled children placed in residential schools were often not visited by social workers or education officers. One education officer told the researchers: 'Once the youngster is at the school, on a day to day basis it's the school's responsibility to ensure the welfare of the child, though we do get reports from the school via the annual review process.' If it was this relaxed with children, it was surely far worse with adults.

Ian Johnston, director of the British Association of Social Workers, told me: 'One of the features is that you have to be a problem before you see a social worker. It's a resource question. There are a lot of well-intentioned people in social work, they want to do a good job, but they are simply stretched too far and the expectations placed on them are unrealistic.'

As for the Longcare residents? 'They were out of sight, out of mind.'

The evidence above was worrying enough. But as I began to draw the years of research for my first Longcare book to a close in 2003, proof began to emerge of an even more serious failure in the system, one that dated back to the introduction of large-scale institutional care for people with learning difficulties in the middle of the nineteenth century.

By the time Gordon Rowe opened Stoke Place in 1983, the country's long-stay hospitals were beginning to return patients to the community. Many of these people had been living in such institutions since they were young children, often for more than 50 years.

The district health authorities, which ran the hospitals, were faced with a drastic shortage of potential placements. They were also acting under the authority of inadequate legislation that was open to widely differing interpretations.

Once a patient was found a home in the community and had spent six months settling in, he or she was 'discharged' by the hospital. Money to pay for their care was passed by the Department of Health and Social Security to the patient's regional health authority, which usually delegated it to its relevant district health authority. This district health authority could then reach an agreement to transfer the funding to the corresponding social services department. But local and health authorities often failed to reach such agreements. Responsibility frequently remained instead with the health authority.

A further complication was that it was not always clear to which area a former patient 'belonged'. If they had been at the hospital since before 1970, they would become the responsibility of that hospital's regional health authority. But if they had arrived at the hospital more recently than 1970, their own previous 'home' regional health authority would become responsible for finding them somewhere to live.

Confused? So, it seems, were the authorities. Nobody seemed to know who was supposed to be looking out for these people. And, if they did know, they didn't seem particularly bothered about it. The former patients were often left at the mercy of the people who ran their new homes, without a social worker or nurse to keep a regular check on their welfare.

Many of the former long-stay patients had spent most of their lives in hospital, denied any independence, education, or opportunity to develop social skills. They often left the hospitals with their few personal possessions in a black, plastic bin-liner, perhaps thinking they were set for a new, brighter life. Unfortunately for 17 of the patients from Botleys Park, in Surrey, they were heading for Longcare.

The former Botleys Park patients moved to Stoke Place during late 1983 and 1984 and were some of Longcare's first residents. Among them were Dorothy Abbott and her boyfriend, Jimmy.

Dorothy moved to Stoke Place in December 1983. She was officially discharged from Botleys six months later. Then, for the next five years, nothing. She was left at Stoke Place in the sole care of Gordon Rowe, a man who had been the subject of a police investigation for sexually assaulting adults with learning difficulties.

Dorothy entered a kind of social care no-man's land. South-West Thames Regional Health Authority – which covered Botleys Park – was still responsible for her welfare. It continued to pay the bills for her care, but, once she was discharged, none of its officers or nurses visited her to check on her welfare. She was finally 'picked up' by the Royal London Borough of Kingston-upon-Thames in 1989, but only after her sister contacted its social services department to express concern about Stoke Place.

Jenny Webb, head of community care services for Kingston, was unable to work out who had been responsible for Dorothy before Kingston took over responsibility for her. 'I don't think it is terribly clear,' she told me. 'I am not clear that anyone took any overview responsibility. Certainly we were not notified of the placement. Obviously, in terms of the standards you would expect with any placement of a vulnerable person, it is a matter of concern.'

Further evidence came from the London Borough of Merton. Two Botleys patients, Edwin and Derek, were placed at Longcare in 1983; again, it seems, by South-West Thames Regional Health Authority. In April 1986, the two men became Merton's responsibility, when the council was asked to provide 'top-up' funding for them, following changes to benefits legislation. In those three years, they hadn't been visited once by a health or social worker.

Merton council's policy was to review out-of-borough clients only every two years, due to 'demand and limited resources', so Edwin and Derek were not reviewed for the first time by a social worker until 1988, five years after moving to Longcare.

Another example of this chaotic approach came from the London Borough of Richmond upon Thames. Three former long-stay hospital patients who originated from Richmond were placed at Longcare.

It took the council more than a year to come up with the following answer to my question: how frequently did you visit your clients while they were at the homes?

'Having searched through all the relevant files, the available evidence suggests that people with learning disabilities who were placed at Stoke Place and originated from the London Borough of Richmond upon Thames were visited on average at regular intervals during the period for which the borough had financial responsibility.'

'On average at regular intervals.' Only a local authority could come up with such a meaningless phrase. When pressed, the reason became apparent.

Stewart Ruston, community services manager for Kingston and Richmond Joint Service for People with Learning Disabilities, told me that at some stage the responsibility for the trio had passed from the health authority (South-West Thames again) to the council. But exactly when it passed, he didn't know. 'I cannot find anything that specifies what, when, where, how,' he admitted. There are no records of any visits to the trio until the early 1990s. And during the 1980s? 'Obviously, there were some visits, but I do not know if there is a lack of information. We probably didn't accept responsibility until they had been there for quite some period. A year or so or more. It's not clear for all three of them.

'The recording practices were not as good as they are now. I don't know if things were done and not recorded... or not done. From our records, we can't prove either way. There were gaps. You can assume neglect, or assume that things would have been done but were not recorded because of poor practice.'

To sum up: a scandalous lack of proper records, no clear idea of whether Richmond's social workers did their job properly, and not the faintest idea of when responsibility for the three residents passed from health authority to council.

One senior social care figure, Anne*, laid much of the blame at the feet of the Department of Health. 'The department used to talk about collaboration. The theory was that if you were in a hospital and you needed to be placed outside, as people with learning disabilities did, there should have been a co-ordinated approach and a suitable placement for you should be found and ongoing support. It didn't work like that,' she told me. 'There is a can of worms waiting to be opened up.'

Dr Jean Collins, at the time the director of Values Into Action, which promotes the rights of people with learning difficulties, told me: 'The (Conservative) government had no grip at all. They didn't do anything about it. They just let it go on. The government had no idea about what was going on on the ground.'

Dr Collins, who described the chaos caused by this process in her book, The Resettlement Game, believes the health authorities that retained responsibility for their former patients during the 1980s simply dumped them in their new placements and forgot about them. 'In many cases they just didn't check up. They would just get a recurring bill and pay it. Residential care for people with learning disabilities is incredibly expensive, but they didn't check up to see what they were getting.'

A Department of Health spokeswoman made it clear that the responsibility for ensuring appropriate arrangements were in place lay with the health authorities. There had been confusion in some cases where placements had broken down as to who was responsible, she admitted, and the department had issued 'clarifying' guidance in 1992.

As for whether the department itself was partly responsible for this foul-up, she declined to comment.

Nobody seemed to know who was supposed to be looking out for the former patients of the long-stay hospitals. And if they did know, they didn't seem particularly bothered about it. They were often left at the mercy of the people who ran their new homes, without a social worker or nurse to keep a regular check on their welfare.

Somehow, the 17 men and women from Botleys Park had been placed in the care of Gordon Rowe and Longcare... and just left there. No social worker checked up on them. Many had no family or friends to look out for them, either. They had spent years – sometimes decades – in secluded, isolated hospital settings, offering them little or no preparation for the distressing and brutal challenges they were about to face at Stoke Place.

But I had also heard stories of coach-loads of patients being shipped up from London to residential homes in the north during the 1980s, because of the drastic shortage of places in the capital. This would have placed these people even further from relatives and friends than the residents of Longcare.

So, in the summer of 2003, I decided to try to find out whether what happened at Longcare was an isolated occurrence, or whether the practice of sending adults with learning difficulties to distant placements far from their original homes was still being repeated across the country.

It quickly became clear that many social care professionals shared my concerns. For example, I was told there were 570 people living in Lincolnshire who were originally from out of county. Many of those from London boroughs, I was told by a senior manager, were believed to be not receiving annual visits from social workers. Many had been placed in homes where they were at serious risk of abuse.

In Kent, the problem was 'rife', said Simon Hewson, head of psychology for East Kent Mental Health and Social Care Partnership Trust. He said it was 'pretty rare' for such people to receive more than one visit a year from their social worker. Often, they did not even get that. 'People are just left,' he said. He said he believed there were hundreds of people in such situations in Kent. And, as in Lincolnshire, some of the homes they had been placed in were 'pretty shady'.

Dr Collins said she too believed, 'anecdotally', that many people in out-of-area placements were not being visited at all by social workers. 'Nobody has any records or statistics, but I think it is widespread. The reason I think it is widespread is that wherever I go in the country, people talk to me about it being a problem. They are concerned that people are being abandoned by their paying authority.'

I spoke to Steven Rose, chief executive of Choice Support, which provides supported living and residential care to people with learning difficulties. He agreed with Collins. 'In my experience,' he told me, 'local authorities' supervision and follow-up of placements after they have made them are absolutely abysmal.' He estimated that every London borough had about 100 clients with learning difficulties in out-of-area placements. 'Even in their own borough, they rarely get round them once a year. I know they do not get to the ones that are miles away. They just haven't got the resources. It is a very real problem.

'We know that any vulnerable person is more likely to be financially, emotionally, physically or sexually abused. We know there is a high incidence of it in terms of people with learning difficulties, not just by the staff, but also by other people living with them. Some organisations are very open about any incidents of abuse, make it public and make sure it is investigated properly, but probably the small, more isolated, probably private, care homes are more high risk areas.

'The care manager, through regular visiting, isn't necessarily going to detect any sort of abuse, but what they can do is satisfy themselves that there are adequate systems and safeguards in place. The more independent people that you have got coming along, the more likely you are to discover something is going wrong.'

The importance of regular visits from social workers was illustrated perfectly by one particular case, which I looked into after it was dealt with by the Registered Homes Tribunal in December 2000.

Alan, who had learning difficulties and high support needs, had been dumped at a care home in Northamptonshire and abandoned by social workers for 12 years, after being placed there by Essex social services.

He was eventually discovered in a locked room, unwashed and semi-naked. An inspector from Northants County Council who visited the home described to the tribunal what he found: 'When I entered his room, AT (Alan) was lying curled up on a plastic-covered chair. He was wearing only a ripped tee-shirt. There was a pool of urine on the floor. The furniture in the room consisted of a wooden bed with a blue plastic mattress, a rickety table with two plastic chairs, a further plastic armchair and two wooden trunks. There was a small mat on the floor in the middle of the room, which was otherwise all lino. There was no bed linen on the bed and the room felt cold.'

A registered mental health nurse visited the same resident three months later and found him sitting unclothed in a pool of urine. She was 'very shocked' at his condition. 'When I went back one hour later there was food in Mr T's hair as well,' she told the tribunal. 'No-one had made any attempt to improve his conditions. He was sitting in the same chair, unwashed and naked. There was food in his hair and urine on the floor.'

The tribunal, which was hearing the home's appeal against the cancellation of its registration, concluded: 'The conditions in which this resident was kept were an affront to human dignity. For years, local authorities who should have been in a position to protect his human rights had ignored him and appear to have failed in their duty of care.'

The tribunal found that Alan had been kept locked in his room in 'conditions of squalor and degradation' and had been denied proper dental treatment for a painful abscess for several years. The co-owner of the home tried to explain the state of neglect by saying that 'nothing more could be done' for Alan, and that he wanted to keep him 'in the same conditions in which he had been kept for the last 40 years'.

The tribunal concluded that Essex social services had 'dumped' Alan in Northants and failed to review his case properly for 12 years.

My research was not by any means exhaustive, but from what I was told, I had no doubt that there were thousands of adults with learning difficulties in out-of-area placements who did not receive any visits at all from their social workers.

Because there were no reliable statistics, I believed then that there should be an independent and thorough investigation of every out-of-area placement in the country, to discover just how many people had been left to fend for themselves.

They were at the daily mercy of the people who owned and ran their homes, and their staff. Many would be living in decent, pleasant homes. Many others would not.

It was a disturbing fact that many of these people – many of whom had already been damaged by decades of institutional neglect in long-stay hospitals – had been so callously cast adrift by the authorities that were supposed to be supporting them.

1   *Disabled Children and Residential Schools – A Study of Local Authority Policy and Practice, by David Abbott, Jenny Morris and Linda Ward; Norah Fry Research Centre, supported by Joseph Rowntree Foundation; 2000*

Chapter Twenty-Four

Guilty

'Two men were behind bars yesterday for killing a man by pushing him into a freezing lake in a 'happy slap' prank. Jonathan Lawson and Sidney Quirke filmed themselves on mobile phones taunting Mark Watts, 44, before pushing him into 25ft-deep water. Non-swimmer Mr Watts, who had a mental age of nine, had been drinking before stripping off and sitting naked on a jetty. A crowd had gathered to watch him. Quirke, 18, who admitted manslaughter, pushed him into the water while Lawson, 20, egged him on, Chelmsford crown court was told. The attack, at Lakeside Shopping Centre in West Thurrock, Essex, last March, was caught on CCTV cameras.'

The Daily Mirror, 15 March 2006

It was not until five or six years after that inspection unit report landed on my desk that the importance of the underwhelming reaction from the readers of the Slough Observer finally began to sink in.

No other conclusion could be drawn from the information I had gathered: the residents' ordeal at Longcare wasn't the fault of Gordon Rowe, or the county council staff responsible for allowing him to open Stoke Place Mansion House. It wasn't the fault of the local authorities that placed clients at the Longcare homes, or Slough police, the Longcare workforce, the criminal justice system, or the NHS. The more the evidence was analysed, the clearer it became who was to blame.

The residents of Longcare had been let down not by a single agency, but by every organisation which had ever come into contact with them. The Longcare scandal wasn't the result of a chain of coincidences or a run of bad luck. It was born out of a deeply ingrained indifference – in every nook and cranny of society – to the fate of people with learning difficulties.

And something even more disturbing slipped into place: the certainty that it would happen again.

Fiona Mactaggart, the Slough MP, who took up the Longcare case after her election in 1997, and ensured there was an inquiry, says she learned a lot from the case. She learned, for instance, that people with learning difficulties can all too easily be treated as 'not people'. 'I was horrified,' she told me years later. 'I have always been a human rights activist and it seemed to me that that is not tolerable in a civilised society.' But she also discovered something else.

'I learned another important thing, which was shocking, which was that there was still a whole bunch of people locally who thought it was all a bit exaggerated, and these were people who worked with people with learning disabilities. It made me understand that there are people who will tolerate uncivilised behaviour when the perpetrator is in their social circle, and they are not going to be found out as someone who is tolerating uncivilised behaviour. It made me much more cynical about seemingly nice, respectable human beings, human beings who had been very nice to me as well. But they were just saying: 'Oh, it's all a bit much, they are all blowing it all up rather. Gordon seemed rather a good chap to me."

She has an explanation for why the Slough Observer was never flooded with letters from its readers about Longcare. 'For a lot of people, the reason they write letters to newspapers is that they feel a direct emotional connection to an issue. I think that lots and lots of people do not feel that about learning disability and if they have learning disability in their family there was then – and less so now but still some – a sense of shame.' There is a sense, she says, that people would rather just not confront the issue and the horror of what was happening at Longcare.

Stoke Place and Stoke Green were scaled-down models of the Victorian and Edwardian asylums and villas for the 'mentally defective'. Their ethos was almost identical: personal possessions were discouraged, food was sparse and of poor quality, vicious punishments were administered by staff, and residents were used as slave labour.

The brutality of Rowe's regime would have concerned even most of the eugenicists of the early 1900s, but its principles were based on the same belief: that such people were not fit to be a part of 'normal' society.

This belief was evident in the horrified reaction of the Somerset villagers when they learned that a home for 'mentally handicapped' people was opening on their doorstep, and in the low priority accorded to people with learning difficulties by Bucks social services. And it was present in the police's failure to launch a proper investigation into the allegations at Longcare in 1992 and 1993, in the GMC's refusal to investigate the complaints about Dr X, and in the care staff who failed to report Rowe's crimes. The callous indifference shown to the fate of people with learning difficulties, and the belief that they should be segregated from the rest of society, were two ignorant sides of the same coin.

PART FIVE

AFTER LONGCARE

Chapter Twenty-Five

The Social Care System

'Disabled people in one of the country's last remaining long-stay hospitals are living in 'shocking' conditions, a former volunteer has told DN. The adults with learning difficulties are often left to sit for hours in their own urine and faeces and staff eat their puddings and snacks, it is alleged... residents on the villa were dirty, dressed in shabby and torn clothes, and rarely kept occupied and stimulated.'

Disability Now, March 2004

Six years on from Bucks County Council's Longcare probe, there were fears that many inspection units were still proving themselves incapable of exposing abuse. This was one of the reasons for the introduction of Labour's Care Standards Act.

The act was strongly influenced by Tom Burgner's Longcare inquiry, and his report two years earlier which had also recommended improvements in the regulation of care homes. One of the most important measures was to set up a National Care Standards Commission to take over responsibility for registration and inspection from councils, and set new national standards for homes and care agencies in England.

The commission would be independent, immune from the politics and constant funding crises of local government, and offer consistently strong registration and inspection. Most importantly, perhaps, its inspectors would spend more time talking to those who used services.

But less than three weeks after the commission's launch in April 2002, the government announced that it would be abolished within two years, and its social care functions merged with the Social Services Inspectorate to form a new Commission for Social Care Inspection. It was a sign of further confusion to come.

The act also set up the General Social Care Council, to regulate the estimated 1.5 million staff in England's social care industry. The council would gradually set up a register of those fit to work in the sector, and regulate training and education. Amazingly, it was the first time there had ever been such a regulatory body.

There was also to be a new list of people considered unfit to work with 'vulnerable adults': the Protection of Vulnerable Adults (POVA) list. This would finally give people with learning difficulties the same protection as children, with employers obliged to notify the government if they dismissed an employee for harming or risking harm to a client. It was hard to believe it had taken so long to introduce such a potentially effective measure.

But thanks to problems in the newly-privatised Criminal Records Bureau (CRB), the government announced in autumn 2002 that POVA's introduction would be deferred indefinitely.

There were other problems. The Care Standards Act had said all care home staff would have to undergo criminal records checks by the end of March 2003. Thanks to the CRB chaos, this deadline was extended to the end of 2004. Deborah Kitson, director of the Ann Craft Trust, said the delays would make abuse more likely. 'It just seems the government are not taking it seriously,' she said. 'We feel like we have taken backward steps.'

The General Social Care Council admitted to me that it could take 10 years before all care workers were admitted onto its new social care register.

Care standards were unlikely to rise until wages and training improved dramatically. By the end of 2000, up to four-fifths of residential care staff in England and Wales were untrained. And in 2002, Stephen O'Kell reported[1]: 'In one of the more affluent areas studied, people could earn more than £10 per hour for working behind a bar, compared with an average £5 an hour for care work.'

Home owners failed to invest, or could not afford to invest, in training. Central government and local authorities failed to fund the higher fees that might have allowed owners to pay decent wages. The result was an unmotivated and poorly trained workforce.

Clare Johnson, one of the Longcare whistleblowers and by now an experienced care worker, was appalled at the attitude of many of her colleagues. There were some genuine care workers, she told me, but many others were bullies seeking power over people in vulnerable situations, or low-skilled workers who couldn't find alternative employment and were terrified of losing their jobs. There had been examples of both at Longcare.

The number of people applying to be social workers had fallen sharply, too, with many councils having to rely on agency staff or recruit from aboard.

Six years after Clare Johnson and Paul Robertson's whistleblowing helped end Gordon Rowe's Longcare regime, the Public Interest Disclosure Act was brought in to protect staff who wanted to raise similar concerns.

The act had, said Fiona Mactaggart, been influenced by the Longcare inquiry, which was published shortly before the act received royal assent and became law in 1998. Although the new legislation led most employers to develop whistleblowing policies, implementation varied widely. In research published in 2005, Rebecca Calcraft[2] concluded that whistleblowing 'continues to be regarded negatively', with staff often reluctant to 'self-identify as a whistleblower' and so failing to access the 'protection and support' their employer offered.

In March 2001, the government published Valuing People, the first learning difficulty white paper since Better Services for the Mentally Handicapped in 1971. It was greeted with enthusiasm, while Community Care magazine described it as a 'defining moment'.

The white paper talked about the importance of civil rights, independence, dignity, choice and inclusion. There was to be a national information centre and help-line for carers, a national network of advocacy services, and targets for combating discrimination in health, housing, education, benefits, public transport and employment.

There would be a new training framework and guidance on restraint techniques for care workers, with a string of other targets, taskforces, support teams and partnership boards. The white paper placed a refreshing emphasis on the rights of people with learning difficulties to make decisions for themselves and to achieve independence, and their right to a decent education, to vote, to have a family life, to be protected by the law.

But where was the money? The white paper said there would be £100 million over two years for a learning disability development fund – much of which would be diverted from pre-existing funding – an implementation support fund of £2.3 million a year and a £2 million research programme. The annual spending on services for people with learning difficulties was about £3 billion, roughly split between health and social services. An extra £30 million or so a year was a rise of just one per cent.

Rob Greig, director of implementation for Valuing People, told me at the time: 'It limits what we can do. It means we have to very carefully prioritise what we work on.'

Gordon Brown, then the chancellor, announced in his comprehensive spending review in July 2002 that social services spending would rise by 29 per cent by 2004, but there was no new money for learning difficulties. Greig told me he had been 'disappointed' by the decision.

Brian White, co-chair of the National Forum of People with Learning Difficulties, set up as a result of the white paper, wrote in Community Care in November 2002: 'People with learning difficulties have never been a priority... I think that in years to come we will see right through the selfishness of governments that have never given us a second thought. They only do something when it is beneficial to them, and if it's not, they don't bother.'

The government's new health and social care priorities, announced in the autumn of 2002, did not include people with learning difficulties, even though they were the most discriminated against, poorest, most 'at risk' sector of society. Instead, the focus was on children, older people and those with mental health conditions.

The Department of Health also admitted to me that it had no plans to fund any research aimed at discovering the prevalence of abuse of people with learning difficulties.

Valuing People came 30 years after its predecessor. That, too, had talked about collaboration between health and social services, supporting carers, phasing out the use of long-stay hospitals, the importance of staff training, and the vital role played by friends, neighbours and voluntary groups. And it, too, had failed to come up with the money necessary to bring about those changes.

One major systemic flaw exposed by the Longcare scandal was the inability of agencies to work together, in particular police, social services and health authorities.

The government tried to address this by issuing No Secrets, guidance on how local authorities should develop 'multi-agency' codes of practice to protect 'vulnerable adults' from abuse. The guidance, which mentioned the Longcare case and was published in 2000, aimed to make adult protection and the investigation of allegations more co-ordinated and coherent.

By late 2002, most councils had produced policies, but No Secrets was inhibited by the government's predictable failure to allocate money towards its implementation. According to research[3], few councils had specific budgets for adult protection, and many of those that did expected them to disappear. Furthermore, the government was showing no interest in monitoring councils' performance, as it did with child protection.

Once again, people with learning difficulties had been relegated to the bottom of the pile.

*

When I returned to this story nearly a decade later, in 2010, I wanted to assess if the changes in legislation, the No Secrets guidance, and the Valuing People white paper, had helped prevent another Longcare.

Despite these positive developments, a stark picture emerged. While there may have been no new scandals on the scale of Longcare, I had still reported on a sickening series of cases of institutional abuse. I was left in no doubt that people with learning difficulties were still being denied their most basic human rights.

In 2004, I revealed in Disability Now that disabled people in one of the country's last remaining long-stay hospitals had been living in 'shocking' conditions.

The neglect at Fieldhead Hospital in Wakefield was again exposed through the courage of a whistleblower. Elizabeth Nassem, who had volunteered on Fieldhead's Brotherton Villa, told me how adults with learning difficulties were left to sit for hours in their own urine and faeces, while staff ate their puddings and snacks. Nassem made repeated, unsuccessful attempts to convince the hospital to improve standards. She told me residents were dirty, dressed in shabby and torn clothes, and rarely kept occupied and stimulated. 'I was absolutely shocked when I first went on the villa,' she said. 'I didn't know people lived like that in my local town. It was like something from Victorian times. It is not just that they do live like this, but that they are allowed to live like this.'

South West Yorkshire Mental Health Trust, which ran the hospital, told me the allegations had been thoroughly investigated and proved 'unfounded'. But later that year, the Healthcare Commission launched a 'fast-track clinical governance review' to examine services run by the trust. The decision had been prompted by Nassem's complaints and a second source who had passed on unrelated concerns.

In a further twist, and one again with worrying echoes of Longcare, the Healthcare Commission admitted to me that, during a visit to Fieldhead, its team had tried to speak to patients in front of staff, and when they were unable to communicate with them, failed to enlist experts to help. Investigators were refused permission to talk to alleged survivors of the abuse who had moved into the community, and failed to question former Brotherton staff.

Dr Jean Collins, director of Values Into Action (VIA), said: 'To simply dismiss the importance of people's experiences and their own perspectives because it is hard to elicit information from them is just mind-boggling.' The commission admitted 'a need to further develop our expertise in this area'.

Despite Nassem's continuing efforts, there never was a proper, in-depth, independent investigation into her allegations, either by the Healthcare Commission or the Commission for Social Care Inspection (CSCI).

It may have been on a smaller-scale than Gordon Rowe's regime, but the abuse suffered by the residents of Bedes View in Hull was still appalling. Seven care workers were jailed, in 2005, for ill-treatment and neglect after subjecting 10 people with learning difficulties to persistent abuse between 1998 and 2001. The abuse took place in two neighbouring bungalows, where residents were kicked and hit, tied to chairs, pinched and bullied. One man was repeatedly kicked in the groin, another had his face rubbed in urine, while a woman was forced to eat her food off the floor.

The law still allowed for maximum sentences of just two years for each offence, so the five women and two men escaped with prison terms of between three and 12 months each.

But in a groundbreaking development, the company that ran Bedes View was fined £100,000 for breaching its duty of care to the residents of the home, under the Health and Safety at Work Act. For the first time that I was aware of – and the Crown Prosecution Service was unable to find any other such cases – a company that had profited from this kind of neglect and ill-treatment had been severely punished, as Longcare Ltd never had been.

The people with learning difficulties who lived at homes and hospitals run by Cornwall Partnership NHS Trust should have been treated with respect and dignity. Instead, they were hit, kicked, over-medicated, mocked, deprived of food and given cold showers. One deafblind man was strapped to his wheelchair for up to 16 hours a day, while another man never had his teeth cleaned, and his toenails became infected because they were never cut. In one home, most of the taps were removed so residents couldn't wash their hands.

A report in 2006 by the Healthcare Commission and CSCI into 'years of abusive practices' – an investigation sparked by concerned relatives, rather than whistleblowing staff – concluded that institutional abuse was widespread and senior trust figures had failed to tackle the problem. The two inspection bodies discovered that the trust had carried out a string of internal investigations.

Allegations included 'staff hitting, pushing, shoving, dragging, kicking, secluding, belittling, mocking and goading people who used the trust's services, withholding food, giving cold showers, over zealous or premature use of restraint', as well as a lack of care, dignity, respect and privacy. There were also allegations of fraudulent use of residents' money.

Although the allegations were not as serious as the worst of the Longcare abuse, the report revealed that the trust had investigated 57 members of staff over 46 separate incidents between 2000 and 2005, while 40 people with learning difficulties had allegedly been abused. It was truly institutional abuse.

The Healthcare Commission and CSCI announced an immediate national audit of learning difficulty health services.

Dr Jean Collins, at the time VIA's director and one of the team who investigated the abuse, said their report showed that people with learning difficulties were still treated as 'second- and third-class citizens'. 'The extent of what was going on there,' she said, 'was really abhorrent.'

Just a few months later, in January 2007, the Healthcare Commission published the findings of another investigation, this time into alleged neglect and abuse at Orchard Hill, another of the last long-stay hospitals and run by Sutton and Merton Primary Care NHS Trust, and some of the trust's community homes.

The investigation found 15 serious incidents of physical and sexual abuse, including allegations that one female resident had been raped. It also found inappropriate use of restraint, including straps on wheelchairs and splints on arms being used to restrict movement, and poor staff training, while the views of people with learning difficulties 'were seldom heard'. The commission said such standards were 'simply not acceptable in the 21st century'.

Later that year, CSCI threatened Bedfordshire and Luton Mental Health and Social Care Partnership NHS Trust with prosecution unless it 'dramatically' improved standards in its residential homes for people with learning difficulties.

Care in nearly all the trust's homes was said to be far below national minimum standards, with problems over training, use of control and restraint by staff, and policies on reporting abuse allegations. Two months later, CSCI successfully applied to magistrates for a court order to shut down one of the homes.

In the same year, an NHS trust began an internal inquiry into serious alleged abuse at one of its day centres.

The results were only made public when the report by Rotherham Doncaster and South Humber Mental Health NHS Foundation Trust (RDaSH) was leaked to a local newspaper three years later, in 2010.

The report included 44 allegations of abuse of 18 people with learning difficulties, high support needs and physical and sensory impairments who used the Solar Centre, a day centre run by the trust. Most of the allegations made against four members of staff were found proven, although all four denied the allegations.

Even though the Healthcare Commission had been told about the allegations in 2007, I discovered, the trust was still given an 'excellent' rating three years running, for 2006-2007, 2007-08 and 2008-09. And so impressed was the Care Quality Commission, which took over the duties of the Healthcare Commission (and CSCI) in 2009, that RDaSH was 'named and famed' as one of 44 high performing trusts in 2009.

South Yorkshire police – like Thames Valley Police in the early 1990s – investigated allegations of physical assault in 2007 but failed to provide enough evidence to press charges. Neither the police nor the Crown Prosecution Service (CPS) would tell me whether they had considered charging staff with ill-treatment and neglect, as had been done with Longcare. As this book went to press, the force had just completed a 'full review', with the file passed to the CPS for a joint decision on whether to press charges.

The families I spoke to were angry that the trust appeared to have 'watered down' the allegations for its report. One 'safeguarding report', carried out by another agency into allegations concerning just one of the service-users, Richie Rowe, revealed that the abuse was far more serious than the trust's report suggested. It described how two members of staff kicked Rowe's wheelchair 'from one side of the room to the other causing Richie to crash into patients and the walls'. In another incident, Rowe was apparently lifted out of his wheelchair and thrown onto the floor. On another occasion, it was alleged that two staff members each grabbed one of his arms and legs and threw him onto a trampoline.

Adrian Milnes, Rowe's step-father, asked: 'What kind of criminal act does somebody have to do before the police will actually take notice?'

I received another safeguarding report, this time about Robert Kirsopp, who was allegedly grabbed and forced to the floor, pricked with needles, and pinned to a wall and hit around the head. Other allegations detailed how he was slapped, punched and threatened. Kirsopp's mother, Valerie, told me: 'It was torture on a daily basis and it continued for a year-and-a-half. I can't believe there were [so many] witnesses and nothing is being done about it.'

Anne Novis, a leading disabled activist and anti-hate crime campaigner, told me the case 'just informs the belief that we cannot have any trust or confidence in our police forces to take seriously the experiences of disabled people when they are absolutely degraded through such hostile treatment'.

There was more to come. I spoke to another whistleblower, Patrick Cawkwell. He had been working as a nursing assistant at a facility near the Solar Centre in 2003. Both services were in the grounds of St Catherine's Hospital, which is run by RDaSH. Cawkwell quit his job because of the abuse he witnessed, but not before making a detailed statement to a manager. He told me he had seen a service-user with learning difficulties locked in a cupboard, another sexually assaulted, and that he had detailed other claims of ill-treatment, neglect, bullying and racism.

The trust told me Cawkwell's allegations had been 'fully investigated' but were found 'not proven'. The trust appears to have failed to pass his allegations to the police. When I asked the trust whether these allegations suggested a wider culture of institutional abuse at St Catherine's, an RDaSH spokeswoman declined to comment.

Cawkwell later contacted the police, after hearing of the Solar Centre allegations, but was told his evidence was 'not required and they had everything they needed'.

The cases above suggest institutional abuse – particularly in NHS settings – is no less likely than when the Longcare scandal was exposed. But evidence of the scale of abuse is hard to find. The Department of Health and Comic Relief are researching the prevalence of abuse and neglect of older people in institutions. But no such work has been commissioned for people with learning difficulties. Nobody knows how widespread the problem is.

Michael Ratcliffe, co-chair of the National Forum of People with Learning Difficulties, although speaking to me in a personal capacity, said there was widespread abuse of people's rights in residential homes. 'I have noticed in a lot of places that they treat them just like children. They send them to bed at seven o'clock.' He said some care staff were really good at their jobs, others were 'just trying and just managing', while some 'couldn't care less'. 'You get older staff that have been there since the year dot and some of them have got really bad habits. The younger ones come in and they learn off the older ones. A lot of these institutions become laws to themselves.'

In 2004, the National Care Standards Commission was replaced by the Commission for Social Care Inspection (CSCI).

In a consultation paper published in its first year, CSCI said its inspectors 'spend too much time 'ticking boxes' and not enough time meeting the actual people who are using those care services', while it spent 'so much time carrying out routine inspections that we do not have enough time to follow up the complaints and concerns that people raise with us'.

Three years later, two CSCI directors – David Walden and John Fraser – described how their approach had become 'targeted, proportionate and flexible'[4]. Rather than inspecting every home twice a year, the idea was to focus on those that were 'performing less well' and increase enforcement activity against 'poorer providers'.

Unannounced inspections became the norm, while CSCI made it easier for prospective residents and their families to see the results of inspections, with up to 200,000 inspection reports downloaded every month. CSCI also developed the idea of 'experts by experience', in which people with learning difficulties and others who had used services would join inspections. And there were new 'tools' to help inspectors communicate more effectively with people with 'profound and multiple disabilities'.

Steven Rose, chief executive of Choice Support, told me that regulation 'improved enormously' under CSCI and moved away from the 'traffic warden tickbox mentality' in which inspectors were only interested in whether the thermometer in the fridge was at the right temperature, while CSCI started to listen to service-users.

But he was concerned about CSCI's successor, the Care Quality Commission (CQC), which took over duties as health and care watchdog in 2009. There have been redundancies, as well as substantial government spending cuts.

Deborah Kitson, of the Ann Craft Trust, was one of the few leading figures I spoke to who praised CQC. 'Safeguarding is very much at the top of their agenda, even in recession times,' she said. 'I am fairly impressed.'

On 1 October 2010, CQC launched a new system for registering services. Instead of the old system of annual inspections, homes will submit written self-assessments. CQC says this will allow homes to review their own services constantly, while it will gather evidence from service-users and other organisations to feed into the 'assessment and review process'.

But John Curry, a former detective inspector with Humberside police and manager of the safeguarding adults board in Hull and East Riding of Yorkshire for eight years, and now an independent safeguarding consultant, believes protection has been 'diluted' since NCSC was replaced by CSCI and then CQC. 'They say they have a focus on poor performing homes, but my view is that this realignment has just been done to save money. There are just not the inspectors walking through the door like there used to be on a regular basis. It's a paper assessment and I do not think that is wholly effective. A lot of it is self-assessing. I know a lot of my ex-colleagues have concerns about the way the regulator operates in terms of safeguarding.' He points, as Rose does, to concerns about the impact of redundancies. The commission agrees that it made 65 inspectors redundant in 2009, but says these were cuts planned by CSCI.

Even more worrying are concerns that residential homes that are good on paper will be able to avoid inspections for up to five years, although this is a suggestion CQC has – almost – denied. It stresses that its focus now is more on a regularly-updated 'quality and risk profile' for each home, including information collected by other organisations, but particularly the views and experiences of residents. 'When providers are failing to meet essential standards,' CQC told me, 'we have strong enforcement powers and will use them where it is necessary.'

Dame Jo Williams, the new CQC chair, told the Commons health committee in September 2010 there was 'no substitute for going in and talking to and listening to people's direct experiences and observing actually what's going on'. Tapping into the experiences of other visitors to the home was also 'very important', she said.

Fiona Mactaggart, then a member of the committee, questioned her closely over how the CQC would ensure this information did indeed feed into its systems. Mactaggart pointed out that these visitors do not always feed that information back. She pointed to Longcare, 'where the local Mencap group thought it was fine and yet patients were being raped in that home and being starved in that home over a number of years'.

Deborah Stuart-Angus, a safeguarding adults expert and chief executive of AssessForCare, is even gloomier than Rose and Curry. She sees the same problems with CQC that there were with Bucks County Council and Longcare. Some homes slip through the net because of a lack of resources. 'Resources are so thin and getting thinner,' she told me, 'with high sickness rates, pressure on staff. The inspection process itself is also complex.'

CQC insists that its sickness levels 'are not unusually high', while staff turnover 'has fallen recently'.

Philippa Russell, who was on the Longcare inquiry team and has since been made a Dame, is also concerned at the shift towards 'much shorter and I think less intensive inspections'. She is concerned that CQC could turn all its attention to the initial registration of homes, 'and not to what happens next'.

Dame Philippa insists that inspections must be about much more than ticking boxes. 'You absolutely need time with the residents and time with the staff and sufficient time to get the confidence of both so that they will speak out.' She believes most of the young, junior staff at Longcare – who were mostly 'very attached' to the residents and did much to try to protect them – would have spoken out if 'someone had got them in a room on their own'. But, she adds, this would never happen 'in a formal, quick CQC whizz round the corridors'.

She would like to see a much greater use of 'experts by experience'. 'Although they are not formal inspectors I think they often pick things up,' she told me. 'I don't think it would have been difficult for lay inspectors to pick up that things were not quite as they should be at Longcare even though superficially they were fine.'

The self-advocacy movement – those organisations run by people with learning difficulties and dedicated to supporting people to speak up for themselves – is strongly in favour of using people with learning difficulties themselves to inspect care and health settings. Andrew Lee, director of People First (Self-Advocacy), told me in the wake of the Cornwall abuse scandal: 'People with learning difficulties in the homes will speak more freely to people with learning difficulties if they have been bullied.'

I talk to the manager of a home where one of the former Longcare residents is now living. She is concerned about the prospect of homes only being inspected every five years. The CQC inspector who visits the home, and told her about this, is 'very concerned' by this possibility. 'She doesn't like the way things are going. She doesn't like the fact that everything is virtually going to become 'desk-top assessments'. She is going to lose out on the opportunity of coming to do assessments, unless people are found to be poor. There is a lot of disillusionment [within CQC]. A lot of inspectors have left.'

Dame Philippa is also concerned. Despite the CQC's near-denial, she says this figure of five years has been proposed. 'Five years is a long time in somebody's life,' she said. 'Five years is too long if there is a problem. A lot of poor care is not deliberate abuse, it is things cumulatively going wrong. The government is determined to lessen the bureaucracy but we have to decide what is bureaucracy and what is necessary.'

She agrees that this drift away from regular inspections risks a return to the attitudes of the 1980s, an atmosphere that allowed regimes like Longcare to thrive. 'Five years... I don't think it is safe.'

CQC says there have not been automatic annual inspections since 2007, when CSCI decided to concentrate on poorer-performing services. A CQC spokesman insists there will be a 'planned review' of every home 'at least every two years', and that this 'may involve an inspection', although it is 'highly unlikely that these reviews would be carried out without a visit to the service'. But he said it was impossible to predict how many inspections there would be under its new system.

Time will tell, but I was not convinced by the CQC's protestations, particularly at a time when the coalition government is attacking 'bureaucracy' and 'regulation' and slashing public sector spending.

When I approached the Department of Health, it repeated much of the information the CQC had given me, but declined to comment when asked if it had any concerns about the new system.

I ask Dame Philippa whether she has seen any improvement in local authorities visiting those people with learning difficulties placed in distant, 'out-of-area' residential settings.

She heard about one case, in which residents from two London boroughs were placed with a family in Sussex, along with a third person from Sussex. When Sussex County Council investigated concerns, they concluded that the three were suffering a 'serious lack of care that was tantamount to abuse', and informed the two London boroughs. But neither showed the slightest interest in moving the two people from the home. 'The two are still there,' she said, 'nothing happened, nobody visited. That seems to me absolutely criminal. And these are increasingly common arrangements. They are even more at risk because CQC is never going to inspect that kind of arrangement.'

She agrees there is still a need for a national audit of people in out-of-area placements, a suggestion I made in my first book. 'Your point about the national audit is particularly important,' she said, 'because we are seeing people moving into smaller, more dispersed places. Local authorities will have less money, and will be more resistant to going out and actually looking at where people are and I think we desperately need some national evidence set of what is actually happening.'

Fiona Mactaggart is also concerned. Now in opposition, she says she wonders whether Labour 'didn't miss a trick' when in power, in failing to create a national network of volunteers to visit isolated people in care settings.

She believes it is homes in which no residents have been placed by local social services where the most serious risks occur. 'I think it's a very, very strong argument for why you need to have local provision,' she told me. 'There's no way social services can properly monitor things a long way away.'

Steven Rose also says there has been 'very little progress at all' on out-of-area placements. He said most of the Department of Health's money and effort went into closing the last long-stay hospitals, and then shutting NHS-run residential campuses. 'In the meantime there has not been a great deal of focus on out-of-borough placements. Most people will acknowledge the quality isn't good. Goodness knows what is going on in many of them. No, things definitely haven't improved in that area.'

CQC agrees that, 'in general', it makes sense for people to live as close as possible to their home area, although some placements will be better quality than those found nearer home. Out-of-area placements, it says, 'should be the subject of regular review and planning'. But it has no idea how many people have been abandoned in placements far from home, a question, it says, that is 'not easy to answer with available data'. It declined to comment when I asked whether a national audit was a good idea.

The Department of Health (DH) was also less than enthusiastic about the suggestion. It said such people 'should be offered a review of care needs in exactly the same way on the same terms as someone living in their home authority. In addition to this someone with high care needs and high cost placements will clearly need particularly attention.'

Yes, but the evidence suggests this is not happening. As for the need for a national audit, the DH declined to comment.

Poor pay among care workers is also still a huge issue, according to Deborah Kitson, of the Ann Craft Trust. 'Poor practice is still there,' she told me, 'but it will not change until we actually put the pay for care staff on a better footing – we pay appalling wages and expect great work.'

Deborah Stuart-Angus believes many of the issues around safeguarding are due to problems with care staff. 'One of the issues you see is huge under-reporting, exceedingly high levels of sloppy practice and few checks and balances being put in place by managers.' She also sees a shortage of quality training because of a lack of funding.

The General Social Care Council (GSCC) will not survive the change of government. The coalition announced in October 2010 that it would be abolished, with its functions transferred to the Health Professions Council, which will be renamed the Health and Care Professions Council (HCPC).

Labour had intended that the GSCC would eventually watch over the entire social care workforce, but it only managed to introduce compulsory registration for social workers, in 2004. Care workers, like those at Longcare, are still outside the regulatory system.

The GSCC told me the problem had been one of 'scale' and that regulating the entire workforce would have been 'a huge job'. Regulating care workers, with daily access to people in incredibly vulnerable situations, was clearly not a high enough priority.

In its Enabling Excellence white paper, published in February 2011, the DH argues that care workers are not untouched by the state. Most are covered by the vetting and barring scheme, which prevents those who pose a known risk from gaining access to children and 'vulnerable adults', while care providers must register with CQC.

The DH told me: 'It does not follow inevitably that compulsory and centralised statutory regulation is the most effective or efficient way of ensuring high quality care.' Its new health and social care bill will allow a voluntary register for social care workers in England, which it describes as a 'proportionate, safe and effective approach'. This register – which the government wants the HCPC to set up by 2013 – could provide an incentive for care home bosses to employ only registered care workers, but they would not be forced to do so.

In the white paper, health secretary Andrew Lansley says 'reducing regulation' is a 'key priority' for the coalition government. 'In a society that trusts and values its health and social care workforce,' he says, 'obliging more of them to pay for regulation should be a matter of last resort.

'By freeing society from unnecessary laws,' Lansley adds, 'the government aims to create a better balance of responsibilities between the state, business, civil society and individuals, and to encourage people to take greater personal responsibility for their actions.' People like Gordon Rowe, perhaps.

The POVA list – those people banned from working with 'vulnerable adults' – was finally introduced for care workers in 2004, four years after the Care Standards Act became law. Employers were now able to discover if their prospective employee was on the list as part of pre-employment checks with the Criminal Records Bureau (CRB). In fact, I discovered only last year, the idea of a POVA-type list for adults was floated by the Conservative government in 1984, but it decided that creating one for children was 'the first priority'. It is unclear why it took another 20 years to introduce a list for people working with adults.

Within a year of POVA's introduction, more than 700 people had been banned from working with 'vulnerable adults'. The charities Voice UK, the Ann Craft Trust and Respond were 'horrified' at the figures, but described POVA as 'a significant development'. An audit by King's College London of the first 100 POVA referrals found 81 per cent were from residential homes, while more than a third concerned male workers, even though they made up only five to 15 per cent of staff. The audit found neglect and physical abuse were more likely reasons for inclusion for residential home staff, while financial abuse was more common in home care.

The following year, CSCI reported that less than three in five residential homes for people with learning difficulties were meeting the standard for vetting and recruiting their staff.

Decisions on 'vetting and barring' care workers is now carried out by the Independent Safeguarding Authority (ISA), set up following the Bichard Inquiry into the murders in 2002 of Jessica Chapman and Holly Wells, and subsequent legislation in 2006. As this book went to press, the government announced that millions of people working or volunteering with 'vulnerable adults' and children would no longer need to have their criminal records checked, in order to 'scale back' Labour's vetting and barring scheme – which would have required more than nine million people to be checked – to 'common sense levels'.

In an echo of its decision on registering care workers, the government said more of the responsibility for 'safeguarding' should be placed on individuals and employers, rather than the state.

The CRB and ISA will merge, while checks will be restricted to those working 'most closely and regularly' with 'vulnerable adults' and children. Care workers will be able to take their checks with them between jobs, through a system allowing for continuous updating of criminal records disclosures that will 'cut down on needless bureaucracy'.

Deborah Kitson told me it 'made sense' to reduce the numbers needing checks but she had concerns about 'how far this may be taken'. She also has concerns about the 'portable' CRB checks and said she would 'need to be convinced that the CRB updates referred to are efficient and prompt and so do not leave people at risk'. But she welcomed the announcement that a balance of responsibility would be shared by the state and the employer, so that employers would have to be 'diligent in their recruitment and safeguarding strategies'.

Lesley Robinson, who manages a residential home for older people in Grimsby, says the vetting and barring system is far from a failsafe. 'Every programme I see or newspaper article I read sends chills down my spine when I realise what awful people there are out there,' she told me, 'and I worry that my 'gut instinct' will let me down badly one day when recruiting, because there is absolutely no way I will rely solely on CRB checks or references. These, at best, are retrospective on the part of references and not always entirely honest if they give any real information at all, as some managers worry about being sued for defamation of character, and at worst on the part of CRBs could simply mean that the candidate has never been caught, again sometimes due to some managers being afraid to report them unless they feel they can prove suspicions beyond a doubt.'

As for whistleblowing, there is some anecdotal evidence that the climate is more supportive for those care workers who want to expose poor practice and abuse. One safeguarding expert, Jane*, who works for an NHS trust, said she had found some improvements in care workers 'recognising abuse and making alerts'. But she said this often only happened when a new member of staff came into a home and was confronted by a regime in which abusive cultures and attitudes had been left 'unchallenged'.

Another professional, Susan*, a former social worker who now trains professionals in identifying adult abuse, says the local authorities she works with have set up safeguarding teams, providing a central point to which concerns can be referred.

This means that anonymous and whistleblowing referrals are 'taken seriously'. Each team has a 'decision maker', who liaises with police and then decides what action to take.

But Susan says that whistleblowing – if you work for an organisation that does not take abuse seriously – can still be 'extremely stressful'. 'There is no doubt in my mind,' she says, 'that some professionals are intimidated not to whistleblow because of [the threat of] reprisals or loss of job, and may leave their employment to avoid taking action, leaving the abuse to continue.' Some organisations still refuse to believe that a member of their staff could have abused a service-user or do not want to damage their 'good reputation'.

Philippa Russell believes the growing number of care staff with immigrant status could also make whistleblowing less likely. 'The threat you could get them thrown out of the country [if they whistleblow] could have a very worrying effect. The young staff at Longcare felt that if they had whistle-blown they would have been dismissed and worse abusers would have come in. I met two young women [who worked there] and they were very young and quite naive and they were just very scared by powerful people. In many care homes and care settings, people are not very well educated, not very confident. They may not have anybody they can talk confidentially to. They are very likely to hang on rather than explode the whole thing.'

Despite the widespread push – both by the Labour and new coalition governments – for greater 'personalisation' of care services, with more choice and control for the individual, many local authorities are still using large residential homes, rather than small, home-like settings.

A CQC report in 2010 found the average size of a residential home (including those for people without learning difficulties) rose from 17.8 places in 2004 to 18.5 places in 2010, although the report stressed that, for people with learning difficulties, about 70 per cent were in homes with less than 10 places. The total number of places for younger adults with learning difficulties in care homes also rose, from 50,235 in 2009 to 50,546 in 2010.

A paper by the National Development Team for inclusion confirmed this trend in 2010[5], warning that 'despite evidence that people want more 'non traditional' housing options, the number of residential care places for people with learning disabilities is continuing to grow'. It pointed to the 6,255 registered homes for people with learning difficulties in England, of which nearly 10 per cent (562) were registered in the previous year.

The paper said that a third of adults with learning difficulties still lived in residential care. 'Good quality residential care should remain a valid choice,' the paper said, 'but it should not be the only or predominant choice just because there is little or nothing else available.'

Although the government's No Secrets guidance was plagued from the start by a lack of funding and the failure to make its recommendations legally binding, it did have an impact. Every area in England now has its own safeguarding adults board, although they do not yet have the statutory force of the equivalent boards for children.

Deborah Kitson says there has been an 'increased awareness' over the last decade. 'There seem to be a wider and wider range of organisations that accept they have a responsibility to look after vulnerable adults,' she says.

Jane, who works for an NHS trust, said her safeguarding team was set up on the back of No Secrets, and had been 'pivotal in raising awareness countywide about abuse, how to recognise it, and how to make an alert'. 'In practice,' she says, 'we have found No Secrets has had an enormously positive impact, enabling clarity in a very grey area.' There is greater awareness and more transparency, she says, and 'life has got more difficult for potential perpetrators', but there are still occasions when organisations are 'intimidated' by the processes and will try to avoid their responsibilities, leaving the victim 'stranded in the middle'. And some large organisations, she warns, particularly in the NHS, have been 'slow to engage' with the agenda, and 'see themselves as having some type of diplomatic immunity from safeguarding'.

John Curry also believes there have been improvements. 'When I started in 2001 there was almost nothing. It was just dealt with in an ad hoc way. No Secrets was the catalyst which started to make things happen. But there was never any funding for it from central government so local authorities just developed as they thought fit. Sad things are still happening. At least now we have an integrated and laid-down process for dealing with those allegations. The amount of training that has taken place has been enormous.' Health bodies are shaking off their reluctance to 'come on board', he added.

Philippa Russell still has her concerns about many safeguarding boards. 'I get the feeling that they are very varied in their... development, and the areas in which they are willing to work.'

The issue of funding has become even more crucial following the 2010 general election and the coalition government's spending cuts. Susan*, who trains professionals in identifying adult abuse, believes many safeguarding adults boards could 'struggle financially'. Because of restricted funding and the lack of legislation, the progress made on safeguarding 'could well be at risk in the future'.

Health secretary Andrew Lansley's new consumer champion for patients, HealthWatch, is set to play a future role in safeguarding, in social care as well as health, although Dame Philippa says she worries about its potential to make an impact as 'everything has been done in such a hurry'. The DH says local HealthWatch organisations will be able to investigate complaints about care standards and if they are not satisfied with the response, 'escalate issues' to HealthWatch England or CQC.

Indeed, in its new 'vision' for adult social care, the government says it wants to 'support and encourage local communities to be the eyes and ears of safeguarding, speaking up for people who may not be able to protect themselves'. 'The risk of abuse,' it says, 'can come from people close to the individual concerned, not just from paid staff or volunteers.'

The DH says HealthWatch England will be based at CQC, and will provide advice to government, CQC and health and local government bodies, based on information from local HealthWatch 'and other sources'. Local HealthWatch branches will have the power to 'enter and view' care homes and could recommend investigations if concerned.

Since No Secrets, there has been continuing tension between those professionals who want stricter, stronger safeguarding rules with more powers for police and social workers, and those disabled campaigners, including many people with learning difficulties, who want the authorities to stop treating them like children and allow them choice and control. They want to take their own safeguarding decisions, but accept that they need help with options, information and support.

Andrew Lee, a leading member of the self-advocacy movement, told me early in 2010 that it was vital to build advice from people with learning difficulties into the safeguarding system. But he said proper training and education across the criminal justice system was vital before the government could even consider giving professionals new powers.

The coalition government, in its 'vision' for adult social care, suggested it was searching for a way to allow people 'to make decisions about risk without becoming intrusive or overbearing'. 'People tell us they wish to be safe,' the document continued, 'but equally they do not want to be over-protected and denied their independence... A modern social care system needs to balance freedom and choice with risk and protection.'

The issue will be addressed – somehow – when the Law Commission publishes its recommendations for the reform of social care laws. Deborah Stuart-Angus, who has been involved in its consultation, hopes it will recommend a new legal duty to co-operate in safeguarding cases. Currently, members of safeguarding adults boards cannot be held accountable because there are no legal requirements on their work, and no legal duty for agencies to co-operate. 'As long as there is no duty to co-operate we cannot hold partners responsible for what they do or don't do,' she says. She has seen a local authority investigator forced to make a request under the Freedom of Information Act to access information in a safeguarding case. She says problems with sharing information are widespread. 'I see it all the time and it is particularly prevalent in health.'

Deborah Kitson says the personalisation agenda has brought the question of freedom and choice versus safeguarding to a head. 'I am absolutely an advocate of personalisation, except when people think you can do it and disregard safeguarding. I don't want to take away people's decisions but at the end of the day there are a lot of people out there who will need safeguarding when they make their decisions.'

Steven Rose says many people are becoming 'very concerned' that the personalisation agenda will leave people with learning difficulties 'without any protection', but he adds: 'Personally, I do not share that view. I don't think the older system worked very well and I think there is scope to make sure that people are protected better.' He says the key will be to ensure that the right checks are carried out on the safety of each person. 'If the planning is right around one person at a time and you are asking the right set of questions around risks and safeguards you can check one person at a time rather than having an inspector coming in once a year or not coming in at all.

'The people responsible for the systems that have worked in a moderate way at best are now saying the new world will leave vulnerable people at risk. I personally disagree. I think the old system has not worked and there are ways of building safeguards into the new one.'

So what about Valuing People, the learning difficulties white paper that was greeted with such optimism in 2001, despite the lack of funding for its implementation?

Jan Walmsley[6] says the setting up of the National Forum of People with Learning Difficulties 'put the voice of people with learning difficulties into the centre of the government process'. But, she adds, any targets in Valuing People were 'vaguely worded, and by any standards hard to measure'.

Jane, who works for an NHS trust, believes the drive to save money has been 'heavily camouflaged' under the 'empowerment' and 'independence' rhetoric advocated in Valuing People, and its 2009 successor, Valuing People Now. She says this cost-cutting is leaving people with learning difficulties more at risk of abuse.

A government report in December 2010 summarised the first annual reports produced by England's 152 learning disability partnership boards, which were set up as a result of Valuing People. Although it praised the 'considerable progress' made across health, housing and employment, it also revealed that the percentage of people with learning difficulties who were known to local authorities and were living in residential homes appears – despite some uncertainty about the figures for 2008-09 – to have risen from about 35 per cent to 39 per cent.

So what should happen now?

Steven Rose believes there must be a greater focus on children and young people, because 'that is where the problems begin'. 'Bearing in mind that all behaviours are a form of communication, there needs to be a proper resourcing and understanding of how to support children who are labelled as having challenging behaviour.' When children cannot be managed, they are often sent to residential schools away from their local authority of origin. And when they become adults, someone has 'conveniently opened a residential care home down the road'. It is those with the most challenging behaviour who are being shut away, he says. 'If we could deal with that, there would be less of a problem.'

'Attitudes and cultures are hard to change,' says Jane, 'but I find through my work that there remain many structures, organisations and people who do not respect people with learning disabilities. Until this changes they will always be viewed as less important and less worthy, making them susceptible within society.'

Richard Curen, chief executive of Respond, believes a major awareness-raising campaign is essential to educate the public about what abuse is, how it can be covered up, and how it affects people with learning difficulties. And, he adds, 'funding for some decent research, funding for some better services'.

Deborah Stuart-Angus says more elected councillors need safeguarding training. 'Saying it is everyone's business needs to be more than just a strap line,' she says. 'Now we are facing huge cuts, in services which are stripped to the bone. There are cultures of excessive working hours, high stress and roles which contain an untold amount of statutory responsibilities, sometimes without people even realising. Unless elected members see the value and lawful requirement of the work being done, we stand the risk of the 20 per cent top slice, just like everyone else.'

Susan, who trains professionals in safeguarding, would also like to see a high-profile awareness-raising campaign, with adverts on television, on the sides of buses, in newspapers and in schools, to spread knowledge about adult abuse and how to recognise the signs, maybe even with DVDs playing in surgeries. 'I would like society to be more aware and not just professionals,' she says.

Michael Ratcliffe says nationally-recognised training of care staff is vital, while 'older staff who are not prepared to change should be told to leave, because they are the ones that cause the problems'. He believes more inspections – and particularly spot checks – are needed, while inspection teams must include people with learning difficulties. The most important measure, he says, is 'strong robust and independent advocacy for all people with learning difficulties in all areas of social care in the community and essential in residential settings'.

Philippa Russell would like to see a 'much clearer and as far as possible independent' method of making complaints about abuse.

She believes Longcare is still 'firmly fixed in the minds' of those who work with people with learning difficulties. 'It had huge publicity at the time and it touched a lot of raw nerves in providers. It was full of awful warnings that most people took to heart and still take to heart when something could go wrong when superficially everything might seem alright.'

*

I returned again, for the first time in many years, to Buckinghamshire County Council. I was keen to discover whether its officers and members had indeed learned the lessons of Longcare, following the humiliation of the independent inquiry in 1998.

In a lengthy written statement – 30 pages long – the council told me that it had taken a 'systematic approach' to the inquiry's many recommendations, coming up with a wide-ranging 'action plan', and that since then it had 'continually reviewed' and tried to improve its safeguarding work.

It introduced multi-agency policies and procedures in 1999, set up a vulnerable adult protection committee in 2001, has produced an annual safeguarding report every year since 2004, and takes the lead in safeguarding work with the area's health bodies, police and CQC. There is a joint-funded adult protection coordinator to organise training, and there have been annual courses with Thames Valley Police since 2001. Its actions sound like those of many other local authorities over the last 12 years.

But if the council has indeed taken the lessons of the inquiry – and its own appalling failings – to heart, why then, in 2008, when CSCI inspected its safeguarding and response to No Secrets, did it conclude that Buckinghamshire's performance was simply 'adequate' (the possible ratings were poor, adequate, good and excellent)?

Again, 10 years on from the Longcare inquiry, Buckinghamshire reacted with an action plan. It claims this led to a string of improvements, with better public awareness, changes in management responsibility, and funding to pay a chair of the independent safeguarding vulnerable adults board. Perhaps most disturbingly, it admitted it had needed to improve in 'learning the lessons' from difficult or complex safeguarding cases [serious case reviews]. Nearly 14 years after Longcare was exposed to the grisly light of day – despite the council's efforts to ensure that Rowe's crimes remained hidden from public scrutiny – Bucks still didn't feel able to learn from cases of serious abuse of adults with learning difficulties. And there was more. It had also concluded that it needed to strengthen joint working with Thames Valley Police – another of the key criticisms from Longcare.

The action plan led, the council says, to the number of cases of potential abuse (safeguarding referrals) passed on to the council increasing from 103 in 2008/09 to 158 in 2009/10, a rise of more than 50 per cent, which it admits 'shows the direct impact of improved practice'. What this means, essentially, is that because it didn't have the correct procedures in place before April 2009, it had almost certainly been failing for many years to pick up scores and scores of cases in which people with learning difficulties were at risk.

Sadly, an assessment by CQC in 2009/10, based partly on the council's assessment of its own performance, found that its safeguarding was still just 'adequate'. It was one of 27 councils (out of 152) that were rated as adequate or poor.

And there was one more depressing sign that Bucks County Council really didn't want to learn the lessons of Longcare, or help anyone else learn them either.

I had noticed that the Longcare inquiry report was not available on the council's website, or anywhere else on the internet. The council told me this was because its website was only created in 1998, the same year the report was published, and the site didn't then have the facility for attaching or uploading documents. But why not add it now?

A council spokesman told me that, since 1998, there had been a 'considerable number of legislative changes' and the council – and others – had 'learned from mistakes'. The report, I was told, was 'readily available in hard copy'. A spokesman added: 'We do not therefore consider it appropriate at this late stage to put the report on our website.'

Perhaps, of all Buckinghamshire County Council's admissions and failures over the last 30 years, that is the most disgraceful one of all*.

*I approached the council in February 2011 to ask it to check the above passage for any factual errors. It had been condensed from a 30-page response littered with jargon, and I wanted to be accurate and fair. In reply, I received a threatening letter, pointing out the 'significant changes' the council had made which had led to 'significantly improved safeguarding practices', and warning that the council reserved its right 'to take any action we may consider appropriate on publication of any material containing references to us'. When I asked the council to clarify its concerns, I received a similar letter, which failed to explain which facts or opinions the council objected to. After nearly 17 years covering this story, I shouldn't have been surprised, but this bullying attitude still seemed deeply inappropriate in the light of the central role the council had played in the Longcare scandal._

1   The Impact of Legislative Change on the Independent, Residential Care Sector, by Stephen O'Kell; Joseph Rowntree Foundation; 2002

2   Blowing the Whistle on Abuse of Adults with Learning Disabilities, by Rebecca Calcraft; Ann Craft Trust and Centre for Social Work, University of Nottingham; 2005

3   *The Response to No Secrets, by Dinah Mathew, Hilary Brown, Paul Kingston, Claudine McCreadie and Janet Askham; The Journal of Adult Protection; Vol 4 Issue 1, Feb 2002*

4   *Reform and Regulation: Two journeys to one destination, by David Walden and John Fraser, in Residential Care: A positive future; The Residential Forum; 2008*

5   *Supported Living – Making the Move: Developing supported living options for people with learning disabilities; National Development Team for inclusion Housing and Social Inclusion Project discussion paper; National Development Team for inclusion; 2010*

6   *Community Care in Perspective: Care, control and citizenship, by John Welshman and Jan Walmsley; Palgrave Macmillan; 2006*

Chapter Twenty-Six

The Criminal Justice System

*'Two Cheshire teenagers who terrorised a vulnerable man
before beating him to death and throwing his body in a river,
have had their life sentences cut... The pair were dubbed as
'feral' when they were jailed for life for the manslaughter
of Raymond Atherton, 40, in Warrington. They beat and
urinated on Mr Atherton before dumping him in the River
Mersey. Despite the severity of their crime, Lord Justice
Rix overturned the life terms and replaced them with
sentences of detention for public protection... The court
heard [they] spent months systematically abusing the
victim, who had severe learning difficulties, in a process
they nicknamed 'terroring'. They regularly broke into his
council flat... where they wrote graffiti on the walls, burnt
his hair and daubed his face with paint.'*

BBC Online, 8 November 2007

One of the female residents of Longcare, one of those the staff called Gordon's Girls, the women Rowe raped and sexually and physically assaulted, moved to a residential home in London after she left Stoke Place.

Like the other women Rowe raped, the abuse had made her an easier target for sexual predators. She was raped again by a care worker in her new home and became pregnant. But despite the evidence provided by an abortion, the judge who heard the subsequent rape case decided she had consented to the attack 'by animal instinct'.

June Raybaud and Justice for Longcare Survivors were horrified when they learned about the case – and the judge's language. They knew the reason the woman might not have appeared to put up a struggle was that she did not understand what was being done to her.

There was clearly something wrong with a legal system that allowed such a miscarriage of justice.

Rowe, of course, had known since Somerset how difficult it was to prosecute a sexual offence committed against a person with learning difficulties.

Rowe killed himself before he could be charged with any sexual offences, but the Longcare case – and the subsequent rape (above) of one of Gordon's Girls – had highlighted a troubling area of the law. Despite the weight of evidence, there was no guarantee Rowe would have been convicted if he had stood trial for rape and sexual assault. And it was even less likely that he would have been handed a fitting punishment.

The law said it was illegal for a man to take part in a sexual act with a 'mental defective' woman (under the Sexual Offences Act 1956). But it was difficult to prove in court that someone was 'a mental defective', apart from the insulting nature of the phrase, so in practice the law only protected women with the highest support needs. And the maximum sentence was only two years. So because prosecutors were usually unable to prove that a victim was 'mentally defective', they instead had to prove indecent assault or rape in the usual way, by proving the attack had taken place and that the victim had not consented. There were very few successful prosecutions.

The Home Office consultation paper Setting the Boundaries concluded in July 2000: 'We were profoundly moved by the extent of sexual abuse against vulnerable people and felt that the law needed considerable strengthening to tackle this while respecting the ability of those who could consent to sexual activity to have a private life.'

This was a crucial point. Introducing a law to make it illegal to commit a sexual act with any person with a learning difficulty would be a dreadful restriction on their right to a sex life, as well as being a throwback to the restrictions of the Mental Deficiency Acts. So the paper recommended that those who were unable to understand the nature or potential consequences of having sex should not be able to consent to it, and that sexual activity with such a person should be a serious offence. Secondly, there should be a new offence of a breach of a relationship of trust, outlawing sex between clients and their care workers. A third new offence would make it illegal to obtain sex with a person with a learning difficulty by threats or deception. All three could have been applied to the crimes perpetrated by Gordon Rowe at Longcare.

These issues were highlighted again in No Justice, a report by the charities Mencap, Respond and Voice UK in September 2001, which made similar recommendations.

In fact, as I discovered while completing my research late in 2010, MPs on the Commons social services committee had recommended in 1985 that the government should order an independent review of the law on 'sexuality and contraception' as it affected people with learning difficulties and those with mental health conditions. Responding, the government had said it would be difficult to devise rules which gave both 'proper freedom and guard against exploitation', while a major review 'might simply attract unwelcome, unhealthy and wholly disproportionate media interest'. This bizarre response delayed the introduction of laws that would have protected women like Tracy, Rachel, Michelle, Janet Ward and Rosie Valton, and of course many of the men at Longcare.

Kathleen Franklin, chair of Milton Keynes People First, told me at the time that at least three members of her group had been sexually assaulted, but none of them had seen their attackers punished. 'They are really scared now,' she said. 'A person that is not going to be nice to the person with learning difficulties and is going to abuse them, I don't agree with. There is a difference between having sex and having it forced onto you.'

The government finally announced plans for new legislation in 2002. The sexual offences bill included three new sets of offences, as outlined in Setting the Boundaries. The first was engaging in sexual activity with a person who was unable to consent due to learning difficulties, with a maximum penalty of life imprisonment. Obtaining sexual activity with someone with learning difficulties by 'inducement, threat or deception' would also carry a maximum penalty of life imprisonment. And thirdly, anyone working in a care setting who engaged in sexual activity with a client with learning difficulties would face a possible 14 years in prison (increased from seven years after pressure from organisations like Voice UK and Mencap).

Some people with learning difficulties were alarmed at the possible criminalisation of their sex lives and outraged at the idea of courts debating whether or not they were able to consent to sex. They also feared the effect of the new laws on the people who ran and worked in care homes and day centres: they were worried that many care workers were ill-qualified to decide whether clients were able to consent, and would take the safer option of forbidding such relationships.

Simone Aspis, a prominent disabled activist with learning difficulties, wrote in Disability Now magazine: 'The new law rests on the issue of consent: did the person agree to the sexual relationship? Mencap would like a test which people with learning difficulties would have to 'pass' in order to prove their consent was informed. There would be outrage if non-disabled people were subjected to such a test during court proceedings, so why should this be different for people with learning difficulties?

'The best way to deter perpetrators is to increase the severity of punishment for people found guilty of unconsented sex with anyone, whether they are disabled or not,' she wrote. Similar concerns were raised by the Learning Disability Taskforce the following year.

But the government had at least tried to close loopholes that were protecting abusers like Gordon Rowe, and sentences were now more likely to reflect the seriousness of the offences.

But there was little point in introducing new offences, with tough new sentences, if the victims of the crimes were unable to give their evidence.

Little attention had ever been paid to making it easier for witnesses with learning difficulties to give evidence in court. In 1998, Charles Pollard, the chief constable of Thames Valley Police, admitted that the criminal justice system was 'failing vulnerable victims'. Parts of the Youth Justice and Criminal Evidence Act 1999 were intended to put that right.

One of the most important sections of the act stated that people with learning difficulties would now be assumed to be competent to appear as witnesses, rather than assumed to be incompetent, as was previously the case. The act would also allow witnesses to give evidence unsworn, if they found it difficult to understand the oath.

Other measures would also, in theory, help more people with learning difficulties give evidence. Lawyers could ask a judge for various 'special measures' to support a witness. These included screens to prevent intimidation by the accused in the dock; court officials removing their wigs and gowns; video-links, allowing the witness to give evidence from outside the court-room; and the use of 'intermediaries', people appointed by the court to assess the needs of a 'vulnerable' witness and help them give their evidence. Although the act became law in 1999, the special measures were not to be introduced in crown courts until August 2002, 13 years after they were recommended by Judge Pigot's advisory group on video evidence.

By the end of 2002, it was clear that the act's full implementation had been further delayed, apparently because of a lack of funding for training. Six months later, Voice UK's Kathryn Stone told me implementation of the special measures had been so patchy that she feared the new laws introduced under the Sexual Offences Act would result in few successful prosecutions.

It was also obvious that magistrates, lawyers, judges and the Crown Prosecution Service (CPS) needed to learn how to deal sensitively and intelligently with people with learning difficulties who entered the criminal justice system.

Unfortunately, the judiciary had refused to undertake specific training, although new guidelines on disabled people were issued to judges as part of the Judicial Studies Board's equal treatment bench book, including advice on reducing the stress felt by 'vulnerable witnesses' and how to take their evidence.

But as Fiona Mactaggart told the Commons in February 2002: 'I have spoken to the chair of the judicial studies training board, who is proud of the fact that judges receive half a day's training on disability. If they receive half a day's training on disability, how much training do they receive in learning disability and ways of communicating with people with learning disabilities? It is not enough. Until we introduce serious training on how to communicate with people with learning disabilities for police, prosecutors and judges, we shall fail to deliver justice.'

This was confirmed by research[1] the same year which showed judges were failing to help witnesses with learning difficulties give their best evidence in court, and rarely intervened to stop prosecuting barristers harassing them or asking confusing questions.

The attitude of the CPS was also a problem, with too many cases dropped because the victim and main witness had a learning difficulty. Sometimes, this reluctance was justified. The courts were heavily tilted against people with learning difficulties. But it also became clear that the CPS lacked specialist knowledge. Sometimes this lack of knowledge reached as far as ignorance and discrimination. Many prosecutors seemed to dismiss the idea of people with learning difficulties appearing as witnesses without even meeting them. Many other cases reached the courts, often because a determined police officer had pushed for a prosecution, only for the CPS to pull out before the trial.

By the end of 2002, the CPS had pledged to improve. The Ann Craft Trust was awarded a contract to train CPS staff. Ann Craft director Deborah Kitson told me she believed there was a 'real commitment' within the CPS to improve, with every lawyer receiving three days' training.

The following year, Sir David Calvert-Smith QC, the director of public prosecutions, told a meeting of the Voice all-party parliamentary group that someone with a learning difficulty faced a 'course of almost Grand National proportions before he or she can get justice'. He said there had been a 'real change of culture' within the CPS but admitted there were 'quite startling differences' in how often prosecutors in different parts of the country applied for special measures. And he said that some judges 'need to have quite strong applications' to convince them to allow special measures to be used.

Later that year, a conference organised by the CPS and Voice UK heard about a scheme that had supported a witness with learning difficulties to give evidence as part of a series of 20 trials in the late 1990s. The trials followed a massive police investigation into abuse in residential homes – mostly for children – in the north-west of England. The scheme – known later as the Liverpool Model of Witness Support, Preparation and Profiling – had provided intensive support for 'Michael', one of the men with learning difficulties who claimed they had been serious sexually assaulted at a large institution. Because

340

of this support, Michael gave evidence in four trials, three of which led to convictions.

But the conference heard of persistent problems in other parts of the country, where police officers and prosecutors continued to write off people with learning difficulties as undependable witnesses who 'tell lies' and 'change their stories'.

Inevitably, efforts to improve the system were hampered by funding problems. One prosecutor told the conference: 'We need more support staff to offer those services and the money just isn't there to do that.'

In May 2003, I was on the verge of sending the final version of Silent Victims to my publisher when the comments of Judge John Baker six years earlier, at the end of the Longcare trial, caught my eye.

Judge Baker had told the court that the Mental Health Act provided him with inadequate sentencing powers, and called for an urgent parliamentary review of the law. Somehow I had failed to follow-up this line of inquiry. I called the Department of Health, which was working on a new Mental Health Act. Yes, they told me, the offences of ill-treatment and neglect were still in the draft act. And no, the maximum sentences had not been increased.

Nearly 10 years on from the exposure of the Longcare regime, and more than six years after the trial, nothing had been done.

*

So if the Longcare case had exposed so many flaws in the criminal justice system, had it also reflected the true scale of crime and abuse against people with learning difficulties?

A survey by Mencap in 1999 found that two-thirds of people with learning difficulties were bullied at least once a month, whether through name-calling, harassment, threats, or physical assaults. Nearly 90 per cent had been bullied in the previous year. The survey quoted one Glasgow woman, who said: 'I get called

341

stupid, teased all the time. Children follow me every day and call me names, threaten to kill me, in the street and at the centre.'

Name-calling often escalated to something more serious, as the perpetrators realised they could get away with less serious offences. Most incidents were unprovoked. They could occur anywhere: at a bus stop, in the street, in leisure facilities, shops, pubs, even in people's own homes.

Three years later, the crime reduction charity NACRO reported that nine out of ten people with learning difficulties questioned for its research[2] had been verbally harassed in the previous year.

In the summer of 2001, another Mencap survey uncovered worrying evidence of human rights abuses within the NHS. In one case, medical staff placed a 'do not resuscitate' notice on the records of a 24-year-old woman with learning difficulties and physical impairments, who had developed a serious respiratory infection, without telling her parents. She was refused intensive care and her parents were told she could not be placed on a life support machine because of her 'age, disability, quality of life and the cost'. She died.

Mencap collected many other examples of such discrimination. Often they involved medical staff placing 'do not resuscitate' notices on patients' records, or judges deciding that lives were 'not worth living'.

Another piece of research[3] also illustrated the need for change. Dr Dinah Murray described how tens of thousands of people with learning difficulties were on repeat prescriptions of anti-psychotic drugs, which could have devastating effects on their bodies. The list of potential side-effects included: difficulty talking, urinating and swallowing, fatigue, jerky movements of head, face, mouth or neck, drooling saliva, skin rashes, sore throat, swelling of feet, trembling of hands, uncontrollable lip movements and weight gain. The drugs – which include some of those used by Gordon Rowe on the Longcare residents, such as Largactil – could also cause sudden death. They were often used as tranquillisers, as Rowe used them, or to calm behaviours that might have annoyed or alarmed other people, such as anger, frustration or shouting, in the mistaken belief that they were showing symptoms of psychosis.

Murray's research showed a frightening tendency among professionals – particularly GPs and care workers – to reach for the drugs when confronted with behaviour they did not understand or did not want to understand, and which was more than likely the result of a frustrated attempt to communicate, simple boredom, or even an undiagnosed health condition.

As for sexual abuse, few cases had reached the courts because of the flaws in the criminal justice system. Often, a successful prosecution was only possible because the offender had been careless.

One successful conviction was of agency care worker Phillip Kambeta, who raped a woman with learning difficulties and high support needs at a Nottingham care home, after using another man's national insurance number to secure his job. Kambeta, who was sentenced to 12 years in prison, was only exposed because he made the woman pregnant.

In November 1999, the charity Respond set up a help-line for people who wanted to report or discuss abuse of people with learning difficulties. By the autumn of 2002, calls had risen from 500 to 1,100 a year.

Alan Corbett was head of clinical services at the charity, which offers psychotherapy and counselling to people with learning difficulties who have been abused. He said the helpline received many calls from mothers who 'find themselves faced with a system that doesn't seem to hear them'.

'They are ringing in about their children, who have been abused, often over periods of years, but certainly no legal justice has been undertaken and no therapeutic justice either,' he told me. 'This is happening across the board – residential, special schools, day centres. Anywhere where people with learning disabilities congregate. We seem to be hearing a worrying number of cases of abuse, deprivation and neglect.'

Corbett said Respond was 'working with more people than we ever have before', with an increasing number of calls about children with learning difficulties. 'We deal with all aspects of abuse – sexual, physical, emotional – but the majority of people who come through the doors have been sexually abused. What we are finding is that we are being asked to work more with people who are clearly traumatised in all kinds of ways. Something terrible has happened to them, but nobody knows quite what. Often that something terrible may be rooted in very early childhood experience. If you are working with someone who lacks words to describe that, you may never know what that is.'

Experts were also convinced that paedophiles were targeting young people with learning difficulties as the tightening of legislation and increased public awareness frustrated their attempts to gain access to children.

An NSPCC spokeswoman told me in 2001: 'It is horrible to think that these young people, who have enough to face in their lives as it is, could become targets for paedophiles. It does happen, and the trouble is that sometimes they cannot communicate when it does happen. I think if the genuine figures were known it would be shocking.'

What was perhaps most shocking was that the vast majority of cases never even resulted in a complaint to the police, let alone a criminal conviction.

Research by Michelle McCarthy and David Thompson[4] suggested that as many as 61 per cent of women and 25 per cent of men with learning difficulties had been sexually abused. Earlier, unpublished, research quoted in their study had found as many as 83 per cent of users of a day service had been abused.

When the problem was so vast, so overpowering, it was unlikely that any of the measures announced by the government to tackle discrimination in the criminal justice system could do anything but make a small dent in what was nothing short of an appalling epidemic of victimisation.

*

At least, that was what I wrote in 2003. But had things improved? And had the special measures, the Sexual Offences Act, and the other measures taken within the criminal justice system made more than a small dent in this 'appalling epidemic of victimisation'?

June is a campaigner with learning difficulties, who lives in London. She told me: 'It's still the same. You still hear about people being abused, being bullied or being ill-treated. There are so many stories about people with disability are getting abused or getting bullied, then they don't get heard.'

She told me this was happening in residential homes and in the wider community. 'It happens all the time if you're on the bus or waiting at the bus stop. They might be on the way home, they get bullied, stones thrown at them, they get called names. They get their bags nicked with their money in it, or mobile phones. Then you go to the police station and they come round and they don't do nothing.'

June is deeply pessimistic about the possibility of reducing the scale of abuse. 'You hear a lot of cases about people have got a disability, but you never stop it because so many people with disability who I know have told me they have been abused,' she says. 'They are afraid to go to report it to the police because they don't get heard. It will never stop.'

Kathryn Stone, chief executive of Voice UK, told me in late 2010 that her charity had taken 90 referrals on its helpline in the previous month, the highest ever monthly number. Nine years ago, there were about six referrals a month. It may be that more people know about Voice UK and are more confident about speaking out, but it certainly doesn't hint at any lessening in the scale of the problem. There have, she says, been 'real increases in the most horrendous murders and very, very serious sexual assaults'.

Andrew Lee is probably the best-known member of the UK self-advocacy movement. He is director of the London-based charity People First (Self-Advocacy), co-chair of the campaigning Learning Disability Coalition, and a member of the Equality and Human Rights Commission's disability committee. Like June, he sees the situation 'getting worse'.

He says many people with learning difficulties are facing what the police would call 'lower-lying issues', the barrage of harassment and bullying that can have the same impact as more serious, isolated offences when it happens on a daily basis.

'There are more people that I know that have actually been attacked than there used to be,' he tells me. 'People First threw a conference for 120 people with learning difficulties, a conference at City Hall [the offices of the mayor of London]. Everybody used the term bullying. They explained what had happened to them. The Met police team were going through the legislation and at the end of the conference every piece of law that was in their book had been broken, but none of the cases had actually been reported. None of them had been reported.'

He illustrates the problem with a stark example. 'When an incident happened to someone I knew, I supported them to go to a police station. They were very frightened. The officer just threw the piece of paper at them and said 'fill that in'. English was her second language. That was enough to make us walk out of the police station.'

When I asked him to clarify how many of the 120 conference delegates had experienced 'bullying', he replied simply: 'All of them.'

Andrew Lee believes the criminal justice system still isn't working for people with learning difficulties. 'We might have individual officers that want to do a good thing, but the system they are working in isn't helpful to disabled people. People with learning difficulties aren't taken seriously and I think that they need to be taken as seriously as if someone from a BME [black and minority ethnic] background would be taken seriously.'

Fiona Mactaggart, a former Home Office minister and now shadow minister for equalities, says the special measures have made a difference in increasing the number of successful prosecutions. 'Talking to police officers who have used them, they just feel so much more confident about nailing perpetrators.' But, she says, there is still resistance from some judges. 'One of the awful things is that we take one step forward and one step back. The rest of the system has made important steps forward, but I don't think some judges have.'

Kathryn Stone believes the laws are better, there is more awareness of the needs of people with learning difficulties, and there is a much closer focus on safeguarding issues. 'Things have improved and they are improving,' she says.

She told the annual Victims and Witnesses conference in October 2010 that the use of special measures had been 'a quiet revolution in the criminal justice system.' Thanks to the scheme, she said, 'thousands and thousands of people have access to justice that perhaps would previously have been denied them.' In 2009, she said, the CPS made more than 30,000 applications for special measures, and more than 28,000 were granted.

But she questions whether this can really be called progress when there have been such appalling cases of rape, murder and other crimes against people with learning difficulties, and when people in residential care homes are 'in daily fear of what is happening to them'.

Margaret Kennedy carried out ground-breaking work in the late 1980s that drew attention for the first time to the hidden abuse of disabled children. A disabled person herself, she became a leading researcher and consultant in this area. She is 'firmly convinced' that institutional abuse is still widespread. Kennedy believes the right legislation is now in place, but that there is a reluctance to take on complex cases, such as those involving people with high support needs. She also believes that many people with learning difficulties decide to put up with abuse because they are genuinely worried about having to leave their home if they complain.

June says too many people with learning difficulties, like her, still face steep barriers to justice. 'They don't know who to turn to,' she says, 'because they do not get heard and they do not get believed.' She knows, because it happened to her. She was sexually assaulted by the friend of a friend. She reported it to the police, but a couple of months before the case was due to be heard in court, she received a letter saying that she was an 'unreliable witness'. The treatment she received at the hands of the criminal justice system left her suicidal, and she had to be admitted to hospital for treatment for depression.

Richard Curen, chief executive of Respond, believes juries – and their ingrained attitudes and beliefs – are often the 'major stumbling block'. He points to two recent cases, in which two women with learning difficulties gave evidence in court of being sexually assaulted. Both took advantage of the special measures and were also supported by Annie Rose, an independent sexual violence advisor (ISVA), who works with Respond across 11 London boroughs and is funded by the Home Office. But in both cases, the jury found the defendant not guilty.

In one of the trials, Rose said her client hadn't seen the intermediary for 11 months between her first interview and the day of the trial. When it was time for her to give evidence, 'there was no relationship built up' and she was 'confused by all the new faces'. In the other trial, the defendant, who also had a learning difficulty, had an expert witness who explained the impact of his impairment, while the victim – the witness – did not. Rose believes the jury would have understood more about the witness if there had been an expert to give evidence about her impairment and level of understanding.

When an intermediary is used well, says Rose, it helps the witness understand what is going on and to communicate, 'enabling them to answer questions and give the best possible evidence'. 'It is invaluable at the early stage of investigations. It helps the victim communicate better and in turn to be taken seriously by the police. Through better communication, the police are able to build up a case and see the victim as a credible witness.'

Rose works with her clients all through the investigation and trial, and afterwards, meeting members of their support networks, making sure they are safe if they have to be rehoused, liaising with the various agencies, building up a relationship of trust and helping them cope with the trauma of the crime, and the trial itself.

The importance of building a relationship with a witness is a crucial part of the Liverpool Model of Witness Support, Preparation and Profiling. It was developed in the late 1990s by Liverpool City Council's new investigations support unit (ISU) as a result of a major investigation into historical abuse, which included many complaints of serious sexual assaults at an institution for men with learning difficulties. The unit was asked to provide intensive support to Michael*, the one witness with learning difficulties who was going to give evidence in court.

The programme the ISU developed through its work with Michael and many other people with learning difficulties aims to ensure equal access to justice. It offers intensive support in the lead-up to the trial, preparing witnesses for their court appearance, explaining what will happen, who will be in court and why, and what sort of questions they will be asked. There are often pre-trial visits to the court building and meetings with the barristers.

A crucial element is the preparation of a witness profile, information the court needs to know about the witness. The profile is given to the judge and the prosecution and defence barristers so they know what they need to do to allow the witness to give her best evidence. The profile might, for example, ask the barristers to maintain eye contact with the witness, or help them spot when she needs a rest.

Geraldine Monaghan, the ISU's investigations manager, says[5]: 'The difference between the service that we offer and that offered by intermediaries is that we would expect during the course of our work with an individual to be able to unlock some of their potential. They would be different in terms of their confidence and their ability to express themselves and to withstand cross-examination by the end of the support and preparation process.' The role of intermediaries, she adds, is restricted to assisting in police interviews and in court. 'They have a meeting to assess the individual but they don't undertake any support and preparation work in the way that we do.'

They often go further than the special measures in court, too, asking the judge for 'additional measures to assist' such as suggesting a particular time of day when the witness is best able to give evidence, and how long they can give evidence for before needing a break. The most frequent measure requested is for Mark Pathak, a social worker and the ISU's investigations officer – who supports the witness throughout the process, building up a relationship of trust and developing the witness profile – to be able to sit quietly next to them in court while they give their evidence.

The scheme has proved hugely effective. Of 47 'vulnerable' witnesses supported by the ISU since 1997, 27 of the 33 prosecutions have led to convictions, a success rate of over 80 per cent. Nearly all these witnesses had learning difficulties, and most had alleged serious sexual assaults. Every witness who has worked with the ISU has said they would willingly go to court again, as long as the ISU was supporting them. The scheme has proved so effective that it is now used with all 'vulnerable witnesses' who give evidence at Liverpool Crown Court.

Martin Decker, district crown prosecutor for CPS Merseyside, says the programme has 'brought a level playing-field... to the type of cases which otherwise defence counsel would have had a field day with dealing with witnesses who are vulnerable and being able to trip them up in cases where they should not be tripped up.'[5] He says the programme has resulted in more than 30 cases going to court that would not otherwise have done so.

Monaghan is puzzled why more regions haven't adapted their work, as the funding necessary is 'not excessive' and the skills involved not specialised, merely 'the practice of social work in a criminal justice context'[5]. A CPS spokeswoman told me the model had been used by one or two other areas, but the reasons it was not more widespread 'vary from area to area'.

'Michael' – the first witness supported by Pathak and the ISU – said years later that his experience had convinced him that people with learning difficulties could go to court and give evidence[6]. 'I was scared but I did it,' he said. 'It was very hard and people can do it but they need support and help from people like Mark. If people with learning disabilities don't get support from someone like Mark they won't go to court. We need people to help us not criticise us.'

*

Despite the real and enduring problems within the criminal justice system, there have been some successes with the new offences and stricter sentences introduced under the Sexual Offences Act.

In August 2010, a Devon man was jailed for nine years after admitting grooming a woman with learning difficulties and forcing her to have sex with him. He admitted three counts of sexual activity with a woman who did not have the capacity to consent, and was jailed for nine years.

The same year, also in Devon, care worker James Watts was jailed after being found guilty of sexual activity with a woman who could not consent, sexual activity with a resident of a care home, and four other sexual offences. His victims, who had learning difficulties and physical impairments, had given their evidence during the three-week trial using the special measures, with one communicating by blinking her eyes – to answer 'yes' or 'no' to questions from barristers – while others used their heads to press buttons on their wheelchairs. Despite the court originally handing down a sentence of 12-and-a-half years, it was later cut on appeal to just four. Kathryn Stone told the Victims and Witnesses conference that the conviction was 'a triumph', while the eventual sentence was 'a disappointment'.

Despite this case, Deborah Kitson, director of the Ann Craft Trust, says social services and police will nearly always shy away from launching investigations where the victim has high support needs or uses alternative forms of communication.

'Very rarely do speech and language experts get called in,' she says. 'As soon as you have someone with a profound disability or with very unclear verbal communication you just hit a brick wall.'

The special measures were also used to allow the victim of a gang-rape to give evidence via video-link. The 16-year-old from north London, who has learning difficulties, was raped by at least three men. One of them then poured caustic soda on her in an effort to destroy the evidence, and added water to intensify the burning. Three of the men were originally jailed in January 2009 for just six, eight and nine years. Outraged by the sentences, the Ann Craft Trust, Respond and Voice UK pushed the attorney general to review them, and two of the men subsequently had their sentences increased by five and three years.

*

At the time Silent Victims was published, in December 2003, I was news editor of Disability Now, which was then a monthly newspaper (it is now a magazine). When I talked to my editor, Mary Wilkinson, about my book, I told her about the judge at the Longcare trial, and the government's subsequent failure to address the pitifully small sentences for those found guilty of ill-treating or neglecting people with learning difficulties. Tom Burgner had also called for much tougher sentences in his Longcare inquiry report, suggesting they should be increased from a maximum of two to ten years in prison, through a new offence of harming or exploiting a 'vulnerable adult', putting them on a par with similar crimes against children.

Disability Now launched its Justice for Survivors campaign, calling on the government to introduce such a law. It immediately won the backing of Central England People First, a leading self-advocacy organisation. Karen Spencer, its chair, told me: 'If the government respects people with learning difficulties, they should change the law and support this campaign.' The campaign also received backing from Voice UK, Mencap and Values Into Action.

Philippa Russell also backed the campaign. She told me she and her Longcare inquiry colleagues had been 'appalled at the inappropriately low sentences' available to the courts, and considered them 'an insult' which 'trivialised' the suffering of the victims. 'We do need to give a very real message that the abuse of people with learning difficulties will not be tolerated,' she said. The charity Turning Point also added its backing, and was later joined by Respond and the Ann Craft Trust.

It soon became clear that many police forces were not even aware of the ill-treatment and neglect offences, which meant they often just conceded defeat when faced with cases of alleged abuse. Greater Manchester Police admitted to me in April 2004 that it had been unaware of the offences when investigating the death of a disabled man in a spa bath in 1998. Malcolm Rowley, who had learning difficulties and high support needs, drowned when the bubbles the care worker put in his bath rose over his face, after he had been left alone. An inquest jury ruled his death was an accident to which neglect had contributed, but no care worker was ever charged, even though Salford social services, which provided 24-hour care at the home, was successfully prosecuted by the Health and Safety Executive and fined £115,000. Although the force did agree to refer the case to the CPS for a second time, no new charges were ever brought.

The campaign was making progress, though. After I raised the issue with the constitutional affairs minister Lord Filkin in 2004 – and following further support from Fiona Mactaggart – the government agreed to increase the maximum sentence for ill-treatment and neglect from two to five years through its planned new Mental Capacity Act. The new offence would only apply to a certain number of carers and care workers with powers under the act, and would protect only those victims seen as lacking the capacity to communicate or make important decisions about their lives. So it might not have made much difference in the Longcare case, but it was progress.

I also wrote to the health minister, Rosie Winterton, about our campaign, pointing out our success with Lord Filkin, and the wide backing for a change in the law – which was soon to include the Longcare trial judge, Judge John Baker. I asked her to introduce a new offence – similar to the one outlined by Tom Burgner – in the government's new mental health bill. Winterton wrote back to say that the government believed the issue was 'an important one' and that it was 'examining the sentence provision' for such offences in the bill.

When the draft bill was published, it included a new, wide-ranging criminal offence, which would have made it an offence for anyone to ill-treat or neglect someone with a learning difficulty or mental health condition who was in their 'care or custody' in any setting – including a private home. Existing laws only covered care homes and hospitals, so this was a substantial improvement. Kathryn Stone described it as a 'huge step forward', which would 'massively raise protection and awareness of the abuse of vulnerable adults'. Again, the maximum sentence would be five years, rather than 10, but it was a welcome gain.

This need for tougher sentences was highlighted in late 2005, when seven care workers who took part in the abusive regime at the Bedes View home in Hull were jailed for between three and 12 months each for ill-treatment and neglect. Government figures secured by Labour MP Joan Humble revealed that the average sentence for cruelty or neglect of a child in 2002 was 19 months, compared with just four months for such crimes against adults with learning difficulties or mental health conditions.

But the campaign took a step backwards the following year. The government was forced to drop its controversial mental health bill and draft a replacement. When the new bill was published, it showed Winterton had dropped the new 'care or custody' clause.

Ivan Lewis, the new care services minister, who had worked in his younger days with people with learning difficulties, promised to examine the issue again. Although the new clause was never restored to the bill, a higher sentence for ill-treatment and neglect was eventually added – thanks to lobbying by Voice

UK and others – before it finally became the Mental Health Act 2007.

When I told Dorothy Thomson about the new act, she made it clear that a five-year maximum sentence for the kind of things that were done to her and her fellow residents at Longcare was still far too low. 'I think that's too lenient a sentence because they don't realise that when they are doing the bullying and the things they do not only hurt the outside, they destroy the inside,' she told me. 'I think 10 years is lenient, actually. Personally, I think they should lock them up and throw away the key.'

*

In Silent Victims, I concluded that the main explanation for the Longcare scandal was that people with learning difficulties were routinely viewed as second- or third-class citizens.

It was these attitudes of indifference, ignorance and outright hostility that had allowed Rowe to set up his brutal regime, and let it flourish for so many years under the gaze of the authorities. But how had these attitudes changed since the scandal was exposed, and in the seven years since my book was published? Surely, with more people with learning difficulties now living in the community and mixing with non-disabled people, there would at least be greater acceptance, and more opportunities for social contact, friendships and, ultimately, protection from abuse and crime.

Dame Philippa Russell told me that, although we were in many ways becoming 'a more equal and more sensitive society', crimes against people with learning difficulties appeared to be on the increase. 'I think they might be going up because people with learning disabilities are more visible and are in society,' she said. 'But there does sadly seem to be a disrespect to people who seem different or not in any way perfect.'

She has had to deal with the fallout from a number of incidents aimed at her son, who has learning difficulties, with 'people arrested for all sorts of unpleasantness'. 'It does make life very difficult for people... and I do not honestly know what the answer is.'

She points to the National Forum of People with Learning Difficulties, and says that 'everybody there has had a bad experience of some kind', often as serious as physical assaults. 'What has always astonished and appalled me,' she says, 'was that the neighbours do not respond, they just walk by on the other side of the road – they say they were frightened.' The same kind of indifference, in fact, that was shown by many of the Longcare staff.

Margaret Kennedy goes further. She says there is a 'cultural unwillingness to perceive learning disabled people as even human'. She sees targeted attacks against them as a 'eugenic crime', the equivalent of their neighbours saying: 'We don't want you in our community.'

It was while working at Disability Now in the summer of 2007, by then as acting editor, that the end product of such attitudes towards people with learning difficulties began to become clear.

This was almost entirely due to the work of Katharine Quarmby, one of the country's most talented and respected social affairs journalists, who by a stroke of great fortune had become our part-time news editor.

Quarmby began to investigate a series of vicious crimes against disabled people – many of whom had learning difficulties – which had clearly been motivated by hostility or hatred. They were, the evidence showed beyond any doubt, hate crimes. But the criminal justice system was refusing to treat them as such. Slowly, Quarmby began to build up a huge dossier of cases, and to ask the question of the criminal justice system: 'If these are not hate crimes, what are?'

Among the victims of these brutal crimes was Rikki Judkins, who was assaulted in an underpass, and subjected to a sustained and fatal attack – later described by a senior police officer as 'brutal, savage and sustained' – that ended with a large stone being dropped on his head.

And there was Raymond Atherton, the victim of a campaign of abuse at the hands of 'feral' teenagers, who regularly broke into his flat, wrote graffiti on his walls, beat him, urinated in his drinks, and poured bleach over him. He was eventually viciously beaten, urinated on and thrown in the River Mersey, where he died.

Barrie-John Horrell was kidnapped by 'friends' who strangled him, hit him with a brick, and kicked and stamped on him, before setting his body on fire.

Then there was Steven Hoskin, who was made to wear a dog collar and dragged around his house by a lead, forced to call his attackers 'sir' and 'madam', before plunging to his death from the edge of a viaduct after being made to hang from railings by his fingertips. A serious case review later found that every part of the adult protection system in Cornwall had been guilty of 'significant failures' in dealing with the 'abuse' Hoskin was experiencing. A post-mortem found he had recent injuries from cigarette burns, neck bruises from the dog collar, and footprints on the back of his hands where they were stamped on before he fell. The review made 17 recommendations for improvements to safeguarding services in Cornwall, and highlighted more than 40 warnings and 'missed intervention opportunities' for the agencies concerned, including the police.

As Quarmby pointed out, these attacks were described by police and prosecutors in markedly similar ways, as 'senseless' and 'motiveless'. But in each case, the victims were treated as less than human, often by people claiming to be their 'friends'. Another common factor was that police forces questioned later about the crimes 'expressed surprise' when asked if they had been investigated as possible disability hate crimes. None of them were. If they had been – that is, if there had been evidence of hostility related to the victim's learning difficulty or other impairment – the sentences imposed by the courts could have been enhanced under section 146 of the Criminal Justice Act 2003.

Quarmby's work helped to raise the profile of the issue of disability hate crime – as did the efforts of disabled activists such as Anne Novis and Stephen Brookes. National media interest was sparked – although only temporarily – in February 2008, when three thugs from Sunderland were jailed for life for the 'sadistic' murder of Brent Martin. Martin, who had learning difficulties, was about to start a new job as a landscape gardener and was preparing to live independently for the first time. Instead, he was repeatedly punched, kicked, head-butted and stamped on by his attackers – all amateur boxers – who partly stripped him and then chased him around a housing estate for several hours, betting each other £5 that they could knock him out, while he pleaded with them to leave him alone. One of the trio would say afterwards: 'I'm not going down for a muppet.' Again, Martin considered his attackers to be his friends. Local self-advocacy groups later told Quarmby that the crime had terrified other people with learning difficulties in Sunderland, with many refusing to go out after dark or visit new places. Yet again, the murder was not treated as a disability hate crime by the police or the CPS.

That autumn, Disability Now, the UK Disabled People's Council and Scope published a ground-breaking report on disability hate crime, written by Quarmby. Getting Away with Murder[7] was a powerful call to arms. 'Many people find it difficult to believe that disabled people are attacked or harassed simply because they are disabled. Most people cannot imagine anyone hating a disabled person enough to want to frighten, hurt or murder them,' Quarmby wrote. But, she continued, 'the roots of disability hate crime lie in contempt rather than fear. Prejudice against disabled people is rooted in the view that disabled people are inferior; in some cases less than human. They are harassed, attacked, humiliated and even killed because their lives are considered less valuable than other people's lives.'

The tragic case of Fiona Pilkington and her daughter Francecca, who had learning difficulties, attracted even greater media interest and political concern than the death of Brent Martin.

Mostly this was not because it was an example of disability hate crime, but because it shone a spotlight on the murky issue of so-called 'anti-social behaviour'. In September 2009, an inquest heard how Pilkington killed herself and her daughter after her family had been subjected to years of disablist abuse and harassment. Pilkington had driven to a layby in Leicestershire in October 2007 and set fire to her car with herself and Francecca inside it.

The inquest heard how the family had been the target of a 10-year hate campaign, which included verbal abuse, stones and eggs being thrown at their house, and fireworks being pushed through their letterbox. The harassment was often aimed at Francecca. Pilkington, her relatives and neighbours made 33 calls to the police, but were not taken seriously and the harassment was never categorised as potential disability hate crime. Instead, the force logged the calls merely as 'anti-social behaviour'. The inquest jury found that the failures of the police, Hinckley and Bosworth Borough Council and Leicestershire County Council contributed to Pilkington's decision to kill herself and her daughter. Julie Newman, acting chair of the UK Disabled People's Council, told me that the failure to treat the offences against the family as hate crimes was 'outrageous' and indicated 'institutional disablism'.

I later discovered that a disabled people's organisation, Leicestershire Centre for Integrated Living (LCIL), had pleaded with Leicestershire police to take disability hate crime seriously five years before Pilkington killed herself and her daughter. Dee Martin, chief executive of LCIL, told me: 'This is not new for us. This is something we have been raising for a number of years.'

Trevor Phillips, chairman of the Equality and Human Rights Commission, described the murders of Brent Martin and Steven Hoskin as 'conspicuous flashes of an often silent bullying menace on our streets, on our housing estates, on our buses and trains, in our schools and, increasingly, online and on mobile phones', and added: 'We all want disabled people to be able to go out and play a full part in their community but too often a trip to the pub, the shops, the swimming pool or work is such an ordeal that it seems easier to narrow their horizons, to stay indoors. This is a hidden catastrophe that we need to address.' In late 2009, the commission announced a major inquiry that aimed to discover the true extent of disability-related harassment and violence.

Mark Brookes, a prominent campaigner with learning difficulties and a senior policy worker at Values Into Action, told a conference in November 2009 that he had had eggs and tomatoes thrown at him and was afraid to leave the house after 8pm, as were many other people with learning difficulties. He called for 'action and not strategies', and said he was tired of 'just repeating and repeating' the same hate crime message.

Andrew Lee and his self-advocacy organisation have also been prominent in calling for action. 'Hate crime is People First's number one campaign,' he told me. 'A lot of our members have been victims of hate crime, including myself.' He says the problem is 'getting worse'.

Anne Novis, who leads on hate crime issues for the UK Disabled People's Council, had been calling for the issue to be taken seriously by the criminal justice system for many years. Over three years, she scoured the media, blogs and internet message boards, and collated personal experiences shared with her by other disabled people, to compile a report on the scale of disability hate crime. Her report, published in 2010 – although it also included many crimes against disabled people who didn't have learning difficulties – found evidence of 68 violent deaths, and more than 500 other potential disability hate crimes. This, she said, was 'the very small tip of a very large iceberg'.

As co-chair of the National Forum of People with Learning Difficulties, although speaking to me in a personal capacity, Michael Ratcliffe's views should carry some weight. The forum, after all, has played an important role in drawing attention to the hate crime issue. He and his wife have had huge problems themselves with young people in Shrewsbury, and have had to call the police on several occasions. 'My wife still gets a bit of aggro,' he tells me. 'She gets names calling. They make fun about her weight and call her 'deafy', because she has a hearing aid. We are careful when we go out. There are some parts of the estate that we have to be really careful about.

'I think it is really something that everybody [with learning difficulties] has to cope with,' he adds. But he says that many people living in the community do not like to report hate crime for fear that they will be sent back to a hostel or other less independent setting. 'A lot of people put up with it and some people put up with it because they think it happens to everybody. It is a terrible thing to think it is just life.'

Distressing cases of brutal and violent deaths kept coming, as did the evidence that the criminal justice system was still failing people with learning difficulties.

In April 2010, four members of a Luton family, and two of their girlfriends, were sentenced to a total of 93 years in prison for offences connected with the murder of a disabled man they had beaten and tortured for years. Michael Gilbert – who is believed to have had learning difficulties – was held captive by the family for 10 years and was regularly beaten, stabbed, tormented, treated 'like a slave' and had his benefits money stolen. Katharine Quarmby – during research for her book on disability hate crime –discovered that Gilbert and his friends reported concerns about his safety to the authorities on at least eight occasions between 2002 and 2009, including reports of three alleged abductions to three different police forces. No official action was taken until the family ended up in court accused of murdering and dismembering Michael Gilbert.

As this book was going to print, a serious case review was published on the events that led to the death of David Askew.

Askew, who had learning difficulties, collapsed and died in March 2010 soon after police received reports that youths had again been harassing him outside his home in Hattersley, on the edge of Manchester.

The review, set up by Tameside Adult Safeguarding Partnership, said the 'teasing and taunting' of David Askew had started shortly after his family moved into their home in Hattersley in 1971, nearly 40 years earlier. Askew had been a repeated victim of thefts, assaults and 'tormenting' when out in the community, and burglary, harassment and other 'anti-social' incidents in and around his family's home. Askew, said the report, 'could get very upset and frustrated over the harassment' and would 'get agitated, shout and bite his hands until they bled'.

Between 2007 and 2010, 26 named young people were identified as taking part in this targeted campaign of hostility. During 2007, 46 incidents involving the Askews were recorded by various agencies, including two burglaries, bricks thrown through the window on three occasions, while David Askew's glasses were broken, and he had his cigarettes and money stolen. The following year there were another 34 incidents, with another 14 in 2009.

One professional said the harassment became 'normal' to the family, who were 'subjected to so much abuse that they learned to tolerate all but the worst', with Askew's mother only calling the police 'when things escalated beyond a certain point, eg if once again she was showered in broken glass'.

Although Askew was known to Tameside social services, which provided some employment and 'day activity' support, the review concluded that he never received the support he needed to ensure his protection.

The Independent Police Complaints Commission (IPCC) also published a report. It found that between 2004 and 2010,

Askew and his family – his mother and brother are also disabled – reported 88 incidents of targeted harassment and hostility, threats and abuse to the police.

The report said there had been a 'total failure' by Greater Manchester Police (GMP) to recognise and respond to any of the incidents as disability hate crimes, even though the force had made tackling hate crime a priority in 2007. Neighbourhood police officers, who had showed 'genuine concern' for the family, had their 'hands tied' by 'organisational shortcomings', while none of the agencies involved had recognised the need to work together 'consistently, cohesively and robustly' to solve the family's problems.

Stephen Brookes, a coordinator of the Disability Hate Crime Network, told me the case showed again the 'serious gaps in the criminal justice system'.

'When so many people have evidence, which was clear and unmistakable,' he said, 'and yet no one works together, there is little wonder that the criminal justice system is not held in high regard by disabled people.'

So what needs to be done across the criminal justice system to ensure that people with learning difficulties secure something approaching justice?

Richard Curen believes the necessary legislation is now in place. What is needed is better implementation and 'changing attitudes'. Nationally, he says, the CPS has a strategy, but locally it is 'very bitty'. 'Similarly, with the judge, it is often down to local decision-making and local culture that will decide whether somebody gets an intermediary or not, whether they get access to the special measures.' He believes there needs to be far better training across the criminal justice system.

Andrew Lee agrees. 'They need to know we need support before, during and after we go to court,' he says.

Annie Rose would like to see intermediaries allowed to spend more time with their clients in the weeks leading up to the trial, and all victims allowed a pre-trial meeting with the prosecuting barrister. And she would like to see expert witnesses used to explain the victim's impairment to the jury.

The CPS says its policy is for all witnesses to meet the prosecuting barrister before a trial, while intermediaries spend as much time with them as they think they need to build a rapport. The intermediary's duty is to the court, and not to the CPS or police, I was told, while expert witnesses may be called 'if necessary', to answer questions on 'competence or capacity'.

Kathryn Stone also stressed the need for better training across the criminal justice system, better public awareness and 'countering very negative attitudes against difference of any kind'. And, of course, better funding.

A CPS spokeswoman told me it was 'committed to training its staff to a high standard', and mentioned three training programmes on special measures, a public policy statement on supporting victims and witnesses with learning difficulties, and legal guidance for its lawyers. She said the CPS was not reluctant to take cases in which the main witness or victim had a learning difficulty, and tried to help them give their 'best possible evidence'. 'We have prosecuted such cases in the past and will continue to do so,' she said, and pointed to the successful prosecution of James Watts.

As for judges, the Judicial Office for England and Wales (JOEW) told me that all judges were 'aware of the special measures' while there had been 'considerable training' for crown court judges on the use of intermediaries. There is information – although it is quite basic – available on JOEW's website, including seven pages on people with learning difficulties, brain damage and mental health conditions, in the Equal Treatment Bench Book – the judicial equalities guide. Judges and magistrates can seek advice from their local diversity and community relations judge. And learning difficulty issues are 'integrated into' case studies and exercises and 'regularly included in induction and continuation training' for judges.

But JOEW accepts that training time is limited and 'priority choices have to be made', and admits that Lord Bradley's 2009 report into how people with learning difficulties and mental health conditions are treated in the criminal justice system called for judges and magistrates to receive awareness training. Since then, 'some adjustments have been made and some further ones are still being considered'.

But, JOEW adds, 'the independence of the judiciary means that ultimately judges will decide for themselves the training that will be delivered to their fellow judges', although they will 'consider concerns from professionals provided they are supported by some form of evidence'.

It was not a response that filled me with confidence.

Andrew Lee – and many others – believe it has to be made easier for people with learning difficulties to report hate crimes. One way is to set up more reporting centres, where people can report hate crimes to a third party, who can pass the details on to the police.

One small scheme perhaps demonstrates the truth of Lee's words. A project to set up the first hate crime reporting centres in Wales saw an immediate sharp increase in reports of offences against people with learning difficulties. Torfaen People First set up the centres with Gwent police, with Home Office funding. Just five weeks into the scheme, in May 2010, there were already four reports. This compared with six in the whole of the previous year. Two were reports of verbal abuse and two of harassment. All four were being investigated by police. The new centres were places where people with learning difficulties frequently met and felt comfortable, including community clubs and education centres. Staff helped people fill in the reporting packs, which were designed to be easy to read and understand. The forms were passed to the police – along with an electronic referral – or the case was referred to the charity Victim Support, depending on the victim's wishes. Police officers trained to work with people with learning difficulties acted as local contacts for the reporting centres.

Lee wants to see more police forces working closely with self-advocacy groups. He told me: 'One thing I would suggest is that every police force has a direct link with a self-advocacy organisation. That way, officers can actually call on the knowledge of those groups.'

Lee told the No More Hate Crime conference in Blackpool in November 2010 that the police needed more training by people with learning difficulties, they needed to understand that 'we need good support to report hate crime', and they had to improve how they interviewed people with learning difficulties. 'They need to know we can be good witnesses,' he said. And, crucially, 'the police and CPS must believe us when we say we have been the victim of a hate incident or crime'.

June, who also has learning difficulties, is convinced that attitudes need to change, particularly those of the police. They have to stop judging people, she says. I ask her how they do this, and she says: 'The way they look, the way they speak. Or if they can't read or write.' She is tired of hearing senior police officers tell conferences how well they are doing in tackling hate crime by visiting schools. The necessary training is still not filtering down to police officers at local police stations. 'Nothing changes,' she says.

Scott Watkin, the Department of Health's national co-director for learning disabilities, who himself has a learning difficulty, says more must be done to encourage greater reporting. His Valuing People Now team has worked with the Home Office on the issue, and he points to the 'brilliant work' carried out by the National Forum of People with Learning Difficulties. But, he says, this is not enough. 'The bottom line is that more still needs to be done to tackle this issue despite progression in the last few years. People with learning disabilities have a right like everyone else to live in a safe environment and feel secure. Everyone needs to understand how wrong and serious hate crime is.'

Michael Ratcliffe, again speaking personally, says dealing with hate crime has to start in schools. 'It must start as young as seven or eight, teaching people the things they say and do upset people with learning difficulties, really upset people.' He would also like to see more police training, but, he says, 'unfortunately they run out of money for these sort of things'.

＊

I contacted Thames Valley Police, keen to find out how they thought the picture had changed since 1994, whether such large-scale abuse was now less likely, and whether there were any changes in legislation they would like to see introduced. Sadly, the response – or the lack of it – did not fill me with confidence. They eventually got back to me with a four-paragraph statement four months later, giving a brief sketch of how they now approached adult safeguarding concerns. No-one seemed to remember the Longcare case, which had so many vital lessons for Thames Valley and other police forces.

A spokesman did finally tell me that the force believes the 'significant changes' that have taken place in dealing with safeguarding adults 'make it far less likely that there will be repeats of such large scale institutional abuse cases', with much of the improvement driven by No Secrets and subsequent good practice standards published by the Association of Directors of Social Services in 2005. And there was a brief mention of their Protecting Vulnerable People Investigation Units, which are also responsible for child abuse, serious sexual assaults and missing persons.

But, as with Buckinghamshire County Council, the Longcare case – and all its crucial lessons for professionals working to protect people in vulnerable situations – seems to have been relegated to a faded historical footnote.

＊

The years of the aftermath of the Longcare scandal span reasonably closely the years of New Labour in government.

Labour came to power in 1997, less than three years after Rowe's regime was exposed. They had 13 years in government to change the way the criminal justice system treated people with learning difficulties.

Fiona Mactaggart, who worked when she was a Home Office minister on how to help witnesses with learning difficulties give their evidence, believes people are safer now than they were when Labour took office.

'I think if people are abused, they have more possibility of getting justice and I think that is because of things we did. Was it enough? Probably not. One of the things I discovered as a government minister is you can never do enough. And I think actually one of the things that we failed to do was to sufficiently confront attitudinal bias against learning disabled people. I think that was a failure. I think government really can lead. We have led on disability discrimination in various ways and I think the attitudes to people with disabilities have changed, partly as a result of having a progressive government which legislated in some of these areas.

'But I think we didn't focus as much as we could have on discrimination against people whose impairment was intellectual rather than physical.' She pauses. 'It's not wholly true, but there is some truth in it.'

1   *Witnesses with and without Learning Disabilities in Court: The role of judge interventions, by M Kebbell, S Johnson and C Hatton; unpublished; 2002*

2   *Access all Areas, by Samantha Cunningham and Susannah Drury; NACRO; 2002*

3   *Potions, Pills and Community Care for People with Learning Difficulties: Hidden costs*, by Dr Dinah K C Murray; Good Autism Practice; April 1999

4   *A Prevalence Study of Sexual Abuse of Adults with Intellectual Disabilities Referred for Sex Education*, by Michelle McCarthy and David Thompson; Journal of Applied Research in Intellectual Disabilities, Vol 10, No 2, 1997

5   *Witness Support, Preparation and Profiling: The Liverpool model*; DVD produced by Mills Media Ltd for Merseyside Criminal Justice Board; 2010

6   *My Life*, by 'Michael', with the assistance of Mark Pathak; Ann Craft Trust, ACT Bulletin; October 2007

7   *Getting Away With Murder: Disabled people's experiences of hate crime in the UK*, by Katharine Quarmby; Disability Now, United Kingdom Disabled People's Council, Scope; 2008

Chapter Twenty-Seven

Speaking Up

'People with learning difficulties sometimes don't know what self-advocacy means... For me it means people must listen to me, I can take a risk, I can have a relationship, that can be hard. I can think for myself, I can go to the shop with support and if I need help, people can help me, I can cry if I want to cry.'

Jackie Downer, in Self-advocacy in the Lives of People with Learning Difficulties; Dan Goodley; Open University Press; 2000

My first contact with a self-advocacy group did not come until near the end of my research for my first Longcare book, *Silent Victims*. I had realised that Dorothy Thomson was the only former resident I had been able to talk to in depth, although I had met two others, Janet Ward and Simon Scott. I had concluded that society must find ways to give people with learning difficulties a voice, but I hadn't been able to do that myself.

I arranged to meet members of one of the most prominent self-advocacy organisations, Central England People First (CEPF). As with other People First groups, CEPF was run by people with learning difficulties, with assistance from paid supporters who took a passive role, giving advice only when asked.

I had met four CEPF members: Ian Davies, Janet Pheasant, Nigel Lott and Craig Hart. After some initial reticence, I remember finding all four insightful about the barriers they faced. Some of their comments about their experiences as disabled people shocked me, although sadly they wouldn't if I heard them today.

Ian told me the group had started 10 years earlier. 'Everyone in this room, everyone here was in day services, in residential care homes,' he told me. 'At that time it was always dominated by professionals. Staff, researchers, health authority, care managers. The problem we were having is our ideas were being dictated by these people. We didn't have a voice of our own... There was a bit of resistance from a lot of people regarding People First. A lot of people. All the regular authorities from social services down to day service managers. They were thinking we couldn't run our own organisation, we couldn't be our own bosses. They didn't think we could do things for ourselves. They wanted to hold all the purse strings. We have proved them wrong.'

'We are our own boss,' Janet added. 'We can make our own choices. There is one thing we do not like. That's being given as a label.'

'People First has a saying,' said Nigel. 'Label jars, not people.'

I asked them that day whether any of them had experienced discrimination or abuse. Yes, said Ian. 'They see something, they just want to make a meal of it. Spastic, four eyes, all those sort of labels, and a lot of that is from the general public. If they were to educate their children in a better sense and direction then the children of today would not be thinking the same way as their parents would.'

'People walk past, looking at you,' said Craig. A few minutes later, he adds: 'I had one last month. I reported it, but since then... I reported it to the police. They have not found any clues. They do not know if it's him or not. I feel angry since after that. He punched me in the face. Just feel like a bit bored or might be a bit drunk. I just said to a friend he might come back and do it again. I feel angry and I just feel being on my own.'

Janet told me how the group aimed to help other people with learning difficulties. 'If that person has a learning difficulty and they are finding it hard to speak up for themselves, that's where we come in, we can talk to them and speak up for them.'

I asked them why self-advocacy was so important. 'I think it is important so we know how they feel,' said Nigel. 'It's their choice. It's their home. They should be saying what they want and what they want to do in it.'

Later, I bumped into Neil Morris – their paid supporter – in the high street. He said the group could have told me far more, but they had only just met me and I was a journalist. Some of their personal experiences of discrimination and harassment were horrific, he said.

The conversation reminded me of what I had been told by former members of Longcare staff, how residents had taken months to trust care workers enough to confide in them. People First members believe that self-advocacy and the use of advocates who themselves have learning difficulties are crucial defences against abuse. People with learning difficulties find it much easier to trust someone else with a similar impairment.

They instinctively distrust 'professionals' – whether social workers, lawyers, or police officers. They hate being talked down to, ignored and patronised.

The self-advocacy movement is about enabling those people without a voice to speak up for themselves. It is about helping people to find their voice, and to use it.

Nearly a decade later, returning to the Longcare story, the self-advocacy movement had become more established. But its members were facing the same funding battles many other disabled people's groups were facing. Just as this book was going to press, People First Lambeth announced that it would have to close after 26 years, following Lambeth council's decision not to renew annual contracts worth £118,000. And I was receiving reports that other self-advocacy groups were under threat, too.

But there were signs of hope, such as the increasing profile of self-advocacy champions like Andrew Lee and other leading figures with learning difficulties such as Simone Aspis, Eve Rank, Mark Brookes and Richard West. Then there was the work of the National Forum of People with Learning Difficulties, the democratically-elected body which represents people with learning difficulties in England and tells the government how its policies are working on the ground. This January, the forum published Staying Strong, a new guide for self-advocacy groups – bringing together the knowledge and experiences of more than 80 self-advocacy groups across England[1].

I wanted to find out more about the history of the self-advocacy movement, hoping to find the seeds of hope for an effective response to the tide of hate crime and abuse that was blighting the lives of people with learning difficulties.

*

The first documents relating to a self-advocacy organisation, according to the academic Dan Goodley[2], come from Sweden in the late 1960s, when a few people with learning difficulties drew up a list of how they wanted their services to be provided. The views of people with learning difficulties were also starting to be recognised at conferences in the US, including one in which a panel of young people discussed how they felt about various supported employment programmes. Similar events were soon held in the UK, including one in 1972 organised by the Campaign for Mentally Handicapped People, which brought long-stay hospital patients together to discuss where they would like to live.

The origins of the name People First came from a self-advocacy conference in Oregon in 1974, says Paul Williams[3]. 'One of the delegates said: 'We are tired of being seen first as handicapped or retarded or disabled. We want to be seen as people first.'' The conference passed a motion to set up an organisation that would promote self-advocacy, to be called People First. Within a year there were 16 branches across the US. But it was not until 1984 that some English people with learning difficulties were inspired to set up their own group, in London.

Lloyd Page was one of those who helped set up that London group. In Goodley's book, Page says: 'Why did I want to get into self-advocacy? Because it's a good thing to do – speaking up for yourself. Being in a group helps you to speak out. By speaking to people in the group it gives you the confidence to speak to other people.'

Another self-advocate, Joyce Kershaw, says people 'look up to us now and listen to us, where before they used to make us look small, and they never listened to what we had to say,' while Patrick Burke describes how being in a self-advocacy group helped him tell individuals and organisations what he thought of them. Before, he says, he was afraid of people. 'Now, I could tell you about the past, the future in 15 years' time, how I'm going to cope, will I cope. I didn't have any idea how to speak out until I met People First.'

In the acknowledgements section of my first Longcare book, I thanked a woman called Mabel Cooper. Like Dorothy Thomson, she was a survivor of a long-stay hospital, a resident for more than 20 years of St Lawrence's Hospital in Caterham, Surrey, where she had shared a ward with 75 other women.

When she came out of St Lawrence's in the early 1980s and moved in with a family, everything was new. She had never been on a bus or a train. She eventually joined a new People First group in Croydon, and later chaired the main London branch of People First.

Cooper became one of the first former long-stay residents to work with an academic – in her case, historian Dorothy Atkinson – to write her 'life story', an important form of historical research which is increasingly being used to ensure that the voices and stories of those people with learning difficulties who lived through the age of the long-stay hospital are not forgotten. 'You've got something to show for your life,' she explained in her life story. 'You've got something so that you can say, 'That's what happened to me.''

Cooper's story must have been read by thousands of people through its inclusion in books such as Forgotten Lives; Crossing Boundaries; and Good Times, Bad Times, and is a striking and powerful example of its type. It is an important historical document.

When the Longcare story first became national news in September 1994, Cooper appeared on the BBC's breakfast TV programme to 'say it's wrong'. 'For people to be tied up and all the rest of it, I saw it in the hospital,' she told me many years later. 'People don't get tied up in this day and age. When it was brought up that that was going on, I went to the BBC to talk about it.'

Despite the different paths their post-hospital lives took, there are many similarities between Cooper and Dorothy Thomson – another woman who spent years in a long-stay hospital – particularly in their determination to fight for their own and other people's rights, their strength of character and their generosity of spirit.

Although no longer associated with People First, Cooper still promotes the virtues of self-advocacy, inclusion and independence. She is still a fervent believer in shutting down all large institutions. 'The big homes they shouldn't have,' she told me, 'because they run them like those long-stay hospitals. They should all be in small homes like when there is five, not when there is 20 or 10 or 11, with supporters or carers to make it so they can go out. It's better because you get that bit of attention that you didn't get if you was in that long-stay hospital.'

Cooper has acted as an 'expert by experience', visiting residential homes as part of their official inspections. 'We sat and talked to the people in them to find out is their life good or bad or whatever.' She also visits schools, to tell the children about her life in a long-stay hospital and to try to persuade them to stop bullying people with learning difficulties.

As well as being a trustee of the charity Walsingham, which supports people with learning difficulties, she has travelled all over the world to discuss her experiences, and talks about her life to students at the Open University, which has awarded her an honorary degree. I ask her what difference shutting down the hospitals has made. 'Because we have been able to go out and do what we want to do instead of what somebody is telling us to do. We can please ourselves now. It makes a lot of difference, John.'

She believes attitudes have changed, at least to her. She thinks the reason that people used to stare at her was because of the clothes she wore when she left St Lawrence's. 'When we came out of the hospital, all the children used to laugh at us because of the clothes,' she says. 'If you look funny then they are going to stare.' She saved her money, and bought clothes of her own as soon as she could, throwing away the clothes and shoes the hospital had given her that had marked her out as different.

She has learned to fit in, a living embodiment of 'normalisation'. 'You have got to be able to fit in, John,' she says, when I meet her at her flat in south London. 'You have got to fit in and be polite to people and if you treat them right they will treat you properly.' She insists that she no longer suffers from the kind of bullying and harassment experienced by many other people with learning difficulties.

Maybe this is because she has learned to dress in the right clothes, and not to venture out too late at night. 'The children on their own are quite trouble or when they have been in the pub, but they do not hurt the learning disability,' she says. 'I don't think the learning disability would be out after 10 o'clock. I can go round and do what I want and people leave me alone.'

When I ask her to describe her life now, she gives me just one word: 'Satisfaction.' But just as there is a part of Dorothy Thomson that will never forgive or forget the wrongs done to her at Stoke Place, so too with Mabel Cooper. I ask her whether spending so many years in a long-stay hospital has made her value her rights more. 'Yes, you have got that spot on,' she says. 'It makes you hard coming out of the hospital. Because I lost a lot of my childhood being in them. You're angry, but you can't take it out on people because you don't know whose fault it was in the beginning that people with learning disability were shut away. If you took it out on everybody you came across you wouldn't have any friends at all.'

As I neared the end of my own investigations, I heard of a research project that seemed to be using the self-advocacy movement to search for answers to some of the questions I had been asking myself.

Lynne Evans and Phillip Morgan are members of RCT (Rhondda Cynon Taf) People First, and are part of a partnership with Glamorgan University and New Pathways, a sexual abuse counselling service in south Wales. Together, they have begun a three-year project to examine abuse from the perspective of people with learning difficulties. Looking into Abuse: research by people with learning disabilities, will investigate physical, sexual, emotional and financial abuse, and neglect. Evans, Morgan and their colleagues spent seven years seeking funding for the project, because they wanted to find out what other people with learning difficulties knew about abuse and what support they needed if they were abused, rather than continuing to ask professionals what they knew and thought.

Asked why the research was important, Morgan said: 'It is important because there is nothing out there for people with learning disability relating to abuse.'

Evans added: 'The project will hopefully let people with a learning disability know where to go and who to see if they, or someone that they know, have been abused. It is also important to help people learn how to stay safe.'

Both of them feel the project is important because people with learning difficulties need to know there are people they can trust and talk to about abuse.

When I asked what they hoped would come out of the research, Evans said: 'We hope that the research will help with educating people with a learning disability on how to keep themselves safe in life and in their community.'

Evans and Morgan say people with learning difficulties can be 'an easy target'. Sometimes, they add, people do not even realise they are being abused. 'It is important for people with learning disabilities to understand what to look for both physically and mentally if people have been abused. We can keep a look out for friends. It is important to be treated exactly like anybody else.'

Despite the many successes of the self-advocacy movement, the experiences of June, a campaigner from London, demonstrate how its work is far from over.

June has spoken up time and time again when she has seen injustice, whether it was her or a friend or a colleague who had experienced it. But her willingness to stand up for herself and speak out earned her a 'reputation'. She told me how she felt unable to accompany a friend to make a complaint to the police 'because they know me and all this, they might think I am making an allegation about a support worker or whatever and you don't get heard.' The police believe she is a trouble-maker. They had told her that she had made up allegations in the past. She made it absolutely clear to me that she had never made up any allegations. It was just that she hadn't been believed.

'I feel I have been punished,' she told me. 'So what if I have got a disability? So what if I made allegations in the past?'

She knows that not everyone is as tough as she is. Some people are scared of speaking up. 'I am a strong character,' she says. The treatment she has received has motivated her to speak up for other people. 'Most people are afraid to speak up for themselves. I'm not afraid to speak up for myself. If people help me, I help them. Most people are not really strong or weak. Might be weak and they feel they can't speak up for themselves.'

This is why she believes that people with learning difficulties must get training to speak up. 'I think it's important that people should get training to say 'no' or 'stop'.'

Although the People First movement did not take root in Britain until 1984, people with learning difficulties had been speaking out and standing up for themselves for many years[4].

Katherine Owen describes how women who had spent many years on a locked ward in an old long-stay hospital found ways to resist the restrictions of the institution[5]. When faced with being made to eat something she didn't want to eat, one of the women would put her food on other people's plates. Another would sit on the floor to avoid being moved back to her seat. A third woman would drag staff off their chairs, trying to force them to go where she wanted to go. Eventually, she would hit herself. After 40 years of 'institutional living', says Owen, 'Francesca was still prepared to fight for who she was and what she wanted, and give her life meaning.'

People with learning difficulties in some long-stay hospitals resisted in other ways. Some made up songs[6]. They sung about the oppression they faced, they poked fun at the staff, and they sung about their desire for a better life.

Sheena Rolph says[7] that new writing by people with learning difficulties 'argues against the 'victim' status so often given to them. In the everyday lives of the people I have been talking to there were ways of retelling, asserting, mocking, and above all, surviving.'

Rannveig Traustadottir and Lisa Spina[8] argue that some residents in institutions would speak up, get angry and display 'challenging behaviour', while others would co-operate to survive, concerned also about the impact speaking up might have on their friends (a valid concern for the residents of Longcare). 'They are neither heroes nor victims but, rather, they make decisions in the context of their families and social lives, as we all do.'

In his powerful testimony about life in three US institutions over 60 years, Thomas Allen writes[8]: 'Living in an institution is Hell. You never know what is going to happen to you. I have seen people die for no reason. I have seen people get punished for no reason. I am one of them. I have been put in a corner, facing the wall, for hours on end simply for talking out of line. To me all institutions are alike. One might be a little better than the other but not by much. You cannot do what you want to do. You have no freedom. You have no respect. You have no dignity. You have very few friends.'

Allen was a survivor, and he did what Dorothy did to survive. He held onto a dream. His, just like Dorothy's, was to find someone to love and who loved him, and to marry them. 'This dream was what kept me going,' he wrote. 'It kept me alive. During times of despair I turned to it and it comforted me and gave me strength.'

John O'Brien has analysed Thomas Allen's strategies for fighting the 'institution trap'[9]. Among the ten lessons he draws from Allen's life – again, startlingly similar to those that Dorothy seems to have lived and survived by at Longcare – are to find safe ways to use your voice and not to give up when others don't listen; to make a positive difference to other disabled people; to reach out and make friends; and to keep your dream alive and guard it from people who try to kill it.

These accounts reminded me more and more of how Dorothy and other Longcare residents had survived Rowe's regime. They made alliances and friendships. Some of the women confided in each other about the things Gordon was doing to them. Tracy would describe how she would worry about SY (a female resident), Janet Ward and Rachel if she wasn't in the same room as them. 'I worried what he was doing and how they were.' She would talk to SY and Rachel about 'what he did to us'.

I also remembered how Dorothy had secretly put food aside for another resident who had been punished by being made to miss his meal. And I read again how she had kept hold of the dream that one day she would get married, and have a home of her own.

When Dorothy was told that Gordon Rowe wanted her to keep the residents awake, she let them sleep. She pestered Rowe about her savings account, and she joked with Jimmy at Angela Rowe's expense. In the incident which led to her escape from Longcare, she told a member of staff she would 'let it all out' about Rowe's regime, and when Rowe threatened her with violence, she grabbed a pair of scissors to defend herself.

The more I looked through the chapters I had written about the regime, the more it became clear that others had resisted, too. There was George, who seemed to have deliberately torn his clothes, no doubt because he didn't like them. Gary Deacon's father, Ron, had described how his son would 'play up' in the car back to Stoke Place after a weekend at home – as many other residents would. I remembered the care worker who described how Stefano held his head in his hands in front of Gordon Rowe and shouted: 'No! No!' And there was Michael, who would challenge Gordon about why he wasn't receiving the same privileges as other residents, even though he must have known he would be punished for his resistance, and how he would secretly eat food his family had given him, and refused to work in the Stoke Place grounds, which he hated. Then there was Jackie, who refused to eat because of a painful medical condition, often spitting the food out when Gordon tried to force-feed her. There was Ben's tussle with Desmond Tully, and the female resident who bought a packet of cigarettes on a shopping trip to Slough, even though she knew it was against the rules.

And then there were the women, and men, who were raped and sexually assaulted by Gordon Rowe. They resisted, too. Rosie would often tell her aunt that she wanted to come home. After a visit, she never wanted to go back to Longcare and would make herself sick. Janet, Rachel, Tracy, Andrew, all described later how they had tried to stop Gordon from raping or sexually assaulting them. Other residents, too, had confided in staff what Gordon was doing to them: Robert and Paul, and I'm sure many others, had resisted Rowe in this way.

The more I read, the less the former residents looked like the passive 'silent victims' I had characterised them as in my first book, and more like survivors, more like people who were abandoned in incredibly vulnerable situations without the support they needed to be safe, and who resisted as they could, in their own ways, the brutal cruelty of the Longcare regime.

1   *Staying Strong: Taking self-advocacy into the future*; The National Forum of People with Learning Difficulties; 2011

2   *Self-advocacy in the Lives of People with Learning Difficulties*, by Dan Goodley; Open University Press; 2000

3   *Two Pioneers of Self-Advocacy: Ray Loomis and Tom Houlihan*, by Paul Williams; in *Exploring Experiences of Advocacy by People with Learning Disabilities: Testimonies of resistance*, by Duncan Mitchell et al (editors); Jessica Kingsley Publishers; 2006

4   *Advocacy as Resistance: Speaking up as a way of fighting back,
    by Dorothy Atkinson, Mabel Cooper and Gloria Ferris; in
    Exploring Experiences of Advocacy by People with Learning
    Disabilities: Testimonies of resistance, by Duncan Mitchell et al
    (editors); Jessica Kingsley Publishers; 2006*

5   *Restriction and Resistance: The experience of life on a locked
    ward for people with learning disabilities, by Katherine Owen;
    in Exploring Experiences of Advocacy by People with Learning
    Disabilities: Testimonies of resistance, by Duncan Mitchell et al
    (editors); Jessica Kingsley Publishers; 2006*

6   *Songs of Resistance, by Sue Ledger and Lindy Shufflebotham;
    in Exploring Experiences of Advocacy by People with Learning
    Disabilities: Testimonies of resistance, by Duncan Mitchell et al
    (editors); Jessica Kingsley Publishers; 2006*

7   *Surprise Journeys and Border Crossings, by Sheena Rolph; in
    Crossing Boundaries: Change and continuity in the history of
    learning disability, by Lindsay Brigham, Dorothy Atkinson, et
    al (editors); BILD Publications; 2000*

8   *Bits on the Life of Thomas Allen, by Thomas Allen with Rannveig
    Traustadottir and Lisa Spina; in Deinstitutionalization and
    People with Intellectual Disabilities: In and out of institutions,
    by Kelley Johnson and Rannveig Traustadottir (editors); Jessica
    Kingsley Publishers; 2005*

9   *Out of the Institution Trap, by John O'Brien; in
    Deinstitutionalization and People with Intellectual Disabilities:
    In and out of institutions, by Kelley Johnson and Rannveig
    Traustadottir (editors); Jessica Kingsley Publishers; 2005*

PART SIX

SURVIVORS

Chapter Twenty-Eight

The Aftermath
[1994-1997]

'I have been in care most of my life. I have been beaten and battered and abused. Just because I have a learning disability and nobody listens to me. I got abused in all them homes. All my life. I got the cane, I got the slipper, started messing around with me. There was a number of prefects, then started messing around with the little fellas, which would be like me as well. But the staff would always batter you. And if you hit one of the staff, you would be in a side ward, and you'd be there for a week. Stripped off, naked, and with no clothes on at all. It would be their word against yours. That's what it would be. Because they are the ones with the white coats on. People with the white coats on tell the truth, and people with learning disabilities tell lies. Nobody would know no better.'

'Michael'; Witness Support, Preparation and Profiling: The Liverpool Model; DVD produced by Mills Media Ltd for Merseyside Criminal Justice Board; 2010

In the first few months after Gordon Rowe was finally forced out of his Longcare empire, the full, terrible impact of his abusive regime began to reveal itself.

Michael was one of those found to be suffering from post-traumatic stress disorder. When he left Stoke Place just a week after the first media reports appeared, he was said to be experiencing fear, helplessness, nightmares, severe depression, anxiety and stress-induced psychosis. Gone was his bubbly and friendly character. He had become withdrawn and secretive, his posture stooped, as if worn down by coping with the horrors of his life. He had given up fighting, resisting, and began self-mutilating. He became moody and uncooperative, would lash out at other residents and became paranoid that the police were after him. He found it impossible to relate to other people. He would bang his head against doors, crying. Afterwards, he would be remorseful, saying: 'I'm sorry, I won't do it again.'

By 1999, he had to be detained under the Mental Health Act in Harperbury Hospital, Hertfordshire. There were reports of his banging his head on the wall, burning his hand with cigarettes and 'uncontrolled screaming'.

Another resident arrived at his new home with only a few, ill-fitting clothes and no personal belongings. He would frequently wet himself, particularly at night. Staff noticed how frightened he was, both of them and fellow residents. He would damage objects in his room, rip his and other people's clothes. He would keep his bedroom light on throughout the night, and would sleep under the bed, insisting that a member of staff stayed in his room until he fell asleep. He would put his arms around his plate at meal-times, watching those around him in case they tried to steal his food, and would eat so quickly that he made himself sick.

Peter, one of the blind residents mentioned by many former Longcare care workers as a frequent victim of Rowe's abuse, left Stoke Place soon after the first media reports. When he arrived at his new home, he was so frightened that he would wet himself rather than asking to use the bathroom. He was only able to answer 'yes' or 'no', his clothes were 'poor quality, outdated and too small', and when there was a confrontation between other residents, he would mimic their voices while rocking and hitting himself. He would shout out, hitting his head with his hands. He, too, was diagnosed with post-traumatic stress disorder.

In the wake of the first media reports about the Longcare regime in the autumn of 1994, the charity Respond – which supports people with learning difficulties who have experienced abuse or trauma – had begun to receive requests for help from local authorities. They wanted to know if their clients had been abused, and whether they should be moved to new homes.

Respond's advice was crucial in persuading many of these councils to find new homes for their clients. Staff in their new placements soon began to notice worrying signs of trauma. By November 1994, Respond was receiving the first in a new wave of enquiries. This time, they were being asked to provide treatment. By Christmas, they were holding their first counselling sessions.

Not all of those Respond treated had been beaten or raped. Many had simply lived for years in an atmosphere of cruelty and inhumanity, witnessing assaults taking place around them every day. As they began courses of long-term psychotherapy, symptoms began to emerge: depression, low self-esteem, an inability to express joy, sadness, or anger. They were showing classic symptoms of post-traumatic stress disorder.

Many were desperately frightened and anxious. One had a phobia of birds. Even the sight of a bird drawn on a piece of paper was enough to spark screams of panic, a reaction no doubt to being locked in the aviary by Gordon Rowe.

'There is no reason at all why someone with a learning disability should display signs of post-traumatic stress disorder,' Alan Corbett – then Respond's head of clinical services – told me. 'Nor did we find people were suffering from psychosis or other forms of mental illness. These were people who clearly showed signs of being traumatised over a long period of time.'

Many of those counselled by Respond shared an 'abnormal' fear of authority and were almost pathologically incapable of disobedience. If another person entered the room, they would cower in the corner. They were jumpy, constantly looking around for signs of danger. Many had eating disorders, suffered from terrible nightmares, or couldn't sleep at all without a light left on, while others were too frightened to go into a bathroom to take a bath.

A key problem in treating people with learning difficulties and high support needs is how to communicate with them. Many of the Longcare survivors could only speak a few words. 'Although the inability to speak may make therapy and counselling a longer and more difficult process, it does not mean that therapy or counselling cannot be used at all,' said Corbett. 'Respond has learned that people who lack verbal skills learn to communicate in many other ways. You can tell someone is clinically depressed by their posture, by how they move, by observing them. If someone is banging her head against the wall, or rocking violently, or cutting her arm, or throwing herself on the floor, those are powerful connections with something that has been done that cannot be put into words.'

'In many ways the most shocking thing about Longcare,' Dame Philippa Russell would tell me later, 'was the persistence, the day-to-day cruelty.' She had been told that, because of how Jackie had been treated at Stoke Place – dragged outside at mealtimes if she talked or refused to eat – she would 'grab a chair and bolt for the door' if she heard a raised voice at her new home. Jackie, I discovered later, had been diagnosed with depression, chronic anxiety, psychosis and post-traumatic stress.

Dame Philippa remembered being shown around Stoke Place by a resident during the Longcare inquiry. Once Longcare had gone, the house was 'actually quite nice', she told me. 'But it was creepy to walk through the private part of the house, where the bedrooms were. There was a beautiful, large sitting-room on the first floor, looking down the park, and the residents wouldn't go into this beautiful room, which was furnished, and carpeted, with pictures, because that is where so much of the abuse took place. Even more horribly, when you walked into this part of the building, you couldn't hear anything. It was all muffled and dull, because of this really thick shag-pile carpet, which in some cases extended up like a sort of dado. A resident said to me, absolutely clearly, with a straight face, 'Well, of course, you couldn't hear anyone coming. You didn't want to go to sleep at night.' It shows you how awful it really was.'

GREG

When Gordon Rowe left The Old Rectory, Norma Adams assumed that her complaints had been investigated by the authorities and proven unfounded.

Within a few weeks, the new management at The Old Rectory asked Norma to find Greg a new home. He had become unmanageable and aggressive and the staff could no longer cope.

Norma agreed to have Greg temporarily admitted to Leavesden Hospital near Watford. She was ill with suspected colonic cancer and it was three weeks before she was fit enough to visit. When she arrived, one of the nurses told her: 'I don't understand what this is all about. Greg is here with a record of aggression, but he is such a sweetie.' Norma believes the heavy use of tranquillisers at The Old Rectory caused the aggression. Once Greg was taken off the drugs, the belligerence vanished.

Ten years later, Greg had settled into a new home. His mother believed he was finally content and stable, and The Old Rectory was a fading memory. That was until she turned on the BBC news one evening and saw a story about Gordon Rowe and Stoke Place. She was appalled, and contacted Slough police. She was assured they already knew about The Old Rectory. Of course they did. Everybody knew.

'I felt so guilty, because I thought I could have done more 11 years ago,' she said. 'I felt all kinds of irrational things. People told me I wasn't guilty of anything, but I was. I will continue to blame myself for the rest of my life, because I could have done more.'

She tried to make up for what she saw as her failure. After Angela Rowe was released from prison, Norma wrote to Jeb Bush, the governor of Florida, the US ambassador in London, and a police chief in Florida, warning them all that Angela might try and open a care home in the state. She also wrote to every social services director in England.

She was furious that the complaints she made in the early 1980s were not investigated more thoroughly, and tried unsuccessfully to find out from Hammersmith and Fulham council whether Greg's social worker ever expressed any doubts about standards of care at The Old Rectory.

Like the Longcare parents, Norma realised that she would never know exactly what happened to her son. He may have been abused. He probably was. She hoped his physical strength protected him. But Greg doesn't talk, and so when Gordon Rowe died, he took his secrets with him to the grave.

GARY

After Angela Rowe 'voluntarily' resigned as a Longcare employee in July 1994, Gary Deacon's behaviour began to deteriorate. The allegations about abuse at the homes had been published in the press and Gary's parents Ron and Doreen were wondering what had happened to him.

Ron remembered how Gary gradually 'seemed to turn against women'. He would become upset very easily, and his angry 'tantrums' of screaming and kicking were always directed at women. 'The worst part of it was that he couldn't talk to you about what the problem was,' Ron told me.

A few weeks later, a detective visited the Deacons. He asked some general questions about Gary and how they felt about the standard of care, but told them there were no allegations so far that Gary had been abused.

'We thought there were a few residents that were OK and Gary was one of them,' said Doreen. 'It must have been nearly a year later when Madeleine Stewart visited and told us what Angela Rowe was supposed to have done to him.'

Lillian, a former care worker, had alleged that she had walked into Gary's bedroom and discovered Angela Rowe masturbating him. Nearly a year later, the CPS decided not to try Angela on the charge of indecent assault – the charge was left to lie on the court's files.

Ron remembered also how his son had been heavily sedated. He had been horrified to arrive one afternoon and find Gary barely conscious and 'zombyish'. Thanks to a new doctor, the medication was gradually reduced and Gary's condition improved.

Ron and Doreen never discovered what happened to Gary at Longcare. All they had was the evidence of the brutality visited on other residents, and Lillian's statement.

Over the 10 years he was at Longcare, Ron never suspected Gary was receiving anything but the best care. 'People say to me now, 'Why didn't you see anything when you were there?' But he was all right when we visited. They are not going to do anything in front of you, are they?'

When Gary lost weight, staff told Ron he had been put on a diet. When his watch, new suede jacket and an electronic keyboard went missing, Ron was told they had been 'put with the good things' for safe keeping. None of these items, or many other presents Ron and Doreen bought for Gary, ever reappeared. It was a story familiar to nearly every parent.

Ron was one of the few relatives who decided to leave their children at Stoke Place after the allegations were revealed in 1994. He believed Gary was better off staying with his friends, and that the standard of care had improved since the Rowes left. Berkshire social services also told him there were no other vacancies near Maidenhead.

'Unless there's a miracle, I know he'll be in a home for the rest of his life,' Ron told me. 'Before this happened, we would have put our trust in a carer immediately, but now we think twice. We are always going to have what happened in the back of our minds, but Gary has to live somewhere.'

SIMON

Avril and Brian Scott knew nothing about the allegations against Gordon Rowe until August 1994, when they received a call from Simon's social worker. She told them she wanted to take Simon away from Stoke Place, but couldn't tell them why. The Scotts drove immediately to Stoke Poges and spoke to Ray Cradock. He told them Bucks County Council was trying to 'stitch up' Gordon Rowe because it owed him money. The truth will all come out in the end, he said, and told them to take no notice of the 'rumours'. They didn't trust Cradock, but decided to let Simon stay at Stoke Place, because they believed he was happy there.

A few weeks later, they received another call from their social worker. She told them there had been an investigation and it was far more serious than Cradock had led them to believe. The council's report mentioned that Simon had been denied treatment for his epilepsy, because staff thought he was faking his symptoms. The Scotts drove to Stoke Place and brought Simon home.

They told me they had been generally 'very happy' with the care Simon received, although the attitude of some of the staff and 'one or two other little things' disturbed them. Once, Simon told them how a care worker smacked his bottom; another time, he was sent to his room because he had been naughty. He also told them about Jackie being dragged out of the dining-room because she wouldn't eat her food. But they believed Gordon Rowe had a 'soft spot' for their son – he used to call him 'Randolph' (after the actor, Randolph Scott), and was always laughing and joking with him when they visited. Brian and Gordon often discussed their mutual interest in videos and filming, and Rowe once showed him his impressive studio in the cottage.

But, sometimes, Simon would return home and they wouldn't be able to get a word out of him – they now believed it was because of the drugs Rowe had fed him. Avril told me Simon was 'one of the lucky ones', because they phoned him so often and Gordon and her husband were so friendly. Brian even said Simon was better off at Stoke Place – he was fitter, because of all the exercise he received working in the grounds as one of the Working Lads, and he seemed to 'thrive' on the harsh regime.

But Avril disagreed. Simon had put on weight after leaving Stoke Place and was much happier. 'He's so much more content, it's incredible,' she told me. 'He doesn't stop talking now – we even have to tell him to be quiet sometimes. He phones us up every night.'

Every now and again, something would happen to Simon to trigger a memory. Avril remembered receiving a phone call from her son. He was upset. A member of staff had told him he would be sent away if he didn't make his bed. When Avril phoned the home, she discovered it was something Simon had remembered being told at Stoke Place.

When I met Simon, his memories of Stoke Place were vague and distant. He remembered the 'big old building' and how he would feed the animals and work in the gardens. But he also recalled his friend Fred being locked in his room because he 'lost his temper'. And he remembered Gordon Rowe. 'He said, 'You must not do that.' He told me off. He taught me to drink beer.' Gordon, he said, called him and Fred 'the terrible twins'.

But Avril remembered the hints of a darker side to Simon's time at Stoke Place. 'Twice he was made to stand outside, because he had dirty shoes on, and he was made to take all his clothes off. Somebody kicked him up the bottom. We visited him one time and there was one lad with Down's syndrome who was being made to stand behind one of the pillars until he was called, and I remember Simon saying: 'Uh-oh, he's been naughty.'

'Every time we went up there, Simon had stitches in his forehead or on his nose or had a burn on his arm. There were so many little niggly things that you accepted at the time, but now it's all come out you realise...' She paused. 'There was another time when we were all together in the car and Simon said to me, completely out of the blue: 'I do not put my fits on.'' She hesitated again. 'He was one of the lucky ones, because we phoned up every week,' she said finally. But it was clear she did not entirely believe what she was saying.

NICKY

Nicky Power's parents waited while the video player clicked into its routine.

A blank screen. The music starts. A jaunty Greek dance. Twanging guitars. A slow rhythm, but persistent.

The first scene: Nicky is seated at a table in a wooden chair, working at a puzzle. She squints, concentrating, behind her black frames. Then she turns and waves at the camera.

The voice begins: friendly, with a country lilt. It is the voice of Gordon Rowe. 'This short film depicts Nicky in various stages of her progress at Stoke Place. It's not compiled in any particular order, but just shows snitbits here and there. Here, of course, she's in the classroom.'

Next to a pub, and Nicky is seated at a table, a glass of Coke in front of her, other residents nearby. She rubs the back of her head with her hand, but is too busy sucking up her drink through two straws to worry about the camera.

The video cuts to a harbour in southern England, where Angela Rowe is untying a rope, and climbing aboard a small motor-cruiser. There are five women, including Nicky, in the boat. Nicky waves at the camera.'Here's Angela, attending to our boat Kasba, when we took the residents on holiday to Bucklesham Bay. Our boat being moored at Chichester, we were able to give the girls who we took some very pleasant rides.'

Cut to the Stoke Place outbuildings. Four of the residents are gathered around a long-eared rabbit. 'Each morning and afternoon the residents go from the classrooms out to see the animals. Nicky loves to make close contact with them.'

Cut to the office. Nicky in a dressing-gown, her hair still wet. Staring at the camera, she suddenly smiles and waves. 'After a bath, Nicky will come down and assist me in the office. She loves me to draw houses for her, in which in the windows must be shown her grannies.'

It was 1996, six years after they had first watched that video, and we were sitting in the Powers' conservatory, talking about their daughter. They remembered watching the video and how they were reassured at how active and happy Nicky seemed.

But they also remembered signs of abuse whose significance would only become clear after the regime was exposed. 'She came home one time with a terrific bruise,' Susan told me. 'All the skin on the back of her heel and her toe was crushed. I rang up Gordon and asked what on earth had happened, and he said: 'Oh, I forgot to tell you, she had a fit and fell down the stairs.' Another time I was told she had had a fit and got her foot caught under the wardrobe. On the amount of epilepsy drugs she was on, she should never have had a fit. And since she moved to her new home she hasn't had a single fit.' She would often come home filthy – her nails were never cut, her ears were dirty, and once there was a huge blister on one of her feet, which had been left untreated. When they arrived for a visit, they would find the residents sitting blank-eyed in front of a television screen, 'as if they had been drugged'. They were not encouraged to visit.

They also remembered Rowe's 'obsession' with Nicky's periods and how he told them he wanted all the female residents on contraceptives. They agreed, because Nicky suffered very badly with PMT.

Hundreds of pounds worth of gifts bought for Nicky went missing, which staff always said were 'in the storeroom'. Rowe insisted that any money they sent Nicky was in the form of a cheque made out to him. Because they trusted him, they agreed.

But they never considered the possibility that Nicky was being abused. 'I never thought about it,' said Susan. 'I suppose we just trust people. Because you would never do it, you don't think other people would.'

Davyd Power remembered Christmases, when Nicky would come home with armfuls of gifts from Gordon. 'Whether it was conscience money, I don't know, but he always said Nicky was one of his favourites.'

Susan and Davyd were on holiday when the scandal broke. Susan's 90-year-old mother recognised Stoke Place in a television report. When one of the family rang Stoke Place, a member of staff told them it was 'all hearsay' and Nicky was fine.

A few days later, the Powers were visited by Nicky's social worker, who told them the truth: Nicky had been beaten and thrown and kicked down the stairs at Stoke Place. 'I was shocked,' said Susan, 'but I took it.' They decided to remove Nicky. Kent social workers visited Stoke Place and were appalled to find there were no records for Nicky's 10 years at the home, including her medication.

Just before Nicky was due to leave, the Powers received a long, rambling letter from Gordon Rowe, begging them not to take her away. He said he and Angela were planning to open a new home with small flats and they would disprove all the allegations. He said they wanted Nicky to join them at the new home, because she was one of his 'special girls'.

Within a few weeks of Nicky leaving, Susan and Davyd were told by her social worker that their daughter had had 'every abuse going'. They were devastated. Susan had to visit her GP for treatment for depression.

'After she moved to her new home, we were told Nicky was having up to eight baths a day and then changing her clothes,' said Susan. 'She refused to look in the mirror. She would have flashbacks and dig and scratch herself.'

Susan handed over another record of Nicky's life, this one a document written several years after the boat trips and pub visits, a time when Nicky was settling into a new home. A more accurate record, it is a diary of Nicky's day-to-day existence as seen by the care workers helping her pick up the pieces of her life.

11 July 1995:

Nicky spilt a cup of tea over herself in the disco. David* and Becky* took her upstairs to change. She was crying and hitting herself. David tried to stop Nicky hurting herself and in the process Nicky bent his thumb by accident. Incontinent at 2am. Perfectly OK when changed. Didn't want to wear a clean nightdress. Threw a wobbly, chewing her fist and hitting herself on the side of the head. Pacified her. Went to bed wearing a polo neck jumper.

12 July 1995 (Nicky visits Respond):

Fine until about 2.20pm. Asked about chips (which we have on the way home). Explained we had to wait for Peter*. Started throwing books about, spitting and screaming. Trashed the waiting-room, pushed the chairs over. Kept hitting me, pulling at my clothes, ripping my dress. After about 20 minutes, she finally calmed down and had a good cry. I gave her a cuddle. Frank* the counsellor made her a cup of tea. She then wanted to change her clothes, so Michelle* fetched her clean clothes from the car. Fine after that, laughing and looking forward to her chips.

14 July 1995:

Nicky wanted to go up and change at 12.40pm. Took her upstairs, where she had several changes of clothes. Started getting agitated, threw one or two things and said, 'Don't do it. Don't like it.' Calmed down after a while, sat waiting for her dinner OK. On coming downstairs at 2pm, Nicky got very upset. Slapping me, Peter (very hard), screaming, spitting and generally very upset. At one stage she threw herself to the floor, *dragging Barbara* down with her. Andrew* and Barbara contained her, while the staff and myself cleared the house. She then calmed down and went down to the kitchen with Lucy* and seems fine now. Blew again this afternoon in the kitchen. Christine* calmed her down, took her up to her lounge in the maisonette. Soon settled again.*

5pm: Nicky wanted to change her clothes again. After supper, Nicky had soaked herself. I changed her and she blew, because she had wet herself. Wouldn't put on her clothes. Sat on her bed and wet herself again, all over me while I was changing her under garments again. Left her for a short while to calm down. Threw clothes and objects at me. Coathanger etc. Calmed down, after a while. Bathed and tried to put nightdress on. Blew again. Soaked her sheets and bedding. Changed them. At last got her into pyjamas with help from Cathy*.

15 July 1995:

Nicky wanted to get changed at midday. Nicky asked to be changed three times this afternoon.

26 July 1995:

Nicky was very happy and relaxed for all the journey to Wandsworth, we even had a terrible storm which she coped with very well! We arrived in good time so that they could have their packed lunch, and still Nicky was relaxed! But when Nicky's counsellor arrived, the first thing Nicky said was 'hair'. Alison then went upstairs for a short while, but on her return she asked Nicky if she was coming upstairs and that was when Nicky started her anger. She blew for a solid half an hour, hitting, spitting, but most of the problem was her spitting at Alison. We did wonder whether anything was brought on by the fact that Alison had had her hair cut very short. All the time Nicky was angry she would look at Alison and repeat 'bye'. After Alison left we calmed her down, changed her clothes and came home, stopping for the McDonald's on the way. No more problems.

1 August 1995:

Because Samantha was shouting, this caused Nicky to 'blow'.
We had cups, pictures flying. She then started to hit herself. After
a few minutes she started to cry and then I gave her a cuddle
and she slowly calmed down and went up to her room. Nicky
very well behaved this evening. Bed wet, washed, changed.
Quilt on the line.*

Legal documents from the civil case taken by the Longcare
families against Bucks County Council provide further evidence
of the abuse Nicky suffered, and its impact upon her. They show
that she was given two anatomically-correct dolls as part of her
therapy. In one session, she undressed the male doll, pointed
to its penis, and said: 'Err, horrid, don't want to kiss it,' and
became angry with the doll.

In another session, she undressed the female doll, pointed
to the genital area, and said: 'Rude... don't want to... ouch!'
She appeared frightened and left the session. She later became
distressed and angry, throwing objects around her bedroom and
bathroom, and screaming: 'Don't want to... stop it.'

On one visit, Susan and Nicky's care workers decided to try
something different. Nicky had shown a deep hatred of all of
the clothes she associated with Stoke Place – particularly the
nightwear – so Susan asked if she wanted to get rid of 'those
nasty clothes'. 'Not nice,' replied Nicky. Susan took Nicky to her
bedroom, but the moment she touched the clothes, Nicky flew
at her, shouting, 'No, no.' It was not until they got downstairs
and one of the care workers asked Nicky: 'Hi, Nick, are you
going to throw those things away?' that she calmed down.

'We had to let her throw them in one of the big green bins,'
said Susan. 'Then she said: 'Gone,' and slammed the lid down.
She would not look at me. She just said: 'Go.' She was so
frightened we were going to take her back to Stoke Place.

'Recently, I bought her a new dress and she put it on and
said: 'Nice, like this, I like me,' and she went over to the mirror

and brushed her hair. I said: 'Is that all right?' and she said: 'I am nice.' That was the first time she had said that for a long, long time.'

At Nicky's new home, she had her own bedroom, a pretty, comfortable place where she was surrounded by her own possessions and favourite toys. She was allowed to spend time on her own at the end of the day's lessons, and was expected to help prepare meals in the small flat she shared with four other adults. Her room had its own television, and videos could be piped straight in if she didn't feel like sitting with her flatmates.

But Susan and Davyd were still not able to have their daughter home to visit. Their house was the place she was taken from to return to Stoke Place. Only recently had she even allowed her mother to hold her hand again. Her mother was the person who always drove her back to Stoke Place.

It was only in the last few weeks that Susan had been able to talk about her daughter's ordeal at Stoke Place. 'The last two years have been a living hell,' Susan said, and brought out a picture of Nicky as a smiling, confident teenager, before she moved to Stoke Place. She looked as if she hadn't a care in the world.

Susan produced two more snaps of her daughter, taken several years later. Nicky had started to put on weight, but the biggest change was in her eyes. The smiling confidence of her teenage years had gone, to be replaced with a haunted, ill-at-ease grimace.

For the first three or four years, Nicky seemed happy at Stoke Place. But then she began to react strangely when it was time to return to Longcare after weekend visits home. She would start to hyperventilate, and say: 'No, Gordon not nice, no, not nice.' Susan told me: 'I thought she just didn't want to leave her mum and dad. When she knew we were on the M25 and heading for Stoke Place, she would just shut up. We would never get another word out of her. Once or twice I brought her back after a weekend at home and I had a job to get her out of the car. I can still see her standing there, just looking so sad.'

Years later, in a letter she wrote to me early in 2011, she was clearly still tormented by her failure to realise what Nicky had been trying to tell her parents. 'After having a nice time at home, we thought it was just the thought of leaving us,' she wrote. 'I just wish she could have been able to tell me. I feel so guilty in letting Nicky down. We just did not know anything was going on... I'm so sorry I took her back. Oh why did I leave her there?'

ROSIE

'When I telephoned Rosie, she would often say she wanted to come home. I told her we would visit her more often. When she did come home for a visit, she never wanted to go back. When it was time to return to Longcare, her face changed and she would make herself sick.'

It was a late summer day in Benedict Alcindor's flat in Tower Hamlets, east London. We were talking in the living-room, surrounded by pictures of her large family. 'I figured maybe she was just missing the family, that she wasn't seeing enough of us,' she told me. 'Then, one Christmas, she gathered all her dolls together and asked me to take them home for her.'

On visits home, Rosie would often touch her belly and tell her aunt that it hurt. Benedict would give her a kiss and a few comforting words. And there were the stitches in an ankle wound Rosie blamed on a fall against a radiator. And the birth control pills Rowe said were to control her periods and 'stop the blood clotting'.

Like most of the Longcare relatives, the first Benedict knew of the council investigation was through television news coverage of the stories my paper and The Independent had run about the leaked report. She was shocked, but never believed Rosie herself had been abused. She rang Tower Hamlets, her local authority, and nothing she was told made her believe anything different.

A few weeks later, Rosie was rushed into Slough's Wexham Park Hospital. She had had a severe epileptic seizure and the hospital was not sure she would pull through. After one visit, Rosie's social worker told Benedict she believed Rosie had been abused. 'I couldn't believe her. I couldn't believe she was one of them,' Benedict told me.

The family were already looking for a new place for Rosie to live, and in February 1995, she moved to a small home in east London, nearer Benedict's home. A few weeks later, Rosie came home to celebrate Mother's Day. It was a weekend Benedict would never forget.

She was in the kitchen on the Saturday afternoon, cleaning some chicken, ready for a big family meal the next day, when Rosie walked in, asked what she was doing and pointed to her belly, as she had done several times before. She told her aunt it was hurting. Then she said: 'He nearly kill me.'

'Who?' asked Benedict.

'Big Dadda,' said Rosie.

'What happened?' asked her aunt. Appalled, she watched as her niece bunched her fingers and performed an unmistakable pumping action with her fist, and pointed to her genitals.

'He nearly kill me,' she repeated.

'Where did it happen?'

'In my room.'

'Who was with you?'

'Only two of us. He put me down on floor. He nearly kill me. He drink milk,' she said, and pointed to her breasts. Then she described how the same thing had happened at the cottage.

'Where was Big Mamma?' asked Benedict.

'She wasn't there,' replied Rosie. 'She went shopping.'

'Where was Baby Ben?'

'He wasn't there. He went shopping with Big Mamma. He put me on the floor. He nearly kill me.'

The next day, Rosie joined the rest of the family in church. 'She was standing next to me as we were singing a hymn and the words were so right that the tears were coming down,' said Benedict. 'Rosie looked at me and said, 'Mamma, you're crying.' I was just a wreck.'

Later, Rosie said she was going to tell her brothers and sisters. 'We were all sitting round the table having dinner and she explained to all of us what happened,' said Benedict. 'It was so sad.

'I was just like a crazy person. I didn't want to believe what she had told me, that she was one of them. I trusted that man so much because he was like a father to her.'

The shock hurt her so badly that her family had to send her away for a holiday. But it didn't work. 'I was crying. My heart was bleeding. I lost weight. I couldn't eat. I couldn't sleep. It was like there was a big brick in my heart that I couldn't get out.'

Her first husband died on the operating table. The pain was terrible, but she pulled through and eventually remarried. This was different, she said. It was a pain that had yet to fade, and showed no sign that it ever would.

Rosie likes to sing and dance and hates to cause problems for others. She can make a cup of tea and put her own clothes on and is clean and tidy. 'She is a nice kid,' said her aunt, 'a happy-going girl. She's not stupid either. She's a clever girl.' Rosie knew Rowe was dead, but the merest reminder of him or Stoke Place was enough to cause an epileptic seizure. She was affected by the regime in other ways, too. After leaving Longcare, Rosie became very protective of her food. She would eat any crumbs that fell onto her clothes and would always finish every bit of her meal, even if she didn't like it.

'She spent 10 years of her life there,' said Benedict. 'At the end, she said nobody loved her no more. Big Dadda and Big Mamma didn't love her no more. I knew Angela was a bit rough, but I always thought Rowe was nice. I couldn't see that he would do anything wrong, that he would take advantage of them.'

Rosie was visited by her social worker three or four times in her first year at Longcare, but after that he left Tower Hamlets and wasn't replaced. 'I was doing all the running, all the chasing, all the visiting,' said Benedict, 'but I didn't have the knowledge to ask the questions.

'It has just finished me. For the kid to be there for 10 years. Damaging her, damaging me. I blame myself. If I had taken any notice of her... she was already damaged, but maybe... Now the more it carries on, the more it hurts me. The feeling is eating me. The way she said it all innocently: 'He nearly kill me. He nearly kill me.''

ANDREW

Andrew's sister and mother would visit him every month, and his mother would phone him every Sunday. They both noticed a gradual change while he was at Stoke Place.

'He became more and more withdrawn,' his mother would say later. 'He had dreadful mood swings and would lose his temper easily.' Like many other residents, his medication 'went up and up'. When Gordon was around, he would become 'anxious and fidgety'. 'I also remember that for a time he used to get the shakes, which was like a nervous habit.' He would ask his mother to keep his birthday money, and often seemed to be wearing other people's clothes.

Andrew was interviewed by the police but refused to say anything. He didn't confide in anyone until months after Gordon had killed himself. It was at a review at Stoke Place, attended by his mother and his sister. 'Andrew just poured out the whole story,' she remembered. 'He said that he had been kicked and slapped by Gordon Rowe, that Gordon had thrown chairs at him and also that Gordon had made Andrew play with Gordon's private parts. Andrew said Gordon had told him not to tell anyone or he would have to leave Stoke Place.' When the subject came up in later reviews, Andrew refused to talk about what had happened, and would just storm out of the room.

TRACY

A couple of weeks after hearing of Gordon Rowe's death, Tracy walked across the grounds of Stoke Place to the cottage where

Gordon and Angela used to live, and threw a brick through the window.

She had remained dry-eyed at Rowe's funeral in 1996. Her behaviour remained 'unpredictable', according to her social worker. She was referred to a clinical psychologist, who said she appeared to be displaying symptoms of post-traumatic stress, as well as anxiety and depression. There were nightmares and angry outbursts.

The following year, in January 1997, the psychologist reported that Tracy appeared depressed and did not want to stay at Stoke Place. 'She also cried two or three times in the session and explained her sadness has got something to do with the past,' the report continued. 'Objectively the client reveals symptoms of depression, anxiety and post-traumatic stress disorder for example irritability, outbursts of anger, difficulty concentrating, depressed mood, anxiety...'

Later that year, four months after finally moving to a new home, her medical notes revealed that she had run out into a road, was scared of staff, was sleeping poorly and was having nightmares about 'the past'. Like many former residents, she would gulp her food down at meal-times. She would often become depressed just by seeing men or talking about the past, and stopped going dry-skiing because the instructor was male.

Her mental health deteriorated to the point where she was seeing large, multi-coloured spiders on her body, and trying to cut the skin off the end of her fingers with a knife.

JANET

One day in 1994, out of the blue, a care worker rang Pauline Hennessey and told her that Janet had started to become 'disruptive' and 'aggressive'. She was having outbursts almost every week.

Pauline drove down to Stoke Place with her dad for a meeting with Janet's social worker, Nigel Rowe, Ray Cradock and the Longcare GP, Dr X. They told her how Janet would often enter a room and start throwing furniture around. On one occasion, she grabbed a knife from the kitchen and threatened to kill herself.

'I told them I didn't understand what was going on because we had never had these problems before,' said Pauline. 'They all looked at each other and said: "We have no idea either."'

Someone suggested that Janet could be placed in a secure unit. Pauline was horrified. Within a month, Cradock and Rowe told Pauline that Janet would have to find a new home.

A few weeks later, Pauline was visited by Janet's social worker. Gordon Rowe was being investigated by Bucks County Council, she was told. Some of the allegations referred to Janet, but details were sketchy. The following day, Havering social services rang back to say the Bucks report had been leaked to the press and that Gordon Rowe had been accused of raping Janet.

'At first I couldn't take it in,' she would say later. 'Not my Janet. It couldn't happen to her. I couldn't stop crying. I had always promised mum I would protect and care for Janet as if she were my own daughter. I had failed them both. How could I have let this happen?'

Janet was moved from home to home in search of a permanent place to live. She moved five times in six months and put on three stone in weight. She missed her friends at Longcare and would wake up crying from nightmares.

Bit by bit, Janet began to tell Pauline what had happened to her. She said Rowe had forced her to have sex with him, that she and other members of Gordon's Girls had been forced to watch pornographic videos with him, and that he had slapped her around the face. She described how Gordon videotaped 'other people' having sex with her and threatened to kill Pauline and take her children away if Janet told her what he was doing.

Pauline and her family began to realise that the signs of abuse had been there, if only they had known what to look for. The burn she 'did in cookery class'. The bruised back where she had 'slipped on the stairs'. The 'sore bottom'. How Janet would say she had 'forgotten' how a certain bruise was caused. How she would return home in shabby, torn and stained clothes, even though Pauline had bought her many bright, fashionable outfits on their frequent shopping sprees. The missing clock-radio, hair-dryer, hi-fi, Walkman, television. The punishments where she was sent to her room for an hour for being rude, but which they now suspect were for days at a time. They remembered how staff had told her how Janet 'lied' and how Gordon told them not to visit so often, to 'help Janet settle in'.

'I used to phone up at 6.30pm and she was always in bed,' said Pauline. 'When she got home, she just wanted to go to bed. It never dawned on me that her medication was too high.'

Pauline remembered the way her sister would talk about Longcare after she left. 'It was fear: pure and utter fear. She told me Gordon was going to come and find her. She talked about men putting her in a van and told me her boyfriend Derek had given Gordon her new phone number.

'Later on, when she discovered Gordon had died, her emotions changed. She would sob her heart out for hours on end. She wanted to know why he had hurt her. She said he couldn't be all bad, because he said he loved her. She said, 'I didn't want Gordon to do it, I asked him to stop'. She was frightened she was going to get the blame for what he had done to her. She was so confused, because she knew that by sleeping with Gordon she had been protected from some of the other things that had been going on, some of the things he had done to her friends. I think she loved Gordon and that is why she was upset when he left, but at the same time she didn't like what he was doing to her.

'He promised her all these things to keep her sweet – a house, getting married and having children. Ever since she was a young child all she ever said was: 'I want a flat like my nan's.' She collected the estate agency adverts in the newspaper. She wanted to be normal. She wanted a boyfriend. She had three older sisters and an older brother. She saw us getting married and having a big white wedding and she wanted to get married.'

Janet often talked about the court case and told Pauline how she would tell the judge about 'the naughty people' and how he would put them in prison and all her friends would be safe. She had even chosen where all her family were to sit in court while she gave her evidence. She still talked about how one day she would get married and have a house and children of her own. But it was clear to her family that Janet no longer believed in her dreams.

On 21 December 1996, Janet died suddenly in her sleep, a few hours after enjoying a Christmas party with other residents. She had finally found somewhere staffed with decent, well-trained people. Pauline believed they had found the permanent 'happy home' she had been seeking for her sister for so many years. The home Janet's mother, Irene, had so wanted to find before she died.

Pauline believed the stress of moving so many times, combined with the guilt and confusion of what happened to her at Longcare, were the real reasons Janet died, rather than the epileptic seizure officially declared as the cause of death.

'I think she just gave up,' Pauline told me. 'She had been in so many different homes. In her last home, they had been giving her some counselling, which obviously pulled up a lot of memories she would rather not have thought about.'

Pauline said her relationship with her sister changed after she found out she had been abused. 'I didn't feel able to give her the comfort, because I didn't want to face the reality of the abuse. If I had the chance now, there are so many things I would do. I was so angry and all my anger was directed at Stoke Place and Buckinghamshire social services. I could deal with that, but I couldn't deal with the emotional side with Janet. If she had opened up and started talking to me, I don't know how I would have coped, because I didn't want to hear it.

'The night she died, I had spoken to her on the phone. Since she left Stoke Place, I spoke to her on the phone five or six times a day. Never once was I angry with her until that night. The children had broken up from school and there were 101 things

I had to do and she had already spoken to me an hour before, so I told her I didn't have time and would speak to her later. Even now, I can't believe I didn't talk to her.

'Earlier in the day she had said to me: 'I'm sorry I upset you.' And I said: 'You haven't upset me.' She said, 'I made you cry.' Then she said: 'Don't worry 'bout me Pauline.' She was so kind and sensitive.'

Chapter Twenty-Nine

Guilt, Nightmares and Depression
[1998-2002]

'A senior detective revealed today that the killing of a tragic young Chinese woman was one of the worst cases of cruelty he had come across in 30 years of policing. Shaowei He, aged 25, was beaten with copper piping, wood embedded with nails, and a broom handle so hard it snapped in half at the King's Chef, Rotherham. The vulnerable woman, who had a mental age of 12 and could speak no English, was subjected to systematic and vicious abuse over a period of weeks by her husband's live-in lover. She was eventually left to die in the freezing backyard of the takeaway on Kilnhurst Road, Rawmarsh, during one of the coldest nights of the year this March.'

The Star (Sheffield), 13 July 2006

In the spring of 2001, I spoke to Alan Corbett again. He told me that Respond had eventually counselled about 10 former Longcare residents. It was still in contact with these survivors and those now supporting them. But there had been no miracle cures. None of them 'got better'.

Instead, therapy provided them with 'the space in which they were believed and a space in which their experiences could be processed', said Corbett. 'What it didn't remove was the terrible reality of those experiences. We were able to provide people with relief from much of the pain of what they had gone through, but when you think of the enormity of the damage, you have to think about a long-term therapeutic plan. For these victims, probably for years and years, people will have to think about their care in a different way.'

They will have to cope with feelings of fear, guilt and shame they will never lose, he said. 'Therapy can help enormously with much of that, but given the severity of the damage, it is not going to stop all of the pain.'

In the autumn of 2002, Corbett told me about a new client, another former Longcare resident who had only recently been put in touch with Respond. Although his social services department had managed to lose all his personal records, the man's new case worker had pieced together his history. He had talked about being kicked and shouted at at Longcare and having his hair pulled. He was also believed to have been sexually abused by Gordon Rowe. He had eating disorders, paranoia and a fear of men. He spent all day locked in his room, watching television with the sound turned down. If he heard a sudden noise, he would immediately 'retreat into himself'. There were serious concerns about his weight, said Corbett. He seemed to be just wasting away.

GREG

For the last few years, Greg Adams had been living very happily with a dozen or so other adults at a care home a couple of hours from London. He had his own room in the big country house and was always happy to see his mum when she came to visit, although he never fussed when it was time for her to leave. He was taken for a 12-15 mile walk almost every day – just a stroll for Greg – and went shopping with staff in the nearby town. He seemed happy.

Although things had improved for parents of people with learning difficulties since the 1960s and 1970s, Norma still saw young mums and dads fighting the same battles she had fought more than a quarter of a century earlier. 'It is slightly easier to get respite care, but they still ask – if not quite so bluntly – 'why do you want respite care?' That attitude is from people who have never looked after an autistic child seven days a week, every week of the year. It is not easy. It can be very rewarding, but it is certainly not easy.

'I think it's awful that after 30 years they are still meeting the same problems. From what I have heard from younger mums, the implication is still there that there is nothing they can do for their child, so why bother.'

STEFANO

Following an unsuccessful couple of years at a residential home near Hastings, Stefano was found a place at a home south of London.

He gradually settled in. The drugs he was taking had been drastically reduced, but, now in his early 30s, his parents wondered whether he would ever return to the happy and sensitive young man they knew before he moved to Stoke Place, the young man who enjoyed going for walks and listening to classical music.

'I feel as though sometimes he doesn't trust anyone, that he's giving up,' said Lidia. 'He is quite depressed and I never know how he will be the next time we see him. He has such a terrible disability to cope with and what happened to him – how can he get over it?' The agency looking after him decided he would not benefit from counselling, but recommended music and art therapy.

Stefano's incontinence had improved, but the Tunstells had been told by the home's owner, a psychologist, that he had almost certainly been sexually abused. 'I know he suffered a lot,' said Lidia. 'It's difficult to know exactly what happened to him there, but there were bits and pieces that happened when he returned home that probably came from his past. He had this habit of pulling us from armchairs when we were sitting down – we just don't know what happened to him there to make him do this. He would also make these strange noises. These were things he never did before Stoke Place.

'He is better now, but I don't think he will ever recover. He was a very happy boy before he went to Stoke Place. Now he hardly ever smiles and he will push us away. He prefers to be on his own now. This is his way of expressing his frustration and the anger he feels that we allowed this to happen, as if it is our own fault.'

A psychologist's report from the autumn of 1998 detailed how the Longcare regime had affected Stefano. It described how he would mimic what must have been Gordon Rowe's voice when he became distressed. 'Get here, Stefano. You're a bastard, Stefano,' he would say. 'Stand in the corner, you bastard.' He would pull and push staff when anxious. He would smear his faeces when he became distressed. Noise, crowded rooms, strangers and the invasion of his personal space would all cause him stress. He would become distressed if someone was behind him when he was naked.

But there were some positive signs. The periods of hyperactivity, in which he would pace around the house and not allow anyone to come near him, had at first occurred nearly every month, but were now less frequent. 'In the early days it could take three to four days before Stefano calmed down,' the report stated. 'This has now reduced to 24 hours and recently if staff can get him to take the medication, he begins to relax in four to five hours. We are working on the assumption that he has flashbacks of his time at Stoke Place and we have also discussed the possibility that he has nightmares which set him off.'

Lidia had been unable to trust anyone after what happened at Longcare. 'We put our extremely vulnerable child in a home, not because we wanted to get rid of him but because we thought maybe they could help him and he would mix with other people,' she said. 'But they abused him in every sense. I don't trust anyone after that place, wherever he goes. I can never relax. When he's not here, I always worry about him. Before he went there, the possibility of abuse never crossed my mind.'

Lidia said she wished Rowe was still alive so he could be punished for his crimes. But he was not the main focus of her anger. 'Gordon Rowe took the money and he treated these people like animals – worse than animals. But to be honest I feel more angry with Buckinghamshire social services. They knew about his record, they knew he had done something wrong.'

Now she only wanted to know what had happened to Stefano at Stoke Place. Amazingly, she had no idea Desmond Tully had been tried in court for allegedly punching her son, until I told her nearly a year after he was cleared of the charge.

'I really want to know what happened,' she told me. 'I don't think I can really be at peace until I know who was responsible for what happened to him.'

Lidia believed that what happened at Longcare proved the need for more frequent and thorough inspections of care homes, paying more attention to how the residents felt about the care they were receiving. But she said the main problem was the attitude of the public towards people with learning difficulties. 'They are second-class citizens. I try not to tell people I have an autistic child. Often when I say he is autistic there is a big, big silence. If I say he is in a home they say that it is their taxes that are paying for children like ours. They say, 'You're lucky not to have to look after him at home.' That's all I get, so usually I don't say anything. We had people say to us: 'Well, being so handicapped, he would never have understood what was happening to him.' But he's a human being and he's very sensitive.

'Logically, I know I didn't have any choice in doing what I did, but as a mother I always have this feeling of failure. I feel that perhaps when I saw the first signs I should have just picked him up and taken him home, but you know that if he loses sponsorship from the local authority it is very difficult to get it back. You have to follow the system. I felt I couldn't possibly manage to look after him all day. That's the situation, but it doesn't make me feel any better.'

Lidia had been taking anti-depressants to help her cope with the feelings of guilt and failure. The horrific abuse Stefano was subjected to wrecked her life, just as it wrecked his. 'I hide myself in my job, but when I am on my own, especially at the weekend, everything comes back to me. I don't like to go anywhere. It's only my job that makes me go out,' she said. She was as isolated as she had been in the late 1960s.

She and her husband worried about what would happen to Stefano when they were dead. 'We are getting older and I have been very ill. We will not be here forever. Who is going to keep an eye on him? Nobody. I can't trust anybody. What if something happened again? It could happen.'

SIMON

It was 1998 and Simon Scott was living 'semi-independently' in a flat in Essex with a friend who has autism, another former Longcare resident. His friend's only communication about his time at the home had been to draw a picture of Stoke Place, with bombs falling on it from the sky.

Simon was well settled into his 'lovely' home in Essex and was gradually returning to the young man his parents used to know. But his mother told me she would never again be able to trust anyone who looks after him.

'We don't trust anybody,' she said. 'Every time they phone up and say he's not very well and can't come to the phone, we question it. Every time he comes home with a bruise, we question it. It's the only way, because if there is one thing we have learned from this, it is that you can't trust anybody.'

It isn't just Simon who has to recover from Longcare. 'We are still trying to get over what happened, because we feel guilty,' Avril told me. 'It was our decision to send him there. Why didn't we see the signs? It is our fault that he went through what he did.'

When I spoke to them again three years later, the Scotts were still finding it difficult to trust anyone who cared for their son, despite the excellent care he now received. 'We still worry about it. It doesn't get any easier,' said Avril.

Life hadn't been easy for Simon in those three years, even if his memories of Longcare appeared to be fading. In August 1998, he had a severe seizure. One of the care workers called an ambulance. While they were waiting, his heart stopped. The care worker managed to resuscitate him, but he spent the next 12 days in intensive care. His kidneys also failed and Simon spent four weeks receiving dialysis. Fortunately, he made a full recovery. 'We nearly lost him,' said Avril.

'It took him a long time to get over it,' said Brian. 'We virtually had to teach him to walk again.'

When he returned to Essex, he was moved to a flat on the ground floor. 'On the floor he is on at the moment, there are wheelchair people who are physically but not mentally impaired and they have not got any patience with him,' said Brian. 'They are going to move him to an upstairs room now that he has settled down, where he will be with people he can communicate with. There is one friend he has with Down's syndrome. They get on really well and Simon is always popping up to see him or he's coming down to see Simon.'

Simon was able to dress, toilet and feed himself, and operate the video, television and music centre his parents had bought him. He seemed happy in his new home. 'He loves it,' said Avril. 'It's his home.' He still called his parents every evening, and was still coming home every weekend to see his parents. And whenever Who Wants To Be A Millionaire? began on television, Simon would ring up his dad to tell him to switch it on. 'He tells me to phone up the number to get on it so I can win lots of money for him,' said Brian.

Brian no longer believed that Simon escaped punishment at Longcare. But he thought his son managed to keep in favour with Rowe, and probably escaped the worst of the abuse. 'I think he knew that if he did what he was told, he kept out of trouble. He was a little bit apprehensive of the Rowes, so he would toe the line.'

At first, Simon would occasionally mention Stoke Place and Gordon Rowe. But in the last couple of years he had stopped talking about Longcare. 'He never mentions it at all,' said Brian. 'A couple of times we have given him an opening when he could, but he hasn't.'

The Scotts were keen to fight for compensation for Simon. 'We will be able to give him holidays,' said Brian, 'but really it's not so much the money as trying to get justice.' He still believed the Rowes escaped justice. 'Rowe was an evil man,' he said. 'I would like him to be alive to take his medicine.'

NICKY

In the spring of 1998, I was sitting again in the Powers' home in Tonbridge. We were talking about the slow improvements Nicky had made since we last met. They were still worried about the heavy doses of anti-epilepsy drugs she had to take – her doctor was apprehensive about weaning her off them after so long. Nicky was gradually losing weight, she changed her clothes less regularly, but still could not stand people coming upstairs or downstairs behind her.

Her parents did not know how long she would continue to receive counselling from Respond, but it appeared to be

419

working, slowly. She even seemed to be getting her sense of humour back.

Despite her progress, Nicky had almost had a 'breakdown' the previous year. She wrecked one of the rooms at Respond during a counselling session. One moment she was totally withdrawn and uncommunicative, the next frenziedly ripping at her dress, scratching, pinching and punching herself and those around her. Alison, the counsellor, wouldn't tell them the content of the sessions. They were confidential, between her and Nicky, she said. For a few months, the counselling had to stop, but it had now started again.

By early December 1999, more than five years after the Longcare scandal first hit the headlines, Nicky still showed no signs of forgetting. She still had nightmares. She would throw her pine bedroom furniture across the room, shouting and smashing the drawers and turning on the taps to try to flood the room. She would pull out clumps of her hair and claw herself. These rages would often occur on Saturday afternoons, after she had had a counselling session in the morning. And while she was raging, she would repeat the words: 'Gordon not nice, don't do it.' Eventually, her parents and staff at the home decided the counselling must stop.

The Powers realised Nicky would never forget what happened to her at Longcare, and they would never know even half of what she had gone through. Now Susan just wanted to know what had happened to her daughter. 'Then if anything happens later on – if she 'turns' again – we could look back and say: 'That's why.''

For a while, Nicky even lost her love of animals. A visit to an animal sanctuary with other residents brought back disturbing memories and, in her mother's words, 'all hell let loose'. But on a recent walk in the forest with her parents, Nicky was able to stroke one of the horses. She could now also visit the pub, enjoy hydrotherapy sessions at the swimming pool and occasionally take part in the dinner parties the residents helped their care workers organise every three weeks. Sometimes the staff took her out for a meal – she liked Indian and Chinese food – and her table manners were improving. And she still loved her Abba tapes.

Nicky's latest care plan showed some improvement. She would go on outings, but still had a problem with people touching her hair. Her periods of being 'distressed' varied from once to six or seven times a day, but occasionally she got through a day without any outbursts. After an episode she would be 'very nice' to staff and apologise. She had also hit out at other residents. She would only wet herself once or twice a week, rather than 'all day, every day', but still had severe depression.

Susan didn't believe Nicky would ever come to terms with what happened to her. 'I think she blames us deep down because I expect she feels that when she said, 'Gordon not nice,' she was trying to tell us in her own way, and we didn't know and we kept taking her back. I just thought she would have a better quality of life there because Gordon would say they were doing this and that and they were having discos and going to the pub.'

Susan said she felt as if she had a brick wall around her, or a large cloud loaded with guilt following her. She found it impossible to trust people. 'I try to trust them at her new home because they were all so horrified at what happened to her and because of the way they have worked with her.'

Her parents were hoping to bring her home for Christmas Day for the first time for five years, although it would depend on how she was feeling on the day. Visits still only lasted about 40 minutes, before Nicky would say: 'Where's Helen* (one of the care workers)? Go see Helen now.' She was happy to see her parents go and waved goodbye from the window.

Susan said that what happened at Stoke Place showed how society treated people with learning difficulties as second-class citizens. 'Quite a lot of people still think they should be put away and not seen. You can see a lot of disgust on people's faces. They tend to pull their children away.'

DAVID

Late in 2000, a consultant psychiatrist, Dr Peter Carpenter, prepared a report on David Jackson as expert evidence for the court case against Bucks County Council. The report described the physical assaults David had suffered at Longcare, particularly at the hands of Gordon Rowe, and how he was punished for his incontinence, deprived of food and hosed down with cold water.

As a result of the abuse, David began to smear and eat his own faeces. 'This,' Dr Carpenter said, 'was a predictable consequence of having little toilet paper supplied and yet being punished for being incontinent – my experience is that the smearing and eating usually occurs as a result of attempting to clear up or cover up the mess, or as a result of new low self-esteem and emotional distress.' In David's case, it re-infected him with the gut parasites he had been suffering from since at least 1990, and made his incontinence even worse.

When he left Stoke Place and moved to the small home where he still lives today, he was at first 'afraid to go anywhere without being told'. He would reject help from staff when he messed himself, which would happen three or four times a week. He appeared frightened that he would be told off and would try to clean himself with washing-up cloths.

The incontinence gradually improved, although it could still be triggered by the anxiety of new situations or new staff.

Dr Carpenter said David appeared to be happy, and that he liked to be busy and enjoyed attending a local day centre, listening to music and collecting photos, which he would spend hours looking through in his bedroom. But occasionally, often at weekends, he would 'clam up' and refuse to move from his chair, except to eat or use the toilet. And he would still experience occasional incontinence, usually triggered by anxiety, pressure or stress.

Dr Carpenter concluded that David's 'days of gloom... may be due to his recall of events if he does not keep himself occupied'.

'The most obvious evidence of the lasting effect of Stoke Place on David is the catastrophic reaction he has to soiling himself, which most often occurs under stress. This soiling is likely to now be a learnt reaction to stress. He then regresses into his past experience when he was so frightened as to try and lick up the evidence of his faecal mess.' There was, he said, 'good evidence that he has still a lot of emotional turmoil about the past and he does not appear to be able to face thinking about the past, living very much in the present.'

ROSIE

When I next spoke to Benedict Alcindor, in the early summer of 2001, I had hoped that the pain over her niece's treatment at Longcare would have faded. But, if anything, it had grown more intense.

As if the family had not had enough to cope with, one of Benedict's nieces had recently been beaten to death in London. Benedict's brother returned from St Lucia to bury his daughter and died suddenly the next day. The family held a double funeral. Benedict had had her own health problems, undergoing an operation on her spine.

Guilt about Rosie was still gnawing at her insides. 'Each time I look at her picture, it is a pain in my heart that is damaging me, eating me up,' she said.

As she talked to me on the telephone, Benedict cried softly. 'It has damaged my life. I can't smile, because I blame my own self. Each time she said she was not going back and she was bringing her dolls and showing her feeling and saying it was hurting, and I didn't take any notice. I thought that she saw my children and wanted to stay home. I didn't want to listen to her, thinking she was playing up... It is doing my head, it is doing my brain, my heart, the burning, the pain, it doesn't go away. I need to move on, but it doesn't feel like I am moving on. All the pain is there, the pressure, the hurt, it is like a lump, something that needs to come out.'

TRACY

In 2000, another consultant psychiatrist, Dr Leila Cooke, had been commissioned to write a report on the impact of the abuse Tracy had suffered at Longcare.

Tracy's mental state, she wrote, had remained 'unstable', and she was still experiencing mood swings, bouts of depression and anxiety. She would frequently run away from her new home, and would often be verbally and physically aggressive towards the staff.

Tracy had told Dr Cooke that she had not liked Stoke Place because of the manager, Gordon Rowe. She told her he was a 'cruel man', who had punched and hit her. She had cried a lot at Stoke Place, she said.

Dr Cooke wrote that Tracy had been 'psychologically vulnerable' even before she moved to Stoke Place, due to a period of depression in 1987. But her behaviour 'changed considerably' after moving there, where she developed 'uncooperative and aggressive behaviour, which was quite out of character'. Dr Cooke said she had had a 'recurrent depressive illness over the last seven years, with associated anxiety, and has also displayed symptoms of post-traumatic stress disorder'. She was likely to continue to experience depression in the future, and would need psychiatric supervision 'indefinitely', as well as psychotherapy. 'She remains anxious, insecure and timid and finds it difficult to trust people.' These, said Dr Cooke, were all a result of the abuse she suffered at Longcare.

JANET

Janet's experiences at Stoke Place persuaded Pauline to set up her own home for adults with learning difficulties. She bought an old farmhouse in Essex and converted it into a small residential home for people with 'challenging behaviour'. She spent thousands of pounds training her staff, and paid them good wages. The residents' care plans were reviewed almost every week to take account of their progress. The reports from social services were exemplary.

'Janet was in six homes in five months after she left Stoke Place,' Pauline told me. 'They were terrible and they smelt. One of them was closed down because it wasn't even registered. I thought that, eventually, once I moved off-site, if Janet was still unhappy, then I would move her here. If she was ever abused or ill-treated I knew that she would have a safe place to come to. All the residents I have here are happy and I have people who have very, very challenging behaviour. They have made such vast improvements. One social worker told us it is the best home in Essex.'

When she heard that some people in the care industry had told me that residential homes were better now, she replied: 'That is crap. There will always be homes and people that are bad, and I think people need to be aware of the potential for abuse, which is why I care so passionately that we must be vigilant. Your loved ones rely on you and if you are aware of the symptoms and the possibilities and the consequences of abuse, then if unfortunately it does happen to a relative, you will know the signs to look for and where to go.

'I think every one of those members of staff that worked there, if they had tried hard enough, could have got that investigated. I say to my staff here: 'If you see something you are unhappy with, bring it to my attention. If I do not deal with it, go to the inspection unit.''

As for Gordon Rowe, she can still be driving down a street and see a man with white hair and think: 'That's him.' But she doesn't hold him as responsible as Bucks County Council. 'They were the safety net and they weren't there.' She was particularly angry that residents' families weren't informed about the incident in 1991 in which Gordon Rowe assaulted Dorothy Abbott.

'I don't think I will ever really get over what happened to Janet. She was like my daughter. I promised mum when she got her into Stoke Place that I would never forget Janet. I felt after Janet died that I had let them both down.

'For eight years I had sole responsibility for Janet. I did everything for her. The fact that she is dead now just makes it so much worse. The last three or four years of her life were such hell and I have got no way of making it better. I can't make Janet feel happy again, because she's not here.'

DOROTHY

Many of the Longcare residents were not able to talk about their experiences at Stoke Place and Stoke Green, although some have been able to give their relatives an idea of what it was like to live there: a half-remembered phrase here, a fragment of an episode there.

But one of the former Longcare residents who was able to give detailed and damning descriptions of life under Gordon Rowe was Dorothy Thomson (formely Abbott).

I first spoke to Dorothy a few days before New Year's Eve 1999, at her home in Hampshire, a flat in a 'sheltered development' she shared with her husband Jamie. Jamie was in his early 40s. He had experienced brain damage as a five-year-old, after contracting meningitis, and also had epilepsy.

The shelves of Dorothy and Jamie's living room were covered with porcelain dolls. Dorothy had more than 50 in her collection. There were dolls dressed as nuns, others in Edwardian costumes. 'To me, everything in here is sort of alive,' she said. 'It's not sort of cold and dead.' The dolls and the soft toys in her bedroom were perhaps reminders of a childhood she was never allowed to enjoy.

Dorothy told me that the abusive regime run by Gordon Rowe had driven her deep into depression. 'I was very suicidal for about two or three years. I used to try and make suicide. When I went to bed, I used to put needles down my arms just so that I could drip blood just like a doctor. I used to hoard tablets up and take them and make myself pretty ill, because the treatment there, you couldn't visualise it being inflicted on a human. I used to say to look at my life just pick up a horror movie, the worst one, and put it in, and you could see my life in reflection.

'I feel sorry for the rest of the residents that are living,' she said, 'because they can't talk about it and the scars are right there. What was annoying is that Gordon Rowe thought that they wouldn't hurt or anything, but they used to come to me and say how much they were hurting. A lot of them would tell me that they were fed up with life and I used to coax them to get on with it and not take any notice. It was my sense of humour that brought them through it in the end.'

One of the things she valued most in her new life was her independence. At Longcare, Gordon Rowe decided at what time the residents should eat and how they would spend every minute of their day. If they didn't conform, they were punished. 'If you wasn't down on time for breakfast, you was hungry for the rest of the day, so time is a big asset.'

Dorothy's years in Stoke Place had also had a lasting impact on how she reacted to seemingly normal situations. 'It takes a hell of a lot for me to trust anybody now,' she said. 'I won't even trust the wardens. I can't go to a doctor's if I was ill.' It had also damaged her ability to react to stress and pain. 'I broke my arm once. I fell on the floor in Stoke Place. I just laughed, because that's the only way that I can beat pain. If you cried (at Stoke Place) you got punished. If you didn't stop crying, you got punished.

'I cannot go into a room now that is crowded or has a party.' Residents were forced to attend parties and put smiles on their faces and 'enjoy' themselves. 'If you didn't go, you had very bad punishments inflicted on you. And if you didn't smile, you had to smile. That's why I'm always laughing now, even when I've hurt myself. To me, life is a joke, and I see it that way. That's the life I was brought up into, the life of a joke.'

I ask her what she hated most about Stoke Place. 'You couldn't have a meal in peace, you couldn't sleep in peace, you couldn't go to your room to have a quiet sit down, because Gordon Rowe had them all rigged up with intercoms and he wanted to know who was in your room and what you were saying.'

Rowe knew the important things in his residents' lives. In Dorothy's case, he knew how much she loved Jimmy. So he split them up and sent Dorothy back from the gatehouse to live at Stoke Place for six months. Dorothy believes this was because she had tried to help other residents. 'Gordon Rowe took me back to Stoke Place and left Jimmy in the group home and I just banged my head on the toilet on the shower room. I just wanted to crush my own brains in. I couldn't stand the hurt anymore. Yeah, I wanted to crush my own skull in. He was a very devious, cruel man.'

She still thinks about Gordon Rowe, and about Angela, and of the 'innocent blood' that is on their hands. 'All Angela Rowe got was two-and-a-half years. But how many years did she give the disabled, how many years of agony, corruption, cruelty, agonising torture?'

But Dorothy says she is most angry with the legal system that allowed Rowe, Desmond Tully and Lorraine Field to get away with such light sentences. 'I'm not angry with Stoke Place, I'm angry with people, I'm angry with the government, I'm angry with the courts.'

Dorothy survived Botleys Park and Stoke Place by clinging onto a 'dream' that one day she would have a flat of her own and would be able to 'settle down'. Her experiences had also given her what she called 'that bitter tinge of life', but also the strength and obstinacy so that 'if anybody says anything or does anything then I will not hesitate to hit back'.

But her horrific experiences of life in the long-stay wards of Botleys Park and under the brutal regime of Gordon Rowe had also made her a more caring person. 'If I go out now and see somebody beating someone up, I wouldn't hesitate to intervene.' Only that morning, she had been helping a new neighbour settle into her flat, Dorothy's social worker told me. She also donated money to the Blue Cross animal charity and performed voluntary work for the disability charity Scope. 'If it was up to me, I would actually work in a mental home,' she said. She had offered to have former Longcare residents to stay in her flat on holiday.

Christianity was one of the factors that helped Dorothy through her ordeal. 'I've got a very big faith, so strong. I think that's what gives me the energy. I mean, even though – you might not understand this bit – they did cruel things to me, Gordon Rowe and Angela Rowe and Nigel Rowe and that, but then if they came to this front door and they said, 'Oh, hello Dorothy, how are you?' I would say, 'Do you want to come in for a cup of tea, Angela Rowe?' I would, yes, because isn't that what Christianity is about – forgiveness?'

But even now Dorothy had married and settled down, she still had to confront every day the reality of what it was like to have a learning difficulty. 'Even now I worry about Jamie. If he goes out for long periods, what'll happen to him? Because I know best of all what the world is like towards disabled people. Even [if] we both go out now we both get insulted, but I taught Jamie not to say anything, so he doesn't. But that doesn't leave the fear inside of you when he goes out.'

Dorothy always vowed that if she married, it would be to a disabled man who needed help and 'guidance for living out in the community'. 'Nothing else matters to me, only Jamie. He's the only one that's really respected me and I have given him my love, too. The fear is there that if anything happened to Jamie, what am I going to do?'

Her experiences had convinced her that society must change how it treats disabled people. 'I think it's about time people started coming out of the Middle Ages and respecting the disabled people, not going round making fun of them, not laughing at them, but showing them a little bit of compassion, because who knows what that disabled person goes through? Who knows they are not going to have a child that will end up the same?'

Chapter Thirty

'She Remembers Everything'

[2003]

'Serious concerns have been raised again about the way the police deal with disability hate crime, after members of a family were sentenced for the brutal murder of a disabled man they had beaten and tortured for years. Michael Gilbert was held captive by the Watt family in Luton for about 10 years and was regularly beaten, stabbed, tormented, treated 'like a slave' and had his benefits money stolen. Four members of the Watt family, and two of their girlfriends, were sentenced to a total of 93 years in prison for offences connected with Gilbert's death in January 2009...'

Disability News Service, 29 April 2010

STEFANO

In the spring of 2003, Stefano Tunstell was still struggling with mood swings, anger, depression and anxiety. His psychiatrist believed they were caused by flashbacks to his time at Longcare. His parents hoped that music therapy would help, but they were concerned about the drugs he had been given to help his mood swings.

A female behavioural therapist had been working with Stefano, and seemed to understand him. 'She says he must be kept very, very busy and must be taken off the drugs he was on,' said Lidia.

Although, he had a good programme of activities and a good key-worker, they wanted to find him a new home. 'It is very, very difficult to find the right place for him,' said Lidia. 'We are really broken-hearted. We have been looking for many places, but we have not been impressed so far.'

They were worried about the future, about what would happen to their son when they were not around anymore. 'We will try to find a better home for him, but there is always change,' said Lidia. 'Suppose the director decides to sell up? What guarantee do we have that they will sell to someone who is really good and caring? When we are old and we can't do anything for him, or when we die... There is not anyone who will look after him. His future is very, very, very bleak.'

The previous year, one of the managers of the home had been suspended after complaints by two care workers of possible physical abuse. Stefano came home one weekend with bruises on his wrists. The manager subsequently resigned after a multi-agency investigation – which included the police – proved inconclusive. Lidia worried that the woman would simply move to a new job at another care home. She and Leslie appeared bewildered and shell-shocked: it had happened again.

SIMON

By the spring of 2003, Simon Scott was happy and settled, with his DVD player, video recorder and wide-screen TV, his collection of James Bond movies, and, most importantly, his own phone. It's his 'lifeline', said Brian, his dad. 'At Stoke, you phoned them up and they would say, 'oh, no, he's in bed'. In the end, he didn't come to the phone at all. But at his new place, if anyone shouts at him, he phones us up and tells us to 'sort 'em out'.'

Simon came home every weekend to see his mum and dad. He had IT and yoga classes at college, and attended a day centre three days a week. A physiotherapist visited him on Friday afternoons to help with his mobility.

The memory of Longcare seemed to have faded for Simon, but not for his parents, who often attended Justice for Longcare Survivors meetings. 'It's a hard slog,' said Brian. 'Every meeting, something comes out.' Avril agreed. 'It's very, very depressing, but now we have got to this stage, there is no way we can turn back. We just hope it will never happen again, but we know darn well that it will.'

Despite all that Simon and his parents had gone through, he did not have his own social worker. Havering Borough Council decided he didn't need one because, a spokesman told me, there was no record of him being ill-treated at Longcare.

NICKY

By the spring of 2003, Nicky Power's parents, Susan and Davyd, had joined the friends committee of their daughter's new home. Gordon Rowe never allowed parents to set up such a group at Longcare.

Susan would often turn up at Nicky's home unannounced. 'I don't phone up anymore, I just arrive.' This was good advice for other parents, she said. 'If you're in a 10 or 20-mile radius of the home, just go and do spot-checks yourself.'

Nicky was now visiting a day centre, learning social skills such as shopping, and visiting the pub. She had hydrotherapy twice a week and had just started aromatherapy, but would only let the therapist touch her hands. For a long time, her dad was the only man she would allow near her.

Her doctor tried to take her off the tranquillisers she was prescribed to cope with her nightmares, rages and tantrums, but she just went 'back to square one', said her mum. She began to self-harm again and repeat the phrase 'not nice'. They had managed to wean her off the massive doses of the anti-epilepsy drug she was on at Longcare, and she hadn't had a seizure since she came off the drug, so her GP believed that she may never have had epilepsy. They believed Rowe used the drug to control her. Some of her speech was finally starting to return, and she was about to begin visits to a speech therapist.

But despite the progress, Nicky was still finding it tough to trust her parents. 'She still will not let anyone walk downstairs behind her,' Susan added. 'I say 'are you happy?' and she says, 'yes, happy'... but she's looking over her shoulder.'

GARY

Gary Deacon had had 'a few bad turns', but his father, Ron, said he hoped they were behind him.

He and Doreen said they were constantly on the look-out for signs of abuse. 'You're investigating all the time in your mind,' said Doreen.

Ron said he was anxious for the civil case to be over, and worried about who would look after Gary once he and his wife were dead.

He said he believed his son still remembered Longcare. 'Gary always has that suspicious look in his eye,' he said. 'When somebody new comes in, he is wondering what they are going to do.'

Gary had not had a social worker for two years. Windsor and Maidenhead council wrote to Ron and Doreen in April

2002, saying he didn't need one because he 'now seems happy and settled in his home'.

If anyone needed a social worker, one would think, it was Gary. If any family needed one, it was the Deacons.

ROSIE

I visited Rosie Valton's aunt, Benedict Alcindor, a few days before Mother's Day 2003.

It had been the day before Mother's Day, eight years previously, on which Rosie had confided in her aunt how Rowe had raped her. 'Each Mother's Day, it just brings grief,' said Benedict. Rosie had been due to visit the previous weekend, but changed her mind and said she didn't want to come, so she would now be with Benedict and her family on the Sunday. 'I hope this Mother's Day it will not be mentioned,' said Benedict.

She wanted the court case to be over. 'Each time I go to a meeting or get a letter, it hurts. It has taken so long, but it is important.'

Rosie still had her 'up days and down days', Benedict told me. 'She can be cheerful when I see her, but sometimes she can be sitting there and all she will want is a hug for comfort.' Benedict said she believed that Rosie remembered what happened to her at Longcare. 'She doesn't forget her mum and she died in 1981. She remembers everything.'

GREG

Greg Adams was 'very happy' in his residential home. 'As far as anyone can tell, he is in a lifetime placement,' said Norma, his mother. 'I hope to goodness he is. He is certainly well-fed, well-housed and happy. I do not expect more than that, although I hope for more. If Greg is happy, he is successful, too, like all my other children.'

She still talked about the Longcare case. It seemed almost a compulsion. 'The more people who know, the less likely it is to happen again,' she said. Her anger with the authorities for not following up her complaints properly in the early 1980s had not abated. 'It took another 10 years before anything was done about it,' she said. 'That evil man was allowed a further 10 years to go on abusing vulnerable people.'

But she had never been able to shake the guilt she felt for not pursuing her concerns about Gordon Rowe more thoroughly.

In a letter she wrote in 2003, she told me how, throughout Greg's life, she had battled with one authority after another. 'There is no doubt in my mind that the need to go on challenging 'authority' will remain, and I am now trying to teach my eldest son (Greg's brother) and a granddaughter (Greg's niece) what I have learned over 38 years... All I am doing is making as sure as I can that Greg will have strong advocacy all of his life.'

TRACY

Nearly a decade after Gordon Rowe had left Longcare, Tracy described in a statement the impact that his regime had had on her.

'Although I like where I am now,' she said, 'I keep thinking about the awful experiences I had at Stoke Place. I keep wondering whether someone is going to hurt me again.'

She didn't trust men anymore, she said, and still became upset when talking about Gordon Rowe. 'No-one knows what that man did to me. People don't understand what I am going through but I still find it difficult to talk about how I am feeling,' she said. She had begun picking at the skin on the palms of her hands, and was on several different drugs to help her cope. For a while, she was receiving counselling.

Tracy remembered going to Butlins in Bognor Regis for a holiday in 1998. The holiday brought back memories of a Longcare holiday in 1987. On her return from Bognor Regis – traumatised by her memories of the abuse she suffered at Longcare – she climbed off the train and began walking down the railway track.

'I still feel angry about everything, being treated badly at Longcare and about specific people being cruel to me,' she said, 'and I would like them to answer for that.'

RACHEL

In the years since leaving Stoke Place, Rachel had needed considerable emotional support. She had low self-esteem and was diagnosed with depression and post-traumatic stress disorder. She had told her social worker in 1998 that she felt 'dirty' and 'disgusting'. As with many other residents, she had nightmares about her time at Stoke Place and had developed an eating disorder, comfort eating to such an extent that her weight increased to 17 stone.

She, too, would make a statement about her treatment at Longcare. 'It has really affected me,' she said. 'I didn't like it. He did it against my will. I was too frightened to say no.' After Rowe had left Longcare, Rachel said that living there reminded her of what he had done to her. 'I was very tearful, unhappy, I was tired all the time, I was suffering from poor sleep and I often had abdominal pain.' Now when she thinks of Rowe, she said, 'I often feel dirty and disgusting.' She described herself as depressed and lonely. 'I am often very tearful and unhappy and I still have anger difficulties. I wouldn't like anyone else to find me as attractive as Gordon Rowe hurt me and this is another reason why I tend to eat so much.'

Now, she said, she was living on her own in a flat with support staff visiting her three times a week. She spoke of her loneliness and her need for female company. 'I can't let myself be close to a man,' she said.

Rachel also talked about the guilt she felt at not being able to help some of the 'less able residents' who she saw being treated badly. She said she was 'up and down in mood' and became depressed when on her own, particularly at night. 'I often cry at night and have difficulty sleeping,' she said, 'and I experience nightmares often about Gordon and Angela.'

DOROTHY

When I called Dorothy again, in 2003, she sounded pleased to hear my voice. She told me she wished the court case was over, and that the public did not care enough about the abuse of disabled people.

Dorothy still thought about the former residents, her friends. If she had to go through her ordeal again, through the years at Botleys Park and Stoke Place, she would. She said it would be worth it, to help her disabled friends escape Gordon Rowe. And she would still invite Rowe in for a cup of tea if he came knocking on her door. But she added: 'I don't think it would be without paying the price of reminding him of what he has done and what he is doing to people.'

Dorothy always said that she survived because she clung onto her dream of an independent life, a husband, a flat of her own. 'It seemed impossible at the time, but I still kept that sort of dream open,' she told me.

She now had that independence, that husband, that flat of her own. 'I have sort of gone into that dream now,' she said. 'I am very happy.'

But the memories were never far away. Stoke Place had 'left a lot of scars'. 'The most thing that comes to mind is the last attack,' she said.

Her experiences at Longcare still affected her behaviour, the way she viewed the outside world, more than 10 years after she escaped. 'I still can't go into a house full of people. I still can't sit in a doctor's surgery,' she said. 'You can't really trust people, you can't trust hospitals, you can't trust crowded rooms.'

She and Jamie had enjoyed a beautiful Christmas. The best ever, Jamie told her. That made her happy.

When I visit Dorothy and Jamie again, there were some new decorations in the flat since my previous visit more than three years earlier, including a cuddly leopard and a monkey named Raja and Buddy, and three pottery angels.

Dorothy said she kept busy, taking Jamie out shopping, visiting his mum, doing the housework, and campaigning. She showed me a newspaper cutting in which she had called on local businesses to do more for disabled people. She told me she deliberately ran over produce in the aisle of the Post Office because they refused to make it more accessible. 'I have had enough of body-abled people shoving disabled people around everywhere, just doing what they think with them.' She said she wanted to see all residential homes closed down. 'I feel as if I have not done enough and they have not listened enough,' she said.

As Jamie sang into his microphone in accompaniment to Jim Reeves' greatest hits, I asked Dorothy whether she still thought about Longcare. 'I think about it quite a lot, but not sad thoughts,' she said. 'I think to myself if I was not a survivor in that place, if I didn't have my dreams of hope then I do not think I would have made it. Suffering like I did had its just reward in the end and its biggest reward was that that dream I held onto came true in the end. I married a man that is disabled. I have a beautiful home. There is nothing else that I want, so compensation would never make a difference to the life that I have got now. This is enough compensation for me. The compensation to be free and live and do what I want and not to be a prisoner now.'

More than a decade after she left Longcare, the only person she was able to trust was Jamie. 'He was the best thing that ever happened to me,' she said.

Although she was happy now, and she had her independent life, her husband, and her beautiful home, the memories were always there, every time she saw a non-disabled man or a crowd of people. The spectres of Gordon Rowe and Longcare, of the life of abuse that she escaped, and the faces of those who weren't so lucky.

Chapter Thirty-One

Survivors

[2004-2010]

'Government spending cuts risk reversing decades of progress towards more independence and control for people with learning difficulties, according to leading members of the self-advocacy movement... Jackie Downer, another prominent activist with learning difficulties, said: 'It is like we are going back to the early 1980s and 1990s and fighting again.' She said people with learning difficulties were having to refight the battles they fought and won for self-advocacy funding. She said: 'It makes you want to chain yourself to one of the politicians. They are taking our lives away, they are taking our resources away.'

Disability News Service, 9 February 2011

GREG

Norma Adams, now in her late 80s and as bright-eyed and sharp-minded as ever, has never stopped campaigning, driven by the guilt she still feels. 'That is going to stay with me for the rest of my life,' she says. 'I could have done more and I didn't.'

She has even taken a short social work course, just to find out what student social workers were being taught.

Her experiences have made her a strong believer in the need for people with learning difficulties in residential care to have advocates, particularly those without relatives looking out for them. And family carers, she says, should be 'kept in the loop and not treated as a damn nuisance'. She says it is 'vital' for service-providers to keep parents and advocates informed about anything that might affect their child or client.

Because Greg lives so far away, she does not see him as often as she would like, and staff often ignore her letters and emails. One of them complained that she was 'curious'. But if there was one thing she has learned over the 30 years since she first met Gordon Rowe, it is that curiosity is a good thing.

The latest CQC report says the home is good and safe, and Greg has been living there for more than 20 years and seems happy and cared for. But she is not about to stop asking questions now.

ANDREW

Andrew's mother tells me that she believes he has blocked out his experiences at Stoke Place. Although he has been having panic attacks since moving from his previous home to Slough – perhaps because it is closer to Stoke Place – he has generally 'not been too bad' and has a job working in a charity shop on Saturday mornings.

She still thinks about Longcare. 'I just kick myself that I didn't know what was going on. But it doesn't do me any good. I just have to think that he's alright now, that he has come through it, because I don't think I could face it again.'

Like many of the other relatives, she finds it hard now to trust her first impressions of people, particularly care workers. When she first met Gordon Rowe, she thought he was 'a nice bloke'. 'I just worry now when I see somebody and think they are nice. Are they really nice or aren't they? It makes you very, very wary. I used to take people at face value, but now I am not sure.'

At Andrew's new home, she says, he is treated like a human being. 'Andrew's really happy there. And I know he would tell me anything now, because I sat down and said, 'If there is anything you are not happy about you have got to tell me,' and I know he would now.'

Andrew received £20,000 compensation from Bucks County Council. But she says the money was never important. What was important was the victory. 'I never even thought about the money. It was just something that shouldn't have happened,' she says. The compensation at least means that her son has treats that he wouldn't otherwise enjoy. 'Anything he wants, I buy it for him,' she says. 'He gets spoilt.'

But she finds it difficult to be pleasant to the Buckinghamshire social workers who occasionally turn up for his annual reviews. They say: 'You know where we are if you need us,' and I say: 'We don't need you. You weren't there for him when he needed you, so why do I need you now?'

LUKE

It took two years after he left Stoke Place before Luke Skiff was able to talk about what had happened to him.

By now living in a hostel in west London, he told a psychologist that a male member of staff had raped him. He gave a detailed and specific account of what had happened, and later told his mother. She remembered how he had started to suffer from rectal bleeding, but had put it down to his long-running skin problems. After Luke left Longcare, he threw away everything that reminded him of Stoke Place, including a photograph.

In the days after describing being raped, he became depressed, 'lethargic and disinterested', and spent a lot of time alone in his room. A few days later, he told his key worker everything, describing how staff had pulled his hair, laughed, swore and shouted at him, and flicked food in his face with a spoon.

Luke rarely talks about Stoke Place, but still refers to it occasionally as 'that horrible house'.

After seven years in the hostel, he wanted more independence. He moved into a shared house and secured a job at McDonald's, where he cleans tables, takes out the rubbish and shows round new recruits, and has now been made a 'manager' in charge of showing new recruits the ropes. He lives in a flat he shares with two other people with learning difficulties. He works three days a week, and knows many people in the area, in the local Tesco supermarket, at the tube station, and at the newsagent where he buys his paper every Sunday to get the football results.

But his progress, which included featuring in a Channel 4 documentary, has not been without its serious setbacks. Early in 2010, Luke claimed he had again been sexually assaulted. The police took his allegation seriously. Their interviews and the repeated questioning initially upset him, but after being reassured that he was not going to prison himself, he said he would be happy to give evidence in court. He and his mother now await a final decision from the CPS.

Luke was at Stoke Place for less than a year, but his mother remembers how he told her the staff were 'horrible' when she was taking him back after Christmas. She thought at the time that it was just because they had caught him stealing a CD. 'I never liked them – and I thought Gordon Rowe was awful from the first time I met him – but I had a great deal of pressure put on me by the social worker. But he never cried or said he didn't want to go back. He liked his friends but he hated the staff.

'Considering all his problems, I would say he is a very well-adjusted, normal adult. He cut Stoke Place out of his life. He doesn't want to talk about it, to be reminded of it.'

Although Luke received £5,000 compensation from the county council, he has yet to need any of the money.

His mother still thinks about Longcare, and still feels angry with herself and with Kensington and Chelsea council. 'I was given all these places to inspect, most of which were entirely unsuitable. The good ones were all full. Most of the private ones were run by people made redundant in the City. They were frightful. Eventually, the social worker said Longcare was wonderful and the people that ran it were simply wonderful. I went down there and met this horrible man [Gordon Rowe] and he was perfectly frightful, and I thought maybe I was just being a snob. Now I feel rather angry at myself that I didn't obey my instincts and that I didn't quite believe Luke when he said the staff were horrible.'

TRACY

More than 10 years ago, Tracy's counsellor described in a letter how she would often arrive for sessions 'too depressed to work' and would sit with her head in her hands in tears, 'unable to express her feelings' and trying to cope with her 'huge feelings of despair and anger'.

The letter, though, suggested that she was improving, and seemed to hold out some hope for Tracy's future. But when I speak to her father, Ken, in the autumn of 2010, he tells me his daughter is still receiving professional help for depression.

'She still hasn't got over it,' he tells me. 'Sometimes she says she is OK and then when she thinks about it that is when she is not very good.' But she won't talk to her parents about what happened to her at Longcare, and she still takes anti-depressants. 'There is no doubt that she will not ever get over it,' Ken says. 'Nor will me and the wife, either, but we try and put it in the back of our minds as long as Tracy is OK.'

He says he is happy with the £30,000 compensation Tracy received. They use it to pay for holidays and clothes for their daughter. But, says Ken: 'We didn't go for the money. We just wanted justice.'

443

LINDA

After leaving Longcare, Linda Dagger was 'terrified', says her sister, Rose. Her weight had dropped from nine-and-a-half stone to just six-and-a-half, and she lost nearly all her teeth because they had not been looked after. She would constantly ask for permission to do simple things like using the toilet or even just sitting down on a chair.

It was only afterwards that Rose could look back and piece together the warning signs. The possessions that went missing, how Linda told her about a female resident who was smacked around the face by Lorraine Field, and how someone had pushed her down the stairs. Rose later discovered that Linda would sit for hours in a quiet corridor at Stoke Place, so she could stay out of trouble. When Rose and her husband took her out on trips, she would eat 'like an animal', eating every last crumb put before her. And she would become 'nervous and anxious' when they told her it was OK for her to put sugar in her tea. Like Michael, she began to walk with a stoop.

If Rose ever asked her too many questions, Linda would clam up and say she didn't know.

'When I used to question things,' says Rose, 'they always had a very good answer.' Like many other relatives, Rose feels guilty now about her failure to realise how bad things were. 'I will never forgive myself, although I never knew.'

In the years after leaving Longcare, Linda would occasionally say something that seemed connected to her ordeal. 'I don't know why they were sitting in the corner,' she would say, or, 'I don't know why they were crying in the corner.'

'I think she went through more than she ever said and she kept it to herself,' says Rose. 'It took her a few years before she went to the toilet or sat down without asking. It took her a long, long time. She had to ask for everything.'

Every time Linda has to move to a new home, Rose is scared about how she will be treated. Now she doesn't trust anybody, so she makes sure she gets to know Linda's care workers, and attends the twice-yearly reviews. 'I have to watch and I am there all the time. That will never go away for me.' And like other relatives, she worries about what will happen if she is no longer around to look after Linda. 'I worry from day to day. It's still there. You can't forget.'

Linda was awarded a few thousand pounds in compensation, but, like one or two of the other former residents, has not yet needed to draw on the money. But it is there if she ever needs it.

Linda has 'come on a hell of a way', says Rose. 'It's been a long, long journey. She always seems happy. She's a very easy person to get to like. She's as lovely a person as you could meet.' Linda now lives with a woman with Down's syndrome in a bungalow in Hackney, attends college every day, visits a day centre, and works on a city farm. Rose can be at Linda's home within 10 minutes. 'She lives a normal life that I never thought she would do. Now she knows about fashion, she knows what she wants to buy, whereas before she was so scared.

'I say: 'Are you OK?' and she doesn't know why I ask these things. I am still frightened. Times are changing, but not quick enough. Linda has an open life but I still have to be there and watch.'

STOKE GREEN HOUSE

Stoke Place survived as a residential home for only five years after the Longcare scandal. It later became a conference centre, and then a hotel.

But the second of Rowe's two homes, Stoke Green House, is still used as a care home today. The building was bought by REACH, the company that took over Stoke Place from Longcare in 1996. REACH now looks after 17 former Longcare residents at a handful of homes scattered across Slough and south Bucks. One of them is Stoke Green, now renamed Sistine Manor.

I ask Nassrin Saeedi, REACH's operations director, whether the former Longcare residents still talk about their old home.

She remembers one of them telling her a year or so after leaving Stoke Place: 'This is my home now. I am not going back to Stoke Place.' But she says such references were rare, and are even less frequent today. 'I think sometimes it must be playing in their mind, but not as much now,' she says.

When REACH took over Stoke Place, Saeedi had to battle with the authorities – and the Slough Observer – to be allowed to keep it open. But she was convinced that the residents who remained needed time to get rid of their emotional 'baggage' before they left their home. There were problems, though, with anxiety, anger and nightmares. Some of them, she says, had 'massive challenging behaviour'. 'A few people were smashing things, throwing things around. I am sure people at the time would have said they should be in a secure unit, but we weren't prepared to give up on them. They gradually calmed down and we haven't seen that behaviour for goodness knows how many years.'

Philippa Russell remembers returning to Stoke Place with Tom Burgner after the inquiry reported in 1998. 'Bucks thought they would immediately want to get out, and they didn't. Part of their recovery was to feel safe in their own home. Once the people had gone, the ghosts had been laid. One or two of them spoke very eloquently about how they now felt safe. This was their home, despite the awful things that had happened in it.'

Gradually, when the time for them to leave grew near, Saeedi and her staff began to point out some of the flaws with Stoke Place. 'When we had the residents' meeting I would say that the carpet doesn't look really good anymore. I was gradually bringing it to their attention that this was not the right place for them to live.'

When moving day arrived in 1999, it was clear that the former Longcare residents were ready to leave. Saeedi arrived at 6.30am to find they had all packed their belongings in plastic bags they had placed in reception. She insists this was the result of the three years' work she and her staff had put in, preparing them for the moment they would leave their home.

'In the long term it has paid off,' she says. 'We have not had any behavioural problems with any of them.' And since the day they left, she has never returned to Stoke Place. 'Since that day, I have not put a foot into that place.'

Gary Deacon is one of the former Longcare residents who lives in a REACH home in Slough. Sadly, both Ron and Doreen had died since I last spoke to them in 2003. Now Gary has no relatives who visit him, although he has an advocate who occasionally takes him to lunch.

There are just four former Longcare residents living at Sistine Manor. All four had previously lived at Stoke Place, rather than Stoke Green. The home's last report from the Commission for Social Care Inspection – following an unannounced inspection – gave it a 'good' two-star rating (out of a maximum of three), and talked about its 'wide range of activities', the 'positive and supportive ethos in the home' and the 'well established safeguarding adults procedures'. Residents 'took their time having the meal', the report said. 'There was time to chat and relax. No-one was rushed.' It mentioned the home's links to a local advocacy organisation.

All of the former Longcare residents took self-advocacy courses after REACH took over. 'I think that was the best thing we ever did,' says Saeedi. 'Making an individual confident enough to talk. Now if any of the staff behave badly they will tell them: 'You are going to be sacked, I am going to tell them.' One of the guys from Longcare wouldn't talk to anybody and would hardly look anybody in the eye. A few years ago, we had a new member of staff and on her second day shift she was sitting in a garden chair and went to sleep. This guy woke her up and said: 'You will be sacked for sleeping on duty. I am going to report you.'

MICHELLE

It took 10 years after the events at Longcare before Michelle Callaway's parents were able to trust anyone to care for their daughter. Because they had visited the home every week, the exposure of the regime had been even more of a shock.

'I think now we can talk about it without getting upset,' says her mother. 'Previously we couldn't have done. It was a chunk out of our lives for a while because it was all we talked about. I think it damaged me emotionally. It has made it very hard for me to let go of her and [let her] lead her own life.'

When they heard the story for the first time on the radio, they thought it must have been something stirred up by a disgruntled employee; but it didn't take long to realise it was far more serious than that.

Michelle had been one of Gordon's favourites, spending time with him in his office in the evenings, and at the cottage. Several members of staff would later tell police how she had indicated that Gordon had raped her.

Her parents had found Rowe a 'dominant character', but had few complaints about the standard of care. They were angry about his refusal to let Michelle attend the local Mencap club, and his decision to cut the number of days every week that Michelle attended the adult training centre in Slough. On one occasion, her mother noticed large bruises on her thighs, but Rowe brushed her concerns aside. Michelle had appeared happy and 'very fond' of Rowe.

But Michelle had become depressed early in 1994, and one weekend in July, two months before the regime was to be exposed in the media, she refused to return to Stoke Place, grabbing the steering wheel as they approached the home. Michelle's parents took their daughter home for a few days, and when they tried again she was 'adamant' that she did not want to return. For several weeks, Michelle would scream in panic if she thought her parents were driving anywhere near Stoke Place. 'After this,' her mother would write later, 'Michelle was in a state of depression for many months and would not leave my side.' Because of Longcare, the family were 'noticed' by social services and Michelle received the support she needed. But they believe it took her at least five years before she fully recovered.

'It was very difficult and quite exhausting,' Michelle's mother says. 'The unhappiness, that was distressing. Not wishing to let me out of her sight made life difficult and restricting.' Because of the sexual abuse she suffered, Michelle still finds it difficult to know how to behave appropriately with a boyfriend.

After she left Stoke Place, Michelle returned to live with her parents, but they eventually decided they had to find her a permanent home. For the last five years, Michelle has been living in her own flat, with 24-hour support, and receives several hours a day of one-to-one care.

I meet Michelle for the first time in October 2010 at her parents' house near Slough. She seems devoted to her parents, particularly her mother. When I ask Michelle to tell me the best thing about living in her own flat, she points to one of her Disney dolls which she has brought down from her bedroom to show me. She likes to cook egg on toast, and helps her mother make us all cups of tea. She seems happy to sit next to me on the sofa for an hour, while I talk to her and her parents, trying to avoid any mention of Gordon Rowe.

Michelle's parents used some of the compensation money from the council to furnish her flat. It meant they were shopping at John Lewis rather than second-hand shops, they said. 'But the money wasn't important,' says her mother. 'We just wanted some sort of justice.'

NICKY

I call Susan and Davyd Power early in October 2010, hoping to hear news of Nicky's steady improvement over the past seven years. Instead, Susan tells me that Nicky has developed a neurological condition. At first, doctors believed she had Parkinson's, but now it is thought she could have dystonia, a movement disorder that can be linked to the heavy use of anti-psychotic medication such as Largactil and Haloperidol. These were the kind of drugs Gordon Rowe and other Longcare staff often used to sedate and control the residents.

At one stage, Nicky's weight fell below six stone, and she now can't talk or walk on her own. Last year, as a doctor tried to work out the correct combination of drugs she needed, she fell into a coma and nearly died.

Susan says her daughter is being looked after well, and has a good social worker who is 'on the ball'. Before her latest health problems, Nicky was still having 'one or two outbursts' but was 'making progress'.

Her mother never mentions Longcare or Gordon Rowe to her daughter. 'She has been through so much,' says Susan. 'I just want her to live from day to day now.'

But Susan still thinks about Stoke Place. 'I shall never ever forget it,' she says. 'It was so horrendous and to see the after-effects, to see what it did to them was so heart-breaking. We didn't know it was going on, so we couldn't stop it. This is the guilty feeling you carry with you and I think you will carry it with you until you die.'

Nicky has at least benefited from her £35,000 compensation. She was bought a state-of-the-art electric bed, which helps with her stiffness first thing in the morning, as well as TVs, music centres, bedroom furniture, and weekly hydrotherapy, which she loves. 'I hope it has made her quality of life that much better than she would have had without it,' says Susan. 'But what I am really keeping it for is if she needs an operation quickly, the money is there to pay for surgery privately rather than having to wait six or eight weeks on the waiting-list.' Susan believes people with learning difficulties are still treated as second-class citizens by the NHS and that she could never be sure that Nicky would receive the surgery she needed if she didn't pay for it herself. 'At least if she is in a private hospital I know I can be with her all day or stay overnight. That's helped a lot.'

I ask her whether her daughter still thinks about Longcare. 'That we don't know, and with the limited speech she had anyway that is something we will never know. She gets very, very depressed, so whether she's thinking of things, I don't know. I just say to her, 'Are you OK?' and she just shakes her head, sometimes for 'no' and sometimes for 'yes'. And I say, 'Are you not happy?' and she shakes it for 'no'.'

STEFANO

When I speak to Lidia Tunstell again in the autumn of 2010, for the first time in more than five years, she tells me she is 'very frightened' about the impact of the government's spending cuts on the support that will be available for Stefano in the future.

She and her husband have already heard of social workers in Surrey being made redundant. 'The county council has got to cut and we are not sure what is going to happen,' she says. Stefano, like every other council-funded care home resident, is set to lose the weekly 'mobility component' of disability living allowance (DLA), which will mean a loss of £49 a week. The DLA allows Stefano and the other four clients to go swimming, horse-riding and bowling, as well as an occasional trip to the pub or McDonald's. And when it stops? 'They will have to do without. I know we need cuts but why do they have to take this out on people with learning disability who can't defend themselves?' says his mother. 'It is absolutely abominable.'

They have used some of the compensation – Stefano received just £15,000 – to pay for a swing for his garden, pictures for his room, and reflexology and massage sessions. Although staff take him horse riding, swimming and bowling, the council decided to stop his music and art therapy when he moved to his new home. 'The council think he doesn't need it,' says Lidia. 'They don't think he's worth it because he is already an adult.'

Things are better for Stefano, though. 'Finally, in the last five years he has got a better home,' she says. But because he can't talk very much, his Longcare experiences are still 'all locked up in Stefano'. 'If someone shouts at him or does something they shouldn't do, immediately it brings it all back and he gets very tense and starts throwing things and shouting. He still wets himself when he is very upset.' But he has at least finally started to put on weight. 'They are feeding him well and they are kind to him, and certainly he is much better, but any little thing gets him all tense. He has good days, bad days, but he suffers when the home occasionally has to replace staff. It is very difficult for him to trust new people.'

Until five years ago, Stefano would often take his anger out on his mother, who is slightly-built herself. 'He used to hit me, kick me and put his hands on my throat occasionally when he was stressed out. He used to hit me so much. Now it doesn't happen so much.'

Lidia still has nightmares about Longcare, still feels the guilt that she didn't protect her son or take him away sooner. 'I have nightmares that someone is trying to take me away or hit me. I just cry a lot to myself, thinking about what happened to him. He was promising as a young man. He is better but he will never recover.'

She still worries about the care Stefano is receiving, even though she knows he is in a better home now. 'If I phone too often, I feel I am disturbing them. They don't phone me as regularly as I would wish. They are nice people but I do not think they realise what we go through, how anxious we are. Even now if he is tense I tend to think something is wrong.'

She worries most about what will happen after she and her husband have died. Stefano has no brothers or sisters, and doesn't even have an advocate. The family's social worker has said there is no need for an annual review. 'If something concerns you, just give me a ring,' she was told. 'We are getting old. What happens to him if nobody keeps an eye on him?'

DOROTHY

When I speak to Dorothy again, she tells me life is still good for her and Jamie. We exchange Christmas cards every year, and we had spoken on the phone several times since my first book was published in 2003, so I knew she had been OK.

She spends her time sewing tapestries for friends, carrying out domestic chores and looking after their two new gerbils, as well as planning a happy Christmas for Jamie. 'Because I have led such a life in the institution and so has Jamie, I tend to think about spoiling Jamie,' she tells me.

She still thinks about Longcare, but tries not to talk about her memories of Stoke Place because they upset her husband. 'I have shoved them in the back of my mind because I do not like getting Jamie upset,' she says. 'There's things that happened in that home that you can't forget but I don't mention it because it makes my Jamie unhappy, so I try to bottle it up as best I can. I try to forget about the life that I led before. I now concentrate on the life that is ahead of me.'

Dorothy still talks about the dream that kept her going at Longcare. 'As soon as you get in an institution, you learn to hate and you have a dream to hold onto and my dream was that one day I would have a flat of my own and I would never marry a body-abled man. That dream has come true, because that is the main thing you have to hang onto to get through these traumas.'

When I suggest that she tried to resist Gordon Rowe and his regime, she agrees. 'I did resist him in a way, yeah. But I was sort of glad I did it because it brought a new life to all the other residents.'

Dorothy received £17,000 in compensation from the county council, but apart from electric beds for her and Jamie and a new chair, most of the money is still being looked after by the Court of Protection. Although there is nothing she needs, she is annoyed that they didn't just put the money straight into her bank account. 'I have got to go through a social worker and she has got to write to the courts and say what I need the money for. I think that is absolute rubbish. Why do I [have to] explain why I need the money?' But she tries not to think about the compensation. 'If I dwell on the money,' she says, 'it just reminds me of what [was] involved to get that money.'

DAVID

It was not until late November 2010 that I finally had the pleasure of meeting David Jackson. David had been so central to the Longcare story – he was mentioned frequently in the inspection unit's confidential report, during the trial, and by so many of the former Longcare staff. The images of him being hosed down with freezing water, tied to a tree and dragged into the woods for a vicious beating by Gordon Rowe had stayed with me all through those 16 years.

I had arranged to visit him one Friday afternoon at his home in south London, with his sister, Janet. Having spoken with Janet on the phone, and talked at length with other members of David's family, I knew he was happy in his new home.

He lives now with six other people with learning difficulties. It is a neat, clean house, with wooden floors and comfortable sofas. When I arrive, just seconds after Janet, we are shown into the living-room, where David is watching television.

Now aged 55, he no longer has the scruffy beard that Gordon Rowe forced him to wear. Instead, he is clean-shaven, smartly-dressed, with short, tidy grey hair and glasses. He smiles a lot. Although he doesn't talk, he uses Makaton signs, and I soon learn that he is missing his housemate and friend Sylvia, who is in hospital. He points upstairs to her room and repeats his personal sign for Sylvia, an expansive and affectionate hug. He had been to visit her in hospital, and took her a picture he had drawn of some flowers. He loves to draw pictures. He is clearly worried about his friend, and again and again he brings the conversation back to her during my visit, at one point describing the bracelet she wears in her hospital bed.

He laughs a lot while we talk. I hear how a male care worker had introduced him to professional wrestling, and how he enjoys other activities such as a Makaton group, a karaoke night, where he plays air guitar, and the Mencap Gateway club, an opportunity for him to meet his other friends, play bingo or bowls, and enjoy a disco. I am told he also enjoys drawing out his weekly allowance from the building society, and visiting charity shops to look for DVDs – he loves Elvis Presley, The Man from U.N.C.L.E. and wrestling. When I am told of his holiday in Weymouth, he shows me the sign for swimming.

I ask David what he likes best, and he points to the DVDs stacked under the television. Janet mentions his birthday barbecue and he signs drinking beer. Laughing again, he holds up five fingers – five beers – and then ten. He seems happy to show me and his niece, who is also visiting, his bedroom, which is decorated with pictures of Elvis, wrestling stars, Spiderman, Superman, and his favourite pop star, Michael Jackson.

Di, the manager, says the progress he has made has not come easy, and there are still reminders of his time at Longcare. 'We know, because of the anxiety Dave experiences, particularly around going to the loo, that that caused a lot of damage to him,' she says. 'We have had to work at building up the levels of trust. We have had to work really hard. He will now come and tell us there has been a problem. Now he will bring his soiled clothes down to the laundry and tell us he has done it.' They have also consulted a continence nurse, who has given them strategies to deal with his diverticulitis.

Di says they aim to give David and the other residents as many opportunities as they can. I ask David if he likes being able to choose things now, and he seems to understand, pointing towards the television. I ask Di to describe how she sees David. 'He is a fun guy with a huge heart and a big sense of humour,' she says. 'He's placid. He likes to tease.'

David was eventually awarded just £16,000 compensation for his terrible ordeal. But at least that money is there if he ever needs anything. Like many other former Longcare residents, he doesn't have a social worker. He hadn't had one at Stoke Place until the regime was exposed.

Janet says David is 'a different person' to the man who left Stoke Place. 'When he first came here, if he was a little late for breakfast, he would be absolutely terrified that he would be told off. He didn't realise that he was allowed to be late.' Now, she says, he has grown in confidence. 'He's happy, he looks great. You wouldn't recognise him as the same person.'

David's brother-in-law, Andy, had told me how David sits in an armchair and cuts out pictures from newspapers and magazines when he comes to visit. He enjoys looking at family photos, and loves animals and babies. Andy remembers how David became withdrawn, pale, gaunt and unkempt at Longcare. He was sure his brother-in-law was being drugged.

Stephen, David's nephew, who is very close to his uncle, remembers how nervous he was after leaving Longcare. 'He would turn his face away from everyone. He was hunched over. He wouldn't even look at people. Now he's got a smile on his face. I take him on the bus and he's looking out of the window, smiling.'

Brenda, one of David's sisters, adds: 'He's a different person altogether. Dave is so happy now you wouldn't think he had been through that horror. I think it is still in his head sometimes. If he sees something on the telly, his face will change. He will go serious, as if he's remembering something.'

Postscript

'Stoke Place is a gorgeous old William and Mary house with Capability Brown gardens, and it couldn't feel more like a treat if it tied itself in a ribbon and put a chocolate on its pillow. Which it probably does (it is also a hotel)...'

Daily Telegraph, August 2008

'On one of the few hot days this year, I lay out in the vast expanse of lawn that makes up Stoke Place's garden and watched, with amusement, as a parade of geese and men in kilts made their way across the front of the hotel... this is one of the most peaceful places I've ever had the luck to stay.'

Marie Claire, 2008

If anything was to underline the message that the Longcare scandal had been relegated to a barely-remembered historical footnote, it was the discovery that Stoke Place had been reinvented as a luxurious boutique hotel.

The new owners appeared unaware of its tragic past, when I contacted them in the late autumn of 2010. Looking at the exquisite images on its website, and the descriptions of 'manicured grounds', 'beautiful views' and 'lazy afternoons on the terrace', it was hard to picture David Jackson being marched across the lawn by Gordon Rowe on the way to a vicious beating in the woods, Jackie being dragged outside by her hair to eat her dinner in the biting winter wind, or the members of Gordon's Girls who were raped by Rowe in Stoke Place's 'lovingly decorated' and 'architecturally elegant rooms'.

Philippa Russell confessed that her heart sank when she saw the website. 'I did wonder what the guests would say if they knew the history,' she told me. She remembered Longcare residents being too scared – they were shaking with fear – to be interviewed in the late 1990s in the first-floor sitting-room where so much of the abuse had taken place.

But this rewriting of history is not restricted to the new – and entirely innocent – owners of Stoke Place and its luxuriating guests. Both Buckinghamshire County Council and Thames Valley Police have shown little inclination to remember the vital lessons of the Longcare scandal. And the new coalition government, and the Care Quality Commission, appear to be drifting away from the tougher regulation and regular and thorough inspections that were introduced in the wake of the scandal, and back towards the laissez-faire attitudes of the 1980s, conditions that had allowed Rowe's regime to thrive. Health secretary Andrew Lansley talks about individuals taking personal responsibility. Who could argue with that? Except when it is at the expense of investment in the kind of firewall that might – just might – prevent another Longcare, or indeed another Bedes View, Fieldhead or Solar Centre.

The spectre of public sector spending cuts hangs over this final chapter. In such a financial climate, how can I justify calling for an expensive national audit of out-of-area placements? But seven years after suggesting such a move in my first book, it is even more urgent today. There must be thousands of people who have been abandoned to their fate in locations far from their home authorities. Many are at risk of serious abuse, but they are not being visited... by anyone. And there is no-one to hear their cries for help.

There is also – still – the need for a study into the prevalence of abuse of people with learning difficulties. My suspicion is that successive governments have shied away from such research for fear of what it would uncover.

Most of the former Longcare residents I have met or heard about have survived what happened to them at the homes. With the help of their families, therapists, counsellors and care workers, they appear to have shaken off the mantle of 'victims', although I am sure they all live with memories and nightmares of Gordon Rowe and Stoke Place, and many still struggle with depression and other psychological by-products of their Longcare years. There are also those, like Nicky Power, whose physical health has probably been affected by the criminal over-medication inflicted on them. Many, though, like Dorothy and David, are now living happy, fulfilling lives.

But other people with learning difficulties are still enduring appalling ordeals. Some have lost their lives. Their names – Brent Martin, Rikki Judkins, Francecca Pilkington, Raymond Atherton, Steven Hoskin, among many others – are a sickening reminder of the hostility and hatred that blight the lives of so many disabled people.

So, nearly 17 years after I started working on the Longcare story, do my investigations suggest that anything can be done? There are no solutions; there is nothing that will suddenly stop people with learning difficulties being abused, or experiencing terrifying hate crimes. But there are lessons to be learned from

Longcare, measures that could – maybe – begin to turn the tide.

Perhaps the most important is around communication. Anything that aids the free flow of information between people with learning difficulties and the wider community, their friends and families, their social workers, the police and health agencies, will make such crime less likely. There is one clear way in which such communication can be supported: advocacy. More money must be invested in advocacy services, and particularly in self-advocacy organisations. Anything that can help people with learning difficulties speak up for themselves will protect them from abuse and crime, and also help them – I hope – become survivors, rather than victims. Sadly, as this book goes to print, increasing numbers of self-advocacy organisations are in dire financial straits as local authorities withdraw their funding.

There is also the need, somehow, to promote respect for people with learning difficulties, and end the social isolation that blights so many lives. The more true friends they can count on, whether those friends are disabled or non-disabled people, the lower the risk of abuse. Attitudes have to change. Yes, there must be awareness-raising campaigns to explain what abuse is and how to spot it. But somehow, whether through government action, educational campaigns, or the use of role models, something must be done to raise the status of people with learning difficulties. This is surely one of the best ways to address the sickening parade of hate crimes against them.

Longcare was a perfect storm. A charming, powerful sadist; an incompetent local authority; a GP prepared to overlook the most obvious signs of abuse; a police force guilty of the worst kind of discrimination; lacklustre legislation; a poorly-trained, uncaring and bullied workforce; an arrogant and ineffective criminal justice system. All came together to create conditions in which abuse of the worst kind could thrive and remain undiscovered.

But police forces are still guilty of discrimination, councils are still incompetent, many care workers are still un-trained and poorly-paid, the criminal justice system is still often arrogant and ineffective, and the scandals just keep coming.

When I was first handed that leaked council report in 1994, I could not possibly have imagined that I would still be working on the story nearly 17 years later. But it was not just the untold stories of the survivors and Longcare's unremitting horror that kept bringing me back. It was also my own uncertainty. How could this have happened? How could Rowe's regime have survived so long? Was this simply due to a unique set of circumstances that would never be repeated? Could it happen again? I still hadn't answered those questions.

Having talked again to contacts I interviewed many years ago, analysed many of the vicious hate crimes that have taken place in the intervening period, and spoken to people with learning difficulties themselves, it is clear that too little has changed.

I may have satisfied myself that many of those abused at Longcare – although not all of them – have survived their horrific ordeal. But I am also now convinced that Gordon Rowe was not the cause of the Longcare scandal.

After focusing for so long on the figure at the centre of the Longcare empire, it is hard to concede that this story is not really about Rowe after all. He merely took ruthless, cruel and vicious advantage of what he saw around him: the discrimination, inequality and hostility that has become ingrained in society over hundreds of years.

The Longcare story, I have finally realised, is about something far less tangible than a sadistic former social worker. It is about a society that deprives people with learning difficulties of their human rights, and about the attitude to difference – the unease, the distrust, the hostility – that allows the kind of abuses that took place at the Longcare homes to continue unchecked.

After 17 years, that is surely the most disturbing conclusion of all.

Useful Contact Details

Ann Craft Trust
Tel: 0115 9515400
www.anncrafttrust.org

Central England People First
www.peoplefirst.org.uk

Disability Hate Crime Network
www.facebook.com/group.php?gid=304401563986

The National Forum of People with Learning Difficulties
www.nationalforum.co.uk

People First (Self Advocacy)
www.peoplefirstltd.com

Public Concern At Work
(free, independent advice on whistleblowing)
Telephone helpline: 020 7404 6609 or
email helpline@pcaw.co.uk
www.pcaw.co.uk

Respond
Telephone helpline: 0808 808 0700
www.respond.org.uk

Voice UK
Telephone helpline: 0808 802 8686
www.voiceuk.org.uk

Bibliography

Abbott, David; Morris, Jenny; and Ward, Linda: Disabled Children and Residential Schools – A Study of Local Authority Policy and Practice; Norah Fry Research Centre, supported by Joseph Rowntree Foundation; 2000

Atkinson, Dorothy; Jackson, Mark; and Walmsley, Jan: Forgotten Lives: Exploring the History of Learning Disability; BILD; 1997

Audit Commission: Community Care: developing services for people with a mental handicap; Occasional Papers, Number 4, The Audit Commission; November 1987

Boyle, Mike and Leadbetter, Mike: Enough is Enough; Elite Recruitment Specialists; 1998

Brigham, Lindsay; Atkinson, Dorothy; Jackson, Mark; Rolph, Sheena; Walmsley, Jan (editors): Crossing Boundaries: Change and Continuity in the History of Learning Disability; BILD Publications; 2000

Brown, Hilary; Stein, June; and Turk, Vicky: The Sexual Abuse of Adults with Learning Disabilities: Report Of A Second Two-Year Incidence Survey; Mental Handicap Research, Vol 8, No 1, 1995

Brown, Hilary; Stein, June: Implementing Adult Protection Policies in Kent and East Sussex; Journal of Social Policy, 27, 3, 1998

Brown, Hilary; Stein, June: Monitoring Adult Protection Referrals in 10 English Local Authorities; The Journal of Adult Protection, Vol 2, Issue 3, September 2000

Burgner, Tom; Russell, Dr Philippa; Whitehead, Simon; Tinnion, John: Independent Longcare Inquiry; Buckinghamshire County Council; June 1998

Burke, Lillian; Bedard, Cheryl: Self-injury Considered in Association with Sexual Victimization in Individuals with a Developmental Handicap; The Canadian Journal of Human Sexuality, Vol 3(3), Autumn 1994

Calcraft, Rebecca: Blowing the Whistle on Abuse of Adults with Learning Disabilities; Ann Craft Trust and Centre for Social Work, University of Nottingham; 2005

Cole, Sandra: Preface to the Special Issue on Sexual Exploitation of Persons with Disabilities; Sexuality and Disability, Vol 9, No 3, 1991

Collins, Jean: The Resettlement Game: policy and procrastination in the closure of mental handicap hospitals; Values Into Action, supported by Joseph Rowntree Foundation, 1993

Commission for Social Care Inspection: Inspecting for Better Lives (Modernising the Regulation of Social Care); 2004

Craft, Ann; Hitching, Marjorie: Keeping Safe: Sex Education and Assertiveness Skills; Thinking the Unthinkable, papers on Sexual Abuse and People with Learning Difficulties: eds Brown, Hilary and Craft, Ann; Family Planning Association Education Unit; 1989

Curen, Richard; Sinason, Valerie: Adults and Children with Learning Disabilities; Domestic and Sexual Violence and Abuse: Tackling the Health and Mental Health Effects; Itzin,C; Taket, A; Barter-Godfrey, S (eds); London: Routledge; 2010

DHSS and Welsh Office: Better Services for the Mentally Handicapped, Government White Paper; 1971

DHSS: Government response to the second report from the social services committee, 1984-85 session: Community Care, with special reference to adult mentally ill and mentally handicapped people; HMSO; November 1985

Diesfield, Kate: Witness Credibility in Cases of Sexual Abuse Against Adults with Learning Disabilities; Tizard Learning Disability Review, Volume 1 Issue 4

Diplock, Monica: The History of Leavesden Hospital; 1990
Dunne, Timothy; Power, Anne: Sexual Abuse and Mental Handicap: Preliminary Findings of a Community-based Study; Mental Handicap Research, 1990, 3:2

Fideler, Paul A: Social Welfare in Pre-Industrial England; Palgrave Macmillan; 2005

Goodley, Dan: Self-advocacy in the Lives of People with Learning Difficulties; Open University Press; 2000

Griffiths, Sir Roy: Community Care: Agenda for Action: A Report to the Secretary of State for Social Services; HMSO; 1988

Gunn, Michael: Sexual Abuse and Adults with Mental Handicap: Can the Law Help?; Thinking the Unthinkable, papers on Sexual Abuse and People with Learning Difficulties: eds Brown, Hilary and Craft, Ann; Family Planning Association Education Unit; 1989

Harris, Bernard: The Origins of the British Welfare State: Society, State and Social Welfare in England and Wales, 1800-1945; Palgrave Macmillan; 2004

Home Office: consultation paper: Setting the Boundaries – Reforming the Law on Sexual Offences; July 2000
Horden, Peregrine; Smith, Richard (eds): The Locus of Care: families, communities, institutions and the provision of welfare since antiquity; Routledge; 1998

Jackson, Mark: The Borderland of Imbecility: Medicine, society and the fabrication of the feeble mind in late Victorian and Edwardian England; Manchester University Press; 2000

Johnson, Kelley; Traustadottir, Rannveig (editors): Deinstitutionalization and People with Intellectual Disabilities: In and Out of Institutions; Jessica Kingsley Publishers; 2005

Judicial Studies Board: Equal Treatment Bench Book; October 2000

Kilgallon W; Day, Dr K; Robinson, N; Community Healthcare North Durham: Report of external review panel into the process and robustness of Community Health Care: North Durham NHS Trust's handling of untoward incidents and the investigation into the learning disabilities service at Earls House Hospital; February 1998

Law Commission Report No 231: Mental Incapacity; 1995

Malster, Robert: St Lawrence's: The Story of a Hospital, 1870-1994; Lifecare NHS Trust; 1994

Mathew, Dinah; Brown, Hilary; Kingston, Paul; McCreadie, Claudine; Askham, Janet: The Response to No Secrets; The Journal of Adult Protection, Vol 4, Issue 1, February 2002

McCarthy, Michelle; Thompson, David: A Prevalence Study of Sexual Abuse of Adults with Intellectual Disabilities Referred for Sex Education; Journal of Applied Research in Intellectual Disabilities, Vol 10, No 2, 1997

McCarthy, Michelle: Sexual Violence against Women with Learning Disabilities; Feminism and Psychology, Vol 8(4), 1998

McCarthy, Michelle: Consent, Abuse and Choices – Women with Intellectual Disabilities and Sexuality; from Traustadottir, R and Johnson, K (eds): Women with Intellectual Disabilities: Finding a Place in the World; 2000; Jessica Kingsley

McGowan, Chandra: A Long Way from Home; The Health Service Journal; April 25, 1996

Mencap: Barriers to Justice – A Mencap study into how the criminal justice system treats people with learning disabilities; November 1997

'Michael', with the assistance of Mark Pathak: My Life; ACT Bulletin; Ann Craft Trust; October 2007

Midwinter, Eric: The Development of Social Welfare in Britain; Open University Press; 1994

Mills Media Ltd: Witness Support, Preparation and Profiling: The Liverpool Model; DVD produced for Merseyside Criminal Justice Board; 2010

Mitchell, Duncan; Traustadottir, Rannveig; Chapman, Rohhss; Townson, Louise; Ingham, Nigel; Ledger, Sue (editors): Exploring Experiences of Advocacy by People with Learning Disabilities: Testimonies of Resistance; Jessica Kingsley Publishers; 2006

Morris, Pauline: Put Away, A Sociological Study of Institutions for the Mentally Retarded; Routledge and Kegan Paul; 1969

Murray, Dr Dinah K C: Potions, Pills and Community Care for People with Learning Difficulties: Hidden costs; Good Autism Practice; April 1999

National Development Team for inclusion: Supported Living – Making the Move: Developing Supported Living Options for People with Learning Disabilities; National Development Team for inclusion Housing and Social Inclusion Project discussion paper; National Development Team for inclusion; 2010

North West Training and Development Team: Sexual Abuse and People with Learning Disabilities – report of a conference held on 18 October 1995 at Bolton

Paige-Smith, Alice: Choosing Inclusion – the power of parents in special education; paper presented at the International Special Education Congress 2000

Peckham, Nicholas Guy; Howlett, Susan; and Corbett, Alan: Evaluating a Survivors Group Pilot for Women with Significant Intellectual Disabilities who have been Sexually Abused; Journal of Applied Research in Intellectual Disabilities; 2007, volume 20 (4), pages 308-322

Philpot, Terry (editor): Residential Care: A Positive Future; The Residential Forum; 2008

Potts, Maggie; and Fido, Rebecca: A Fit Person to be Removed: Personal Accounts of Life in a Mental Deficiency Institution; Northcote House; 1991

Pritchard, D G: Education and the Handicapped: 1760-1960; Routledge and Kegan Paul, 1963

Quarmby, Katharine: Getting Away With Murder: Disabled people's experiences of hate crime in the UK; Disability Now, United Kingdom Disabled People's Council, Scope; 2008

Quarmby, Katharine: Scapegoat (draft version); Portobello Books; 2011

Report of the Committee of Inquiry into Allegations of Ill-Treatment of Patients and other irregularities at the Ely Hospital, Cardiff; HMSO; March 1969

Report of the Committee of Inquiry into Normansfield Hospital; HMSO; November 1978

Report of the Committee of Inquiry into South Ockendon Hospital; HMSO; May 1974

Report of the Farleigh Hospital Committee of Inquiry; HMSO; April 1971

Richardson, M: Reflection and Celebration – Neal (1960-1987): Narrative of a Young Man with Profound and Multiple Disabilities; Journal of Learning Disabilities for Nursing, Health and Social Care, (1997) 1(4)

Rushton, Alan; Beaumont, Kay; and Mayes, Debbie: Service and Client Outcomes of Cases Reported Under a Joint Vulnerable Adults Policy; The Journal of Adult Protection, volume 2, issue 2, June 2000

Rushton, Peter: Lunatics and idiots: mental disability, the community, and the poor law in North-East England, 1600-1800; Medical History, 1988, volume 32, number 1, pages 34-50

Sanders, Andrew; Creaton, Jane; Bird, Sophia; and Weber, Leanne: Home Office Research and Statistics Directorate, Research Findings No 44 – Witnesses with Learning Disabilities

Sellin, Birger: In Dark Hours I Find My Way – messages from an autistic mind; London: Victor Gollancz; 1993

Sinason, Valerie: Secondary Mental Handicap and its Relationship to Trauma; Psychoanalytic Psychotherapy (1986), Vol 2 No 2

Sinason, Valerie: Uncovering and Responding to Sexual Abuse in Psychotherapeutic Settings; Thinking the Unthinkable, papers on Sexual Abuse and People with Learning Difficulties: eds Brown, Hilary and Craft, Ann; Family Planning Association Education Unit; 1989

Sobsey, Dick; and Doe, Tanis: Patterns of Sexual Abuse and Assault; Sexuality and Disability, Vol 9, No 3, 1991

Social Services Inspectorate, Department of Health: Inspection of Local Authority Social Services Department Inspection Units: Buckinghamshire; May 1995

Social Services Inspectorate for Wales: Social Services in Wales 1999-2000 – The Report of the Chief Inspector; January 2001

Speaking Up For Justice – Report of the Interdepartmental Working Group on the Treatment of Vulnerable or Intimidated Witnesses in the Criminal Justice System; June 1998

Stanley, Nicky; Manthorpe, Jill; and Penhale, Bridget (Eds): Institutional Abuse – perspectives across the life course; Routledge; 1999

Thane, Pat; Memorandum submitted to the Commons health committee inquiry into social care; 2009

Tsuchiya, Takashi: Eugenic Sterilizations in Japan and Recent Demands for an Apology: A Report; Ethics and Intellectual Disability, Vol 3, No 1, Autumn 1997

Varley, Christopher: Schizophreniform Psychoses in Mentally Retarded Adolescent Girls Following Sexual Assault; American Journal of Psychiatry; April 1984

Voice UK, Respond and Mencap: Behind Closed Doors: Preventing Sexual Abuse against Adults with a Learning Disability; 2001

Wagner, Gillian (chair): Residential Care: A Positive Choice: Report of the Independent Review of Residential Care; National Institute for Social Work/HMSO; 1988

Walmsley, Sandra: The Need for Safeguards; Brown, Hilary and Craft, Ann (eds): Thinking the Unthinkable, papers on Sexual Abuse and People with Learning Difficulties; Family Planning Association Education Unit; 1989

Welshman, John and Walmsley, Jan (eds): Community Care in Persepctive: Care, Control and Citizenship; Palgrave Macmillan; 2006

Wetherall, Grant: Investigation of Abuse of People with Learning Disabilities at Stoke Poges, Buckinghamshire; practice study for diploma in social work, Brunel University; June 1995

Williams, Christopher: Invisible Victims – crime and abuse against people with learning disabilities; London: Jessica Kingsley Publishers; 1995

Wright, David and Digby, Anne (eds): From Idiocy to Mental Deficiency – Historical Perspectives on People with Learning Disabilities; Routledge; 1996

CL

362.
230
942
59
PRI

5001553617

LONGCARE SURVIVORS

The Biography of a Care Scandal

College Lane, Hatfield, Herts. AL10 9AB
Information Hertfordshire
Services and Solutions for the University

For renewal of Standard and One Week Loans,
please visit the web site **http://www.voyager.herts.ac.uk**

This item must be returned or the loan renewed by the due date.
A fine will be charged for the late return of items.